D1169585

GetBackers

3

GetBackers

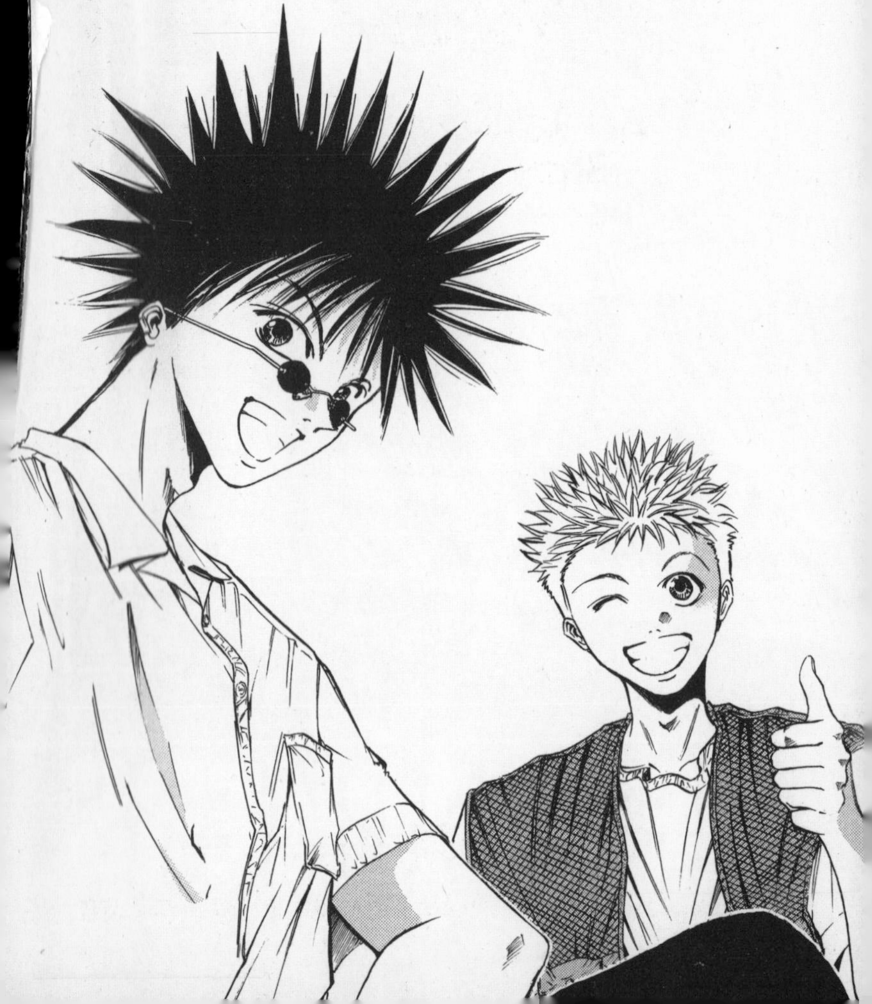

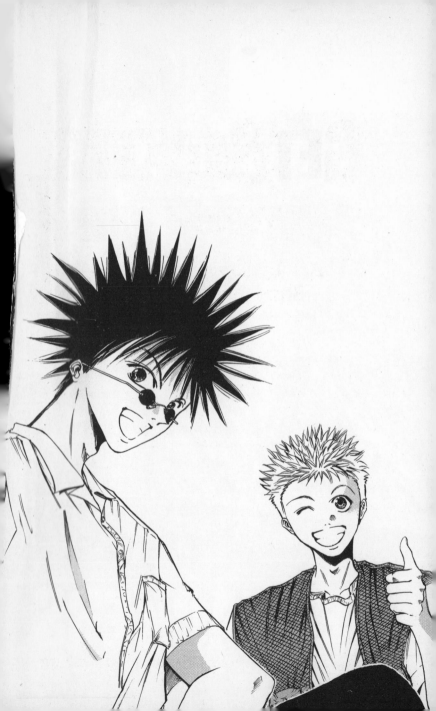

GETBACKERS

Volume 3

Art by Rando Ayamine
Story by Yuya Aoki

Los Angeles • Tokyo • London • Hamburg

Translator - James Cohen
English Adaptation - Ryan Shankel
Associate Editor - Arthur Milliken
Retouch and Lettering - Deron Bennett
Cover Layout - Patrick Hook

Editor - Luis Reyes
Digital Imaging Manager - Chris Buford
Pre-Press Manager - Antonio DePietro
Production Managers - Jennifer Miller, Mutsumi Miyazaki
Art Director - Matt Alford
Managing Editor - Jill Freshney
VP of Production - Ron Klamert
President & C.O.O. - John Parker
Publisher & C.E.O. - Stuart Levy

E-mail: info@TOKYOPOP.com
Come visit us online at www.TOKYOPOP.com

A  Manga

TOKYOPOP Inc.
5900 Wilshire Blvd. Suite 2000
Los Angeles, CA 90036

GetBackers Vol. 3

©1999 Yuya Aoki and Rando Ayamine, All rights reserved.
First published in Japan in 1999 by Kodansha Ltd.
English translation rights arranged by Kodansha Ltd.

English text copyright ©2004 TOKYOPOP Inc.

All rights reserved. No portion of this book may be reproduced or transmitted
in any form or by any means without written permission from the copyright
holders. This manga is a work of fiction. Any resemblance to actual events
or locales or persons, living or dead, is entirely coincidental.

ISBN: 1-59182-635-7

First TOKYOPOP printing: June 2004

10 9 8 7 6 5 4 3 2 1

Printed in the USA

Story Thus Far:

Ginji Amano can amplify the electrical currents in his body. Ban Mido has the power to create illusions in people's minds for one minute. Together they are the GetBackers, a retrieval agency whose motto is, "We get back what shouldn't be gone." For the right price, they'll return anything that's been taken.

Recently hired by the wealthy Eichiro Ohtaki to retrieve a mysterious box, the Getbackers found themselves on the road to riches. But jobs don't come that easy for the duo. To get the box, they had to take on the notorious Transporters, comprised of the relentless Mr. Unstoppable, Lady Poison, and the sinister Jackal.

The battle turned out to be a dangerous one, and Ginji was taken hostage by the Transporters gang. Desperate times call for desperate measures, and Ban Mido is just the desperado to get the job done. Using his "Evil Eye," Ban rescues his best bud and gets the goods. Looks like smooth sailing from now on...or is it?

Ya caught up? Then here we go.

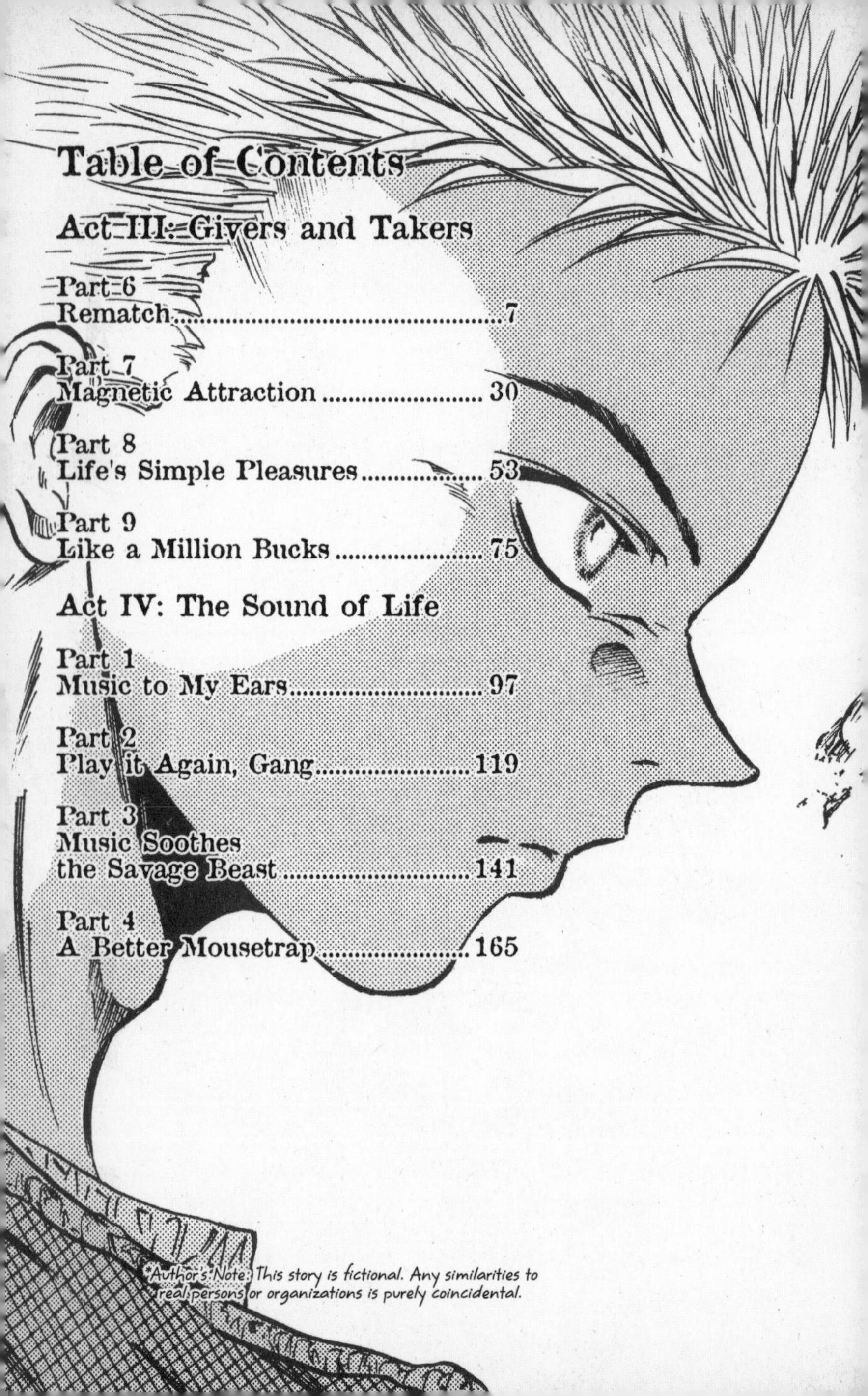

Table of Contents

Act III: Givers and Takers

Act IV: The Sound of Life

*Author's Note: This story is fictional. Any similarities to real persons or organizations is purely coincidental.

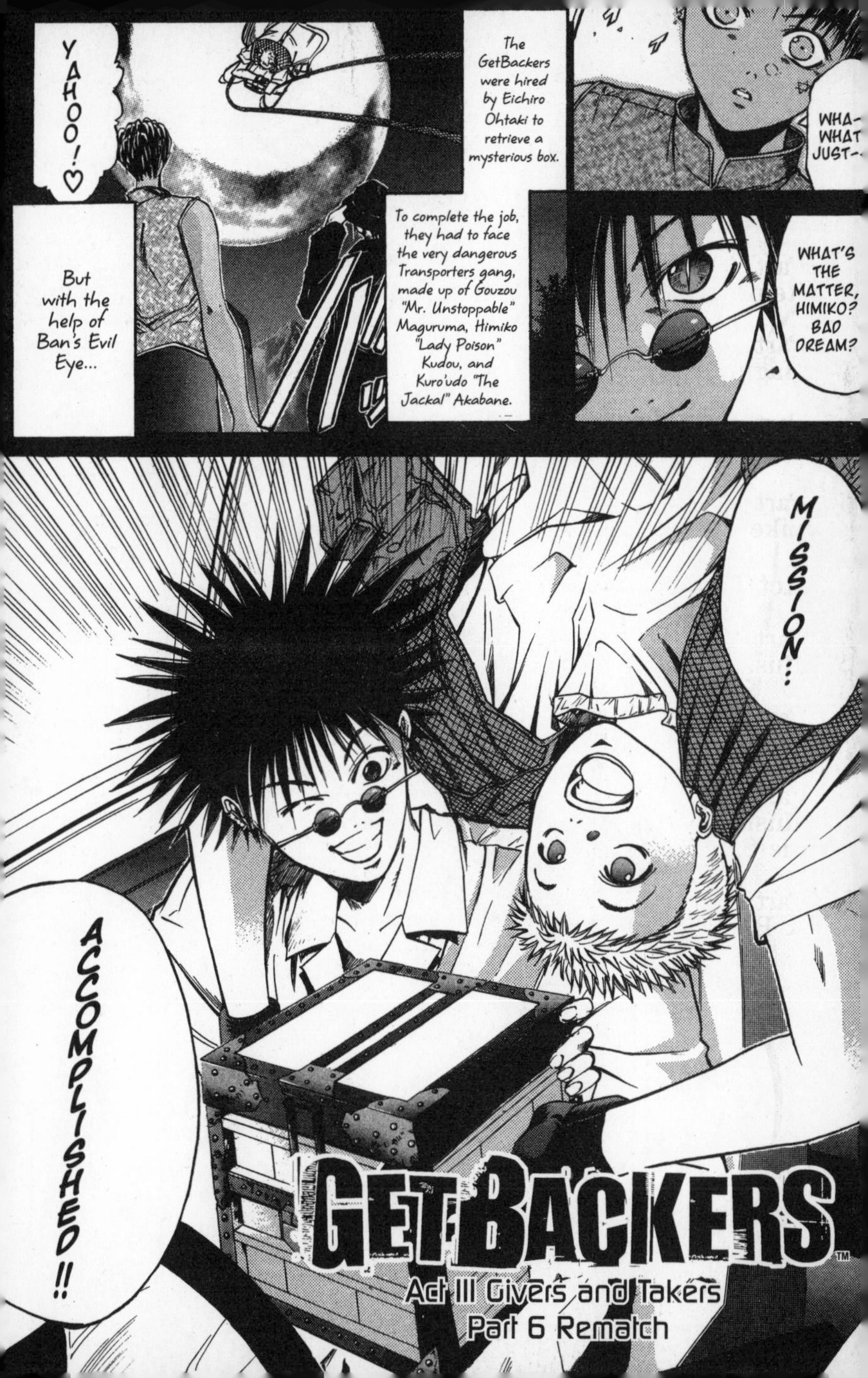
WHA-WHAT JUST--
WHAT'S THE MATTER, HIMIKO? BAD DREAM?
The GetBackers were hired by Eichiro Ohtaki to retrieve a mysterious box.
To complete the job, they had to face the very dangerous Transporters gang, made up of Gouzou "Mr. Unstoppable" Maguruma, Himiko "Lady Poison" Kudou, and Kuro'udo "The Jackal" Akabane.
YAHOO!♡
But with the help of Ban's Evil Eye...
MISSION...
ACCOMPLISHED!!
GETBACKERS™
Act III Givers and Takers
Part 6 Rematch

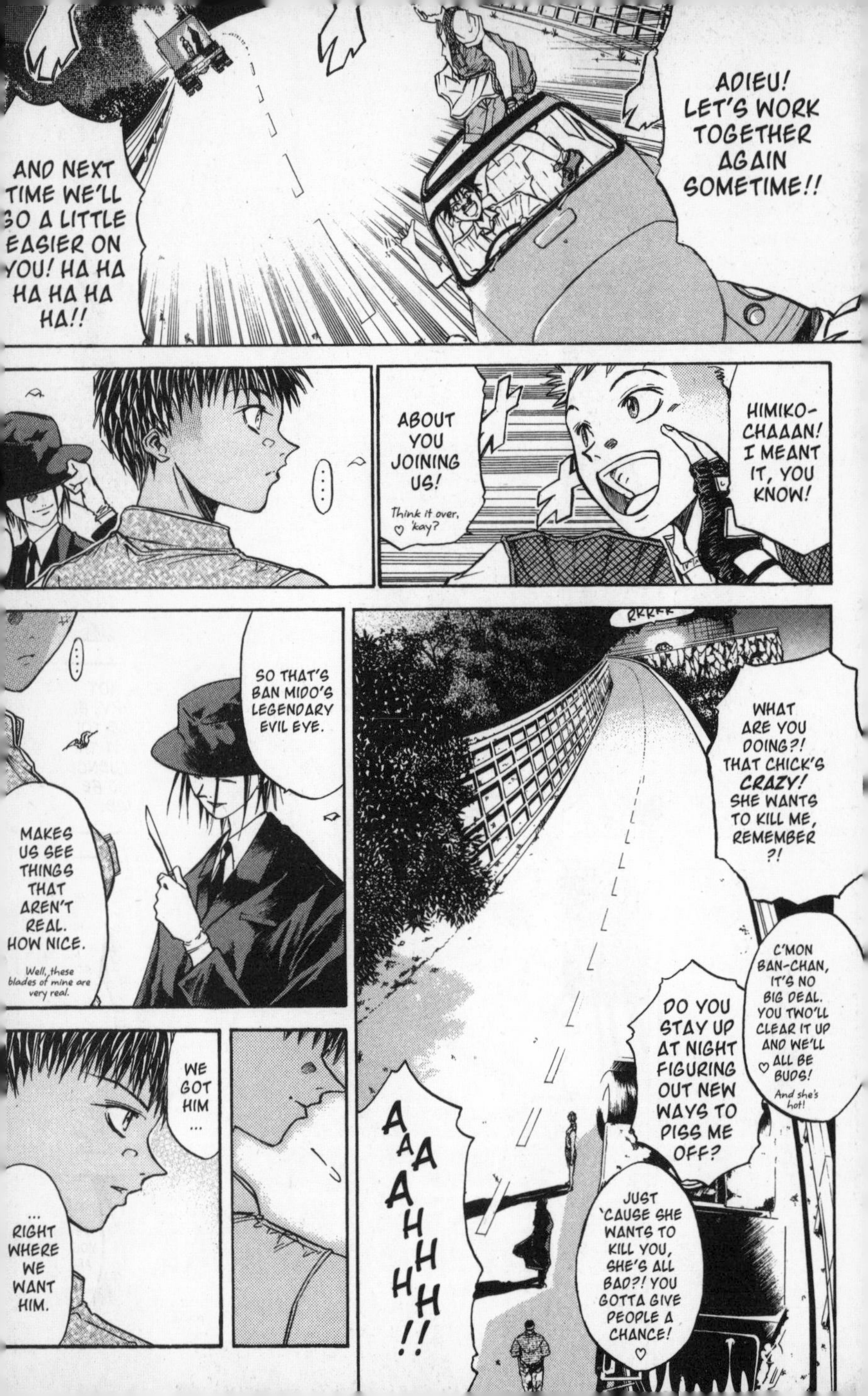
ADIEU! LET'S WORK TOGETHER AGAIN SOMETIME!!
AND NEXT TIME WE'LL GO A LITTLE EASIER ON YOU! HA HA HA HA HA HA!!
HIMIKO-CHAAAN! I MEANT IT, YOU KNOW!
ABOUT YOU JOINING US!
Think it over, ♡ 'kay?
....
RKKKK
WHAT ARE YOU DOING?! THAT CHICK'S CRAZY! SHE WANTS TO KILL ME, REMEMBER?!
C'MON BAN-CHAN, IT'S NO BIG DEAL. YOU TWO'LL CLEAR IT UP AND WE'LL ALL BE BUDS! ♡
And she's hot!
DO YOU STAY UP AT NIGHT FIGURING OUT NEW WAYS TO PISS ME OFF?
AAAAHHHHH!!
JUST 'CAUSE SHE WANTS TO KILL YOU, SHE'S ALL BAD?! YOU GOTTA GIVE PEOPLE A CHANCE! ♡
...
SO THAT'S BAN MIDO'S LEGENDARY EVIL EYE.
MAKES US SEE THINGS THAT AREN'T REAL. HOW NICE.
Well, these blades of mine are very real.
WE GOT HIM ...
... RIGHT WHERE WE WANT HIM.

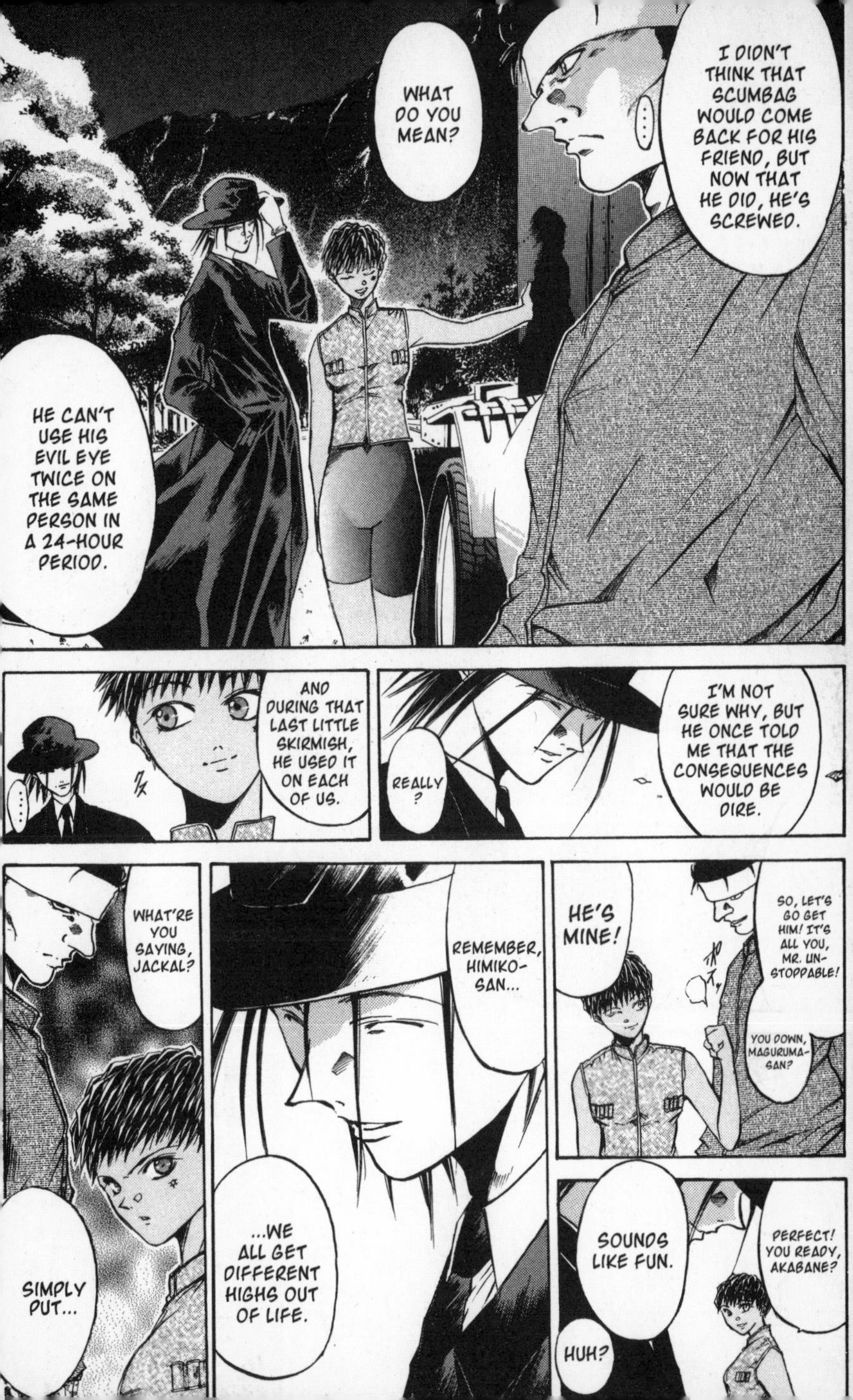
I DIDN'T THINK THAT SCUMBAG WOULD COME BACK FOR HIS FRIEND, BUT NOW THAT HE DID, HE'S SCREWED.
...
WHAT DO YOU MEAN?
HE CAN'T USE HIS EVIL EYE TWICE ON THE SAME PERSON IN A 24-HOUR PERIOD.
I'M NOT SURE WHY, BUT HE ONCE TOLD ME THAT THE CONSEQUENCES WOULD BE DIRE.
REALLY?
AND DURING THAT LAST LITTLE SKIRMISH, HE USED IT ON EACH OF US.
...
SO, LET'S GO GET HIM! IT'S ALL YOU, MR. UNSTOPPABLE!
HE'S MINE!
YOU DOWN, MAGURUMA-SAN?
PERFECT! YOU READY, AKABANE?
SOUNDS LIKE FUN.
HUH?
REMEMBER, HIMIKO-SAN...
...WE ALL GET DIFFERENT HIGHS OUT OF LIFE.
WHAT'RE YOU SAYING, JACKAL?
SIMPLY PUT...

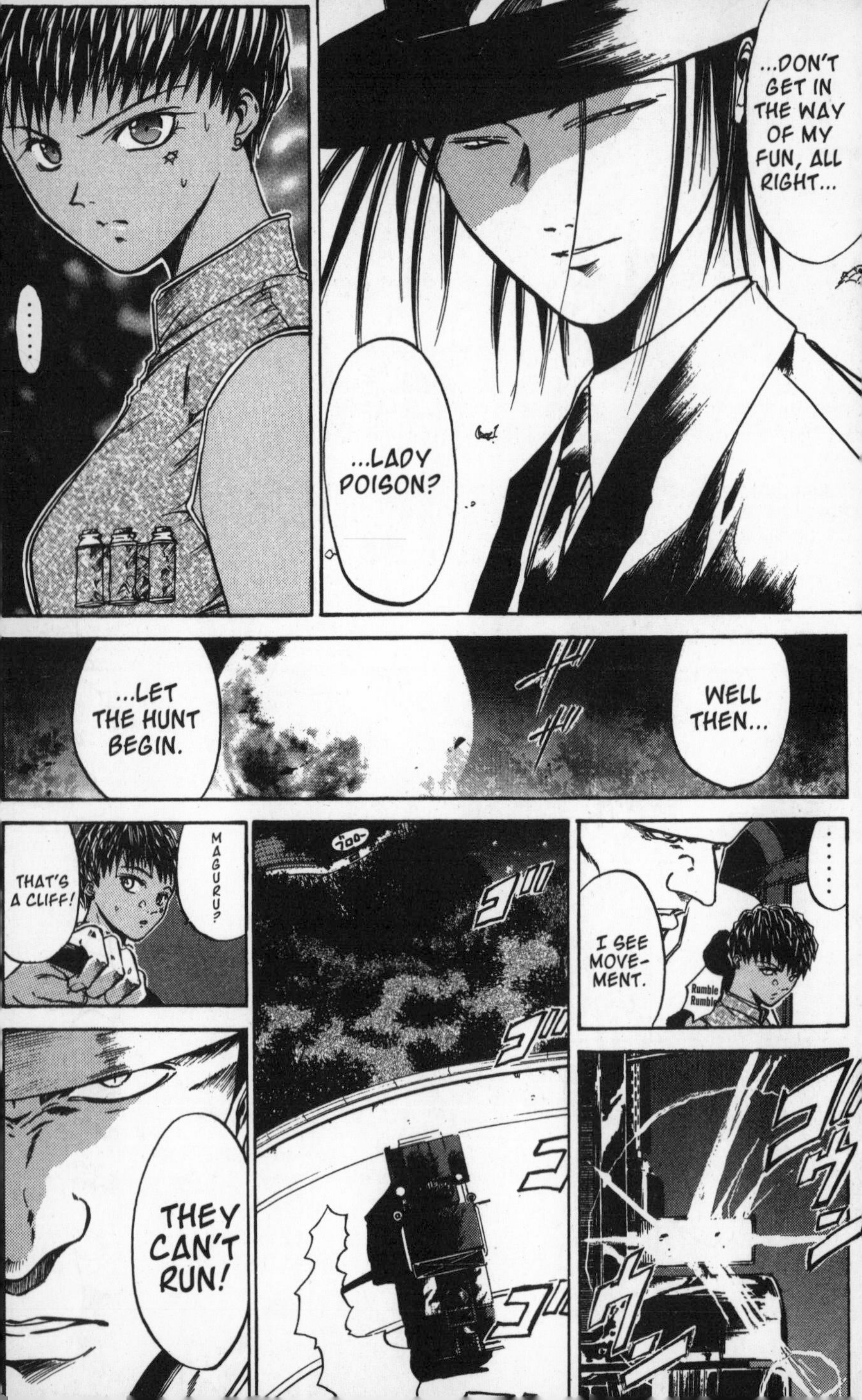
...DON'T GET IN THE WAY OF MY FUN, ALL RIGHT...
...LADY POISON?
......
WELL THEN...
...LET THE HUNT BEGIN.
......
I SEE MOVEMENT.
Rumble Rumble
MAGURU?
THAT'S A CLIFF!
THEY CAN'T RUN!

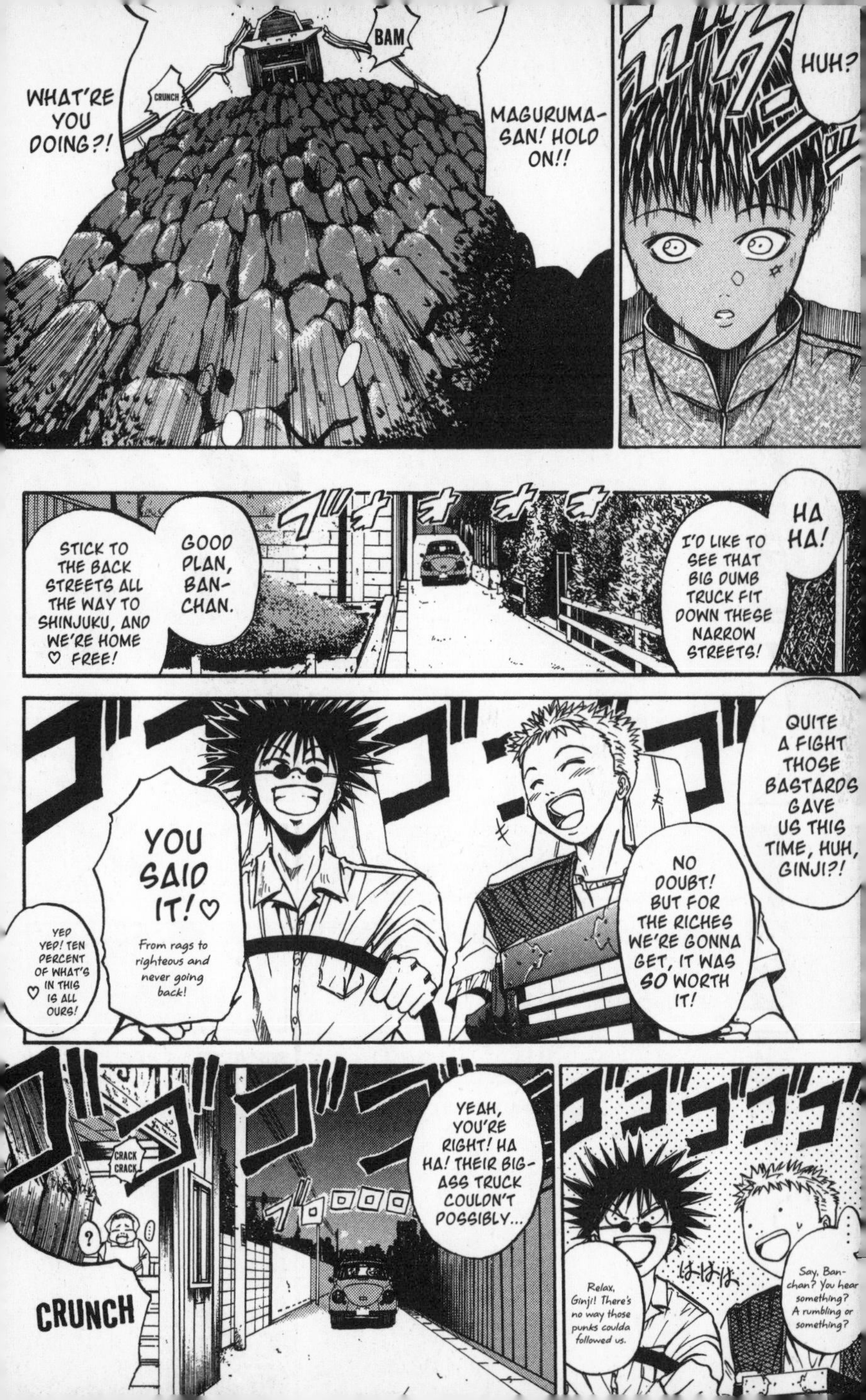
HUH?
MAGURUMA-SAN! HOLD ON!!
BAM
CRUNCH
WHAT'RE YOU DOING?!
HA HA!
I'D LIKE TO SEE THAT BIG DUMB TRUCK FIT DOWN THESE NARROW STREETS!
GOOD PLAN, BAN-CHAN.
STICK TO THE BACK STREETS ALL THE WAY TO SHINJUKU, AND WE'RE HOME ♡ FREE!
QUITE A FIGHT THOSE BASTARDS GAVE US THIS TIME, HUH, GINJI?!
NO DOUBT! BUT FOR THE RICHES WE'RE GONNA GET, IT WAS SO WORTH IT!
YOU SAID IT! ♡
From rags to righteous and never going back!
YEP YEP! TEN PERCENT OF WHAT'S IN THIS IS ALL OURS! ♡
Say, Ban-chan? You hear something? A rumbling or something?
ははは
Relax, Ginji! There's no way those punks coulda followed us.
YEAH, YOU'RE RIGHT! HA HA! THEIR BIG-ASS TRUCK COULDN'T POSSIBLY...
CRACK CRACK
?
...
CRUNCH

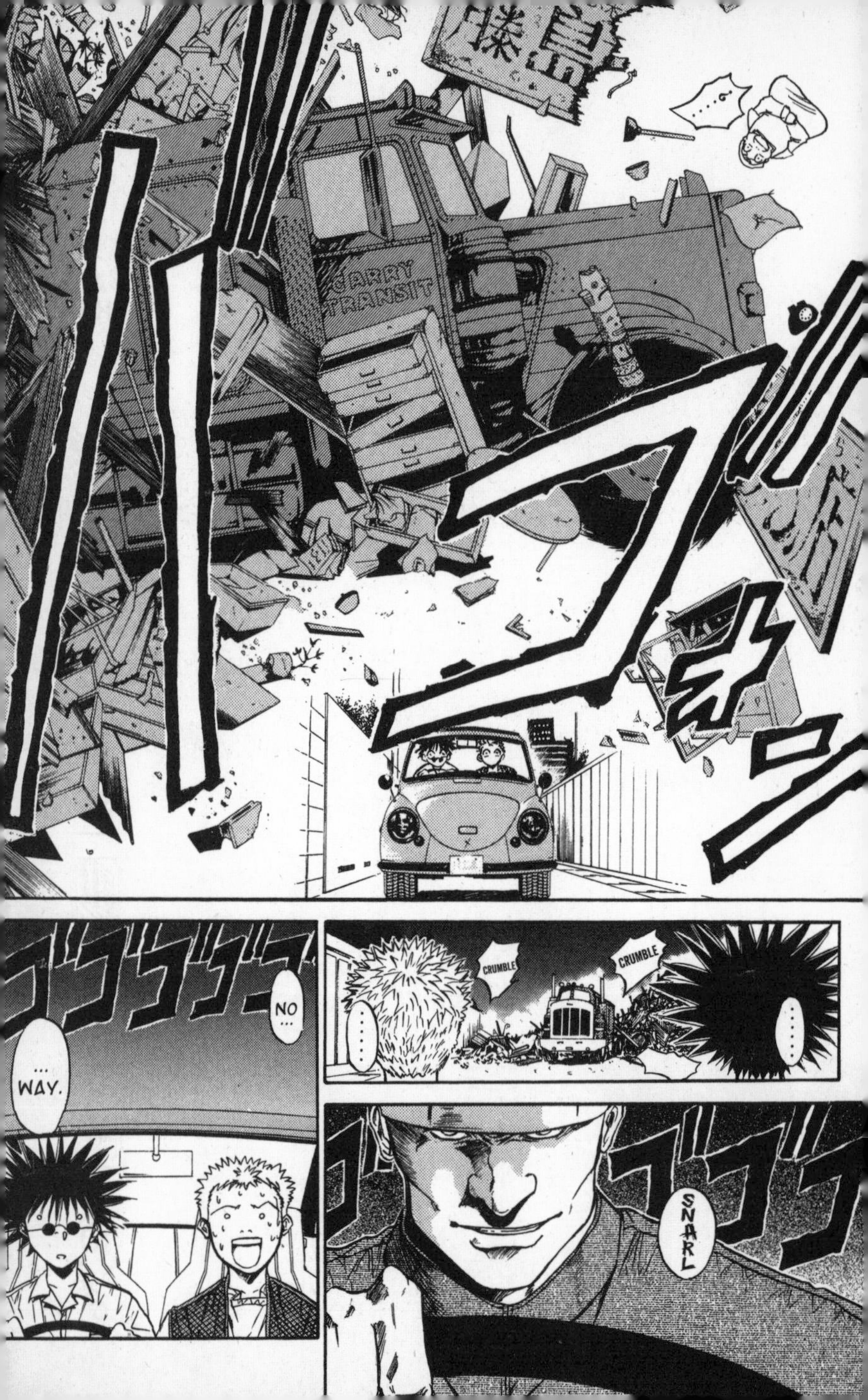

...?
CRUMBLE
CRUMBLE
......
......
SNARL
NO ...
... WAY.

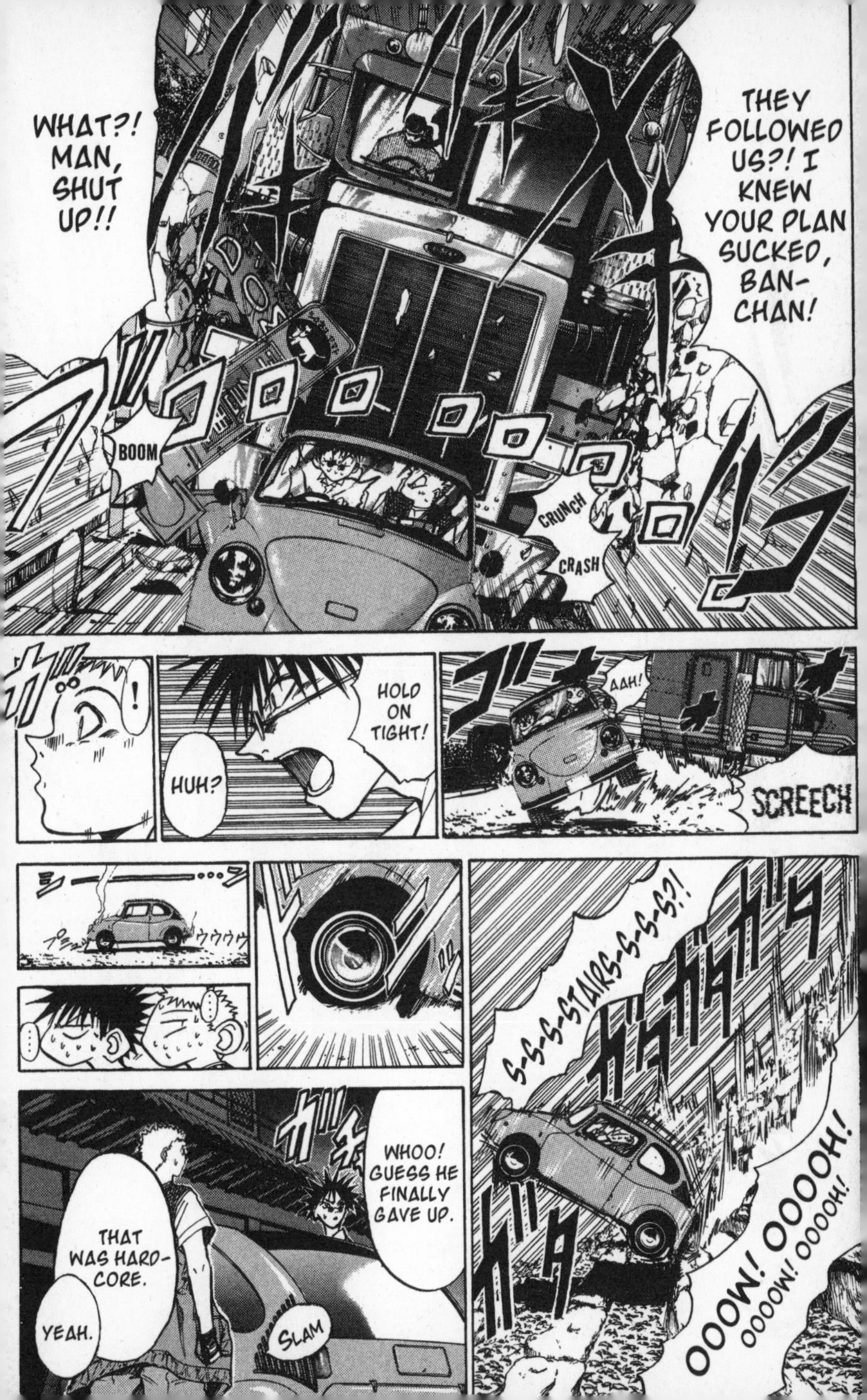
THEY FOLLOWED US?! I KNEW YOUR PLAN SUCKED, BAN-CHAN!
WHAT?! MAN, SHUT UP!!
BOOM
CRUNCH
CRASH
AAH!
SCREECH
HOLD ON TIGHT!
HUH?
!
S-S-S-STAIRS-S-S-S?!
OOOW! OOOOH!
OOOOW! OOOOH!
...
...
WHOO! GUESS HE FINALLY GAVE UP.
THAT WAS HARD-CORE.
YEAH.
SLAM

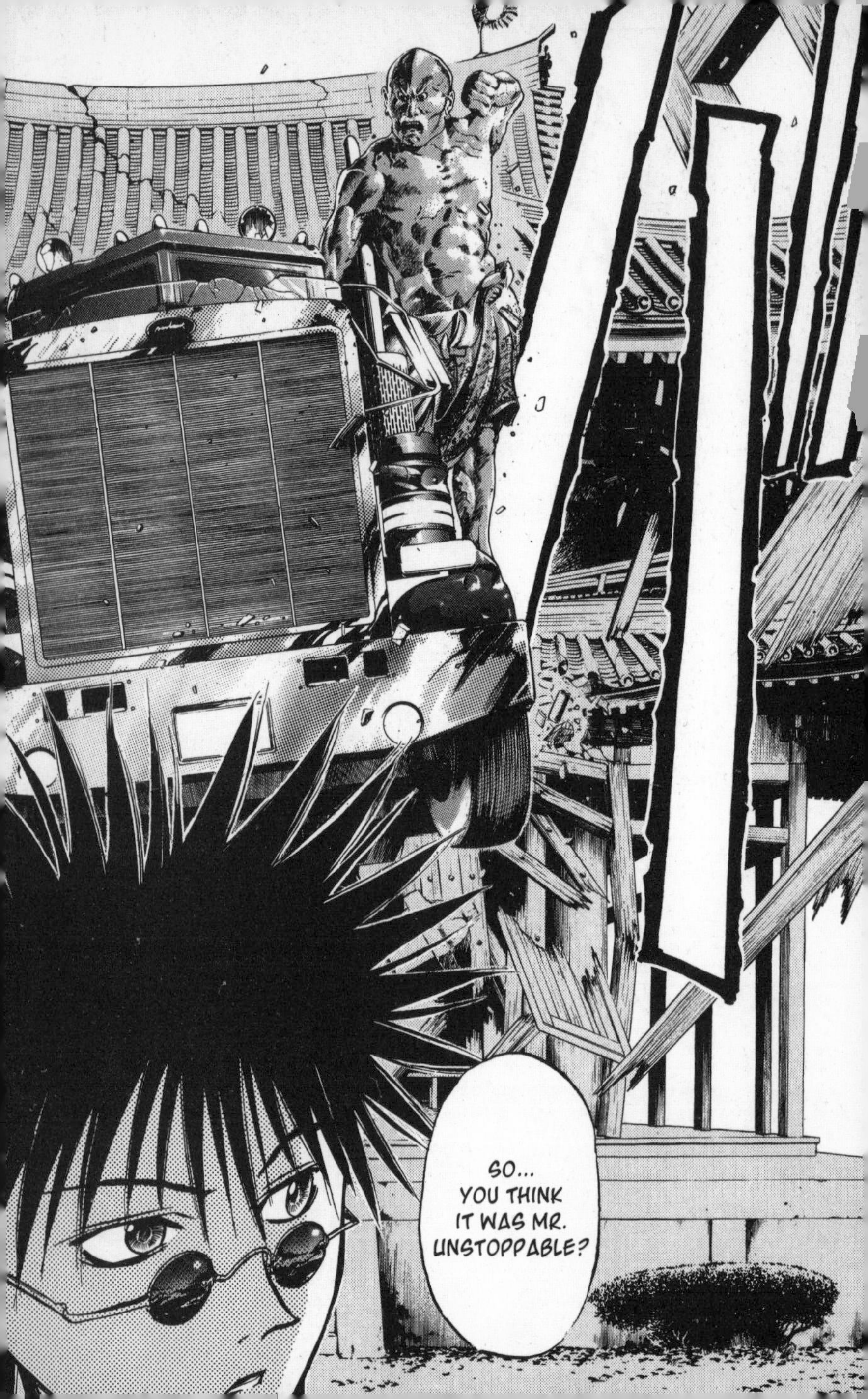
SO... YOU THINK IT WAS MR. UNSTOPPABLE?

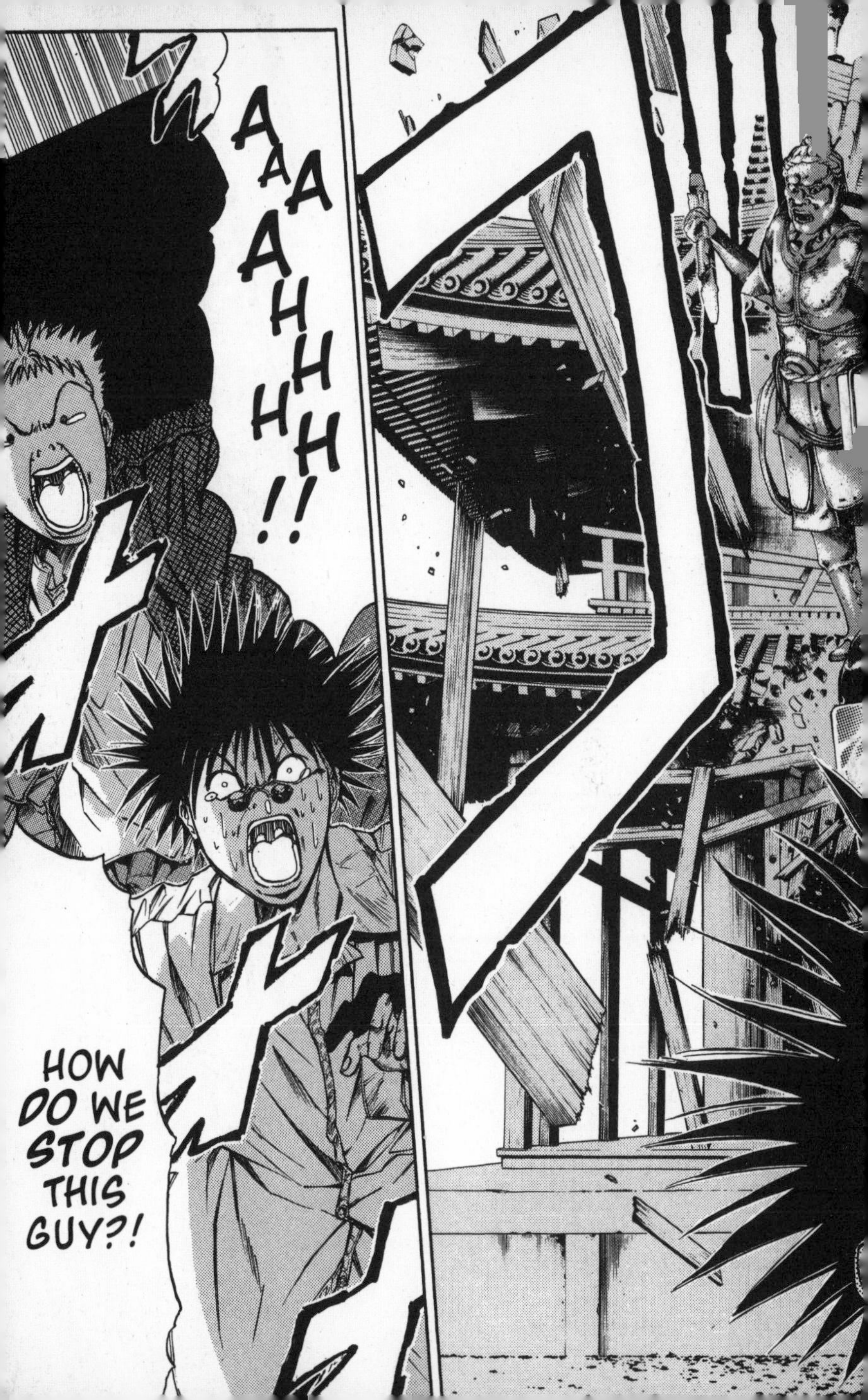
AAAAHHHH!!
HOW DO WE STOP THIS GUY?!

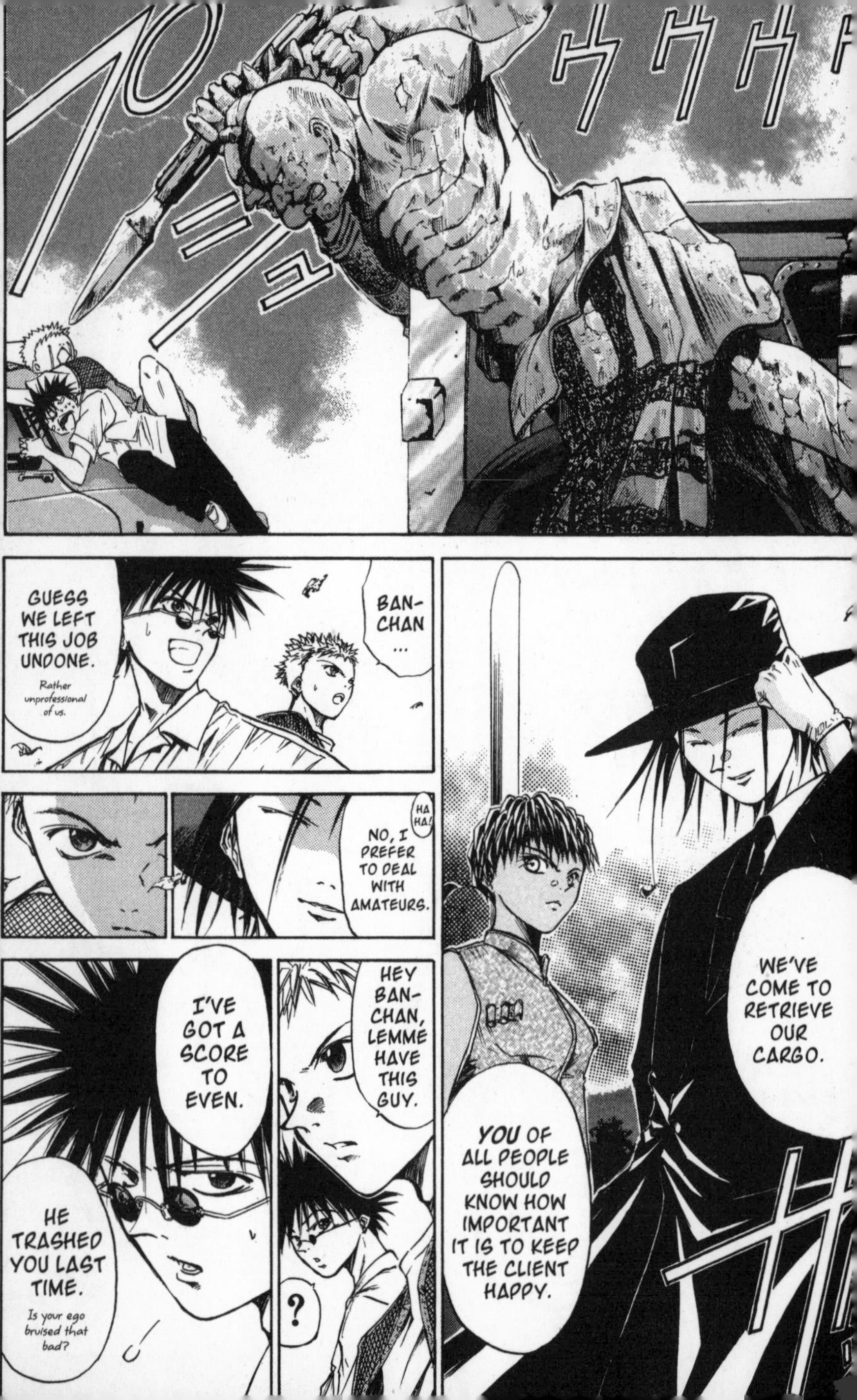
WE'VE COME TO RETRIEVE OUR CARGO.
YOU OF ALL PEOPLE SHOULD KNOW HOW IMPORTANT IT IS TO KEEP THE CLIENT HAPPY.
BAN-CHAN ...
GUESS WE LEFT THIS JOB UNDONE.
Rather unprofessional of us.
HA HA!
NO, I PREFER TO DEAL WITH AMATEURS.
HEY BAN-CHAN, LEMME HAVE THIS GUY.
?
I'VE GOT A SCORE TO EVEN.
HE TRASHED YOU LAST TIME.
Is your ego bruised that bad?

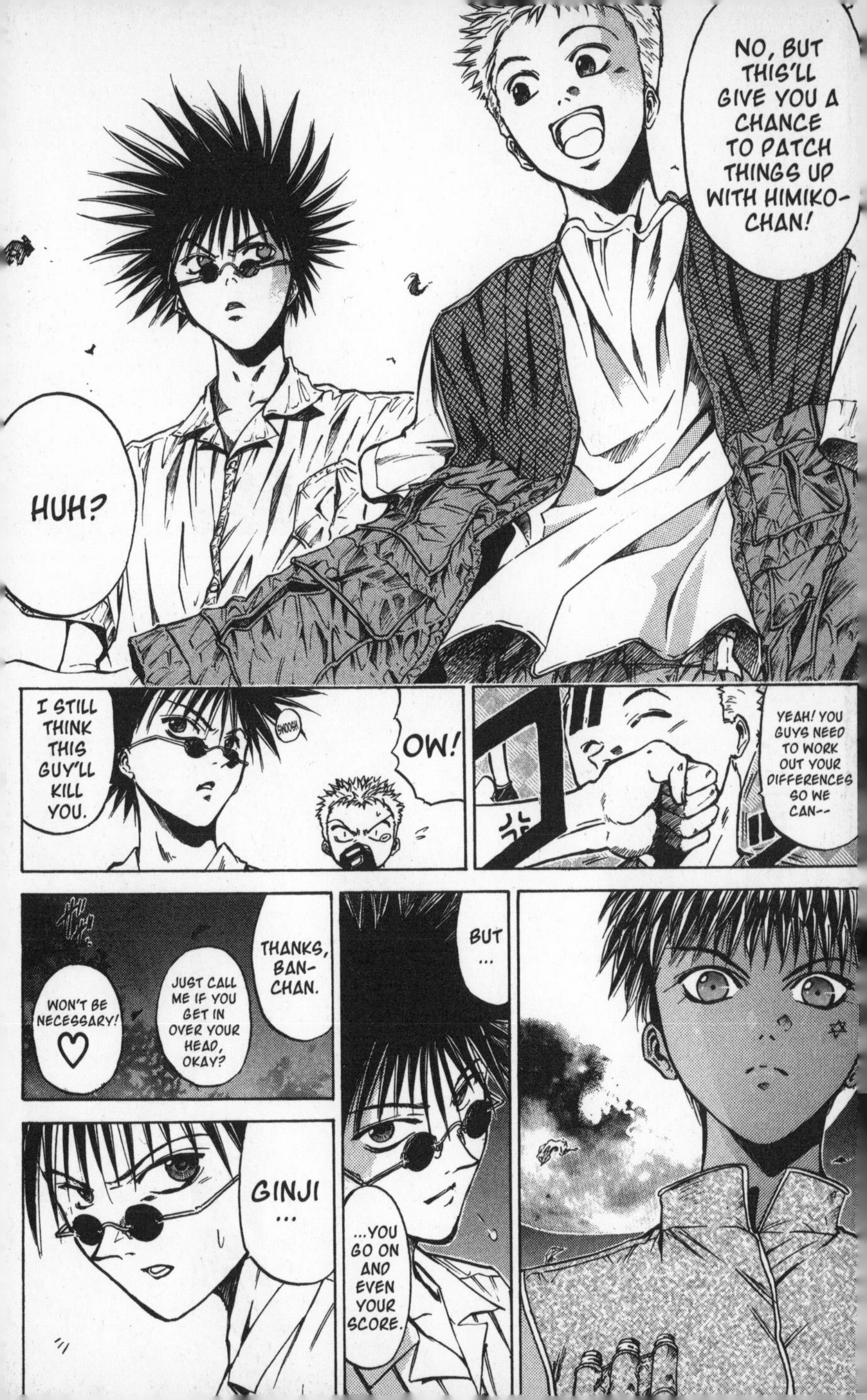
NO, BUT THIS'LL GIVE YOU A CHANCE TO PATCH THINGS UP WITH HIMIKO-CHAN!
HUH?
YEAH! YOU GUYS NEED TO WORK OUT YOUR DIFFERENCES SO WE CAN--
OW!
I STILL THINK THIS GUY'LL KILL YOU.
BUT ...
...YOU GO ON AND EVEN YOUR SCORE.
THANKS, BAN-CHAN.
JUST CALL ME IF YOU GET IN OVER YOUR HEAD, OKAY?
WON'T BE NECESSARY! ♡
GINJI ...

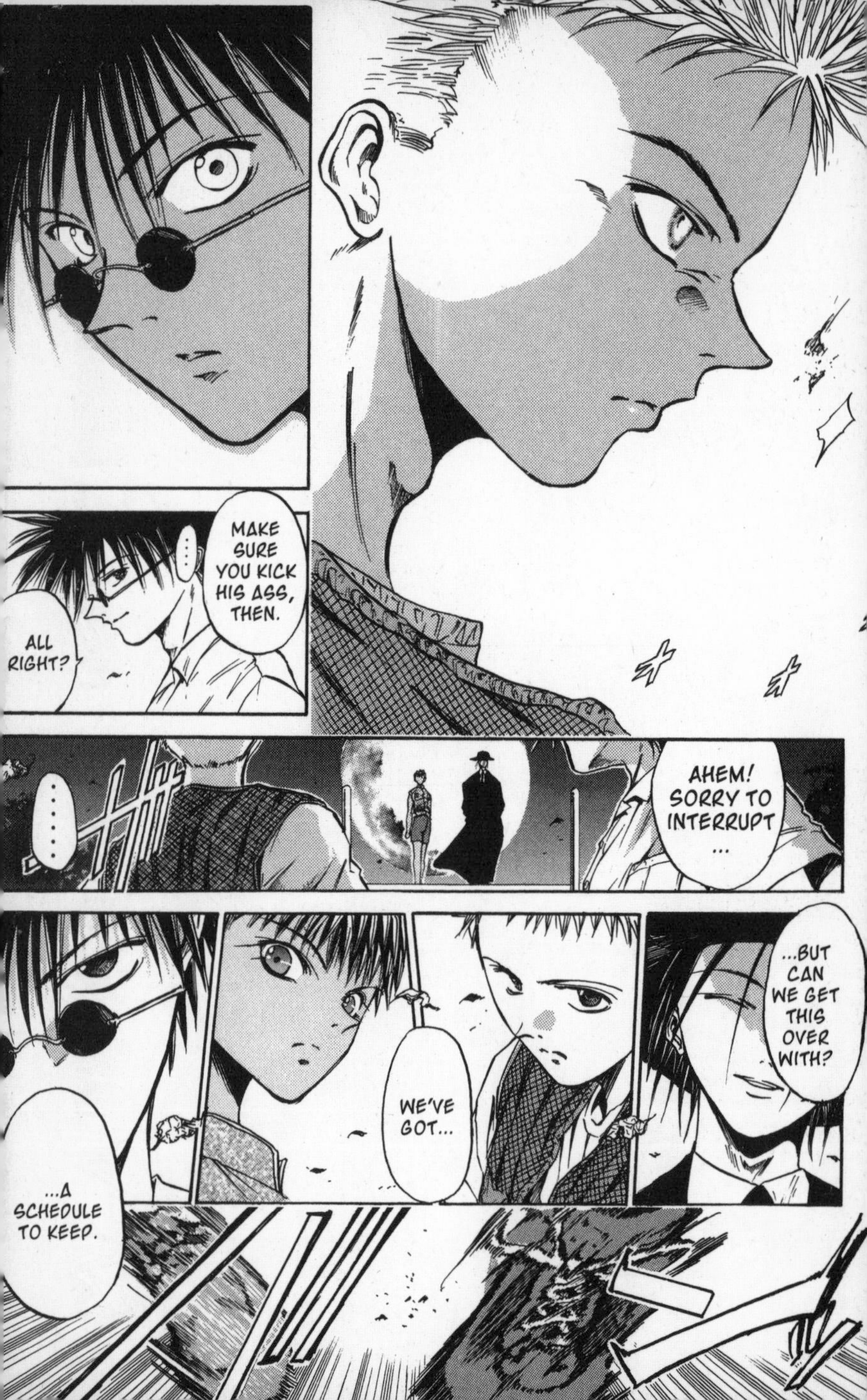
MAKE SURE YOU KICK HIS ASS, THEN.
...
ALL RIGHT?
AHEM! SORRY TO INTERRUPT ...
......
...BUT CAN WE GET THIS OVER WITH?
WE'VE GOT...
...A SCHEDULE TO KEEP.

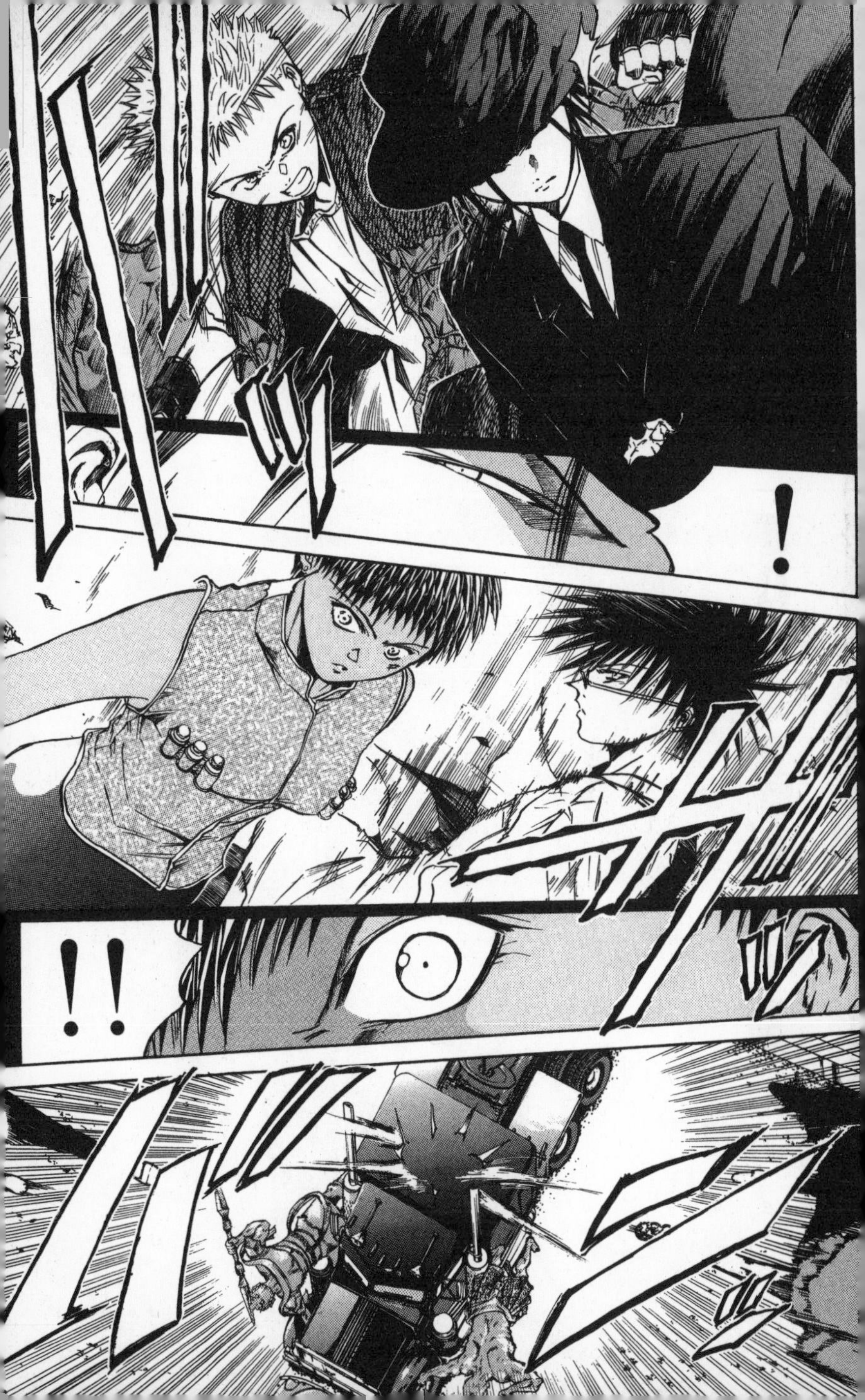
!
!!

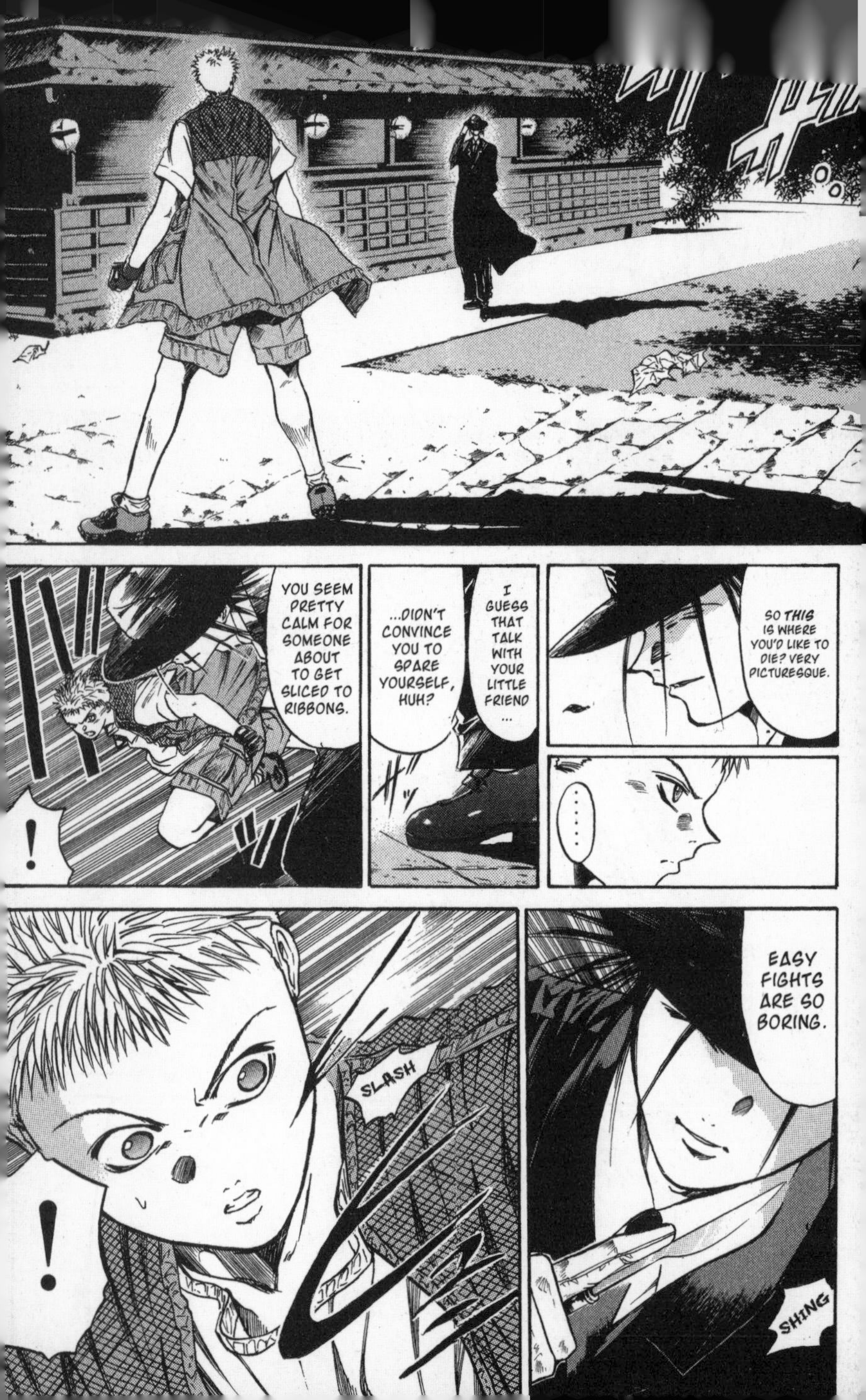
SO THIS IS WHERE YOU'D LIKE TO DIE? VERY PICTURESQUE.
......
I GUESS THAT TALK WITH YOUR LITTLE FRIEND ...
...DIDN'T CONVINCE YOU TO SPARE YOURSELF, HUH?
YOU SEEM PRETTY CALM FOR SOMEONE ABOUT TO GET SLICED TO RIBBONS.
!
EASY FIGHTS ARE SO BORING.
SHING
SLASH
!

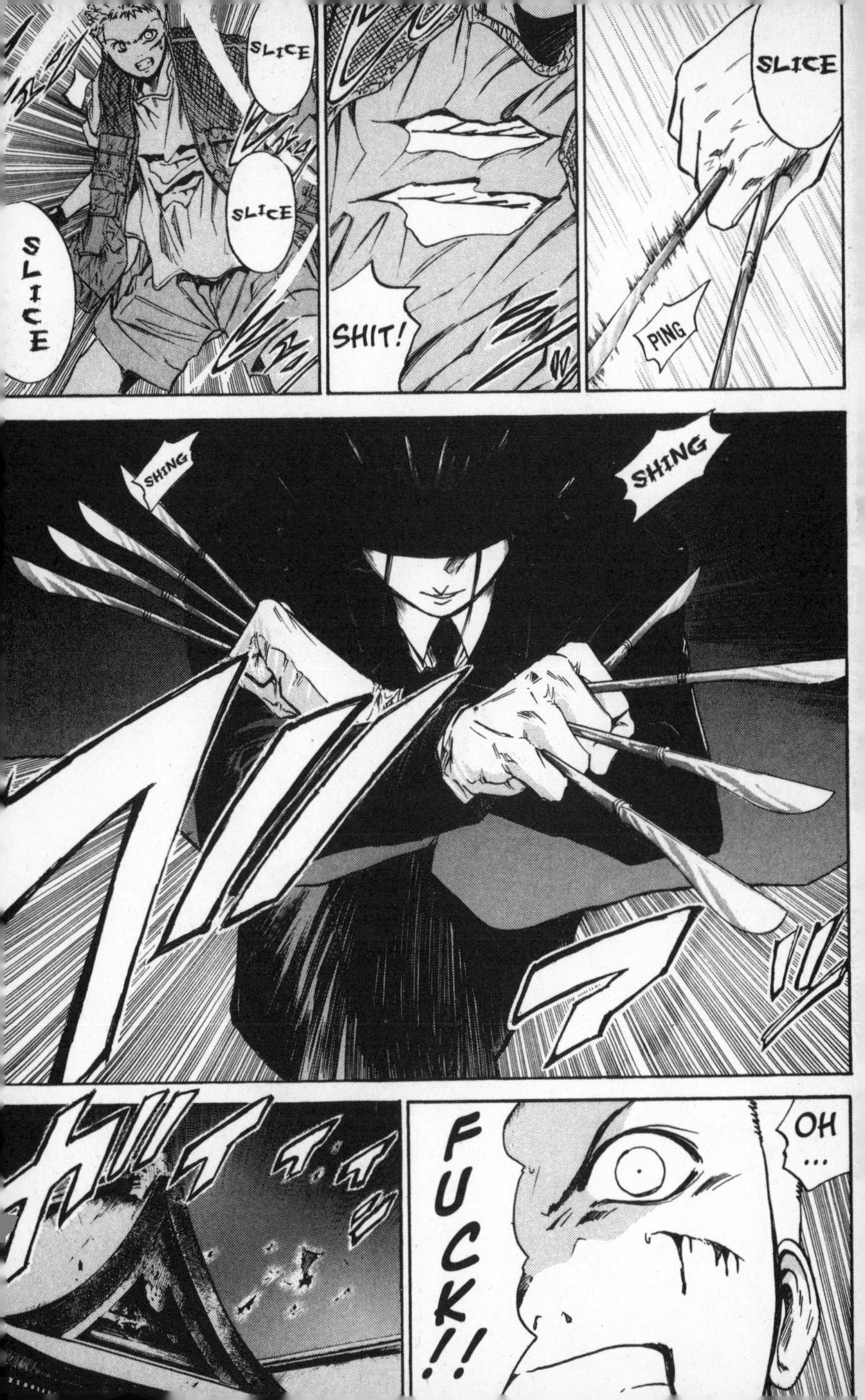
SLICE
PING
SHIT!
SLICE
SLICE
SLICE
SHING
SHING
OH ...
FUCK!!

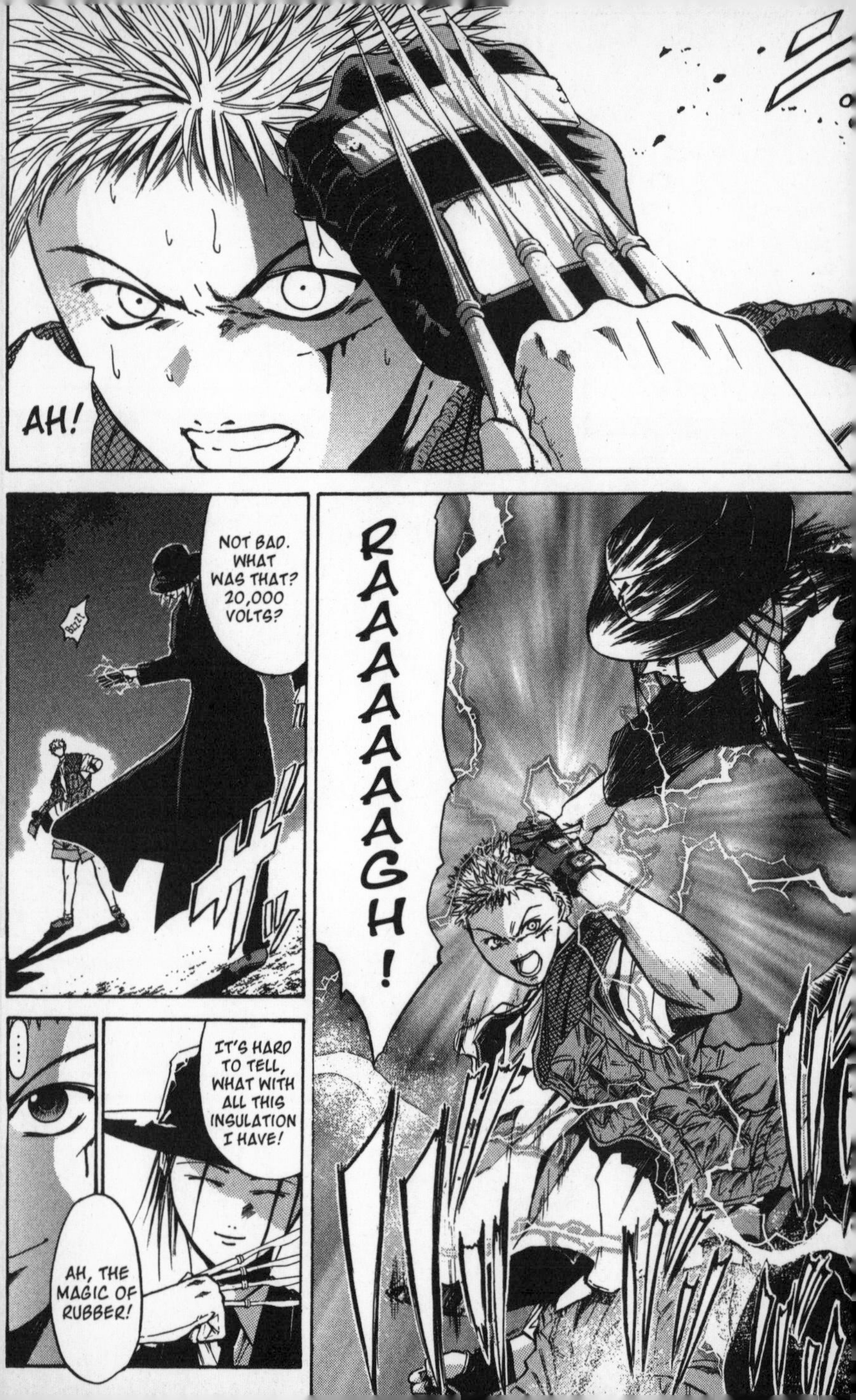
AH!
RAAAAAAAAAGH!
NOT BAD. WHAT WAS THAT? 20,000 VOLTS?
IT'S HARD TO TELL, WHAT WITH ALL THIS INSULATION I HAVE!
AH, THE MAGIC OF RUBBER!
...

....

YES
...

CLANG
CLANG
CLANG

...INDEED!

STILL
BORED?

?!

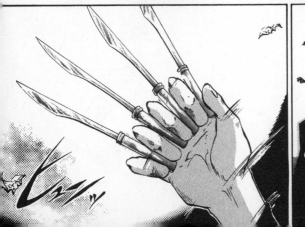

NOT
AT ALL,
NOW.

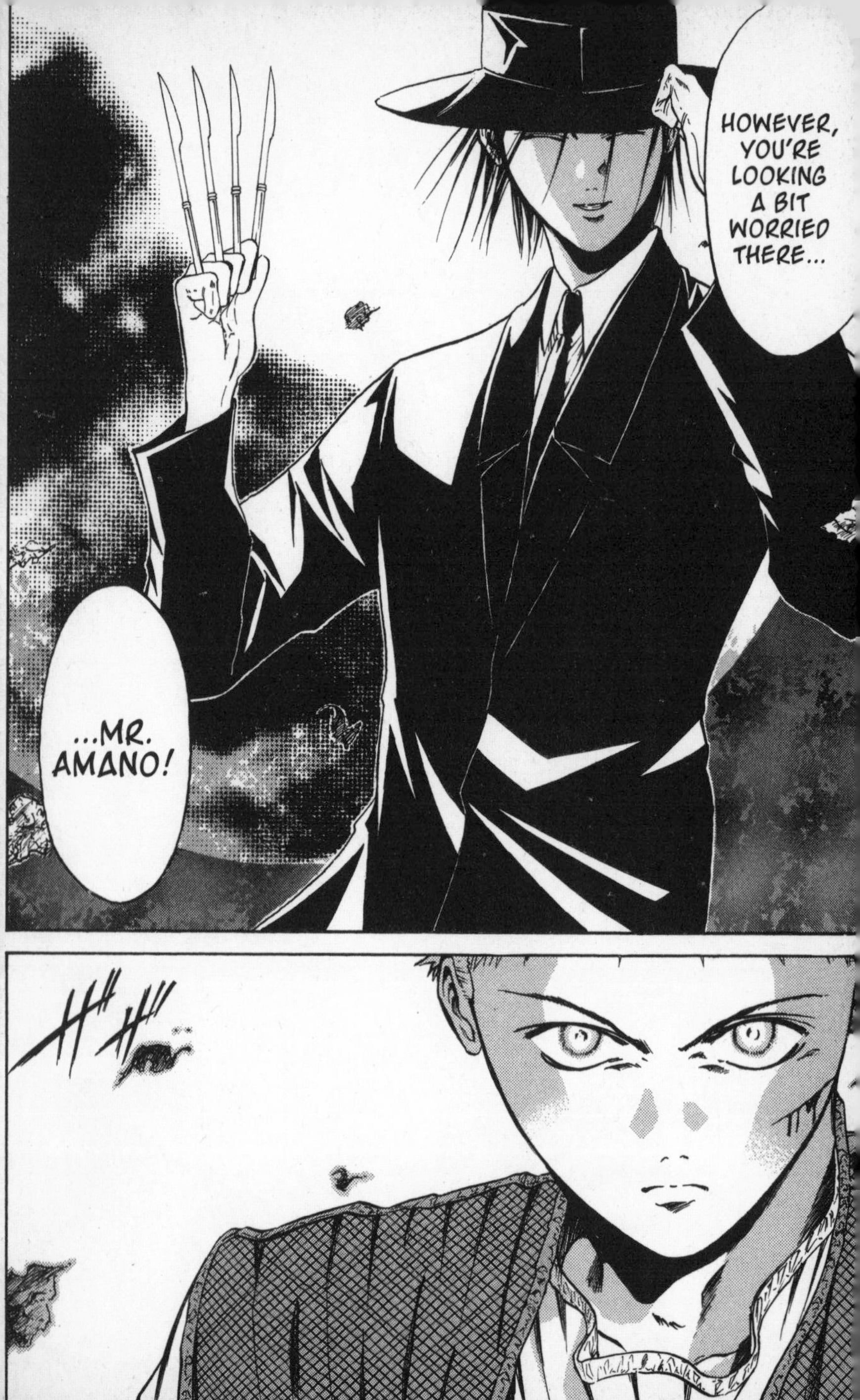
HOWEVER, YOU'RE LOOKING A BIT WORRIED THERE...
...MR. AMANO!

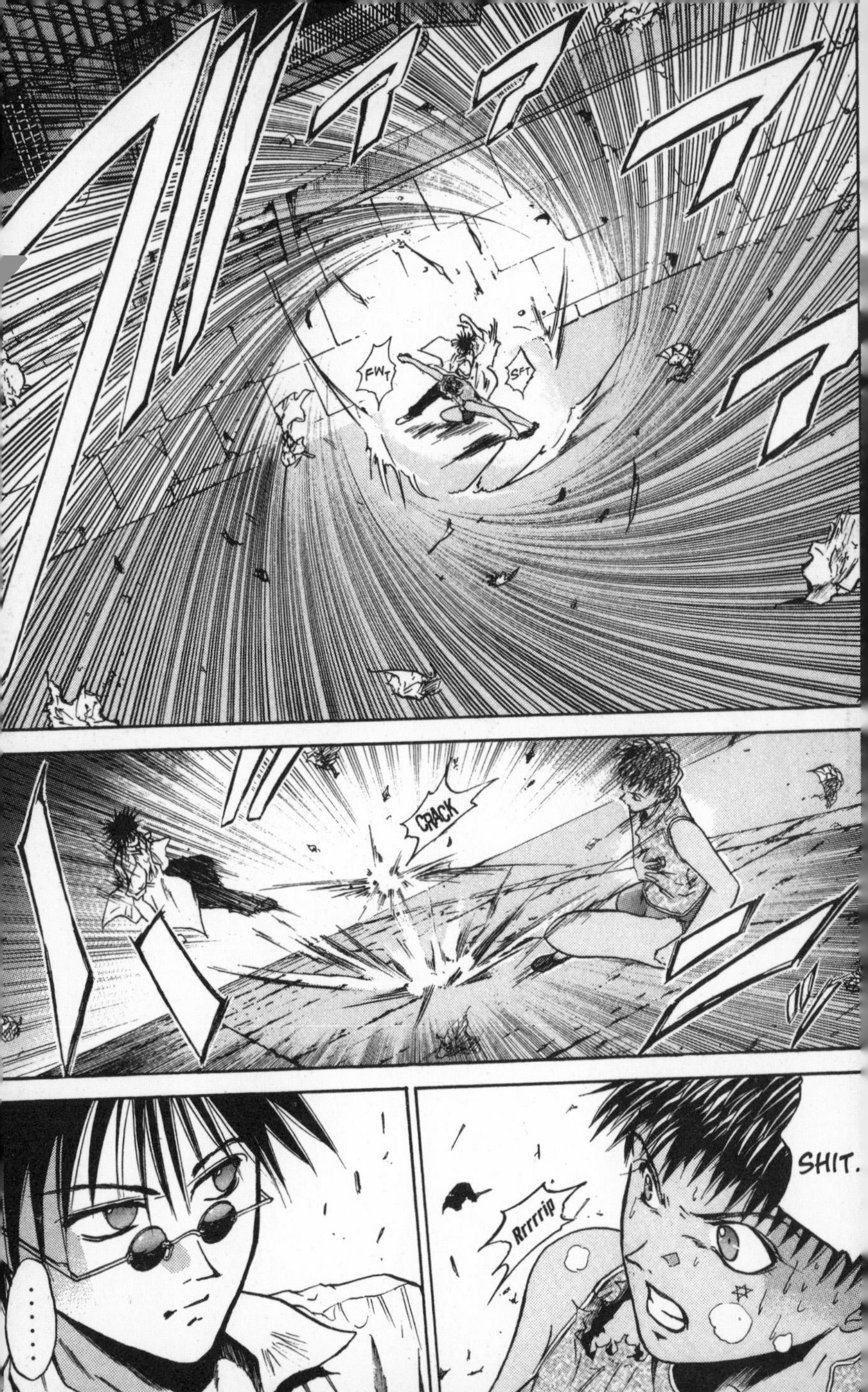
SFT
FWT
CRACK
SHIT.
Rrrrrip

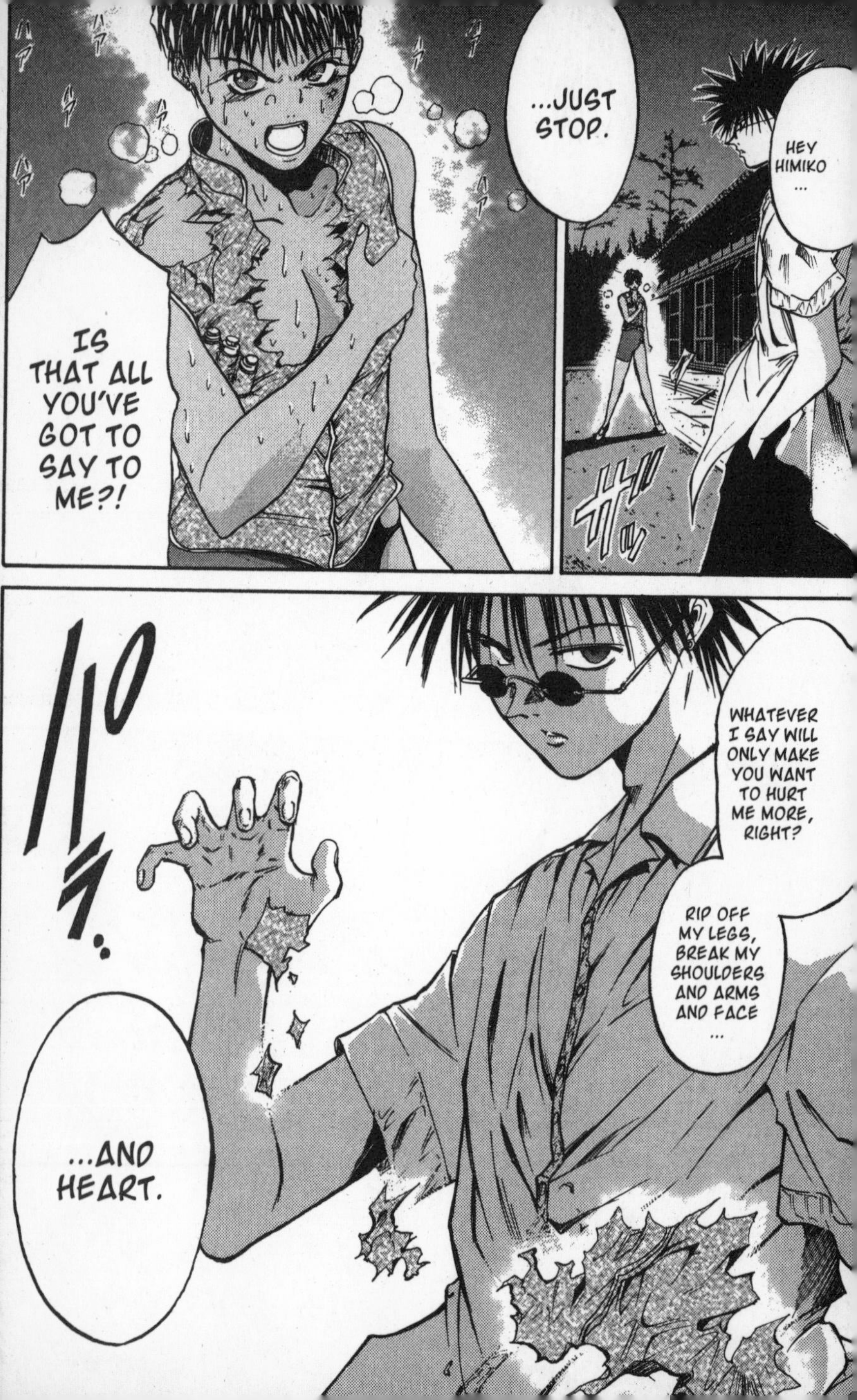
HEY HIMIKO ...
...JUST STOP.
IS THAT ALL YOU'VE GOT TO SAY TO ME?!
WHATEVER I SAY WILL ONLY MAKE YOU WANT TO HURT ME MORE, RIGHT?
RIP OFF MY LEGS, BREAK MY SHOULDERS AND ARMS AND FACE ...
...AND HEART.

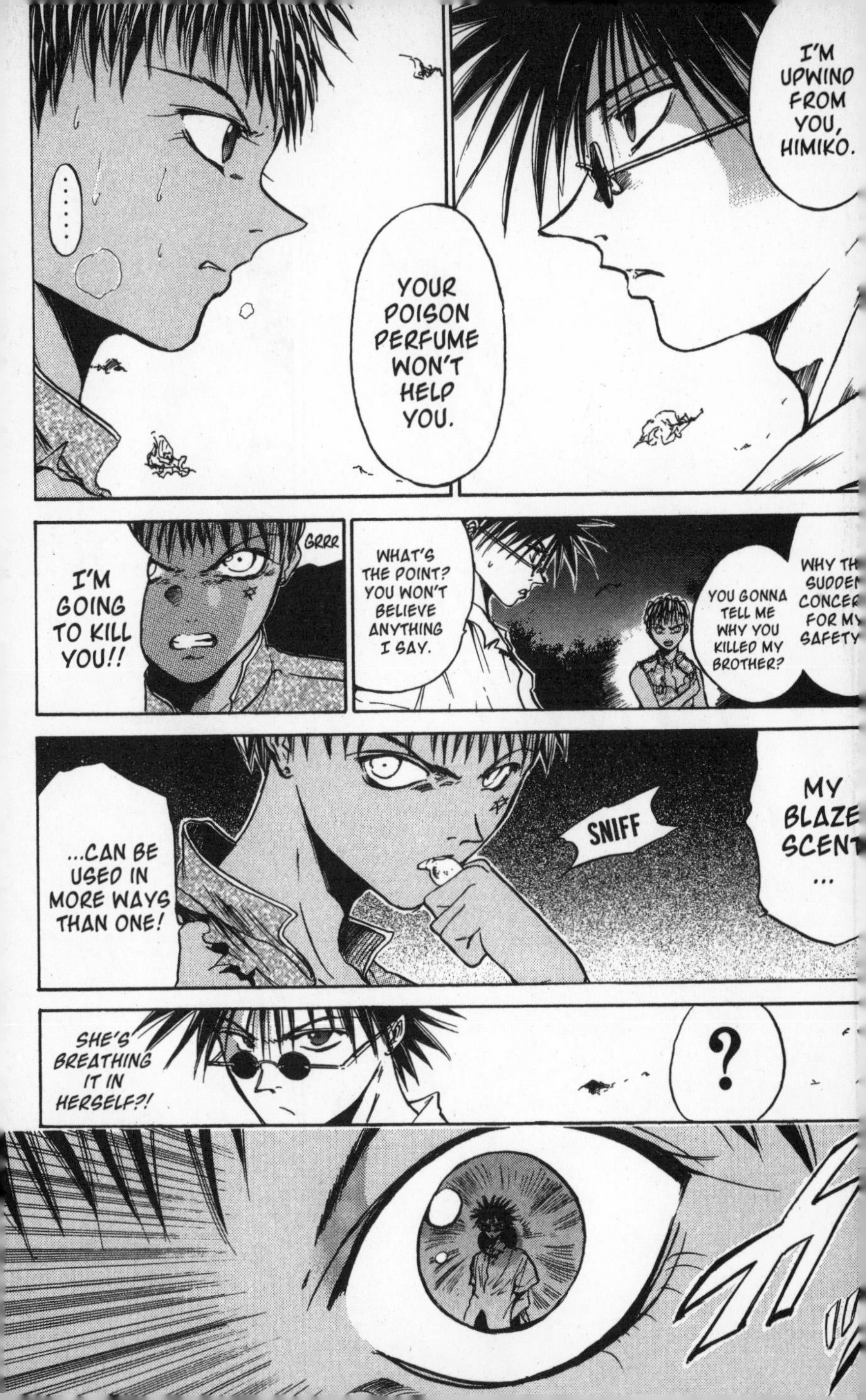
I'M UPWIND FROM YOU, HIMIKO.
YOUR POISON PERFUME WON'T HELP YOU.
......
WHY TH SUDDEN CONCER FOR MY SAFETY
YOU GONNA TELL ME WHY YOU KILLED MY BROTHER?
WHAT'S THE POINT? YOU WON'T BELIEVE ANYTHING I SAY.
GRRR
I'M GOING TO KILL YOU!!
MY BLAZE SCENT ...
SNIFF
...CAN BE USED IN MORE WAYS THAN ONE!
?
SHE'S BREATHING IT IN HERSELF?!

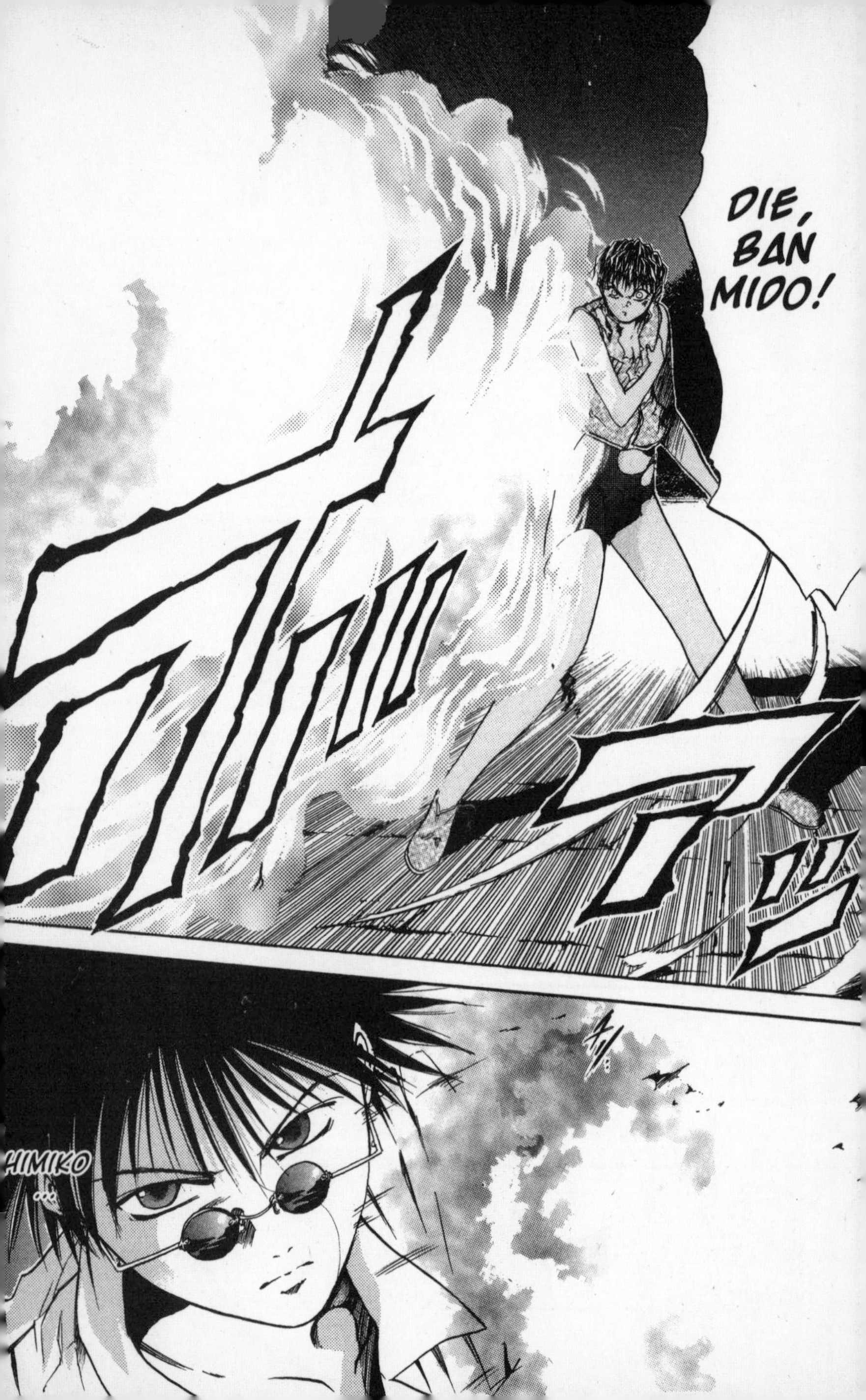
DIE, BAN MIDO!
HIMIKO ...

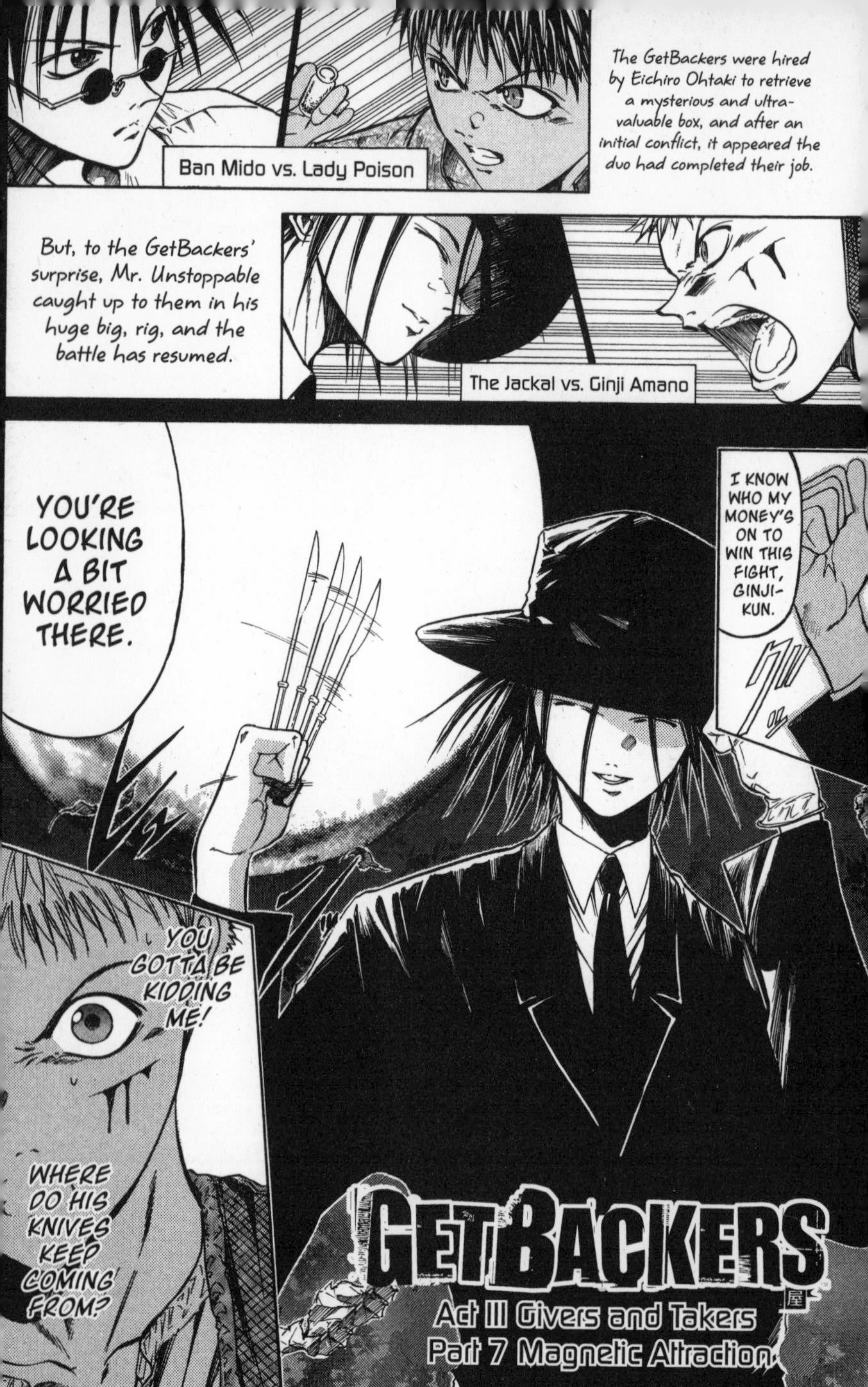

The GetBackers were hired by Eichiro Ohtaki to retrieve a mysterious and ultra-valuable box, and after an initial conflict, it appeared the duo had completed their job.
Ban Mido vs. Lady Poison
The Jackal vs. Ginji Amano
But, to the GetBackers' surprise, Mr. Unstoppable caught up to them in his huge big, rig, and the battle has resumed.
I KNOW WHO MY MONEY'S ON TO WIN THIS FIGHT, GINJI-KUN.
YOU'RE LOOKING A BIT WORRIED THERE.
YOU GOTTA BE KIDDING ME!
WHERE DO HIS KNIVES KEEP COMING FROM?
GETBACKERS
Act III Givers and Takers
Part 7 Magnetic Attraction

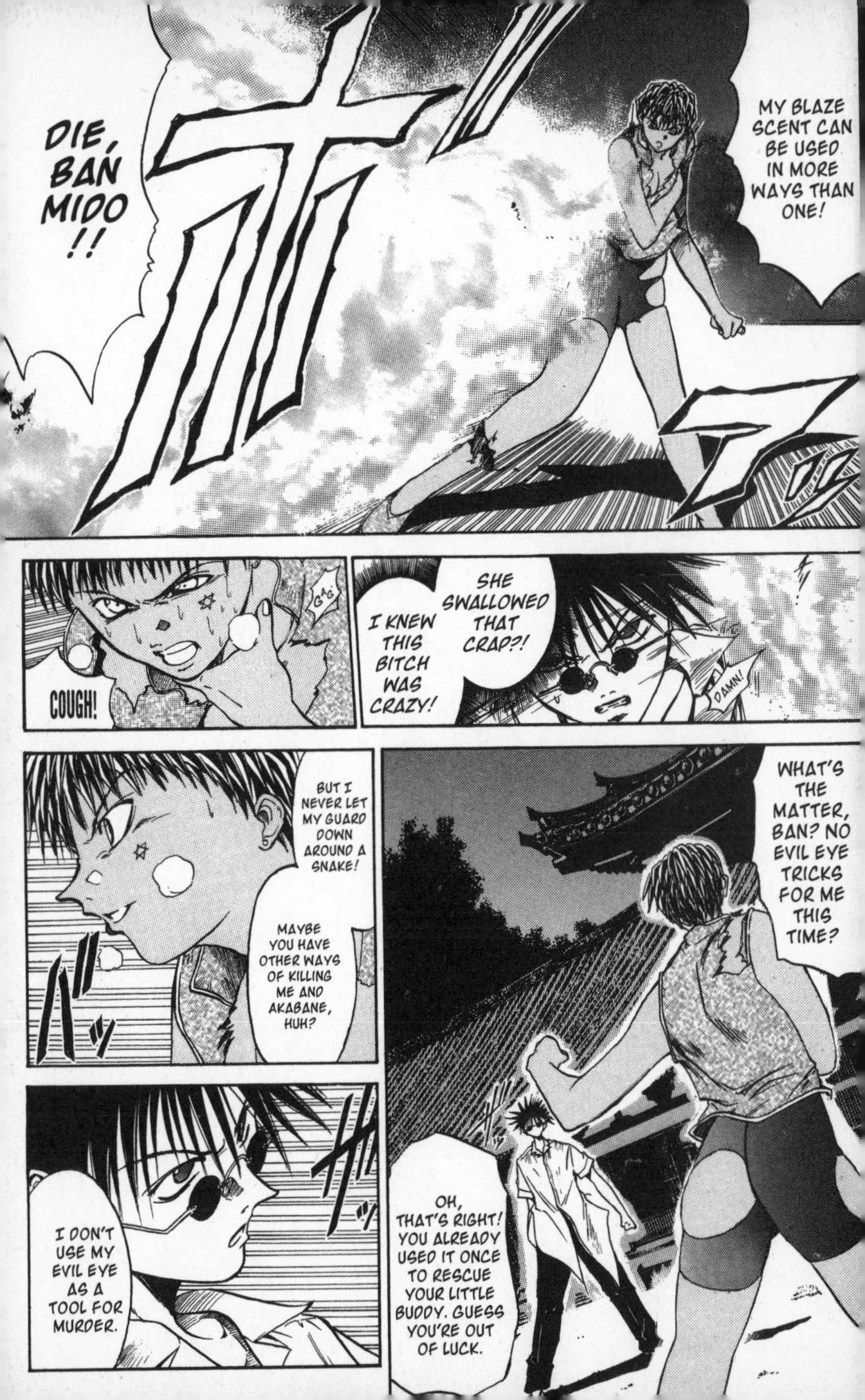
MY BLAZE SCENT CAN BE USED IN MORE WAYS THAN ONE!
DIE, BAN MIDO!!
SHE SWALLOWED THAT CRAP?!
I KNEW THIS BITCH WAS CRAZY!
DAMN!
GAG
COUGH!
WHAT'S THE MATTER, BAN? NO EVIL EYE TRICKS FOR ME THIS TIME?
OH, THAT'S RIGHT! YOU ALREADY USED IT ONCE TO RESCUE YOUR LITTLE BUDDY. GUESS YOU'RE OUT OF LUCK.
BUT I NEVER LET MY GUARD DOWN AROUND A SNAKE!
MAYBE YOU HAVE OTHER WAYS OF KILLING ME AND AKABANE, HUH?
I DON'T USE MY EVIL EYE AS A TOOL FOR MURDER.

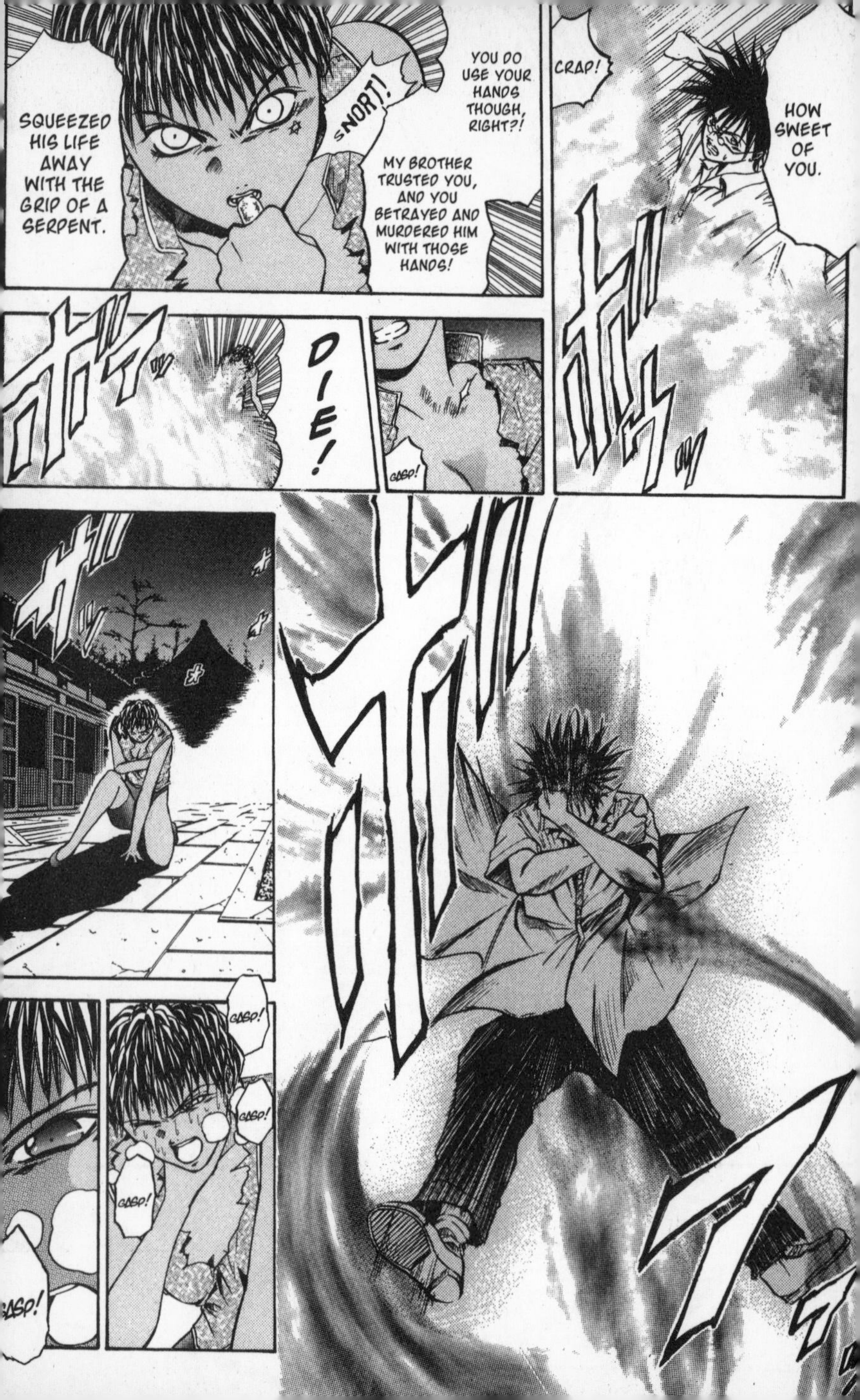
CRAP!
HOW SWEET OF YOU.
YOU DO USE YOUR HANDS THOUGH, RIGHT?!
MY BROTHER TRUSTED YOU, AND YOU BETRAYED AND MURDERED HIM WITH THOSE HANDS!
SNORT!
SQUEEZED HIS LIFE AWAY WITH THE GRIP OF A SERPENT.
DIE!
GASP!
GASP!
GASP!
GASP!
GASP!

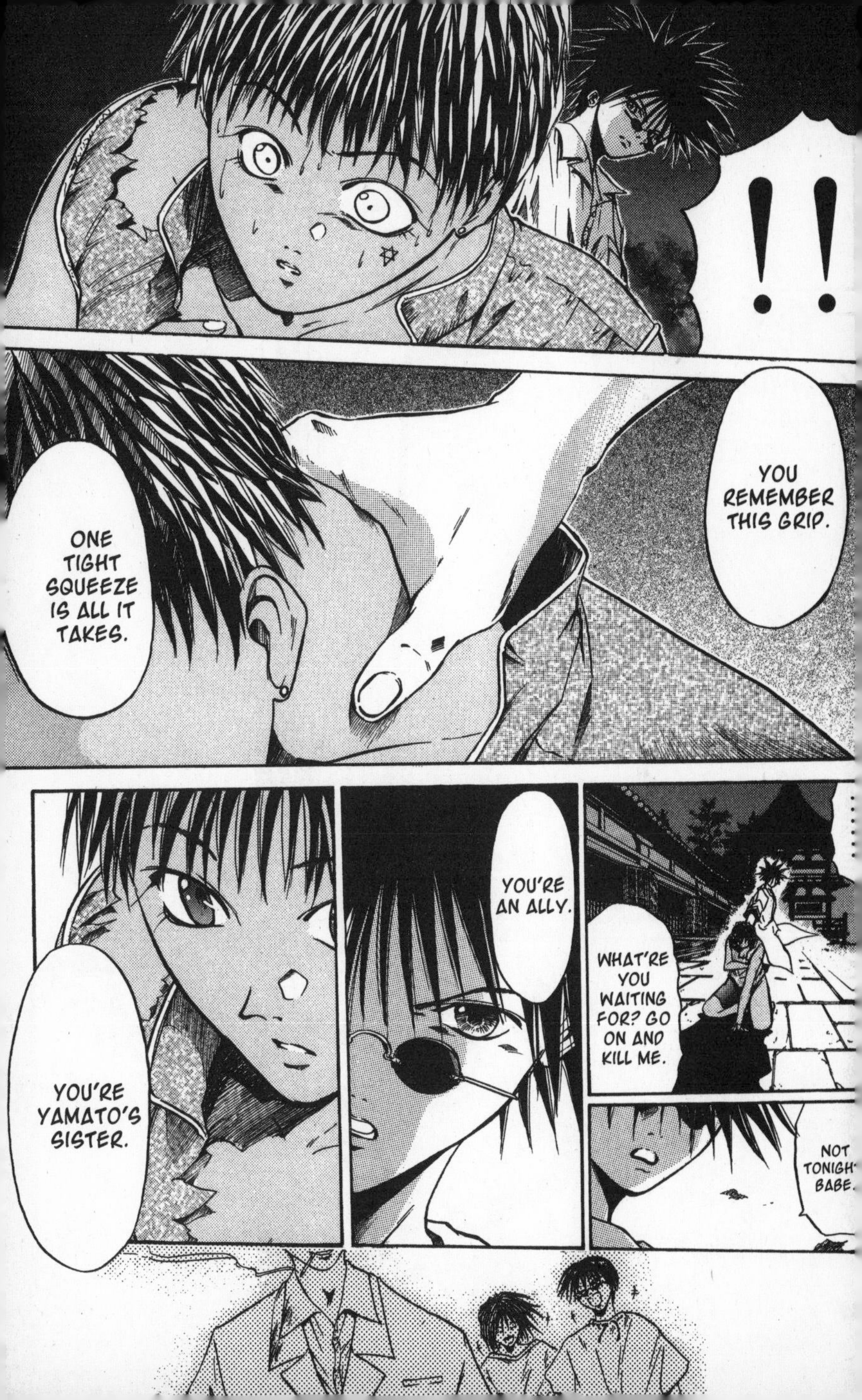
!!
YOU REMEMBER THIS GRIP.
ONE TIGHT SQUEEZE IS ALL IT TAKES.
WHAT'RE YOU WAITING FOR? GO ON AND KILL ME.
NOT TONIGH BABE.
YOU'RE AN ALLY.
YOU'RE YAMATO'S SISTER.

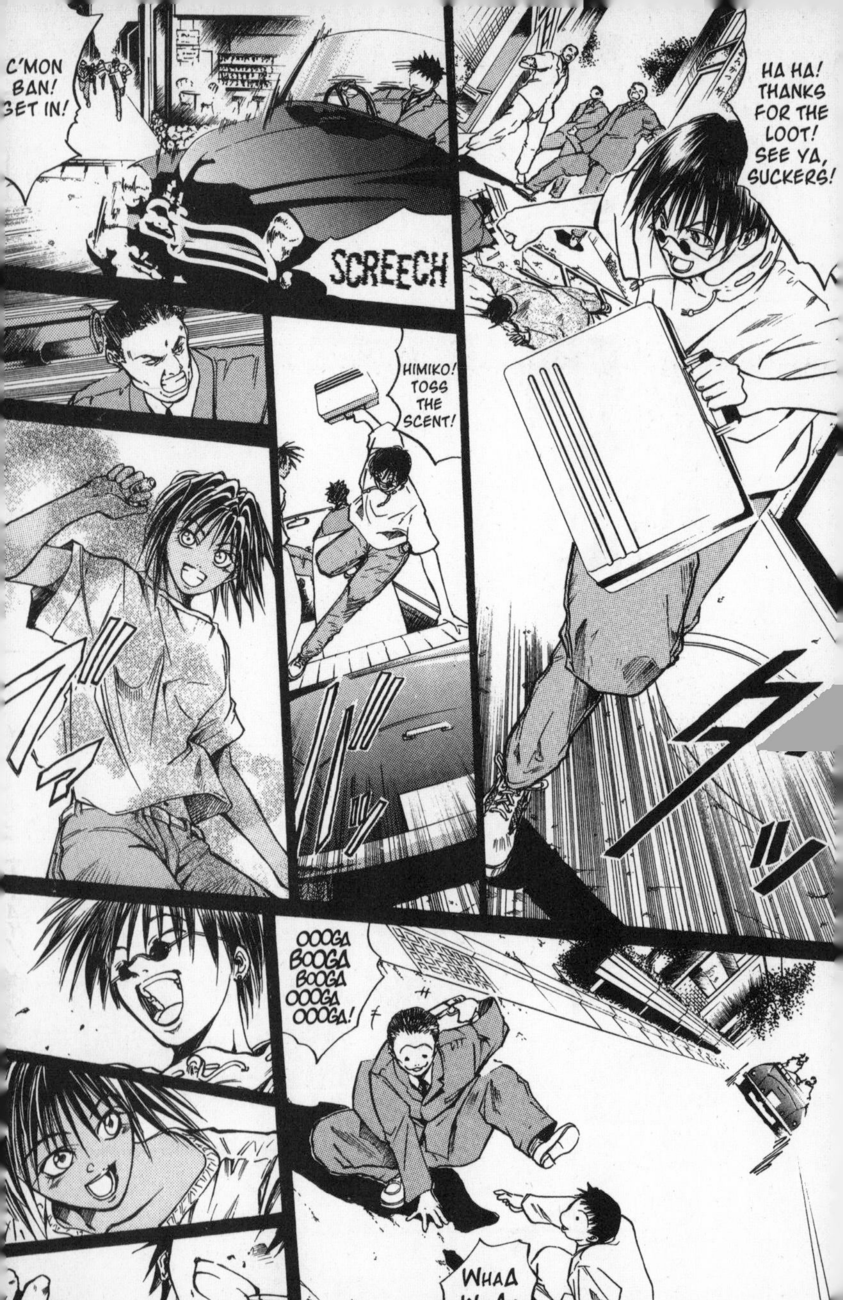
HA HA! THANKS FOR THE LOOT! SEE YA, SUCKERS!
C'MON BAN! GET IN!
SCREECH
HIMIKO! TOSS THE SCENT!
OOOGA BOOGA BOOGA OOOGA OOOGA!
WHAA WHAA WHAA!

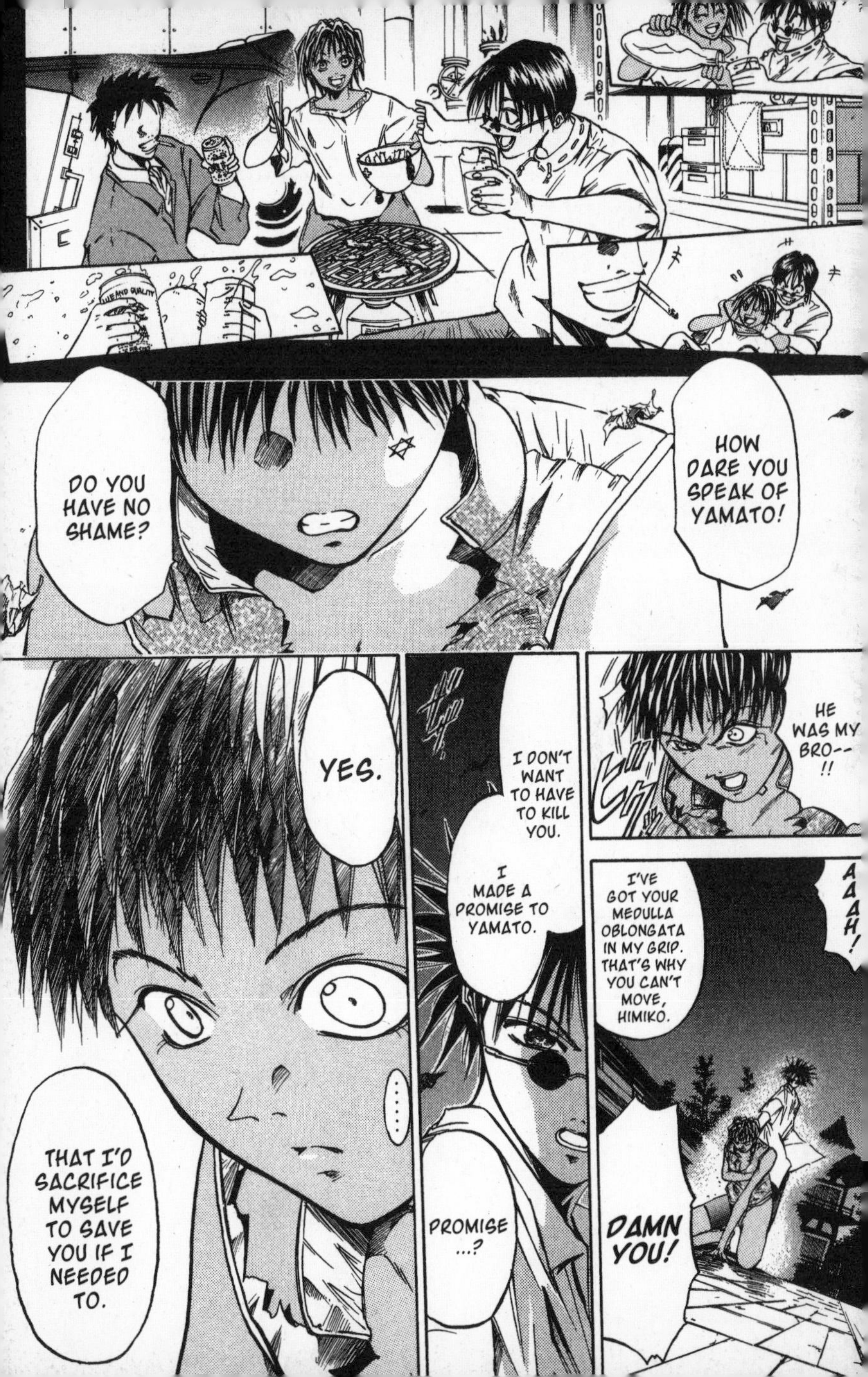
HOW DARE YOU SPEAK OF YAMATO!
DO YOU HAVE NO SHAME?
HE WAS MY BRO--!!
AAAH!
I'VE GOT YOUR MEDULLA OBLONGATA IN MY GRIP. THAT'S WHY YOU CAN'T MOVE, HIMIKO.
DAMN YOU!
I DON'T WANT TO HAVE TO KILL YOU.
I MADE A PROMISE TO YAMATO.
PROMISE ...?
YES.
......
THAT I'D SACRIFICE MYSELF TO SAVE YOU IF I NEEDED TO.

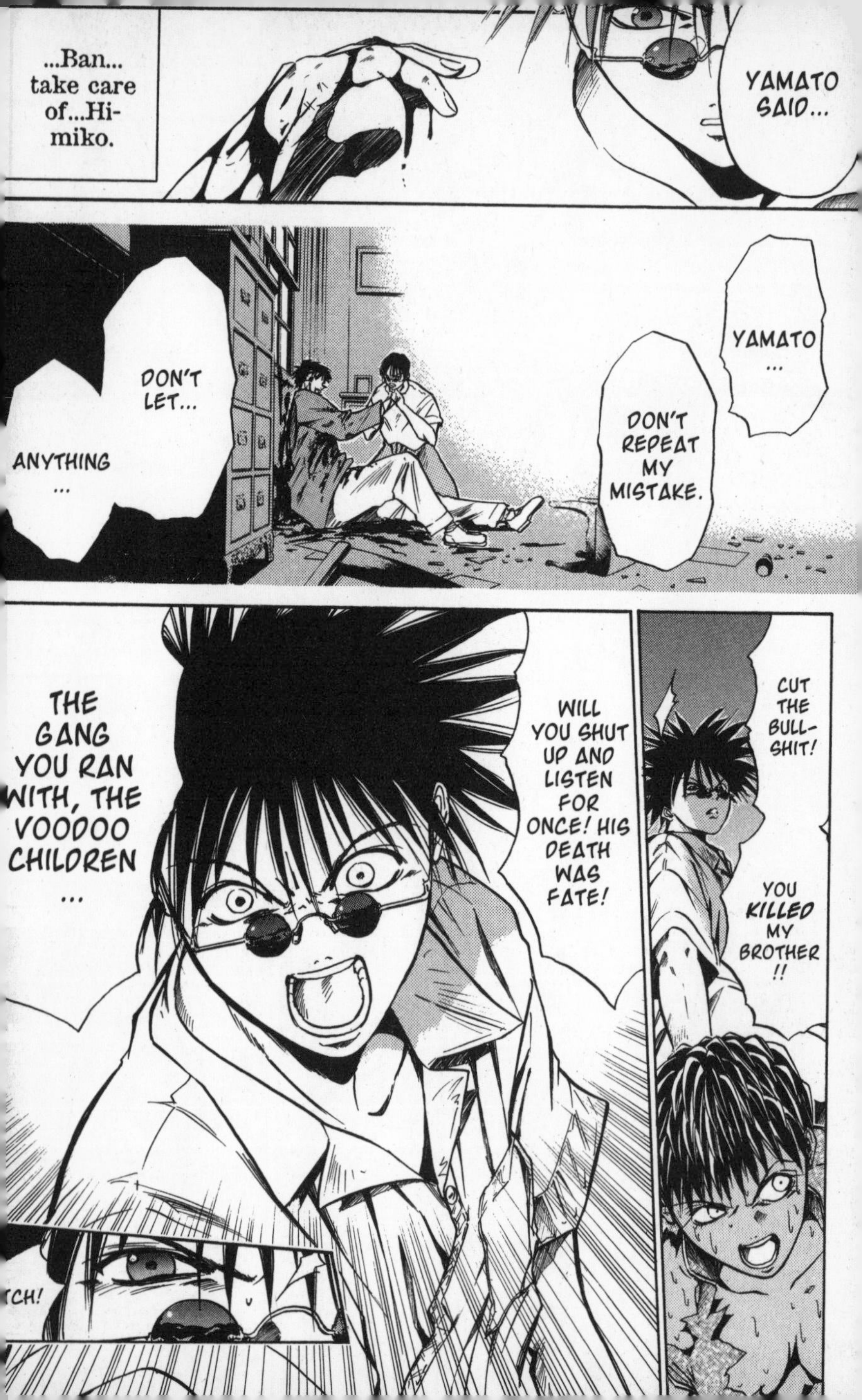
YAMATO SAID...
...Ban... take care of...Hi-miko.
YAMATO ...
DON'T REPEAT MY MISTAKE.
DON'T LET...
ANYTHING ...
CUT THE BULL-SHIT!
YOU KILLED MY BROTHER !!
WILL YOU SHUT UP AND LISTEN FOR ONCE! HIS DEATH WAS FATE!
THE GANG YOU RAN WITH, THE VOODOO CHILDREN ...
CH!

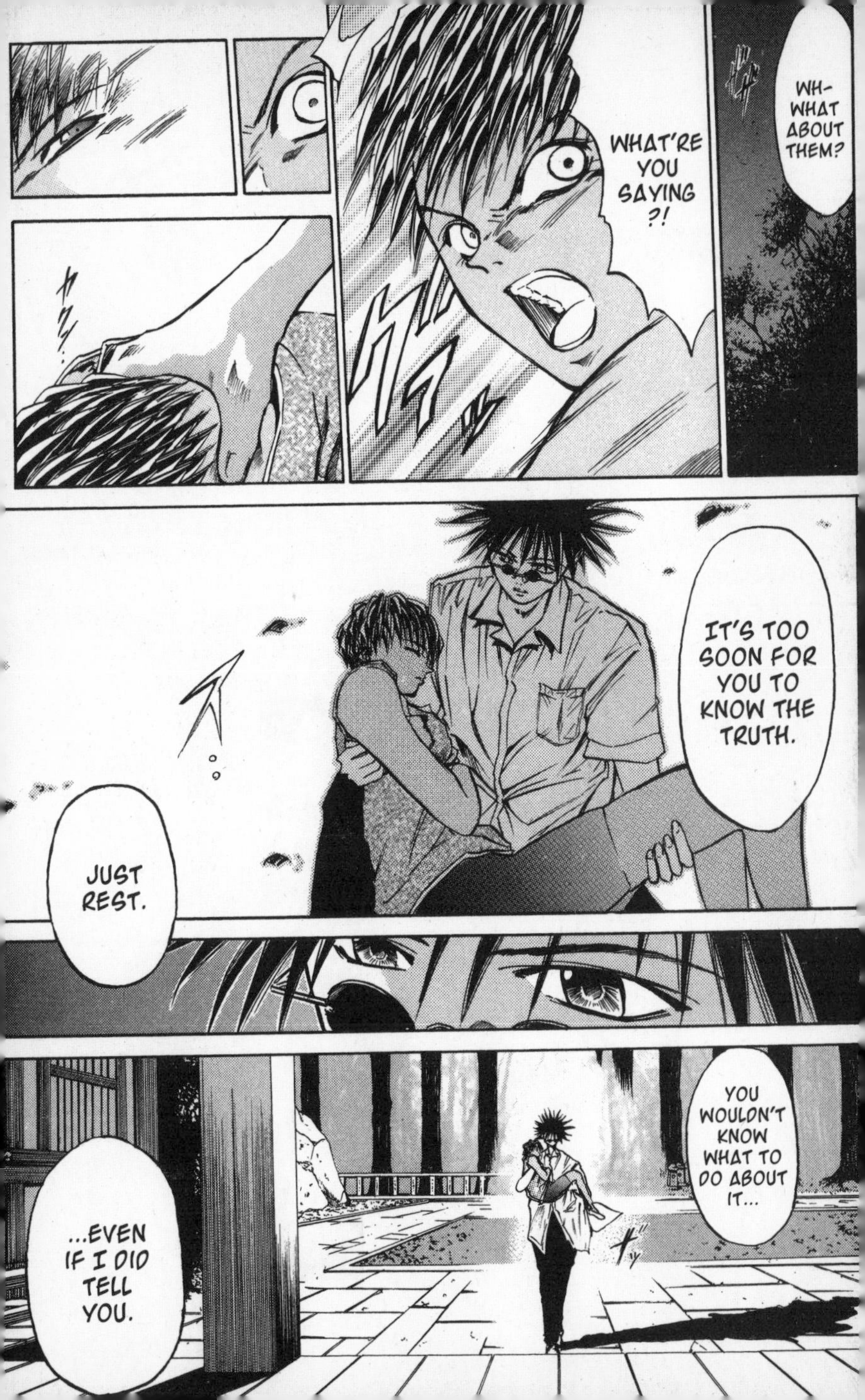
WH-WHAT ABOUT THEM?
WHAT'RE YOU SAYING?!
IT'S TOO SOON FOR YOU TO KNOW THE TRUTH.
JUST REST.
YOU WOULDN'T KNOW WHAT TO DO ABOUT IT...
...EVEN IF I DID TELL YOU.

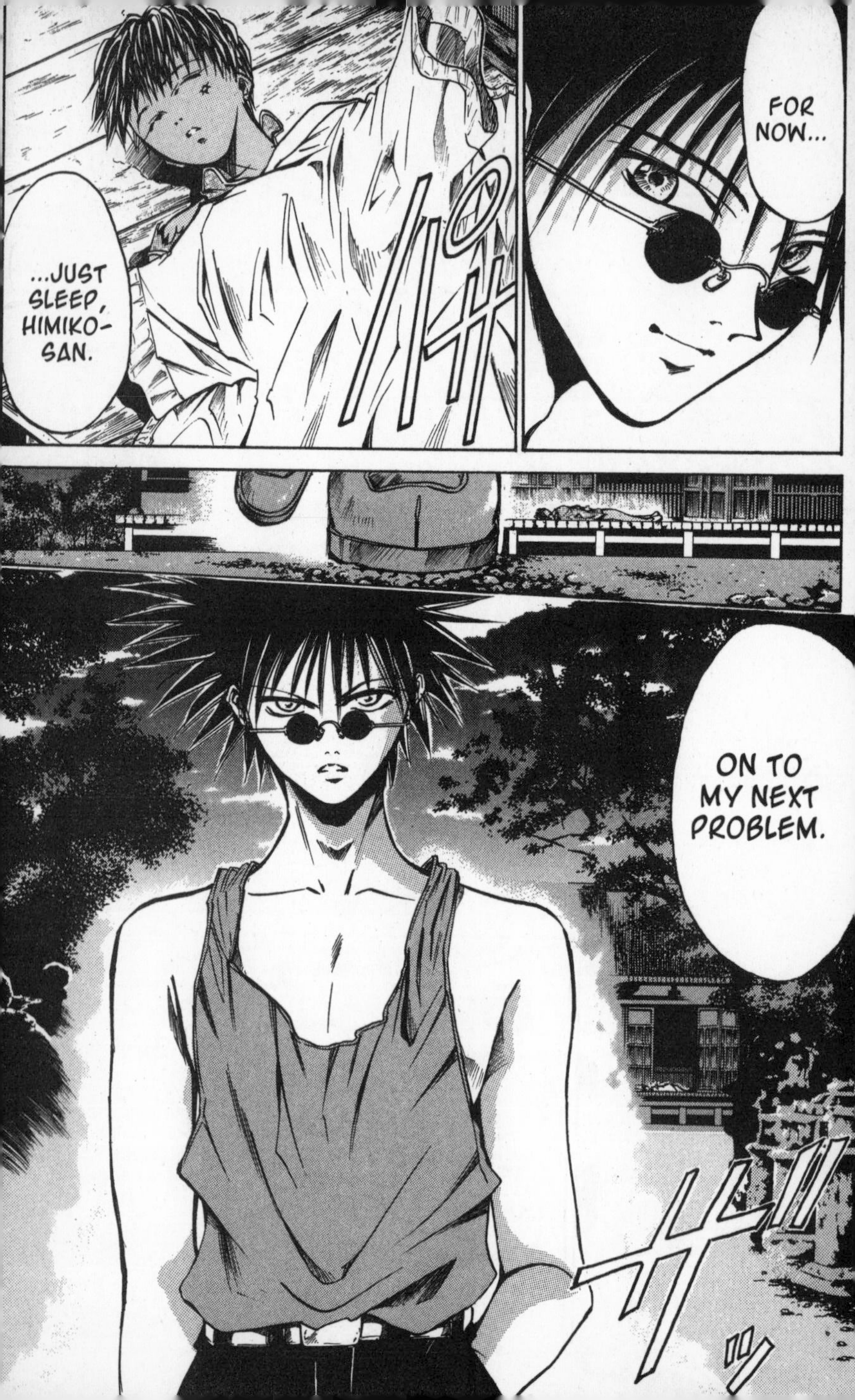
FOR NOW...
...JUST SLEEP, HIMIKO-SAN.
ON TO MY NEXT PROBLEM.

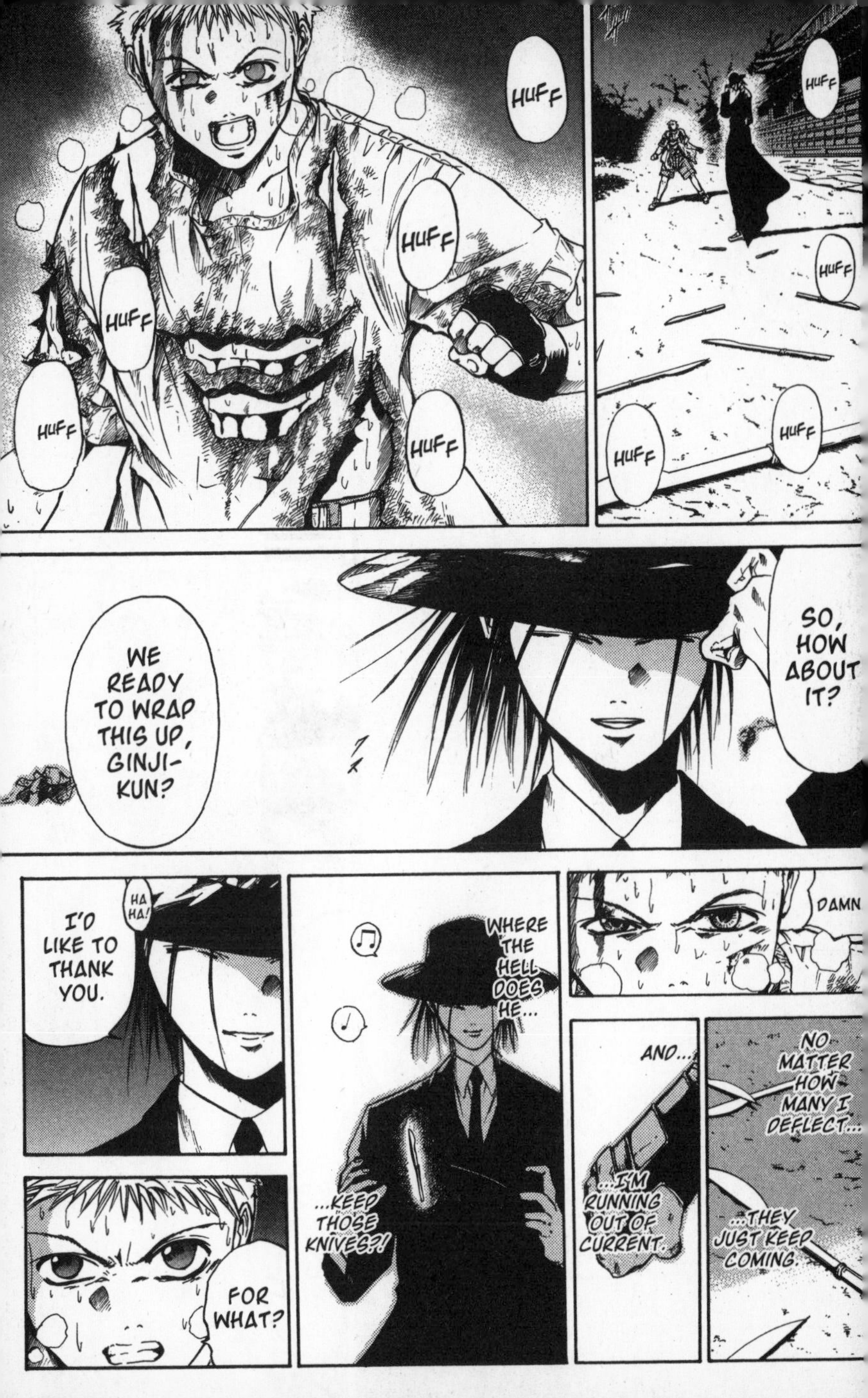
HUFF
HUFF
HUFF
HUFF
HUFF
HUFF
HUFF
HUFF
HUFF
SO, HOW ABOUT IT?
WE READY TO WRAP THIS UP, GINJI-KUN?
DAMN
NO MATTER HOW MANY I DEFLECT...
...THEY JUST KEEP COMING.
AND...
...I'M RUNNING OUT OF CURRENT.
WHERE THE HELL DOES HE...
...KEEP THOSE KNIVES?!
HA HA!
I'D LIKE TO THANK YOU.
FOR WHAT?

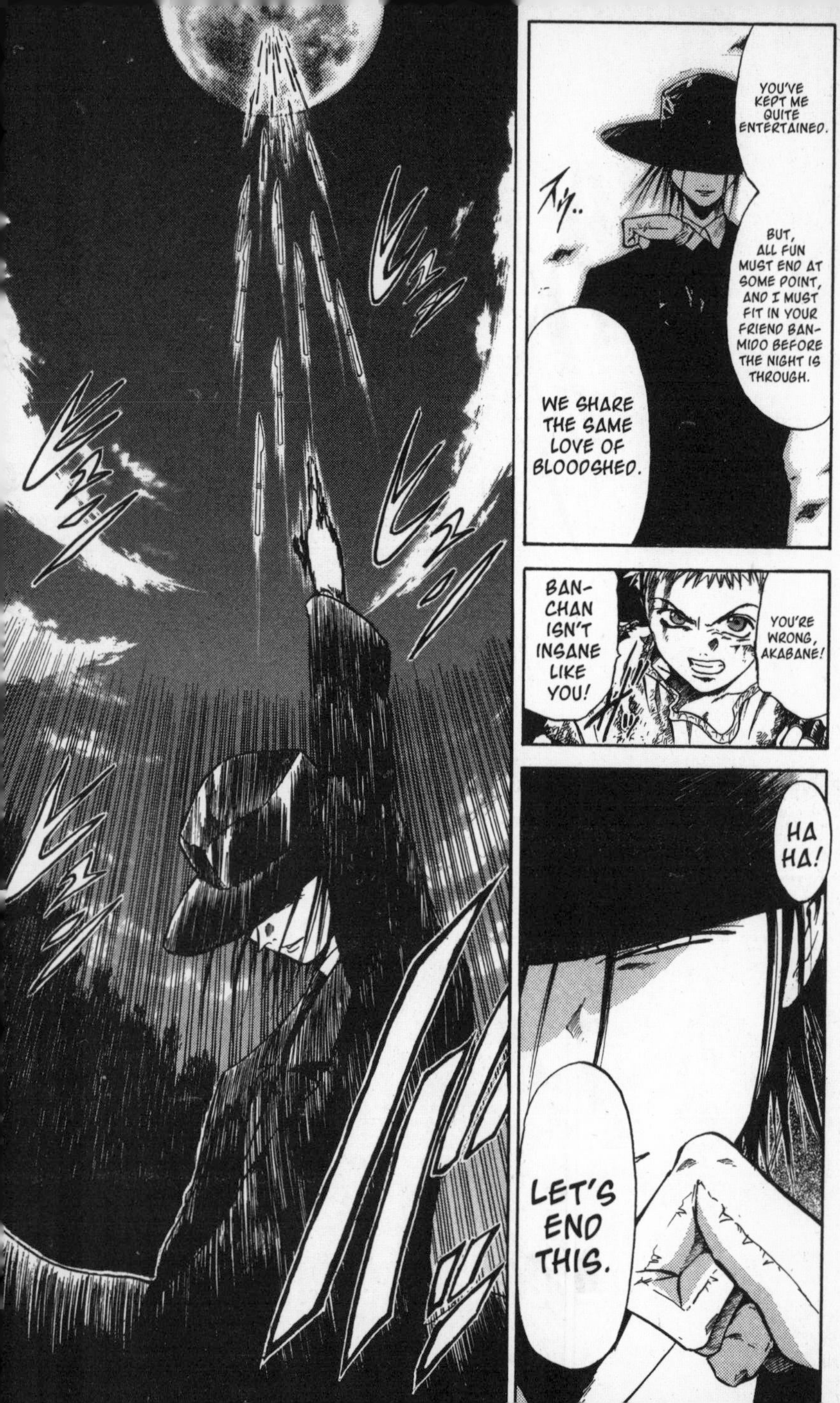
YOU'VE KEPT ME QUITE ENTERTAINED.
BUT, ALL FUN MUST END AT SOME POINT, AND I MUST FIT IN YOUR FRIEND BAN-MIDO BEFORE THE NIGHT IS THROUGH.
WE SHARE THE SAME LOVE OF BLOODSHED.
YOU'RE WRONG, AKABANE!
BAN-CHAN ISN'T INSANE LIKE YOU!
HA HA!
LET'S END THIS.

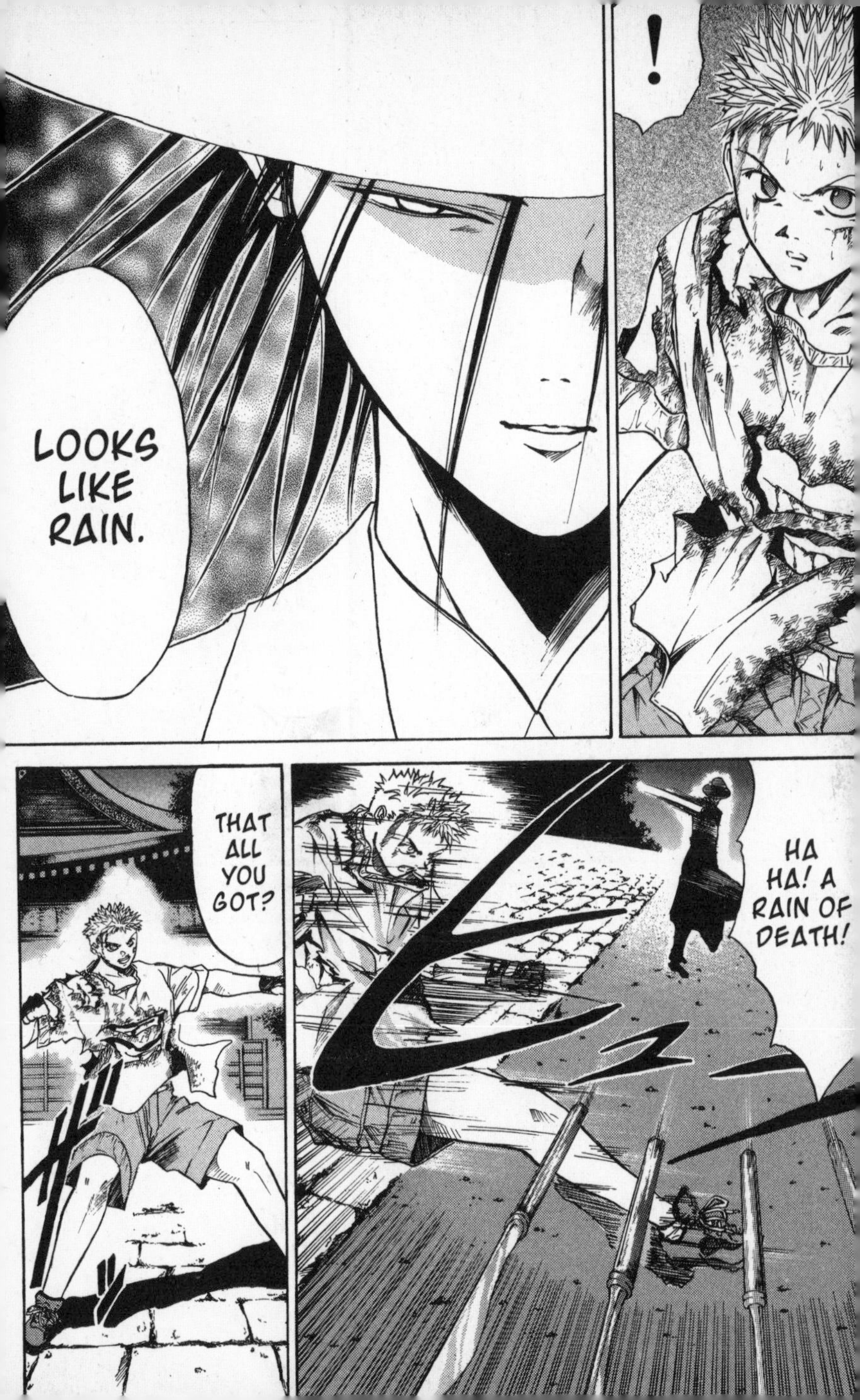
!
LOOKS LIKE RAIN.
HA HA! A RAIN OF DEATH!
THAT ALL YOU GOT?

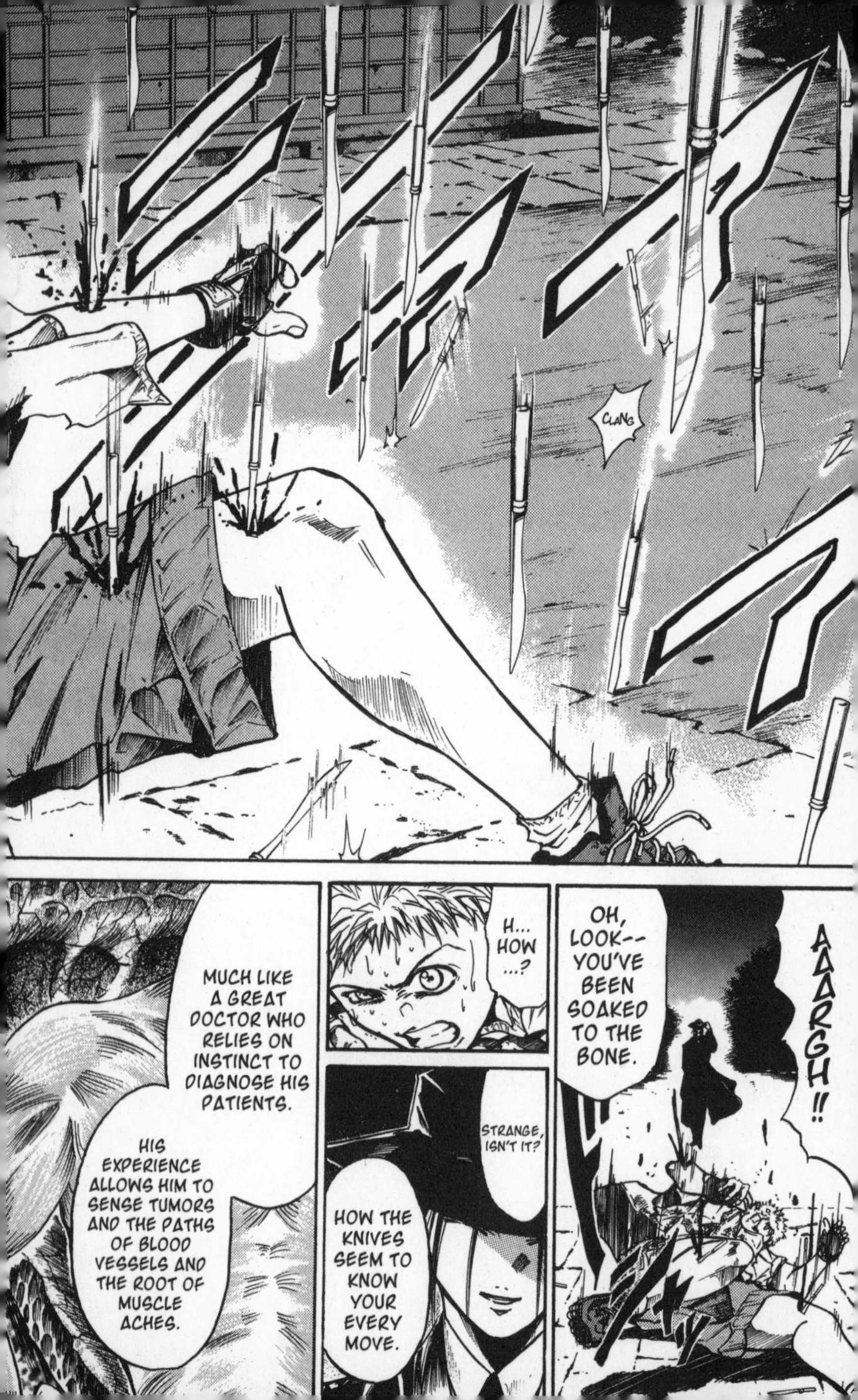
CLANG
AAARGH!!
OH, LOOK--YOU'VE BEEN SOAKED TO THE BONE.
H... HOW ...?
STRANGE, ISN'T IT?
HOW THE KNIVES SEEM TO KNOW YOUR EVERY MOVE.
MUCH LIKE A GREAT DOCTOR WHO RELIES ON INSTINCT TO DIAGNOSE HIS PATIENTS.
HIS EXPERIENCE ALLOWS HIM TO SENSE TUMORS AND THE PATHS OF BLOOD VESSELS AND THE ROOT OF MUSCLE ACHES.

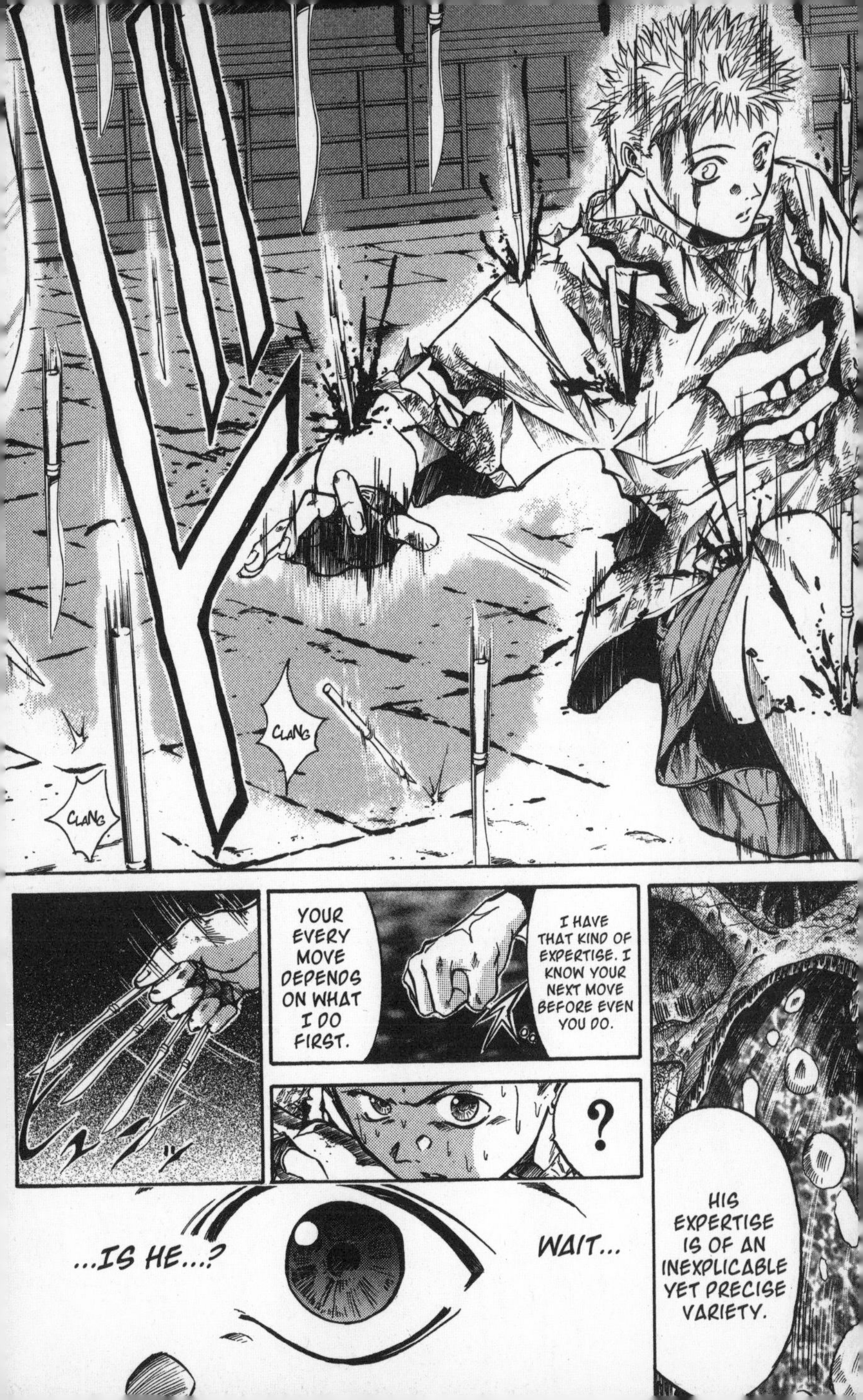
CLANG
CLANG
HIS EXPERTISE IS OF AN INEXPLICABLE YET PRECISE VARIETY.
I HAVE THAT KIND OF EXPERTISE. I KNOW YOUR NEXT MOVE BEFORE EVEN YOU DO.
YOUR EVERY MOVE DEPENDS ON WHAT I DO FIRST.
?
WAIT...
...IS HE...?

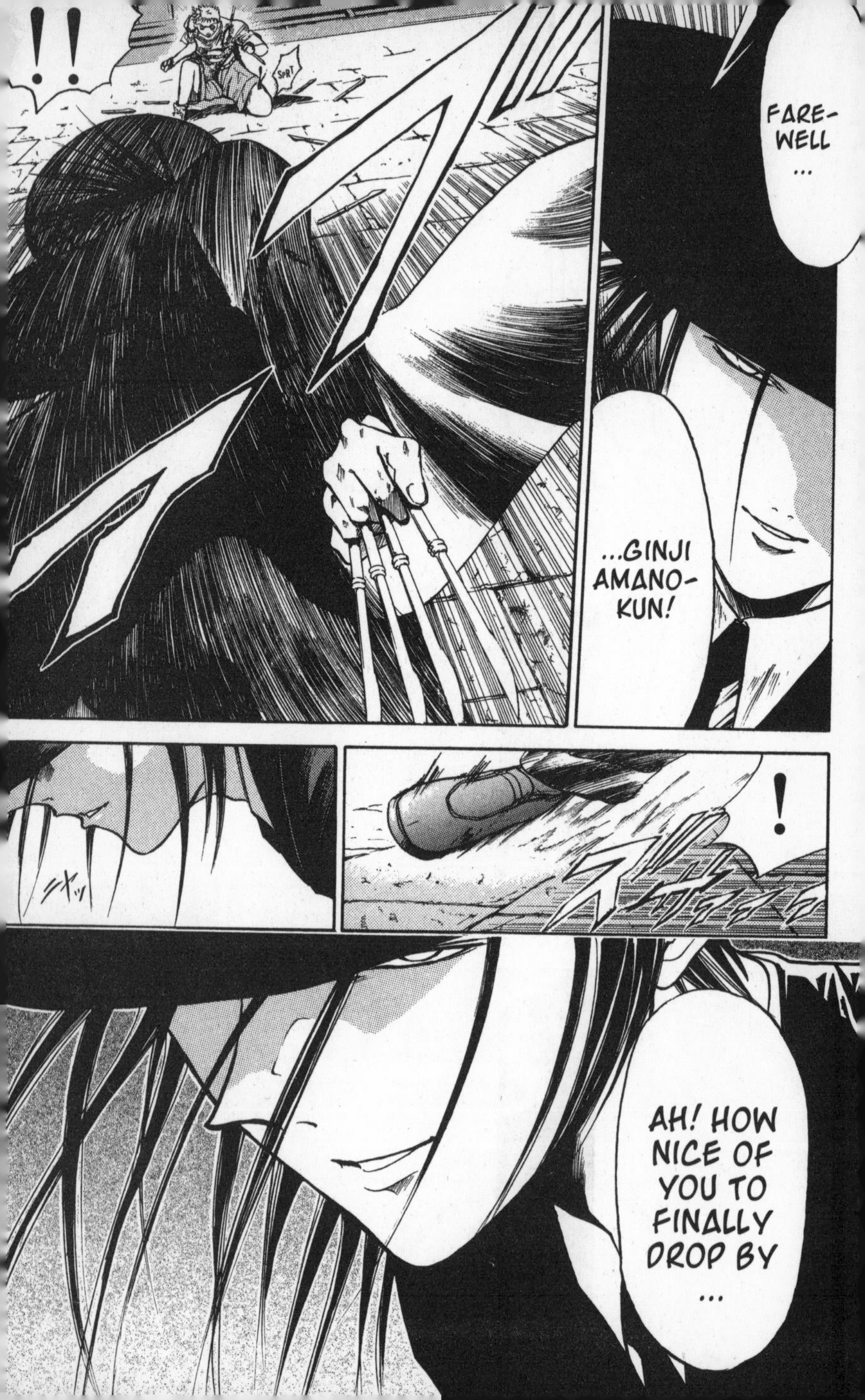

FARE-WELL ...
...GINJI AMANO-KUN!
!!
SPRT
!
シャッ
AH! HOW NICE OF YOU TO FINALLY DROP BY ...

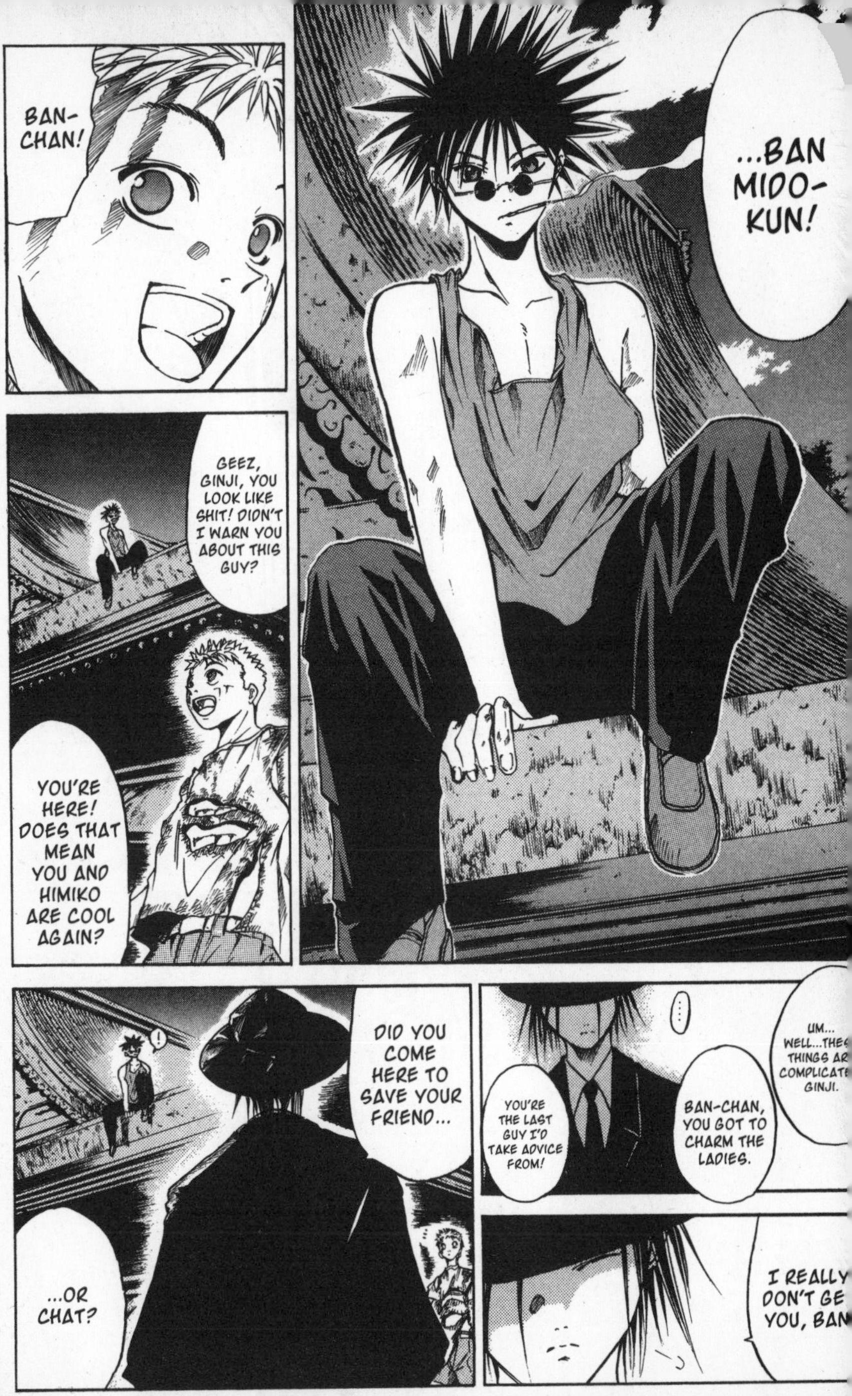
...BAN MIDO-KUN!
BAN-CHAN!
GEEZ, GINJI, YOU LOOK LIKE SHIT! DIDN'T I WARN YOU ABOUT THIS GUY?
YOU'RE HERE! DOES THAT MEAN YOU AND HIMIKO ARE COOL AGAIN?
UM... WELL...THES THINGS AR COMPLICATE GINJI.
...!
BAN-CHAN, YOU GOT TO CHARM THE LADIES.
YOU'RE THE LAST GUY I'D TAKE ADVICE FROM!
I REALLY DON'T GE YOU, BAN
!
DID YOU COME HERE TO SAVE YOUR FRIEND...
...OR CHAT?

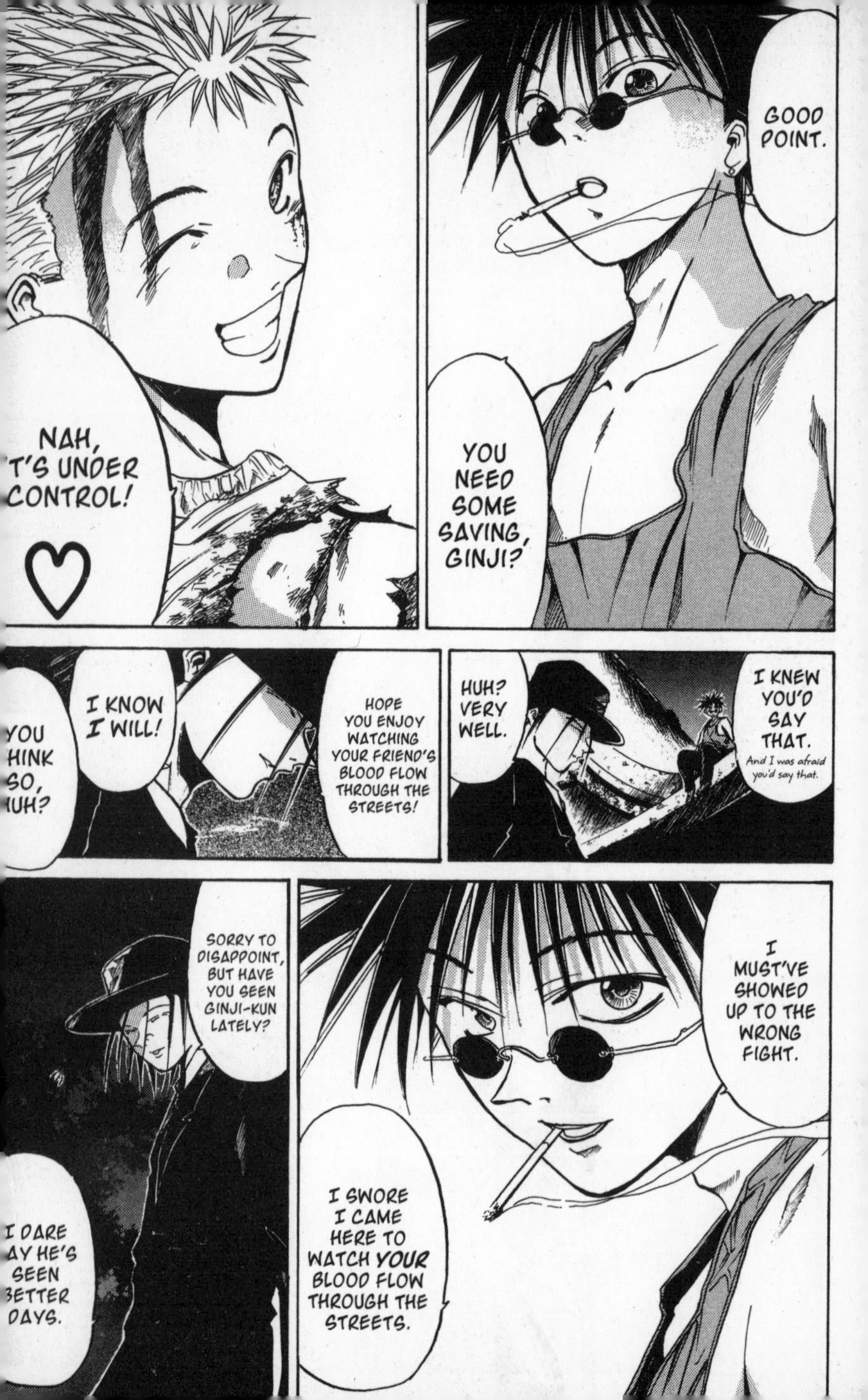
GOOD POINT.
YOU NEED SOME SAVING, GINJI?
NAH, T'S UNDER CONTROL!
I KNEW YOU'D SAY THAT.
And I was afraid you'd say that.
HUH? VERY WELL.
HOPE YOU ENJOY WATCHING YOUR FRIEND'S BLOOD FLOW THROUGH THE STREETS!
I KNOW *I* WILL!
YOU HINK SO, HUH?
I MUST'VE SHOWED UP TO THE WRONG FIGHT.
I SWORE I CAME HERE TO WATCH *YOUR* BLOOD FLOW THROUGH THE STREETS.
SORRY TO DISAPPOINT, BUT HAVE YOU SEEN GINJI-KUN LATELY?
I DARE AY HE'S SEEN BETTER DAYS.

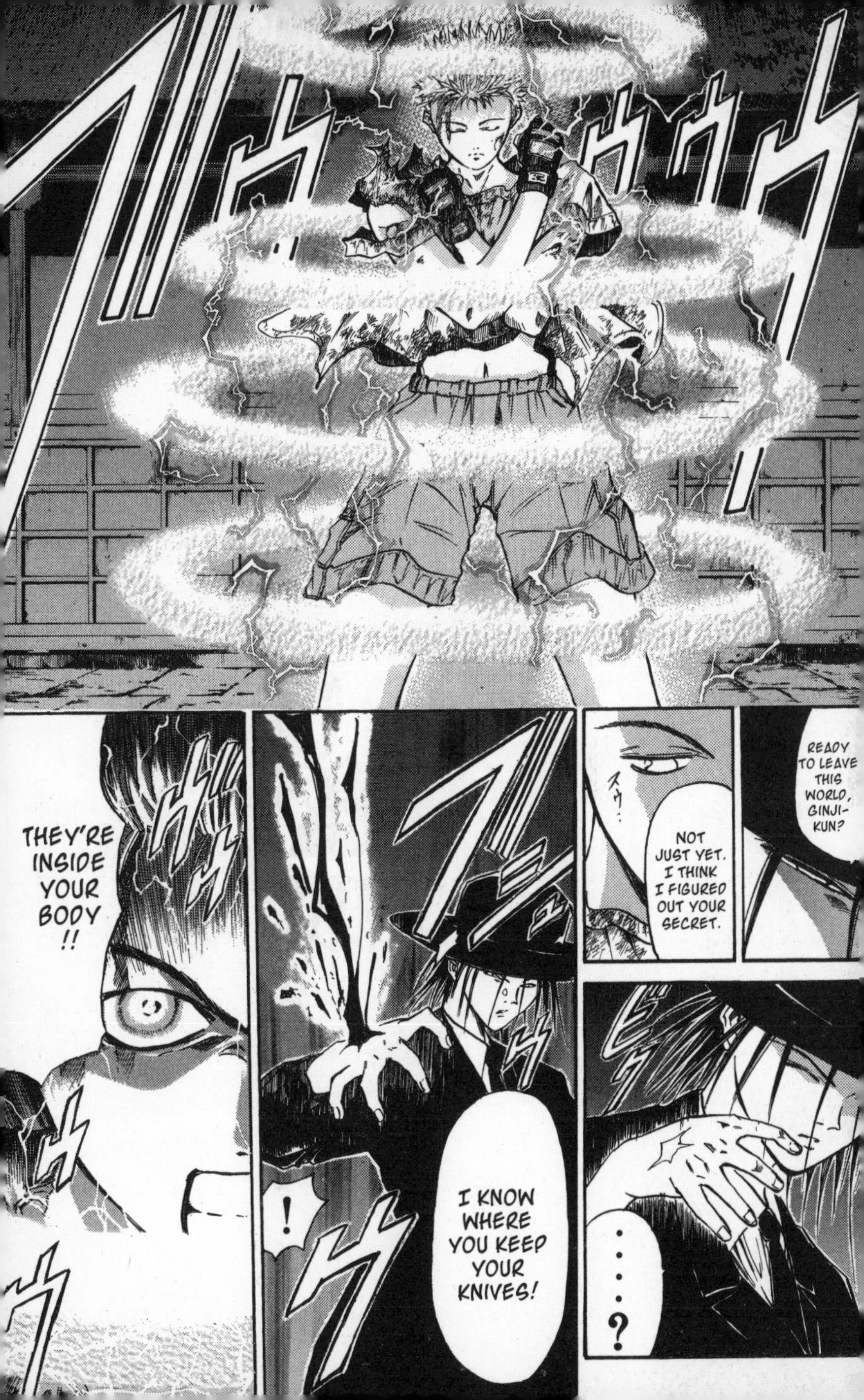
READY TO LEAVE THIS WORLD, GINJI-KUN?
NOT JUST YET. I THINK I FIGURED OUT YOUR SECRET.
...?
!
I KNOW WHERE YOU KEEP YOUR KNIVES!
THEY'RE INSIDE YOUR BODY!!

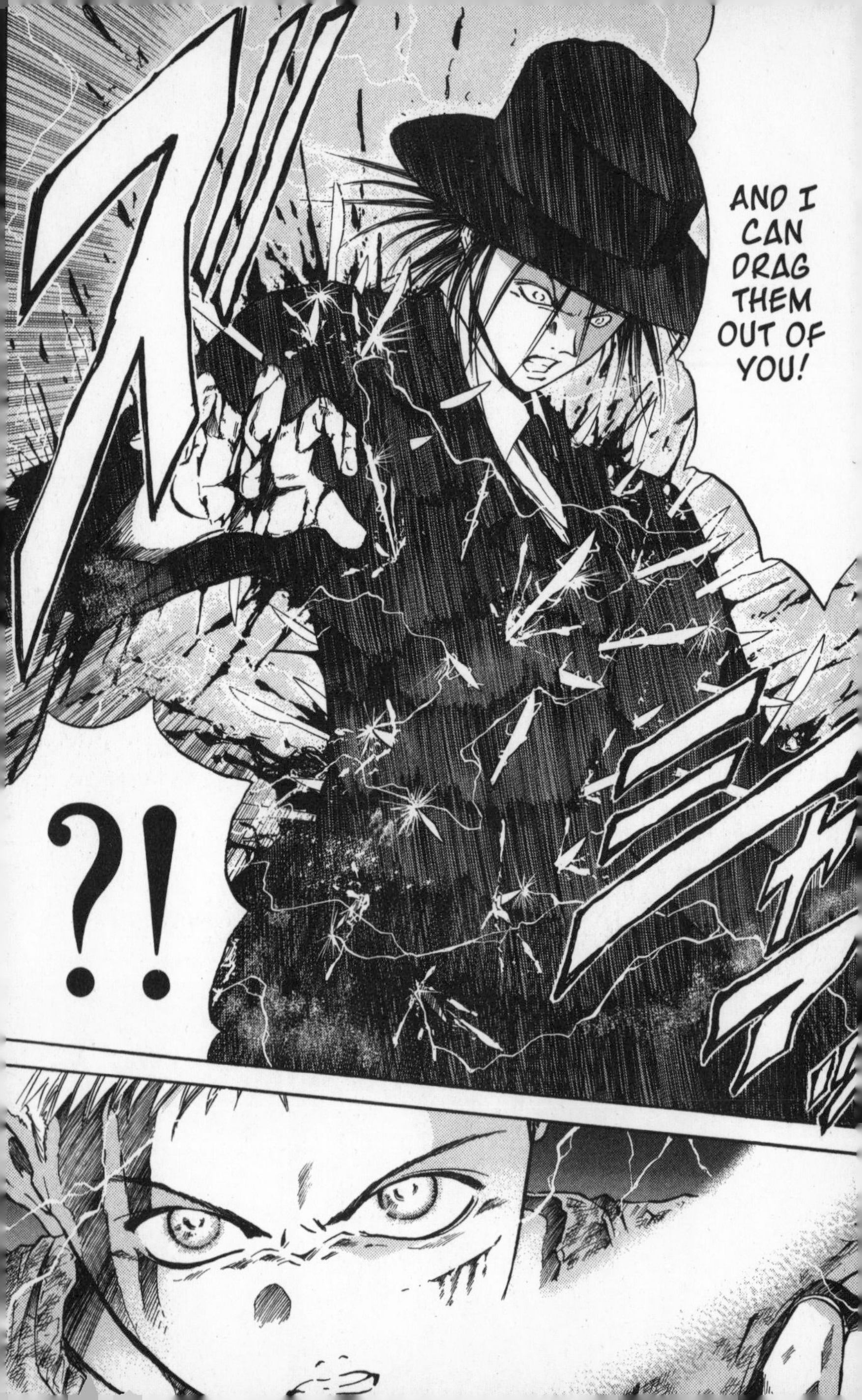
AND I CAN DRAG THEM OUT OF YOU!
?!

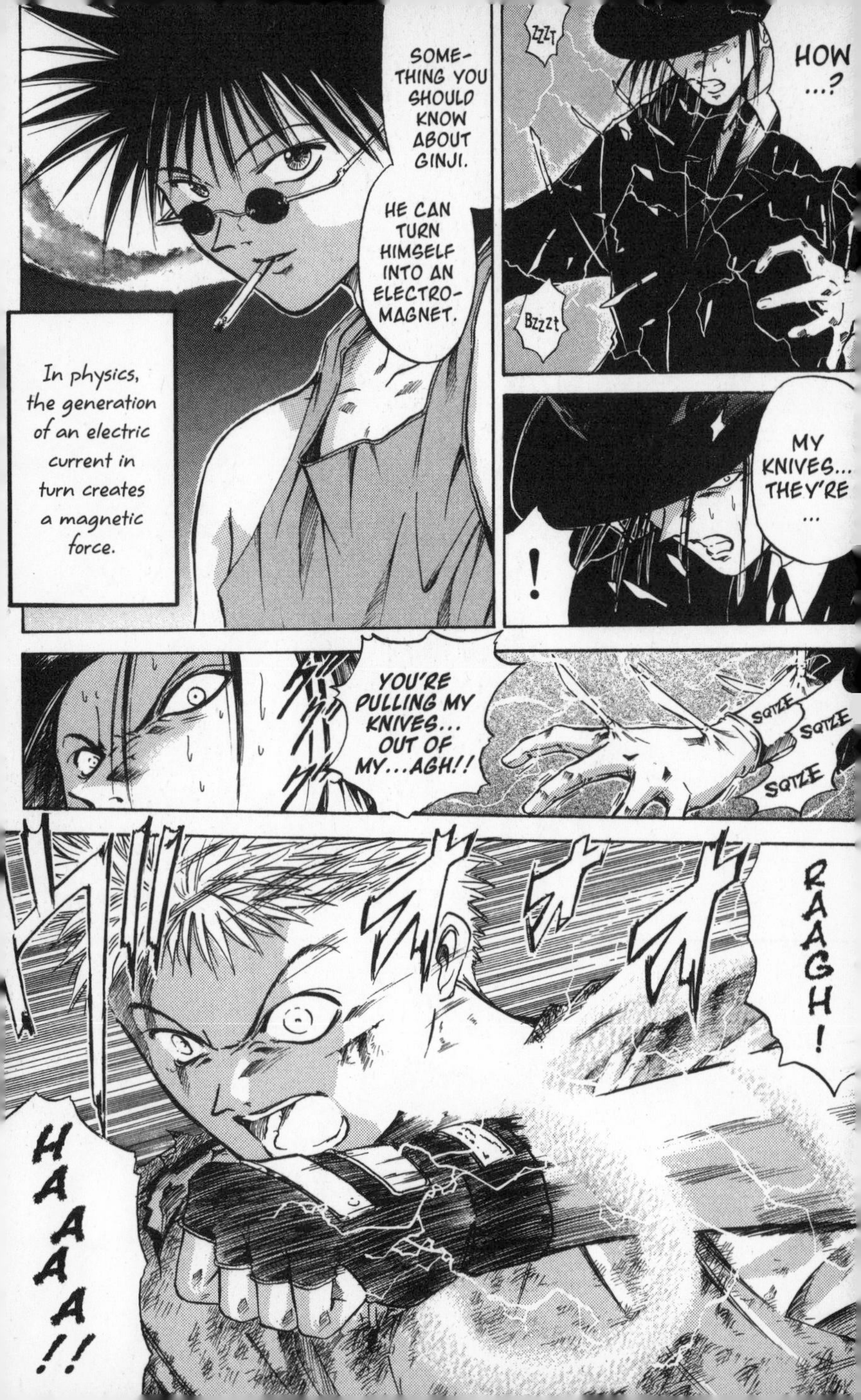

ZZZT
HOW ...?
Bzzzt
MY KNIVES... THEY'RE ...
!
SOME-THING YOU SHOULD KNOW ABOUT GINJI.
HE CAN TURN HIMSELF INTO AN ELECTRO-MAGNET.
In physics, the generation of an electric current in turn creates a magnetic force.
SQTZE
SQTZE
SQTZE
YOU'RE PULLING MY KNIVES... OUT OF MY...AGH!!
RAAGH!
HAAAAA!!

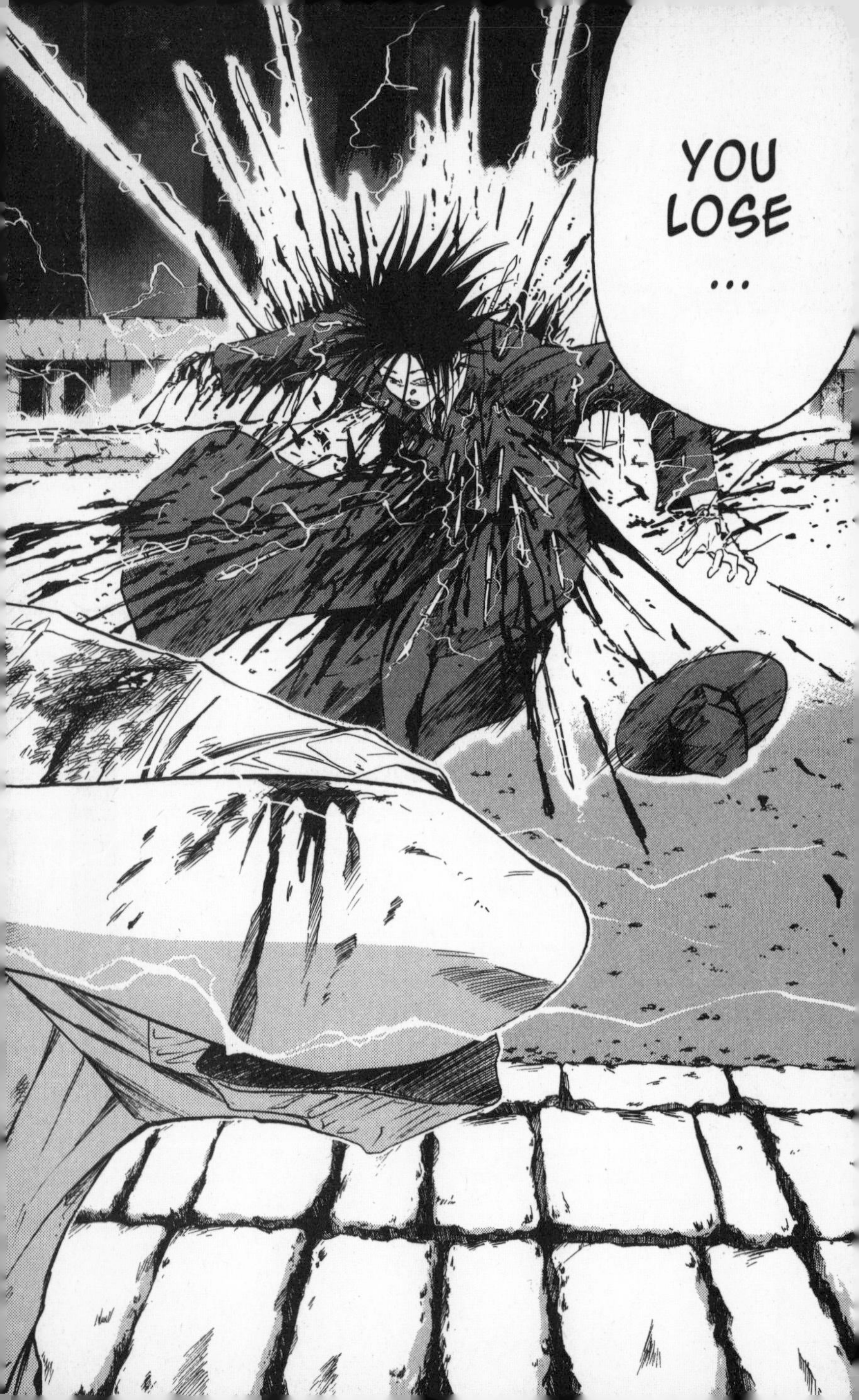
YOU LOSE ...

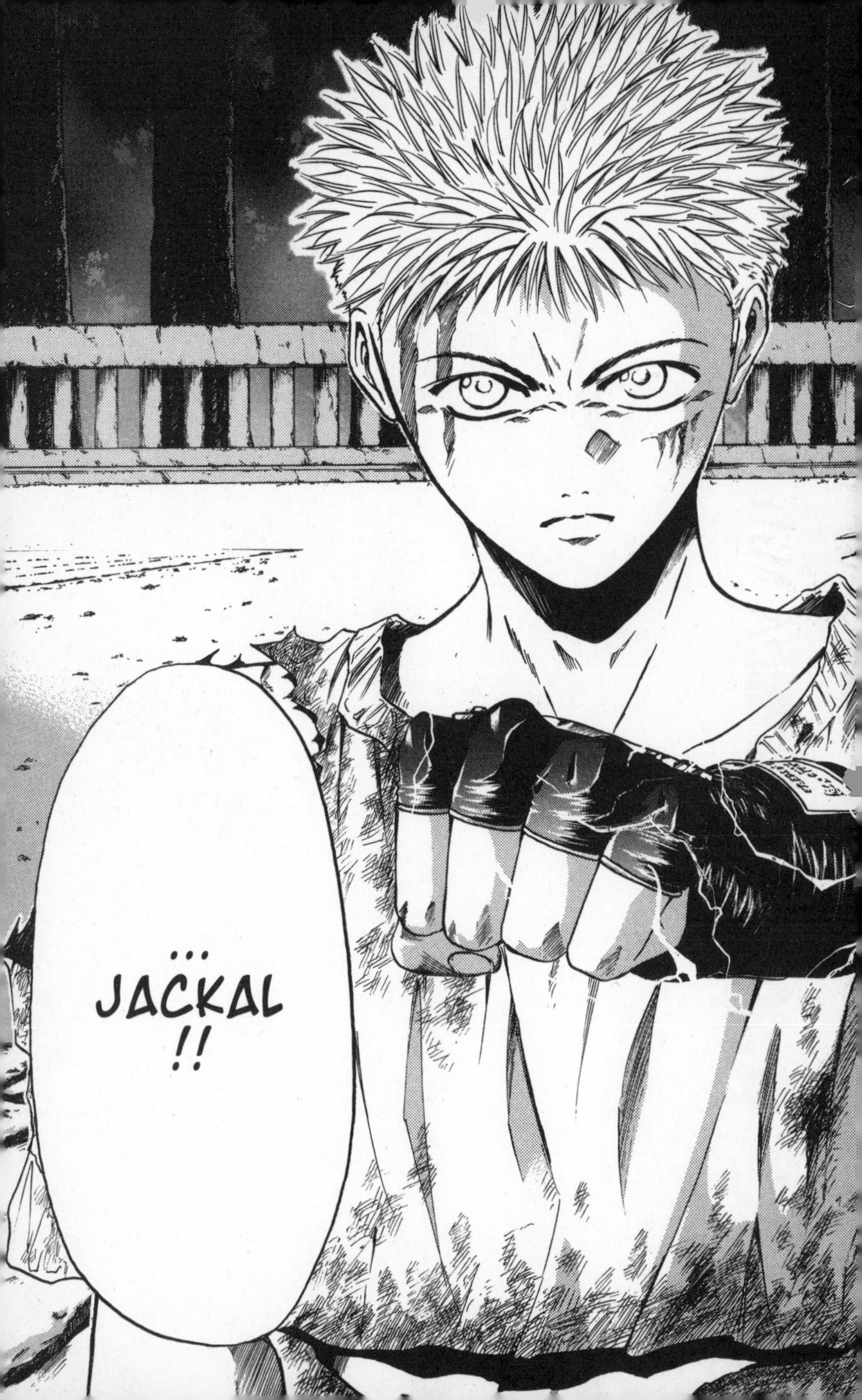
...JACKAL !!

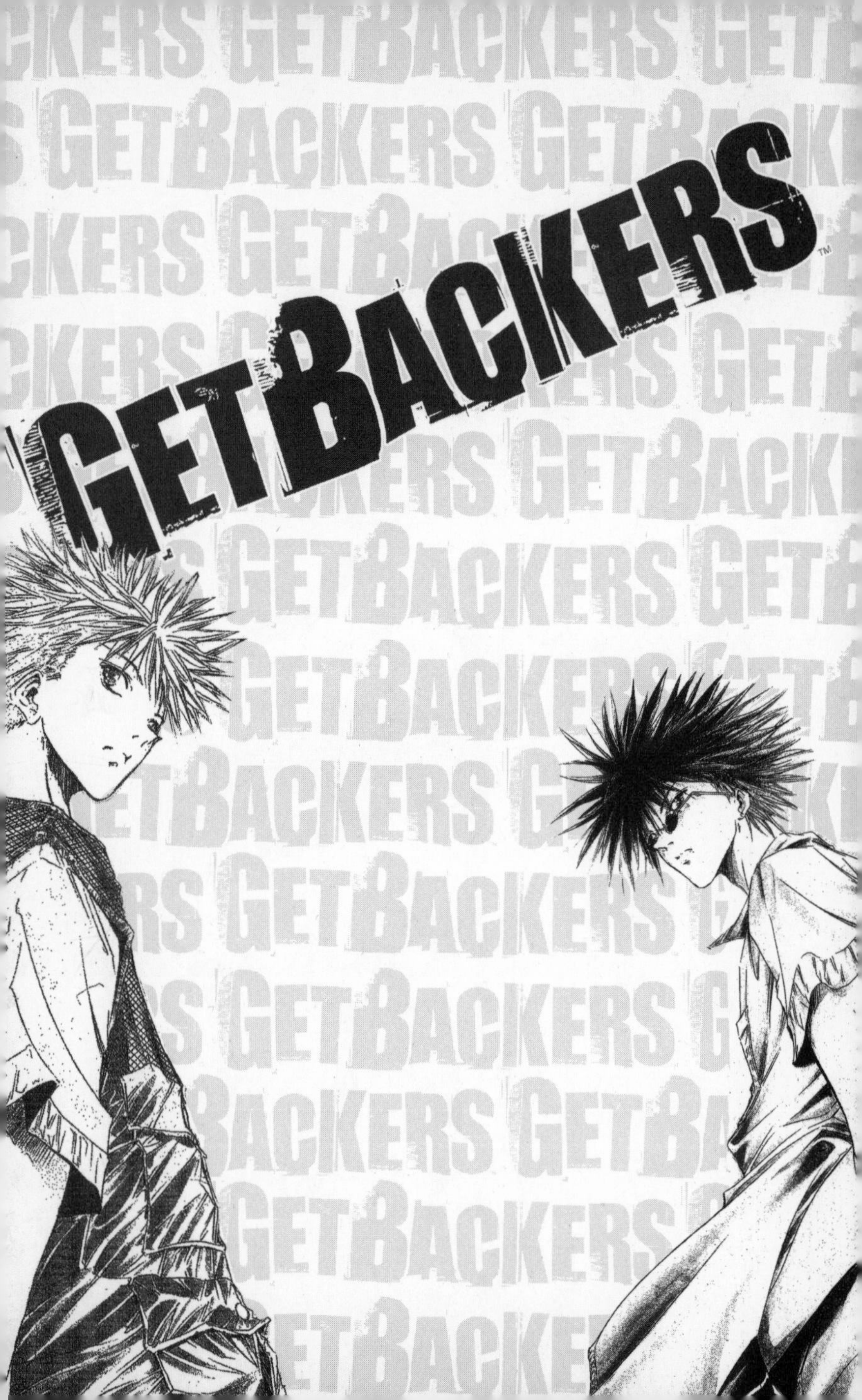
GETBACKERS™

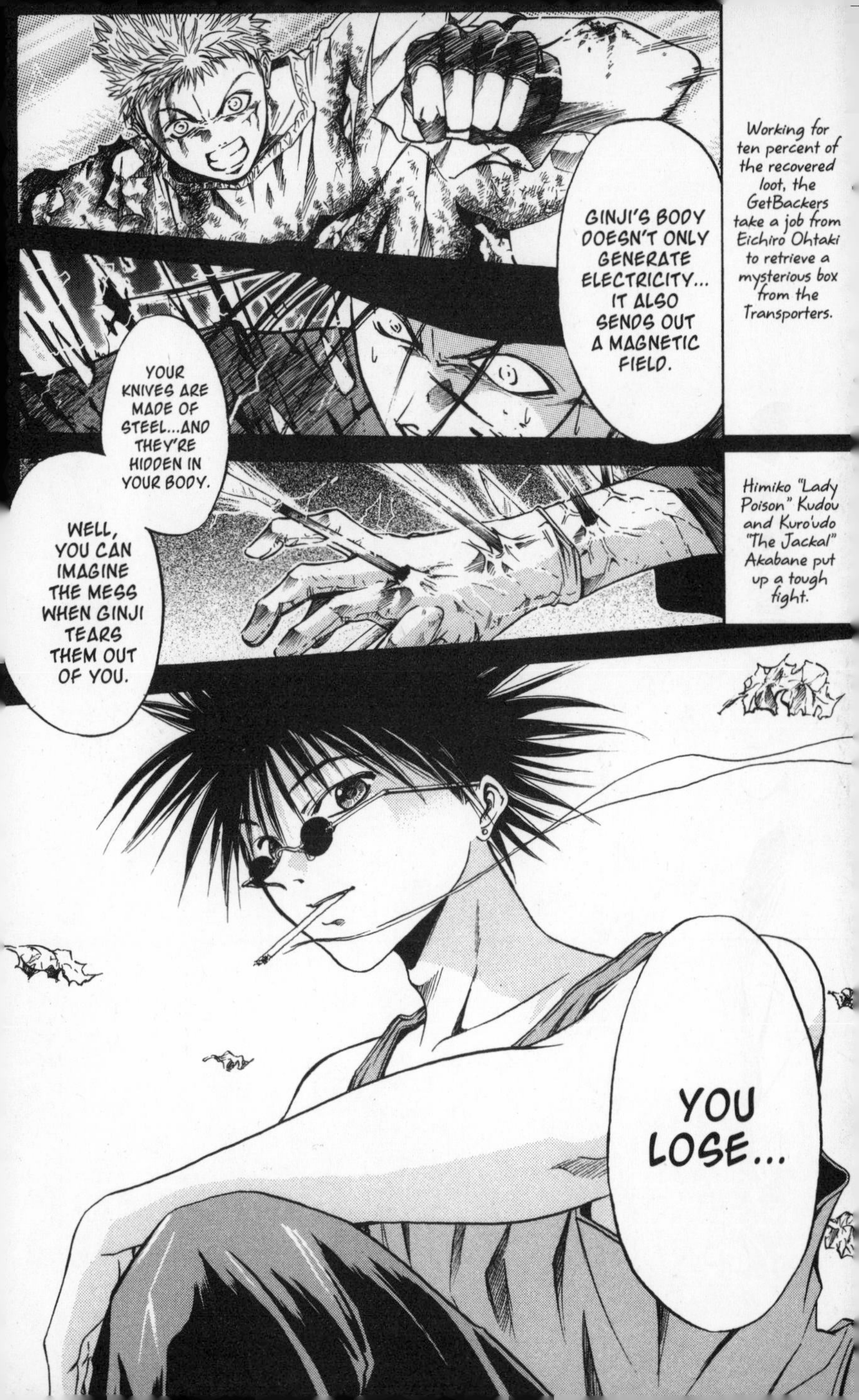
Working for ten percent of the recovered loot, the GetBackers take a job from Eichiro Ohtaki to retrieve a mysterious box from the Transporters.
GINJI'S BODY DOESN'T ONLY GENERATE ELECTRICITY... IT ALSO SENDS OUT A MAGNETIC FIELD.
YOUR KNIVES ARE MADE OF STEEL...AND THEY'RE HIDDEN IN YOUR BODY.
Himiko "Lady Poison" Kudou and Kuro'udo "The Jackal" Akabane put up a tough fight.
WELL, YOU CAN IMAGINE THE MESS WHEN GINJI TEARS THEM OUT OF YOU.
YOU LOSE...

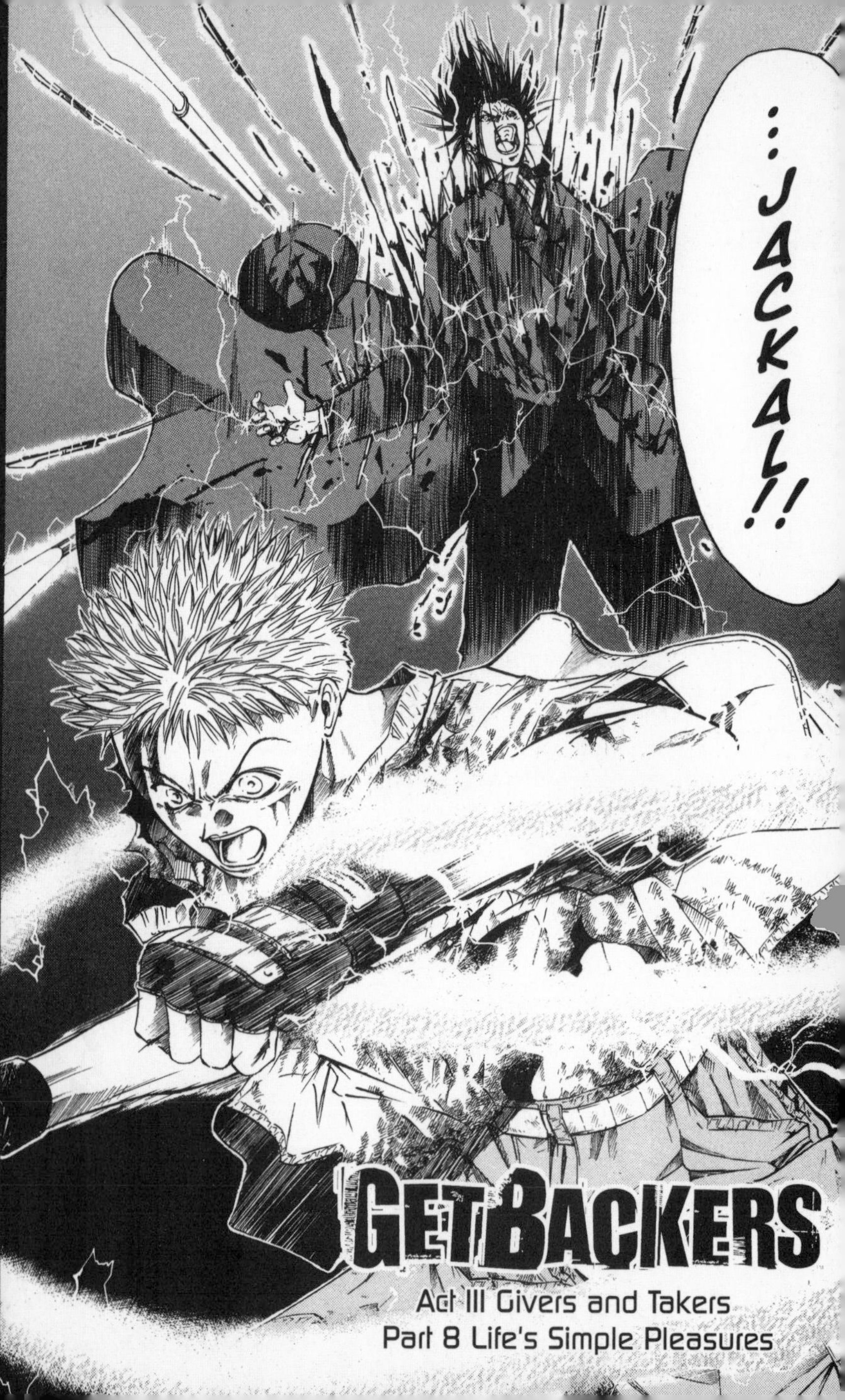
...JACKAL!!
GETBACKERS
Act III Givers and Takers
Part 8 Life's Simple Pleasures

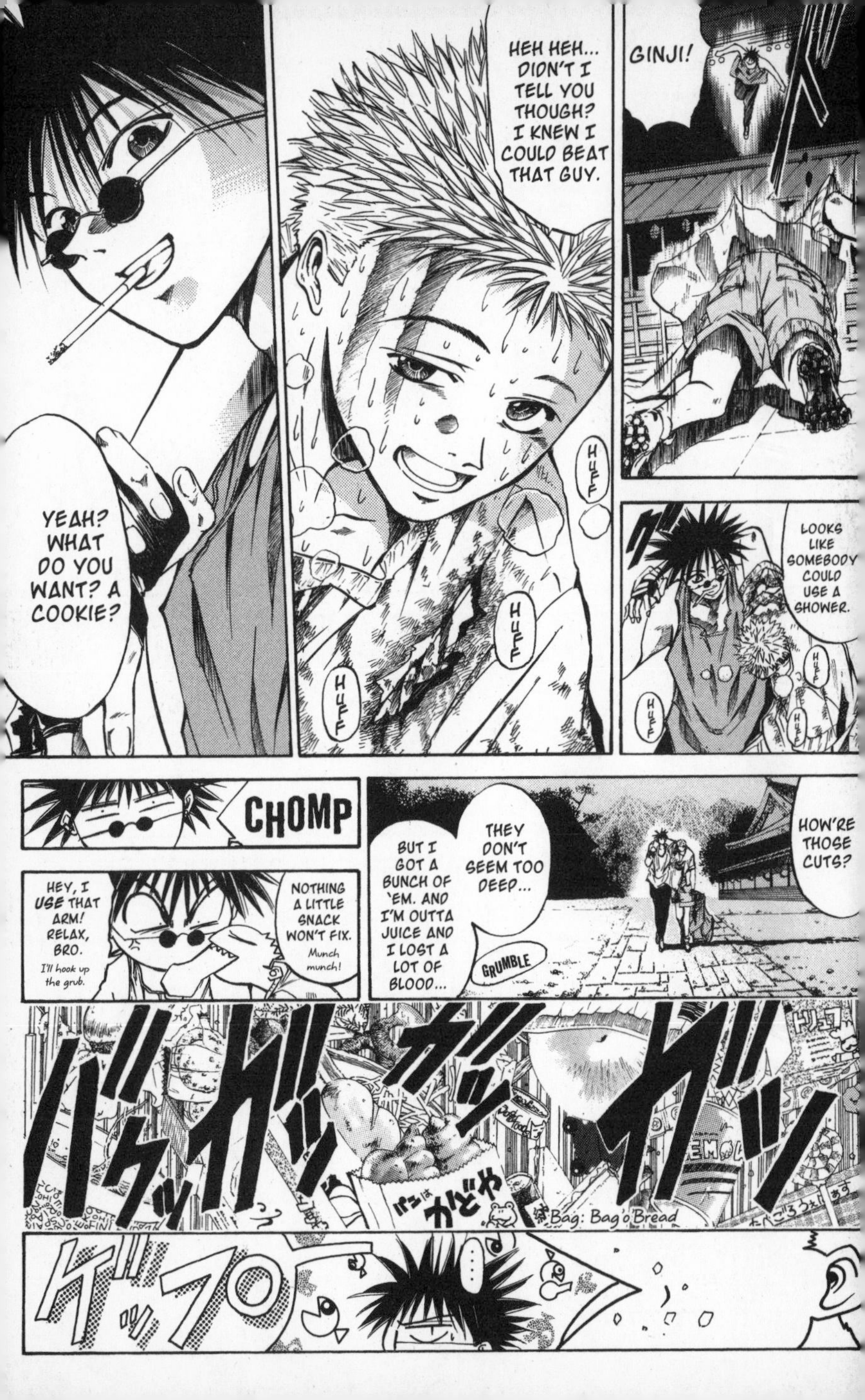
GINJI!
LOOKS LIKE SOMEBODY COULD USE A SHOWER.
HUFF
HUFF
HEH HEH... DIDN'T I TELL YOU THOUGH? I KNEW I COULD BEAT THAT GUY.
HUFF
HUFF
HUFF
YEAH? WHAT DO YOU WANT? A COOKIE?
HOW'RE THOSE CUTS?
THEY DON'T SEEM TOO DEEP...
BUT I GOT A BUNCH OF 'EM. AND I'M OUTTA JUICE AND I LOST A LOT OF BLOOD...
GRUMBLE
CHOMP
NOTHING A LITTLE SNACK WON'T FIX.
Munch munch!
HEY, I USE THAT ARM! RELAX, BRO.
I'll hook up the grub.
Bag: Bag'o Bread

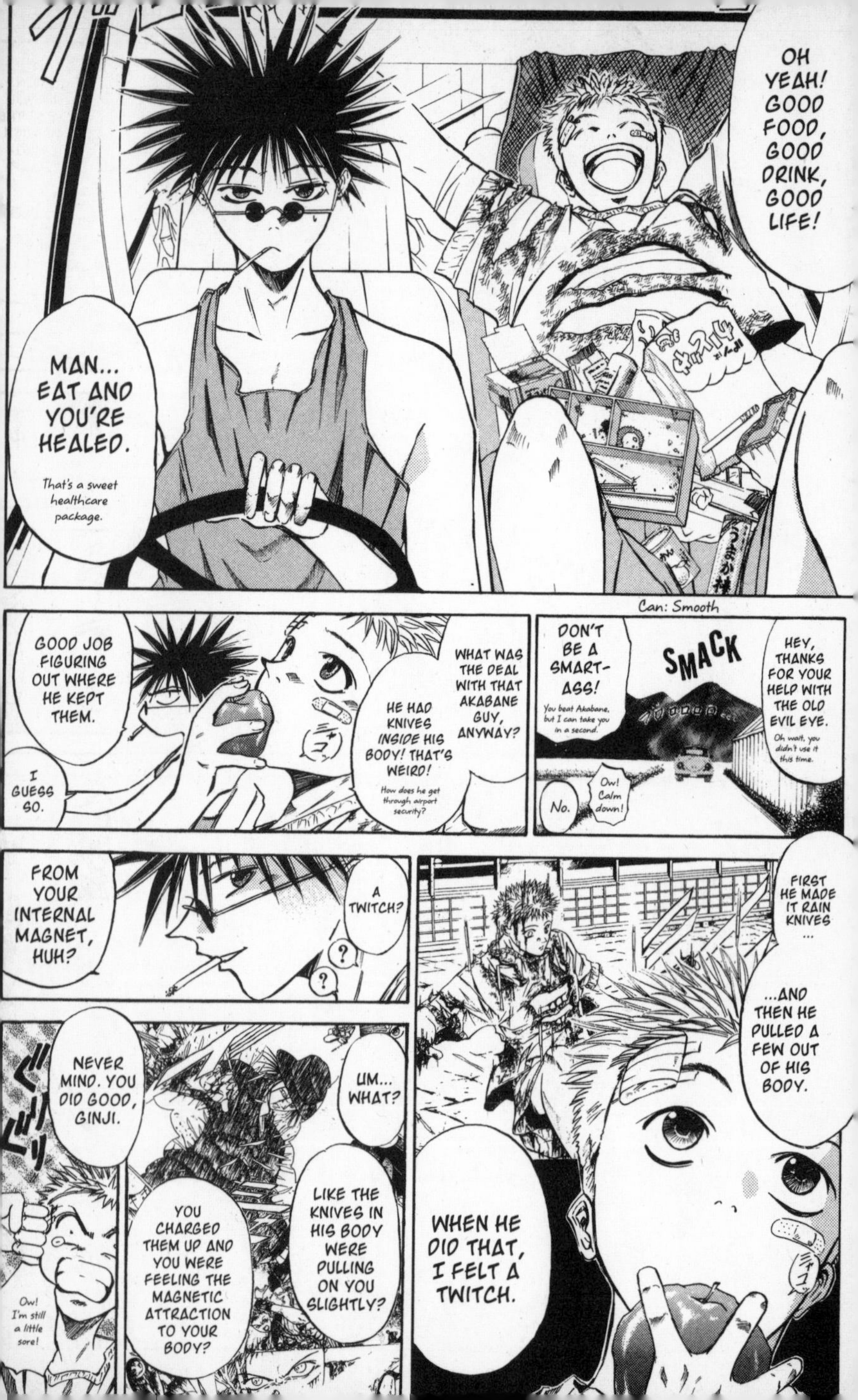
OH YEAH! GOOD FOOD, GOOD DRINK, GOOD LIFE!
MAN... EAT AND YOU'RE HEALED.
That's a sweet healthcare package.
Can: Smooth
HEY, THANKS FOR YOUR HELP WITH THE OLD EVIL EYE.
Oh wait, you didn't use it this time.
SMACK
DON'T BE A SMART-ASS!
You beat Akabane, but I can take you in a second.
Ow! Calm down!
No.
WHAT WAS THE DEAL WITH THAT AKABANE GUY, ANYWAY?
HE HAD KNIVES INSIDE HIS BODY! THAT'S WEIRD!
How does he get through airport security?
GOOD JOB FIGURING OUT WHERE HE KEPT THEM.
I GUESS SO.
FIRST HE MADE IT RAIN KNIVES...
...AND THEN HE PULLED A FEW OUT OF HIS BODY.
WHEN HE DID THAT, I FELT A TWITCH.
A TWITCH?
FROM YOUR INTERNAL MAGNET, HUH?
LIKE THE KNIVES IN HIS BODY WERE PULLING ON YOU SLIGHTLY?
YOU CHARGED THEM UP AND YOU WERE FEELING THE MAGNETIC ATTRACTION TO YOUR BODY?
UM... WHAT?
NEVER MIND. YOU DID GOOD, GINJI.
Ow! I'm still a little sore!

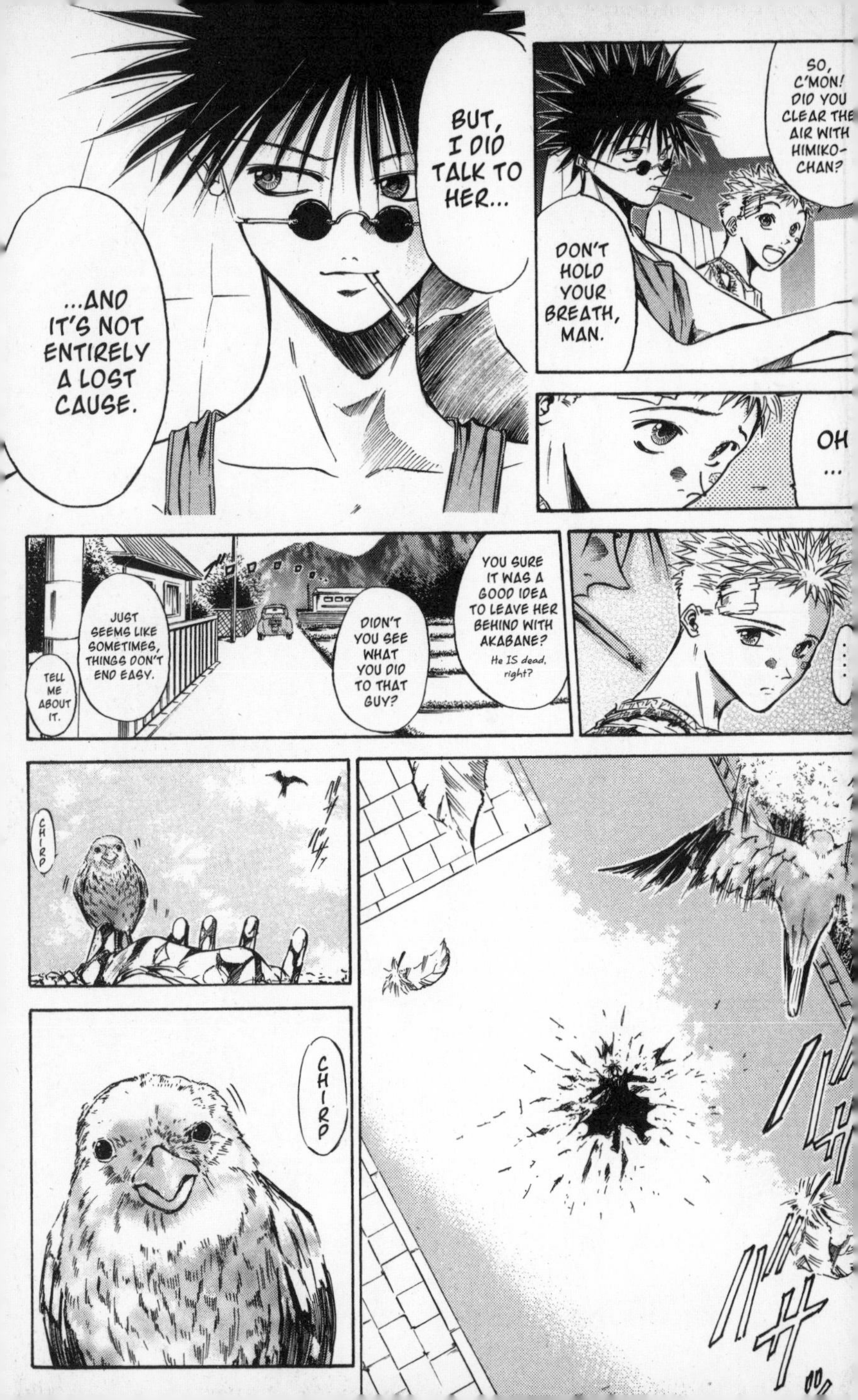
SO, C'MON! DID YOU CLEAR THE AIR WITH HIMIKO-CHAN?
DON'T HOLD YOUR BREATH, MAN.
OH ...
BUT, I DID TALK TO HER...
...AND IT'S NOT ENTIRELY A LOST CAUSE.
...
YOU SURE IT WAS A GOOD IDEA TO LEAVE HER BEHIND WITH AKABANE?
He IS dead, right?
DIDN'T YOU SEE WHAT YOU DID TO THAT GUY?
JUST SEEMS LIKE SOMETIMES, THINGS DON'T END EASY.
TELL ME ABOUT IT.
CHIRP
CHIRP

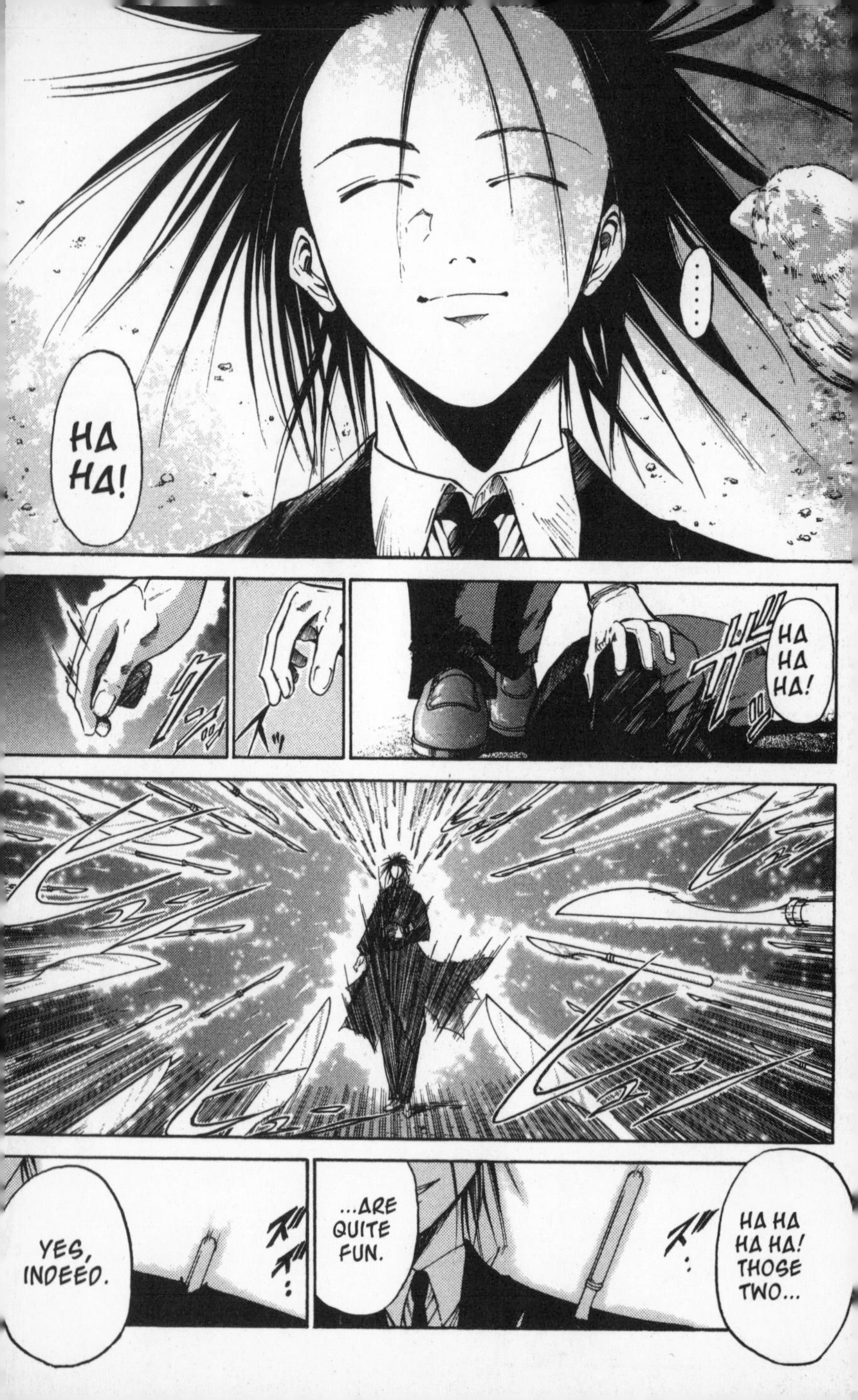
......
HA HA!
HA HA HA!
HA HA HA HA! THOSE TWO...
...ARE QUITE FUN.
YES, INDEED.

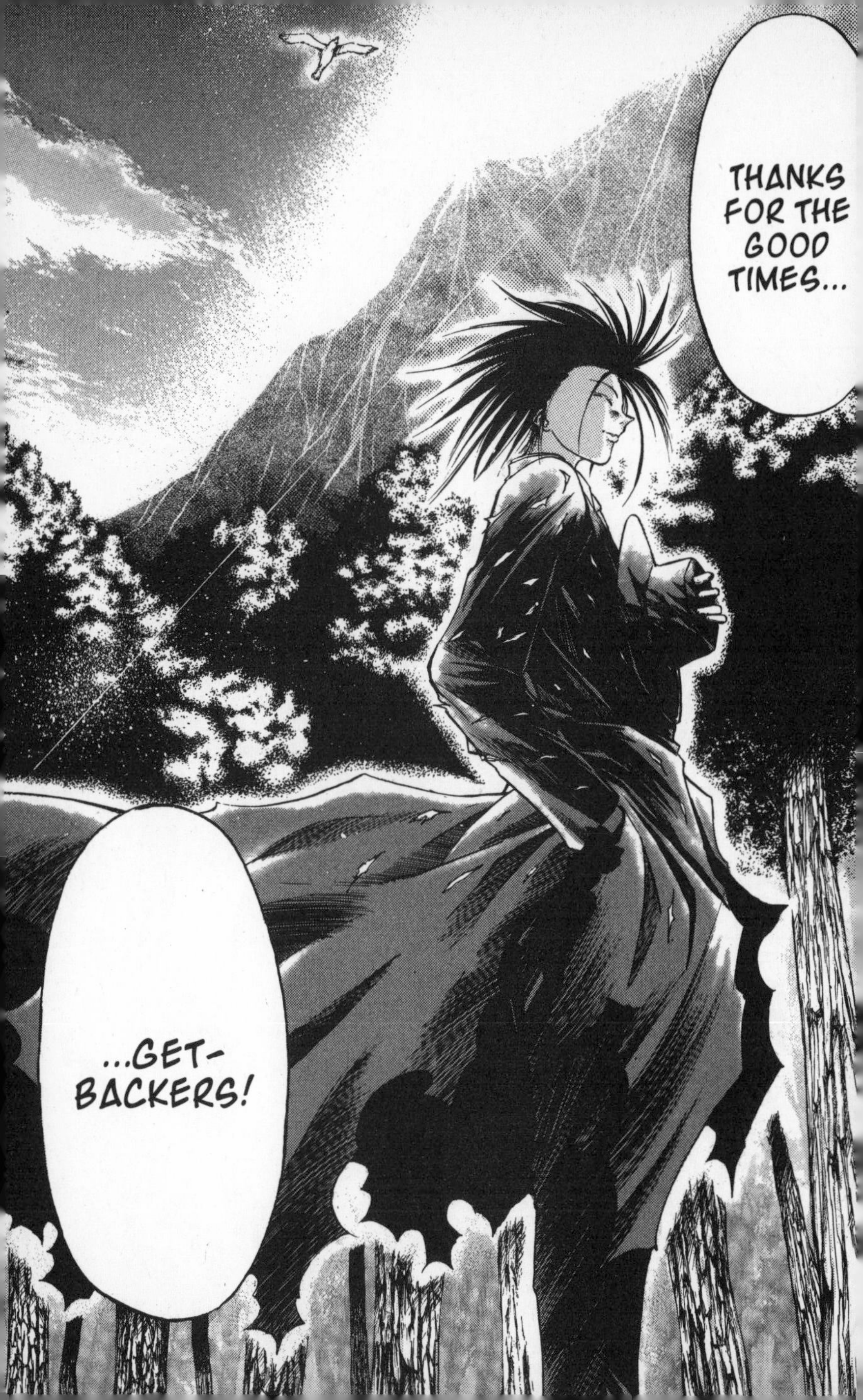
THANKS FOR THE GOOD TIMES...
...GET-BACKERS!

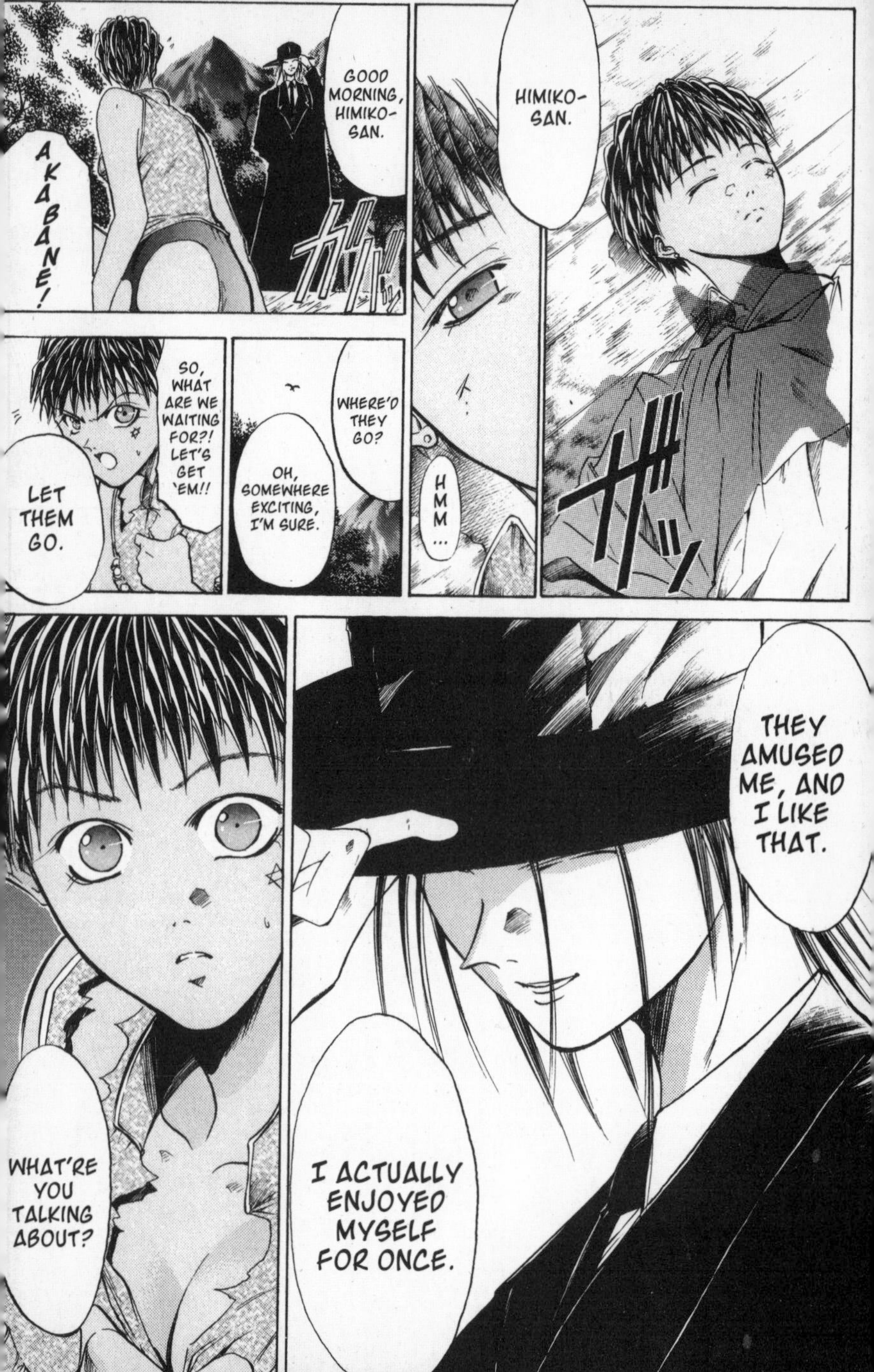
HIMIKO-SAN.
HMM...
GOOD MORNING, HIMIKO-SAN.
AKABANE!
WHERE'D THEY GO?
OH, SOMEWHERE EXCITING, I'M SURE.
SO, WHAT ARE WE WAITING FOR?! LET'S GET 'EM!!
LET THEM GO.
THEY AMUSED ME, AND I LIKE THAT.
I ACTUALLY ENJOYED MYSELF FOR ONCE.
WHAT'RE YOU TALKING ABOUT?

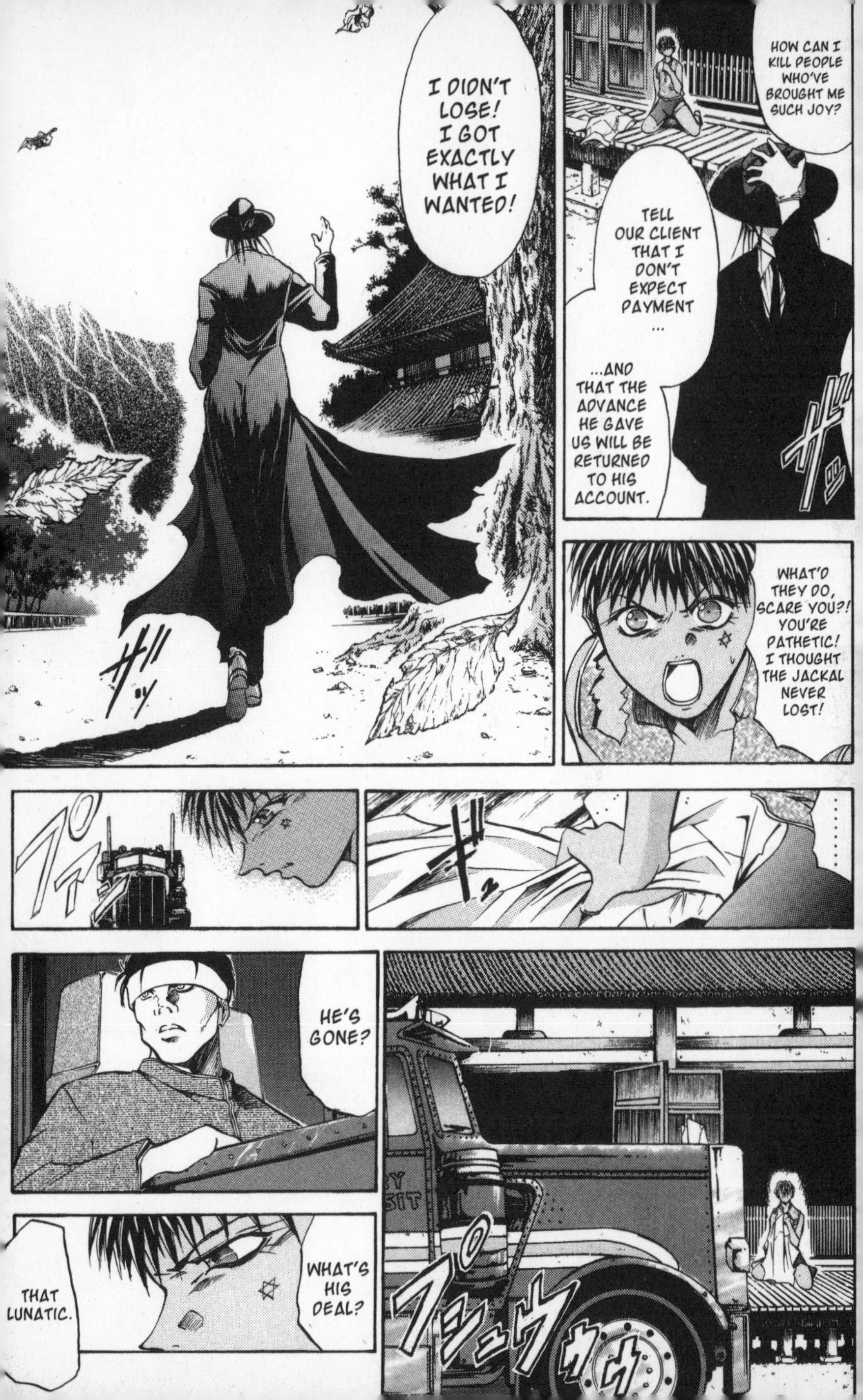
HOW CAN I KILL PEOPLE WHO'VE BROUGHT ME SUCH JOY?
TELL OUR CLIENT THAT I DON'T EXPECT PAYMENT ...
...AND THAT THE ADVANCE HE GAVE US WILL BE RETURNED TO HIS ACCOUNT.
WHAT'D THEY DO, SCARE YOU?! YOU'RE PATHETIC! I THOUGHT THE JACKAL NEVER LOST!
I DIDN'T LOSE! I GOT EXACTLY WHAT I WANTED!
HE'S GONE?
WHAT'S HIS DEAL?
THAT LUNATIC.

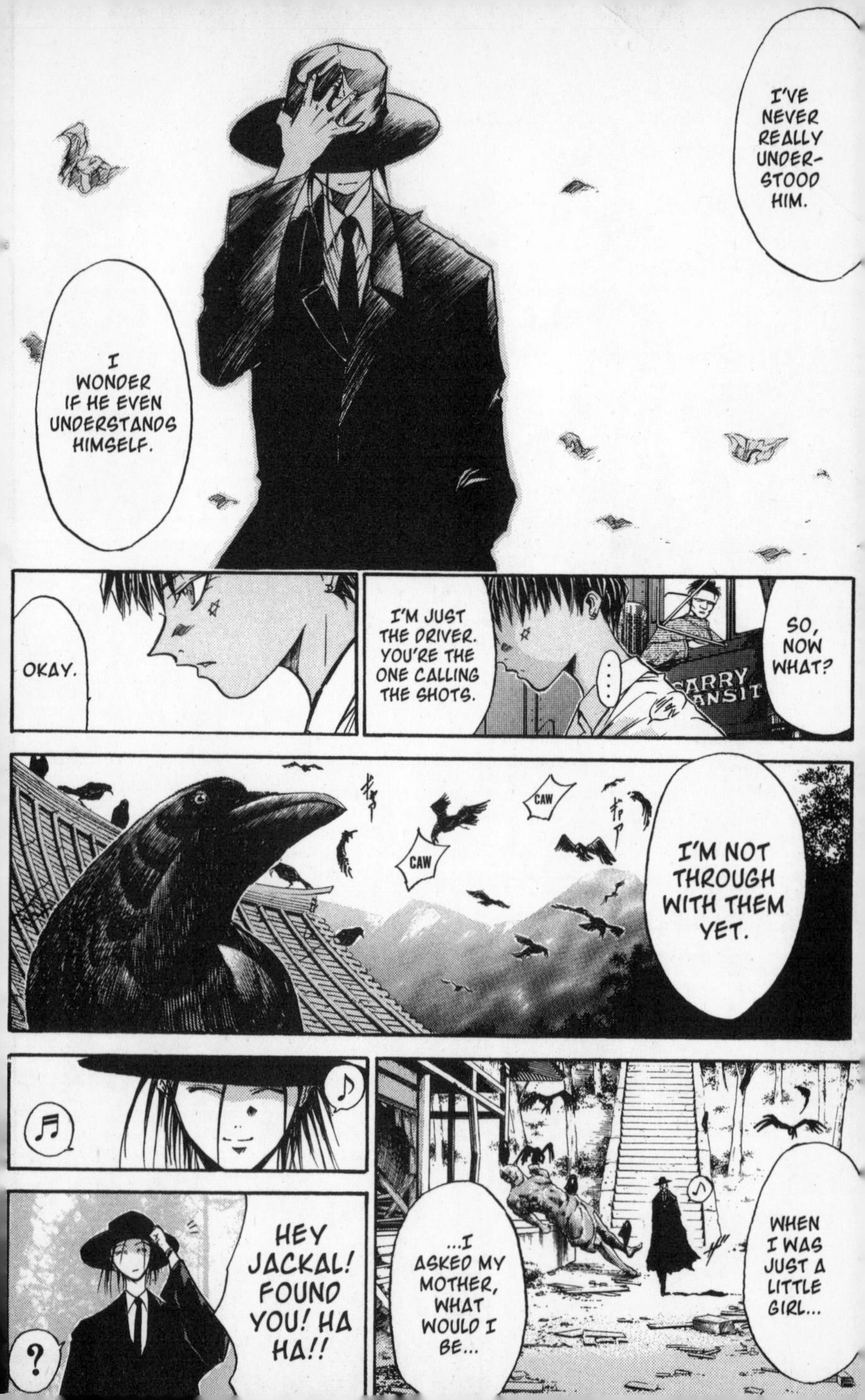
I'VE NEVER REALLY UNDER-STOOD HIM.
I WONDER IF HE EVEN UNDERSTANDS HIMSELF.
SO, NOW WHAT?
...
I'M JUST THE DRIVER. YOU'RE THE ONE CALLING THE SHOTS.
OKAY.
I'M NOT THROUGH WITH THEM YET.
CAW
CAW
WHEN I WAS JUST A LITTLE GIRL...
♪
...I ASKED MY MOTHER, WHAT WOULD I BE...
♪
♫
HEY JACKAL! FOUND YOU! HA HA!!
?

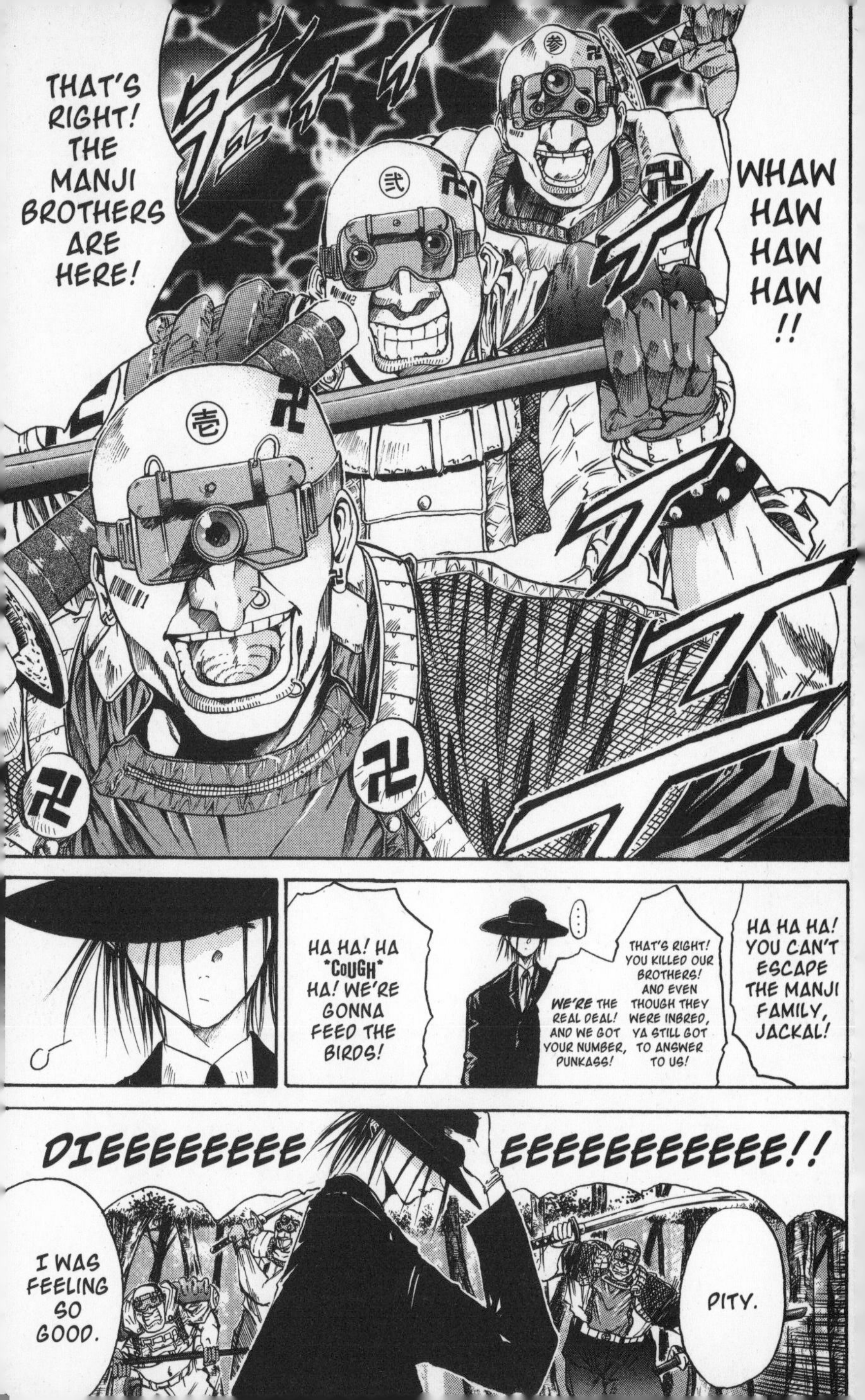
WHAW HAW HAW HAW !!
THAT'S RIGHT! THE MANJI BROTHERS ARE HERE!
HA HA HA! YOU CAN'T ESCAPE THE MANJI FAMILY, JACKAL!
THAT'S RIGHT! YOU KILLED OUR BROTHERS! AND EVEN THOUGH THEY WERE INBRED, YA STILL GOT TO ANSWER TO US!
...
WE'RE THE REAL DEAL! AND WE GOT YOUR NUMBER, PUNKASS!
HA HA! HA *COUGH* HA! WE'RE GONNA FEED THE BIRDS!
DIEEEEEEEEE EEEEEEEEEEEE!!
PITY.
I WAS FEELING SO GOOD.

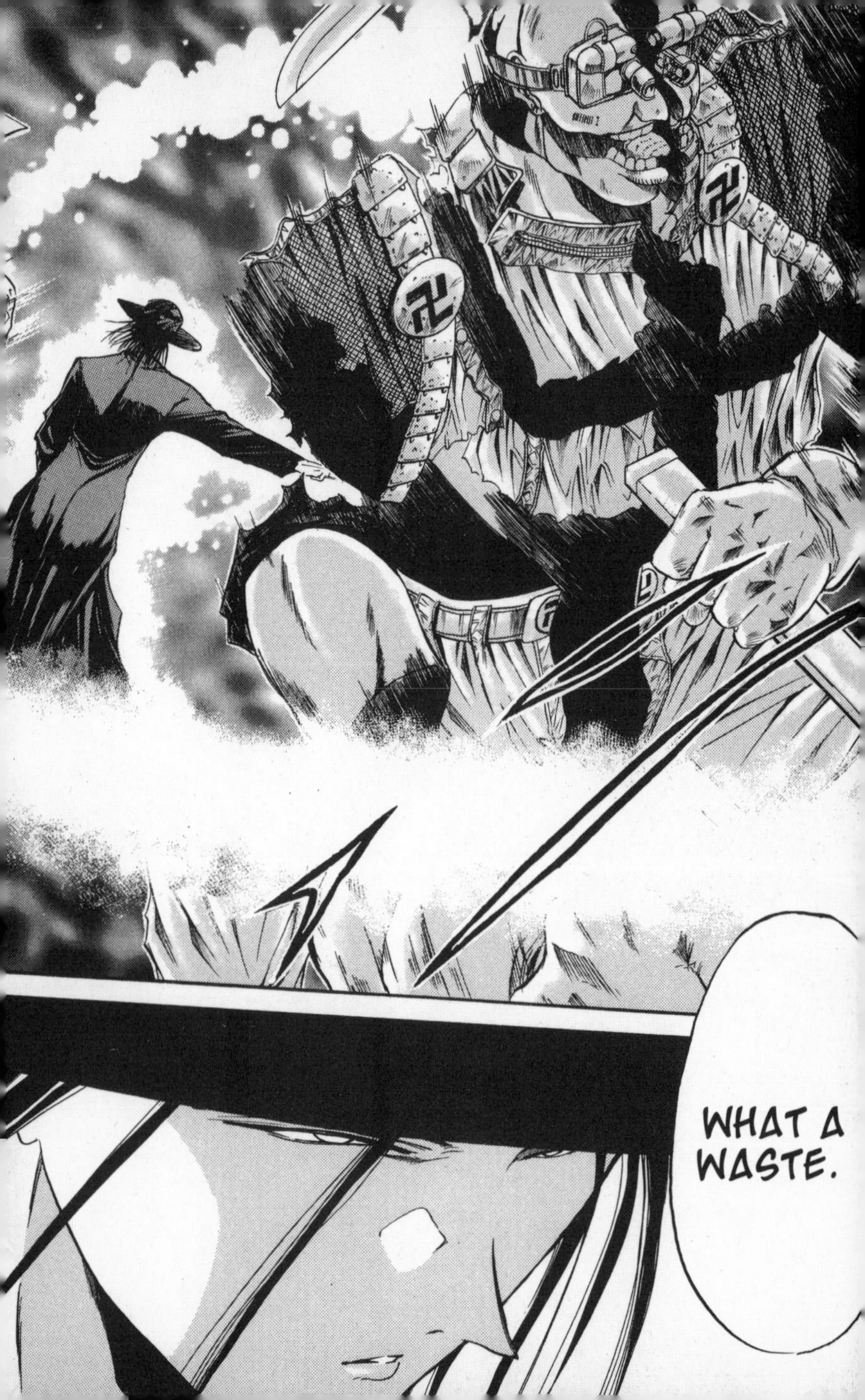
WHAT A WASTE.

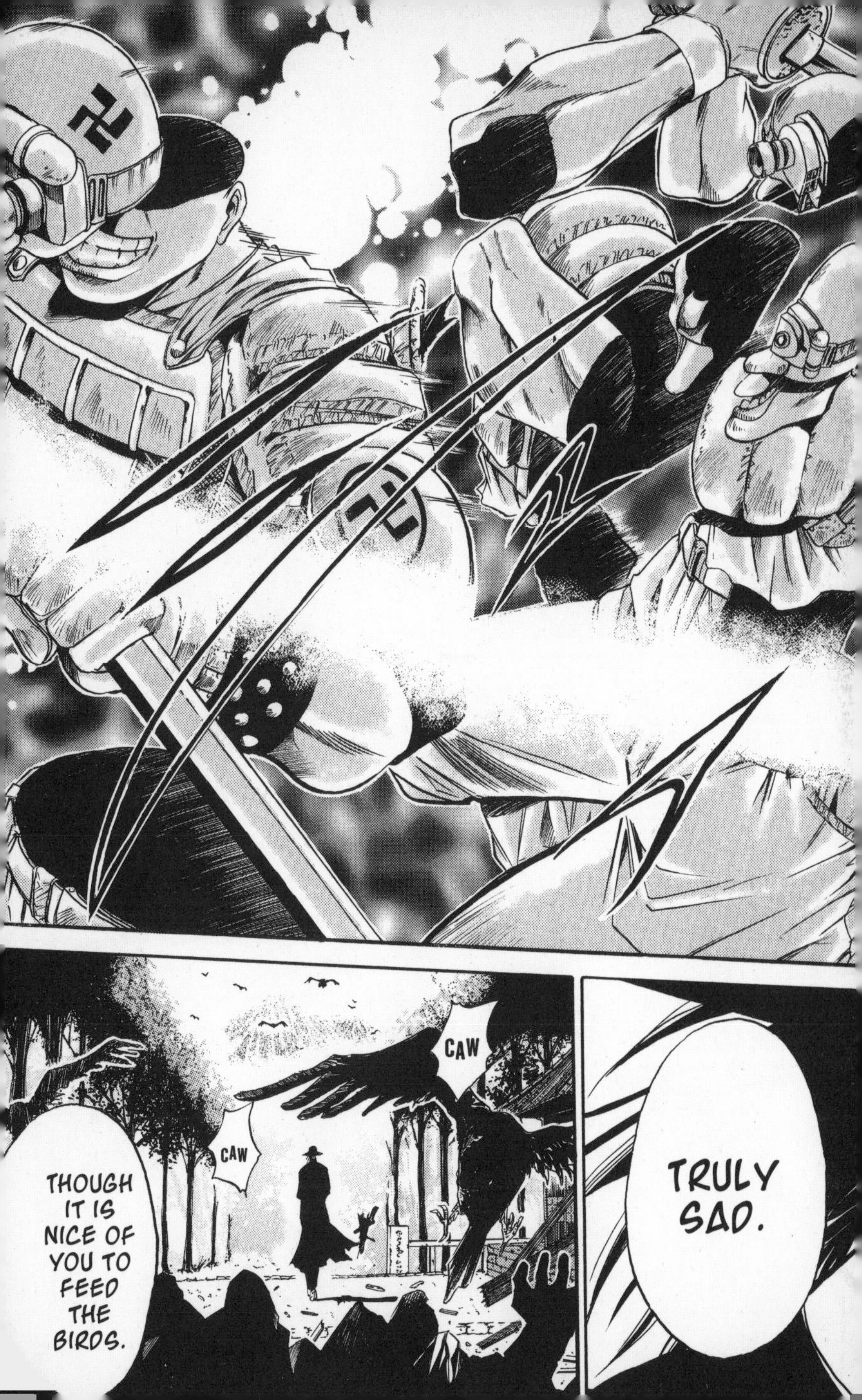
TRULY SAD.
CAW
CAW
THOUGH IT IS NICE OF YOU TO FEED THE BIRDS.

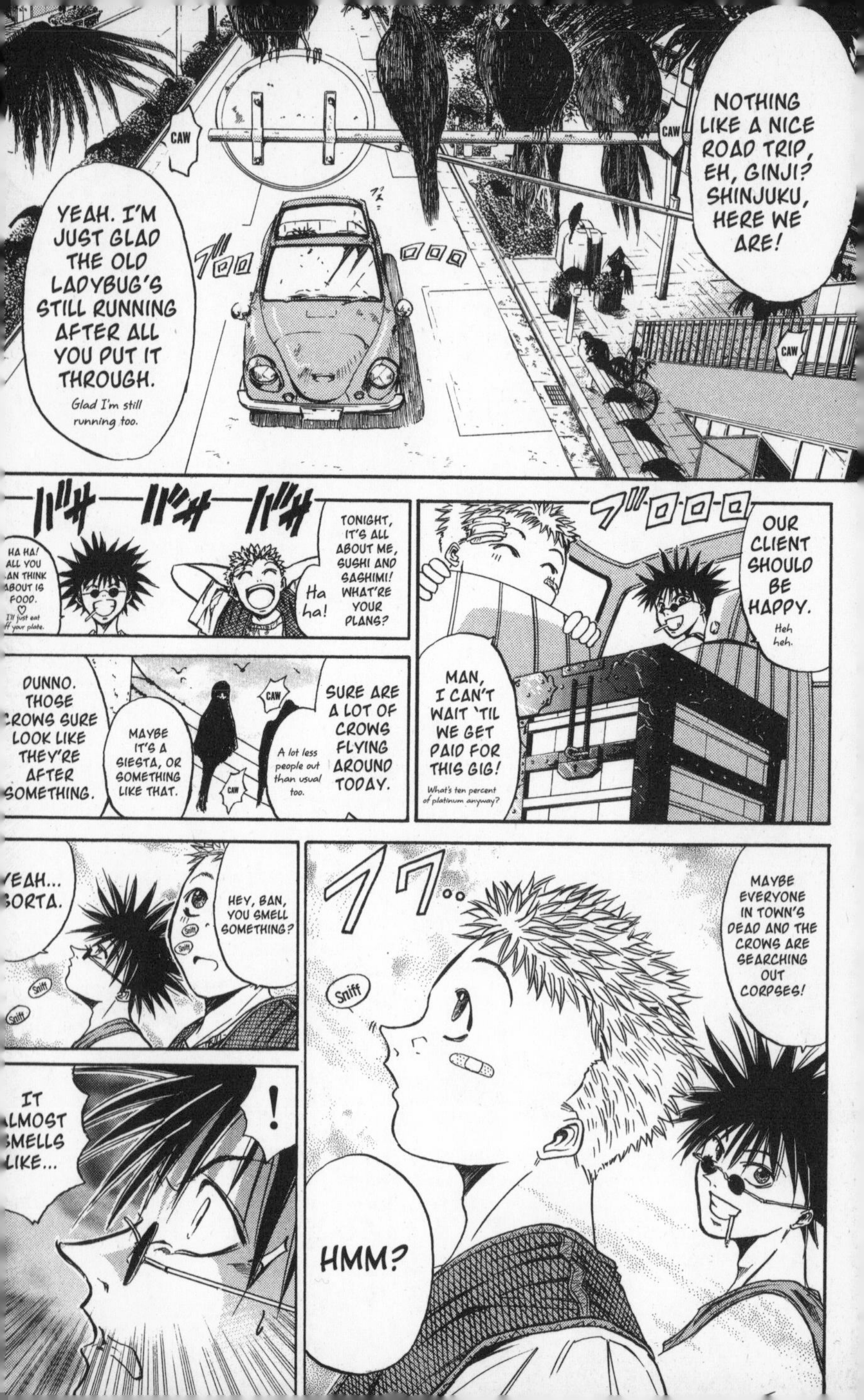
NOTHING LIKE A NICE ROAD TRIP, EH, GINJI? SHINJUKU, HERE WE ARE!
CAW
CAW
YEAH. I'M JUST GLAD THE OLD LADYBUG'S STILL RUNNING AFTER ALL YOU PUT IT THROUGH.
Glad I'm still running too.
CAW
OUR CLIENT SHOULD BE HAPPY.
Heh heh.
TONIGHT, IT'S ALL ABOUT ME, SUSHI AND SASHIMI! WHAT'RE YOUR PLANS?
Ha ha!
HA HA! ALL YOU AN THINK ABOUT IS FOOD. ♡
I'll just eat ff your plate.
MAN, I CAN'T WAIT 'TIL WE GET PAID FOR THIS GIG!
What's ten percent of platinum anyway?
SURE ARE A LOT OF CROWS FLYING AROUND TODAY.
A lot less people out than usual too.
CAW
CAW
MAYBE IT'S A SIESTA, OR SOMETHING LIKE THAT.
DUNNO. THOSE CROWS SURE LOOK LIKE THEY'RE AFTER SOMETHING.
MAYBE EVERYONE IN TOWN'S DEAD AND THE CROWS ARE SEARCHING OUT CORPSES!
Sniff
HMM?
HEY, BAN, YOU SMELL SOMETHING?
Sniff
Sniff
YEAH... ORTA.
Sniff
Sniff
!
IT LMOST MELLS LIKE...

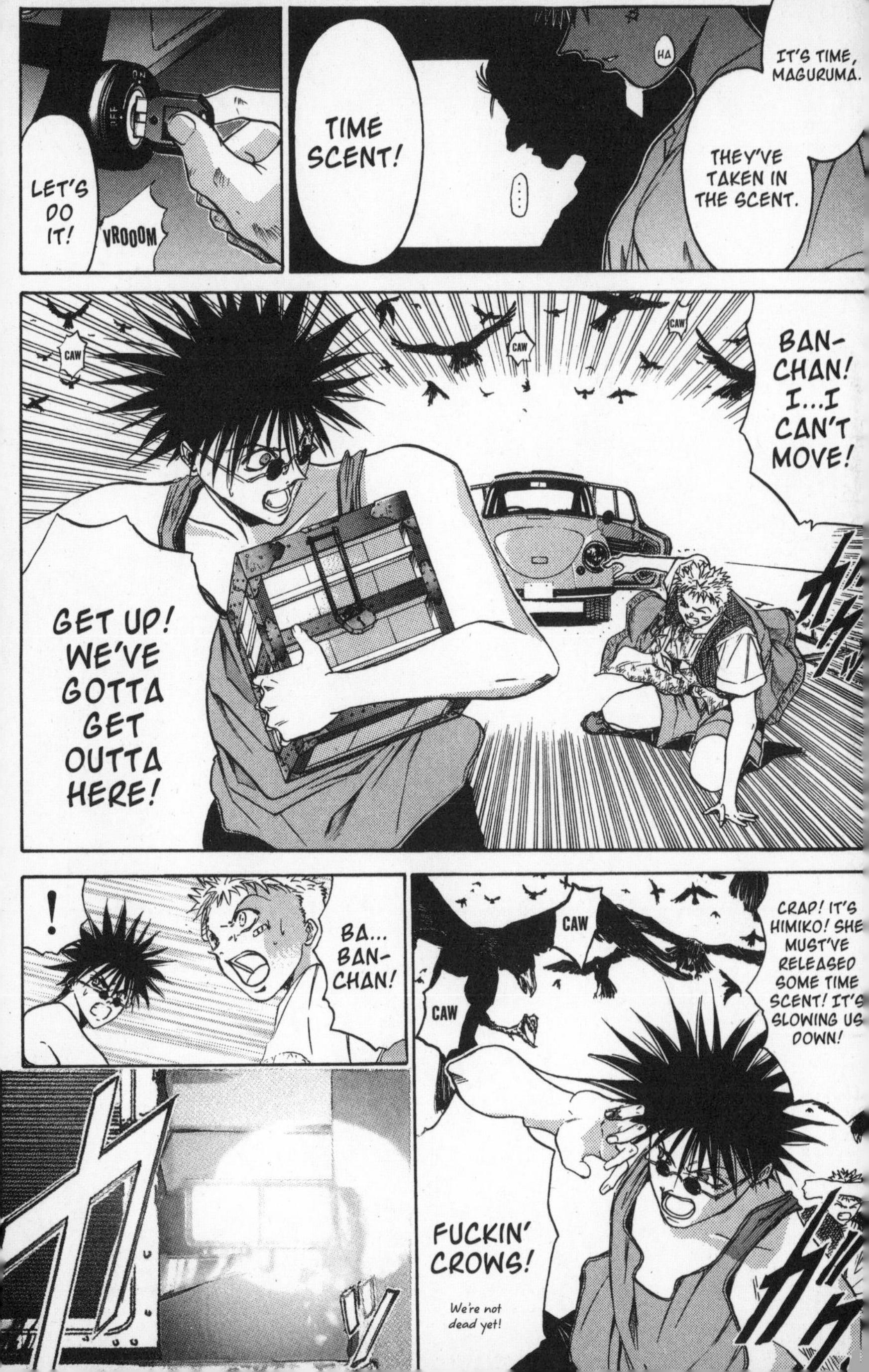
HA
IT'S TIME, MAGURUMA.
THEY'VE TAKEN IN THE SCENT.
TIME SCENT!
...
LET'S DO IT!
VROOOM
CAW
CAW
CAW
BAN-CHAN! I...I CAN'T MOVE!
GET UP! WE'VE GOTTA GET OUTTA HERE!
CRAP! IT'S HIMIKO! SHE MUST'VE RELEASED SOME TIME SCENT! IT'S SLOWING US DOWN!
CAW
CAW
FUCKIN' CROWS!
We're not dead yet!
!
BA... BAN-CHAN!

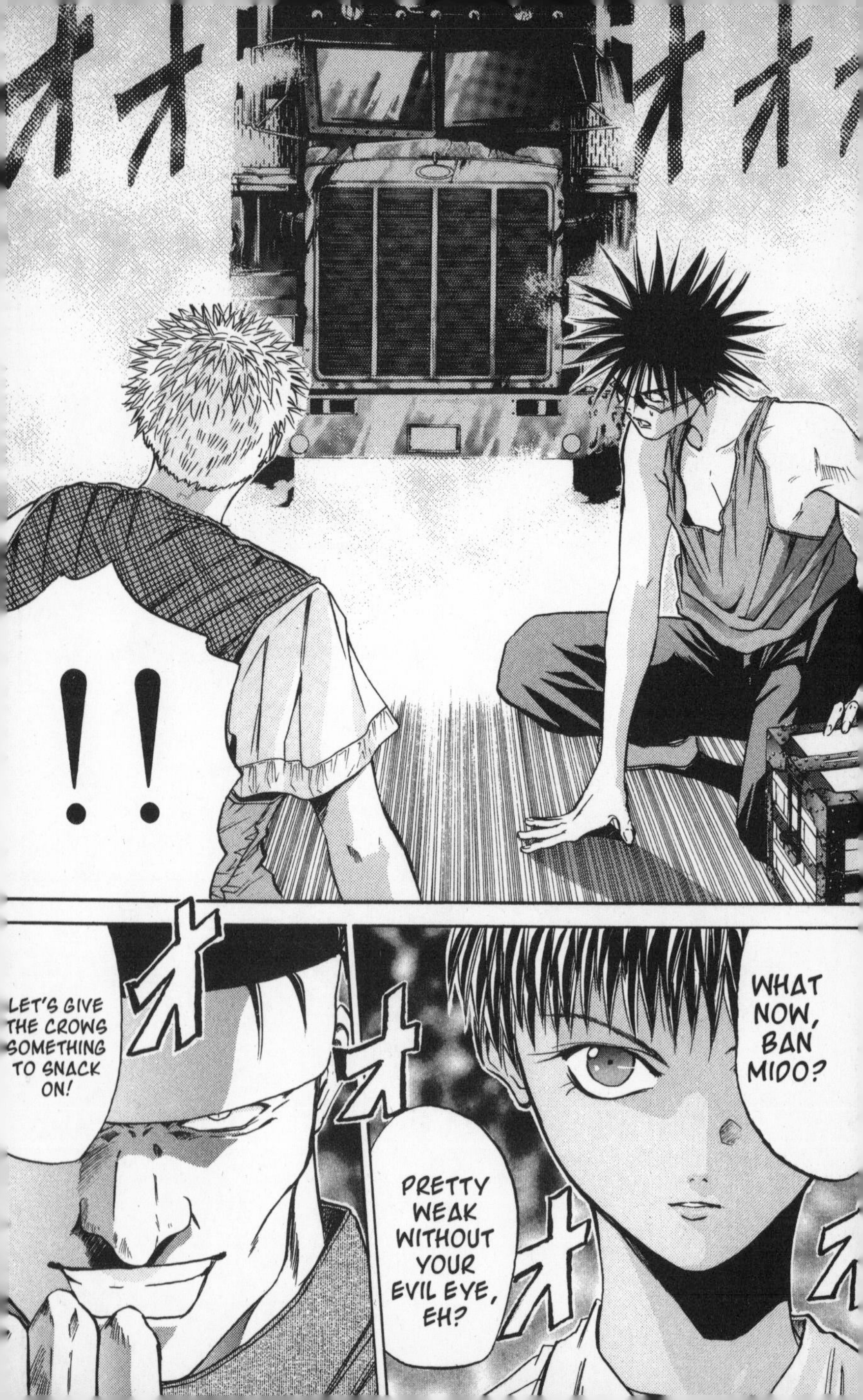
オオオオ
!!
オオオオ
WHAT NOW, BAN MIDO?
PRETTY WEAK WITHOUT YOUR EVIL EYE, EH?
LET'S GIVE THE CROWS SOMETHING TO SNACK ON!

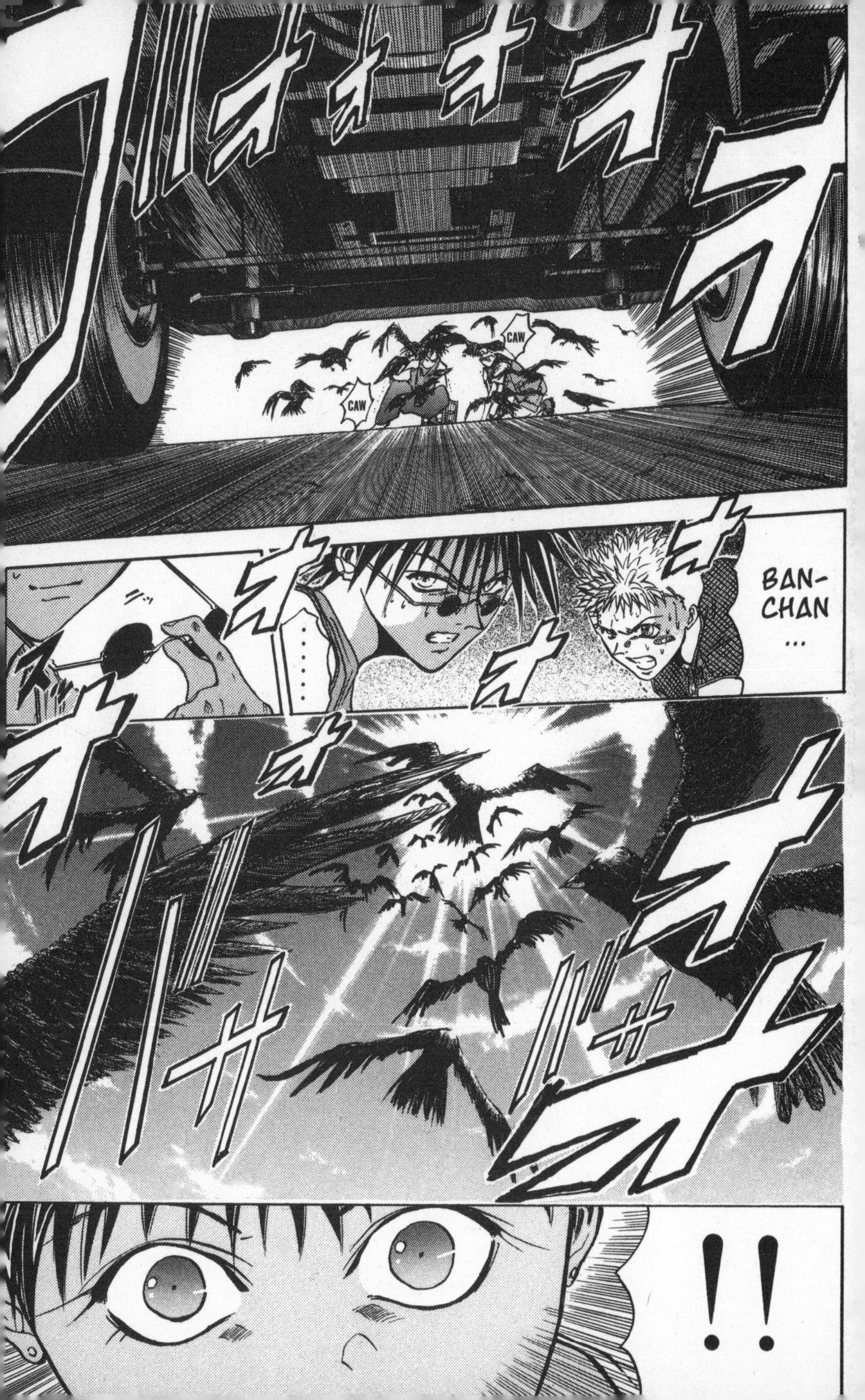
CAW
CAW
BAN-CHAN ...
!!

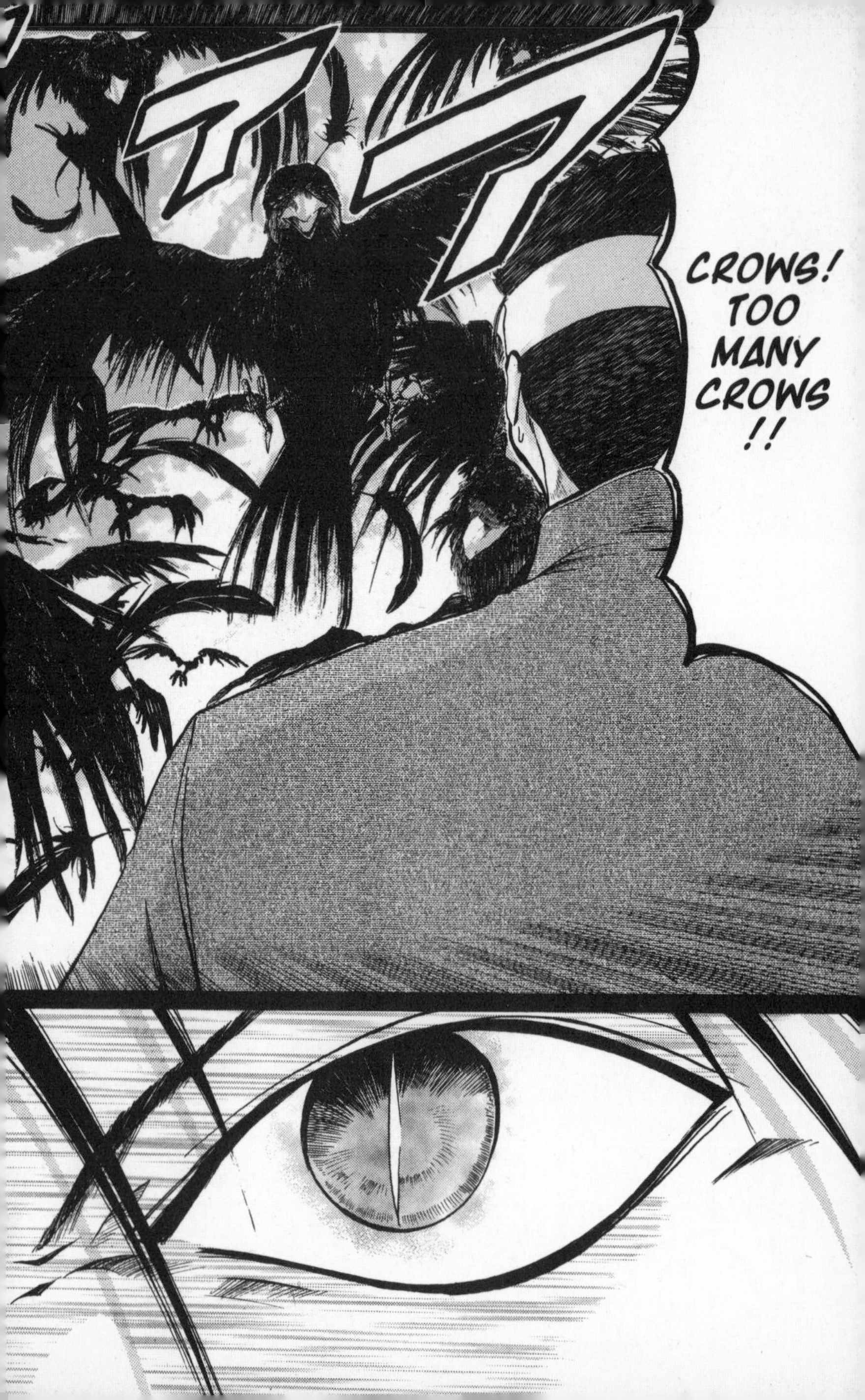
CROWS! TOO MANY CROWS !!

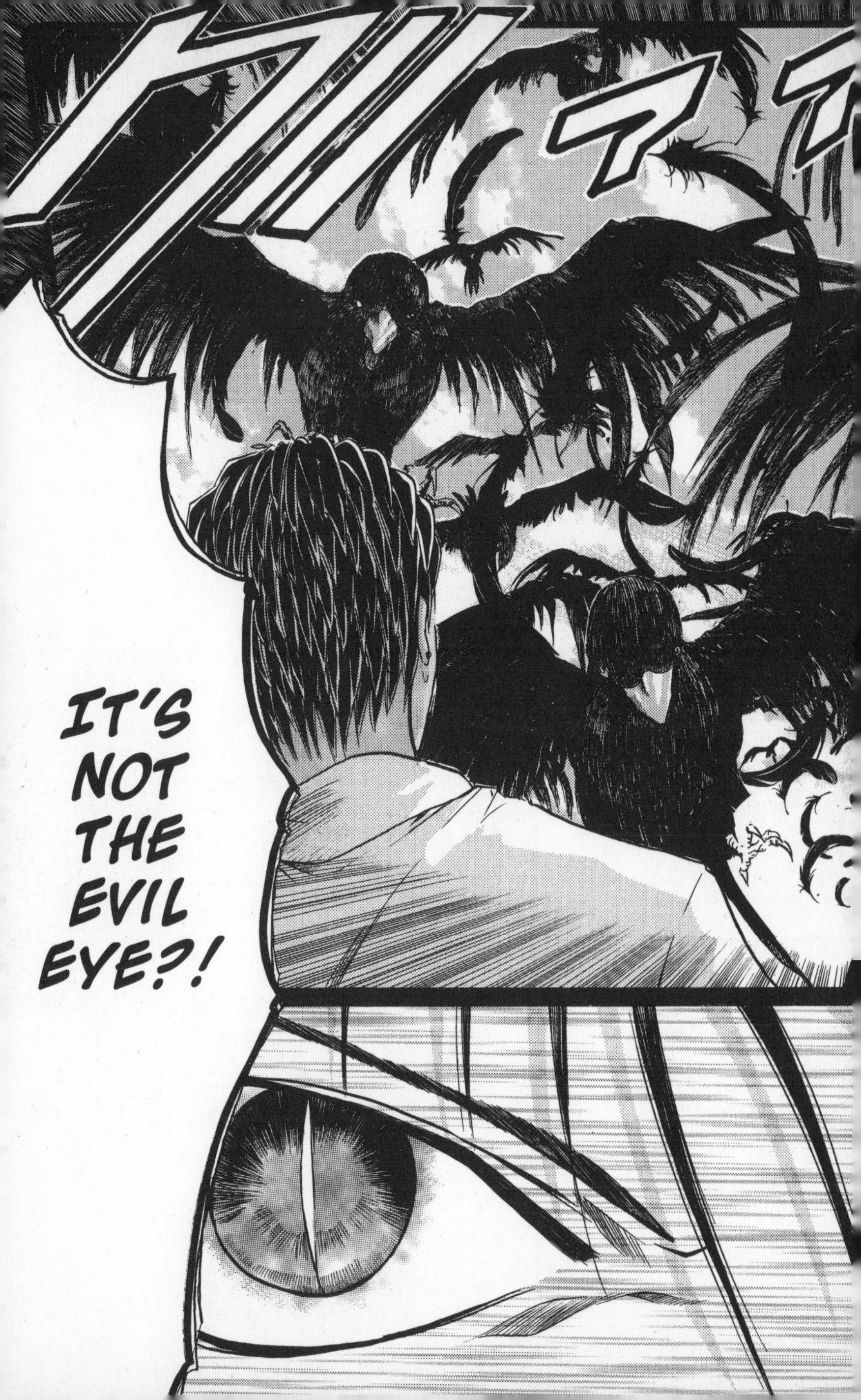
IT'S NOT THE EVIL EYE?!

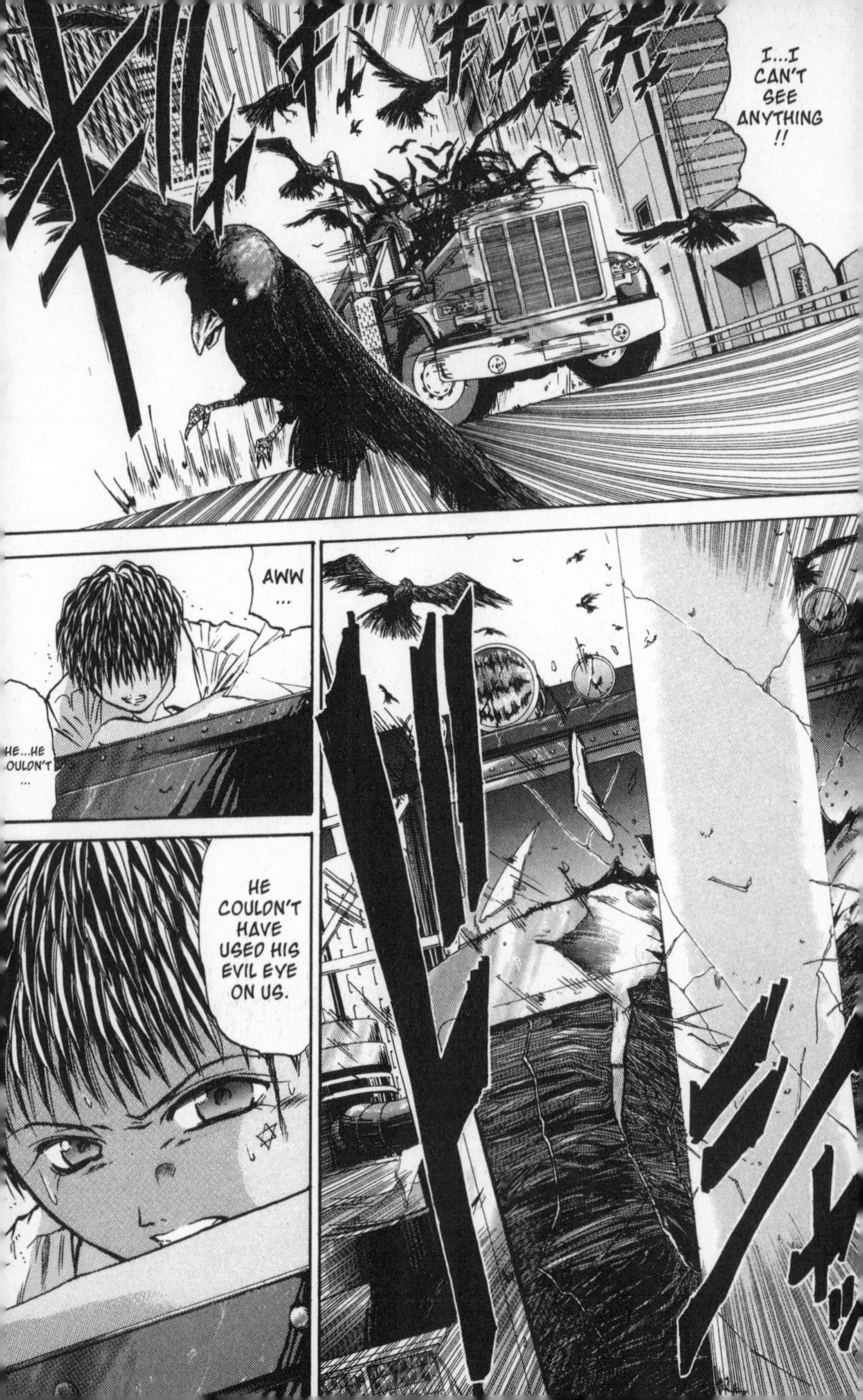
I...I CAN'T SEE ANYTHING!!
AWW...
HE...HE COULDN'T...
HE COULDN'T HAVE USED HIS EVIL EYE ON US.

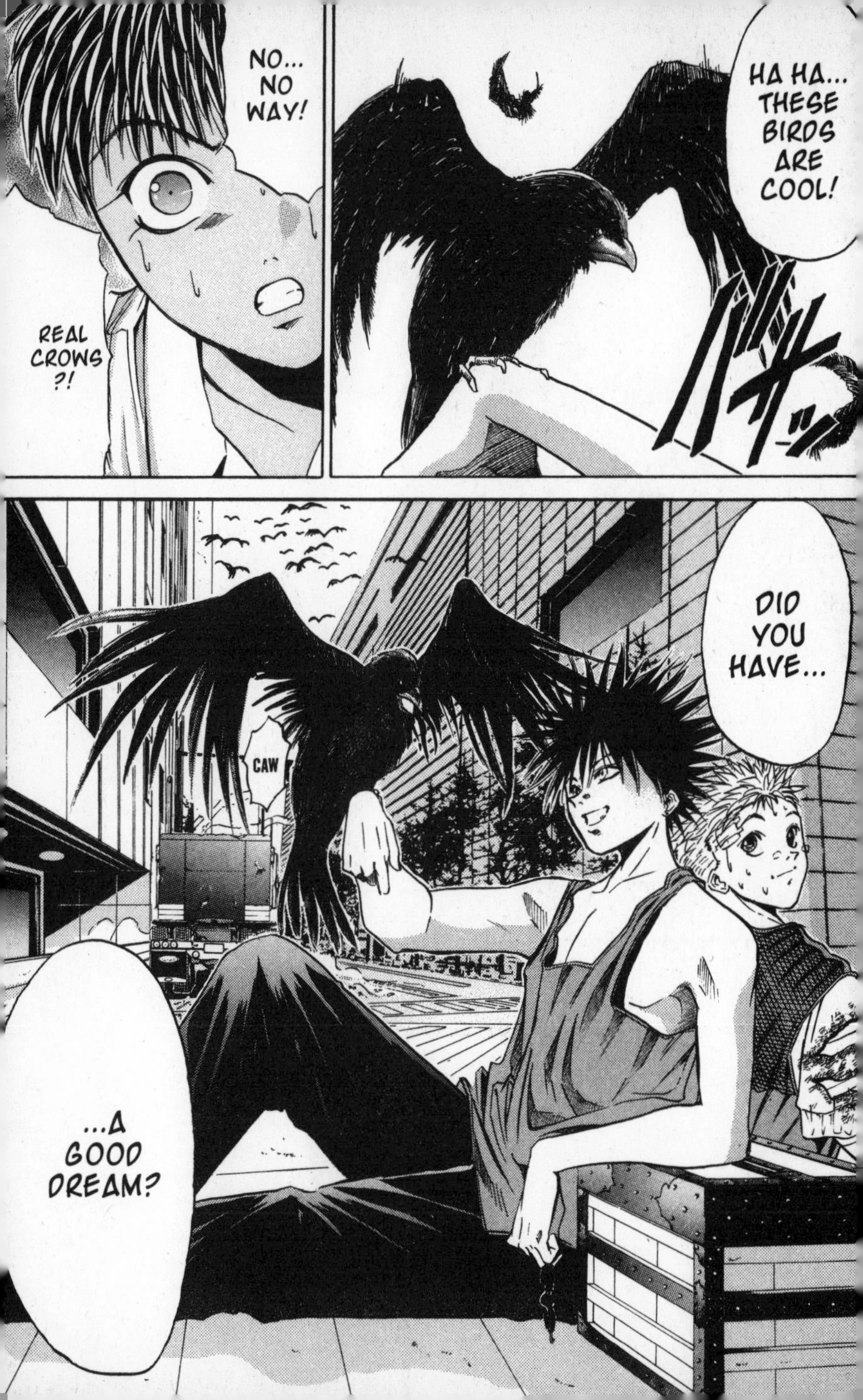
HA HA... THESE BIRDS ARE COOL!
バサッ
NO... NO WAY!
REAL CROWS ?!
DID YOU HAVE...
CAW
...A GOOD DREAM?

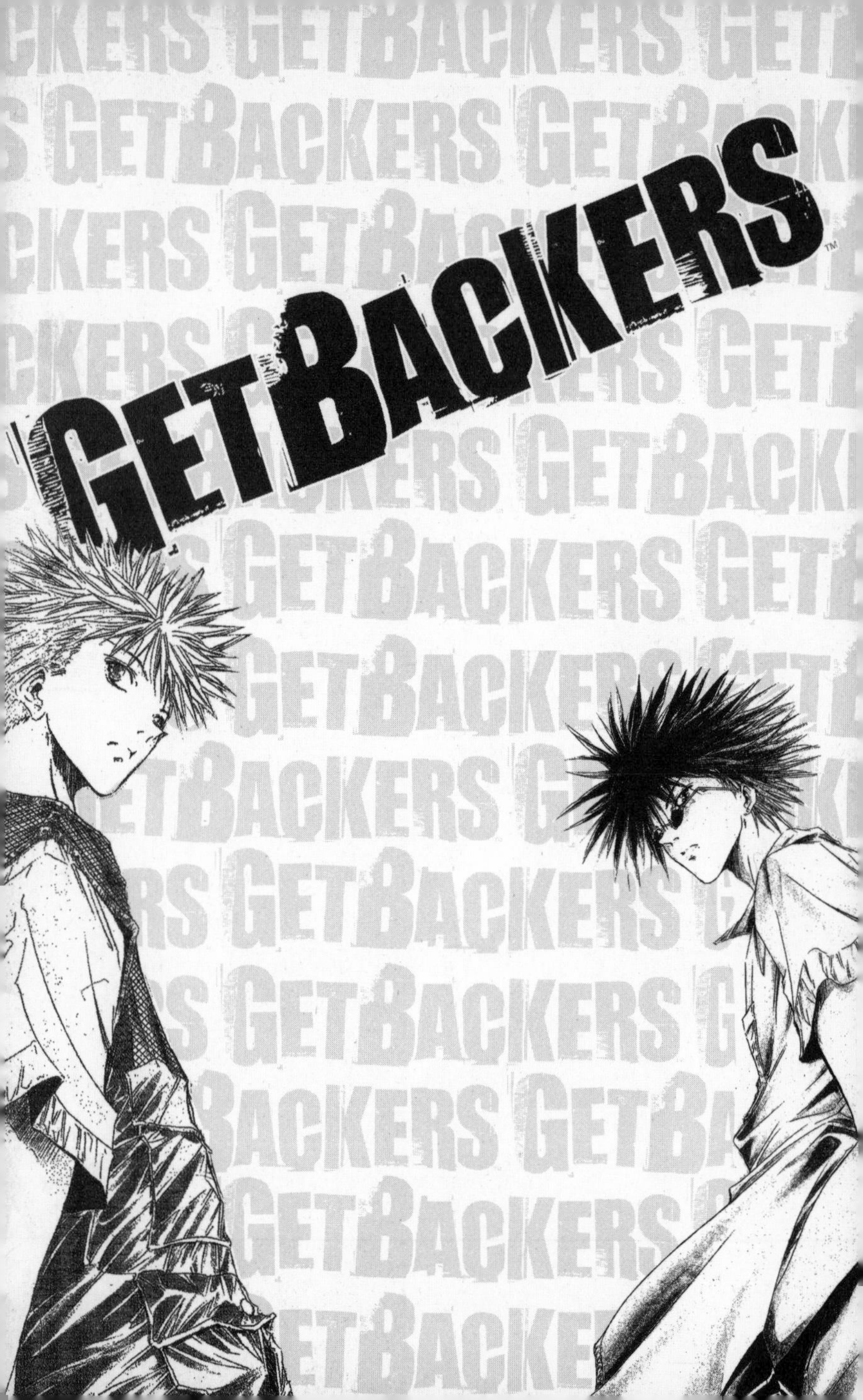
GETBACKERS™

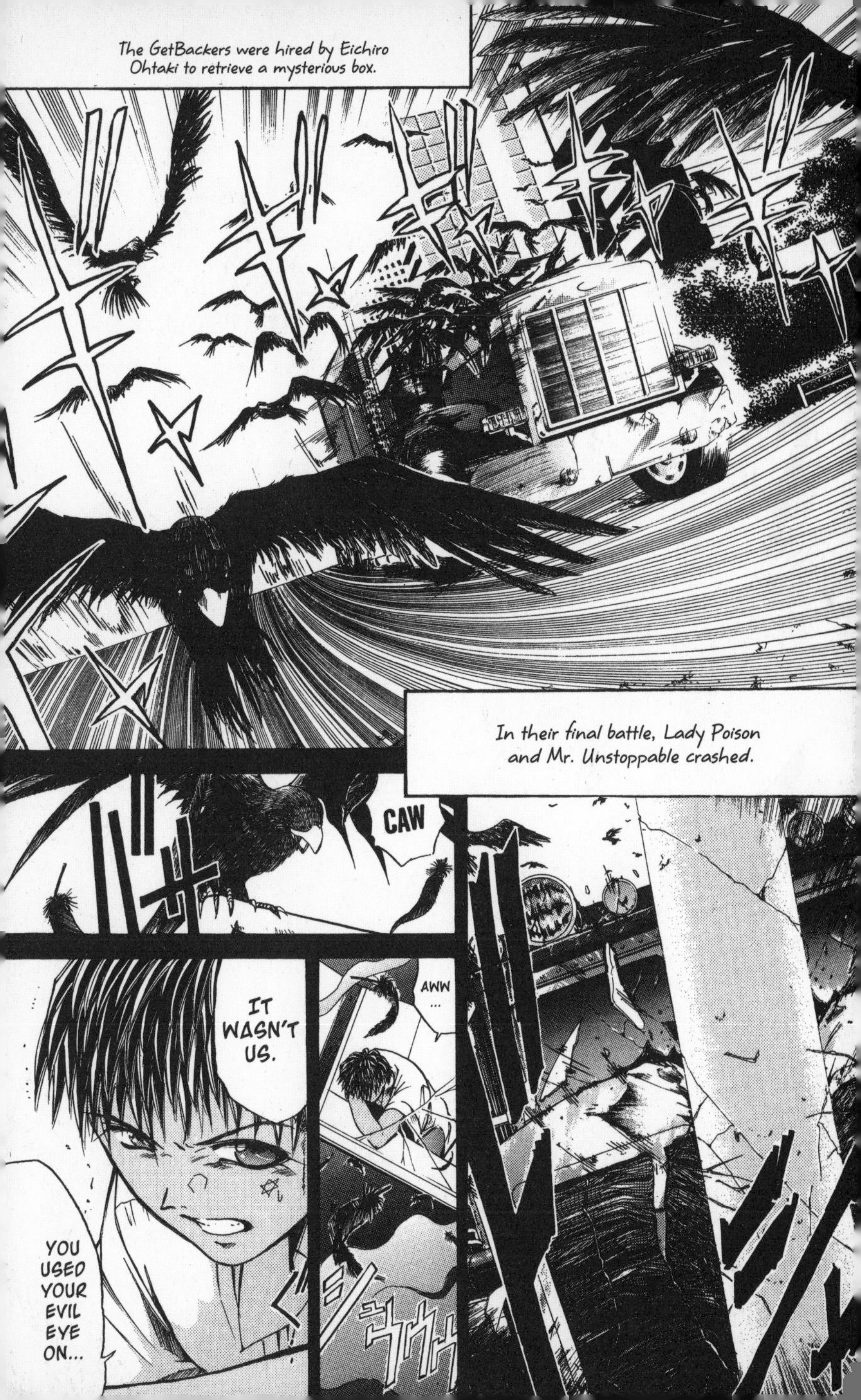
The GetBackers were hired by Eichiro Ohtaki to retrieve a mysterious box.
In their final battle, Lady Poison and Mr. Unstoppable crashed.
CAW
AWW ...
IT WASN'T US.
YOU USED YOUR EVIL EYE ON...

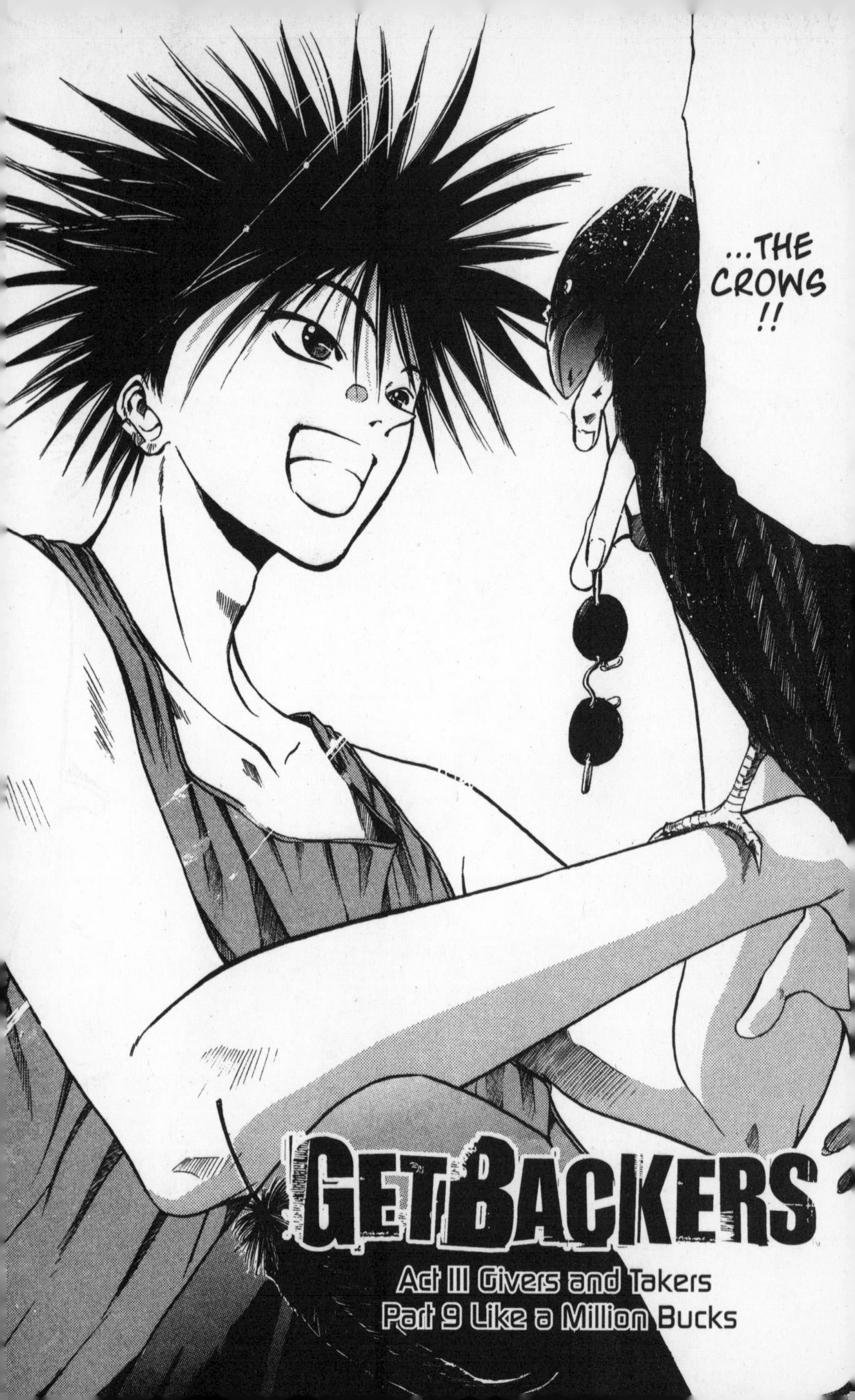
...THE CROWS !!
GETBACKERS
Act III Givers and Takers
Part 9 Like a Million Bucks

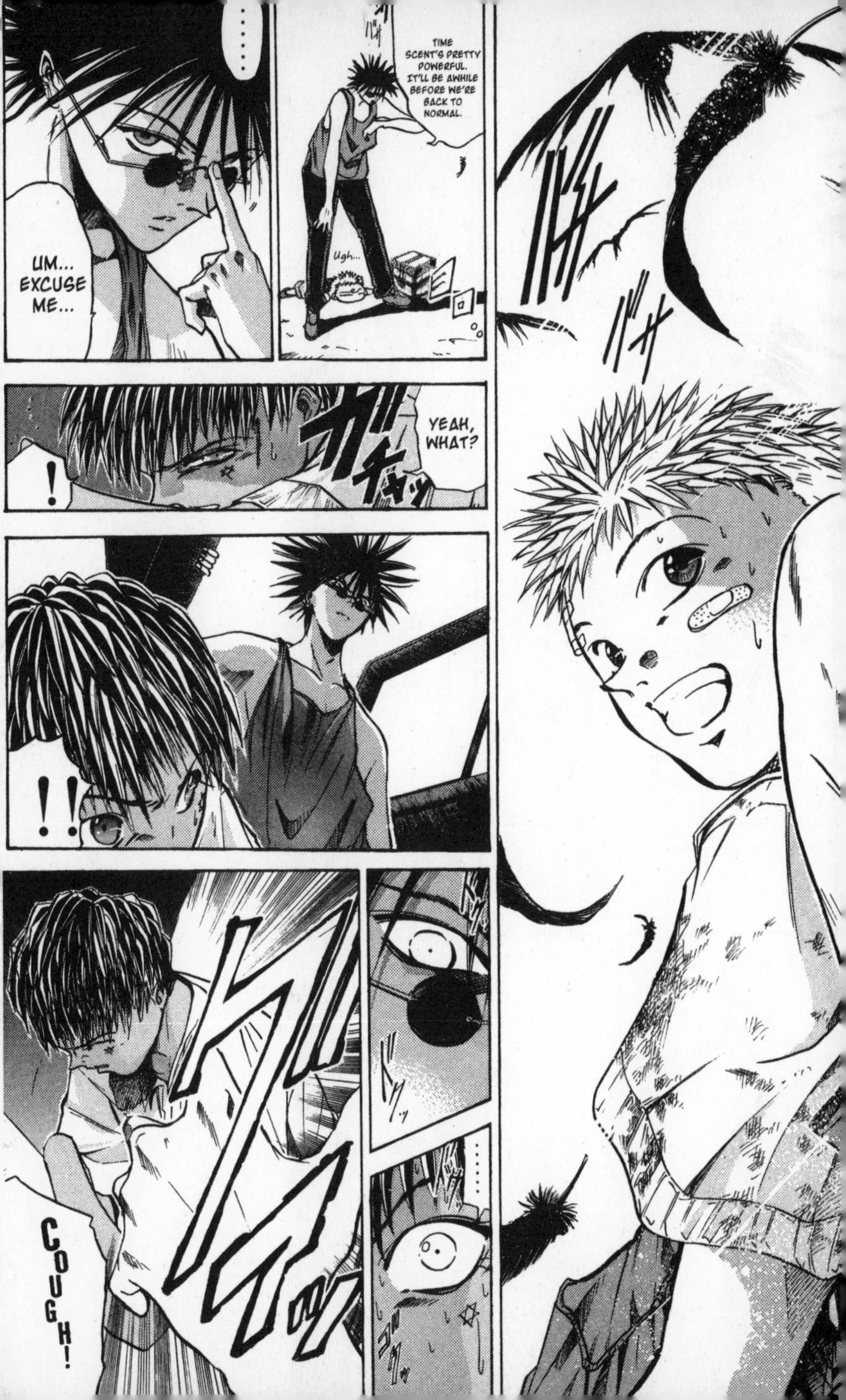
TIME SCENT'S PRETTY POWERFUL. IT'LL BE AWHILE BEFORE WE'RE BACK TO NORMAL.
Ugh...
......
UM... EXCUSE ME...
YEAH, WHAT?
!
!!
......
COUGH!

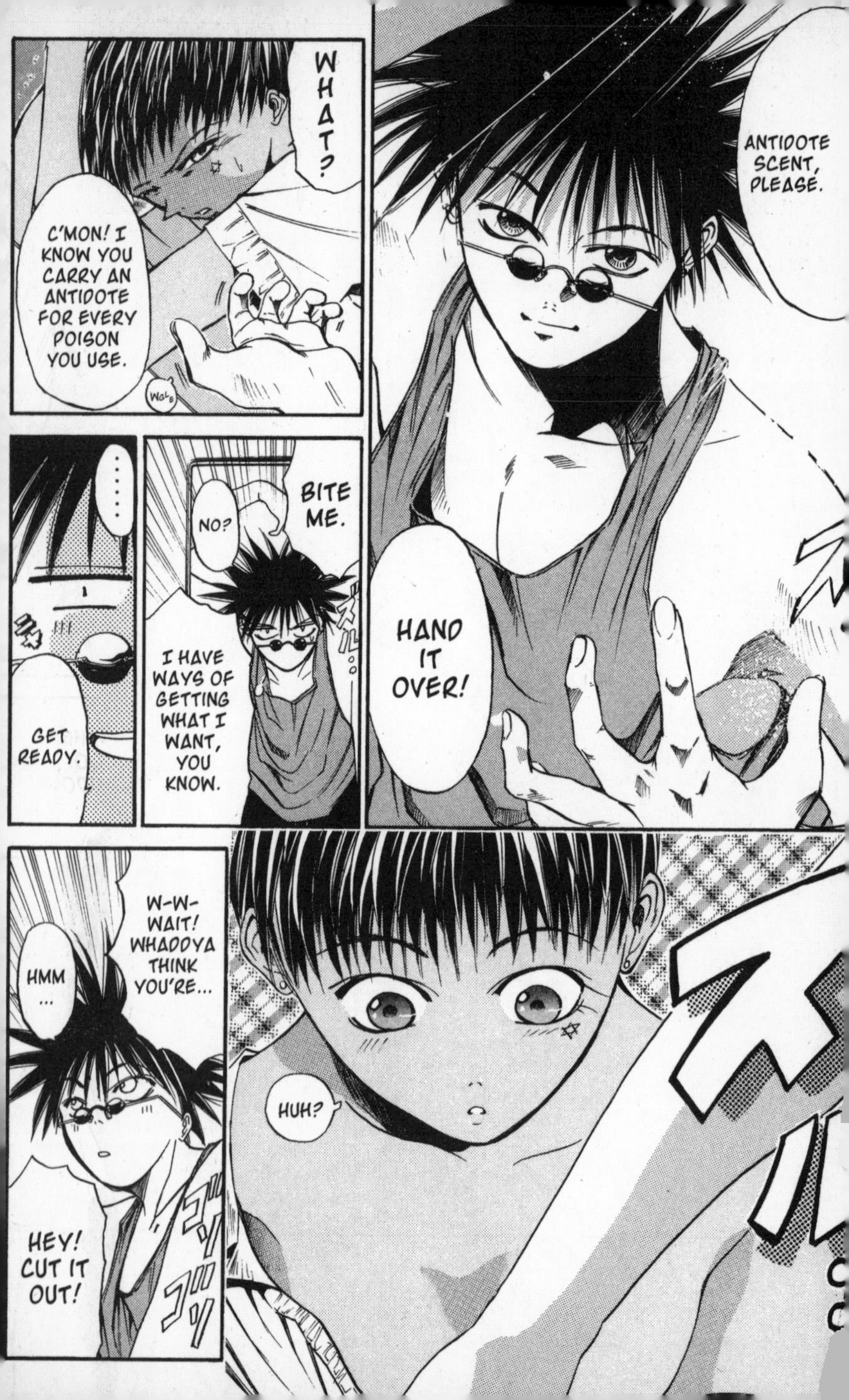
ANTIDOTE SCENT, PLEASE.
HAND IT OVER!
WHAT?
C'MON! I KNOW YOU CARRY AN ANTIDOTE FOR EVERY POISON YOU USE.
BITE ME.
NO?
I HAVE WAYS OF GETTING WHAT I WANT, YOU KNOW.
......
GET READY.
HUH?
W-W-WAIT! WHADDYA THINK YOU'RE...
HMM ...
HEY! CUT IT OUT!

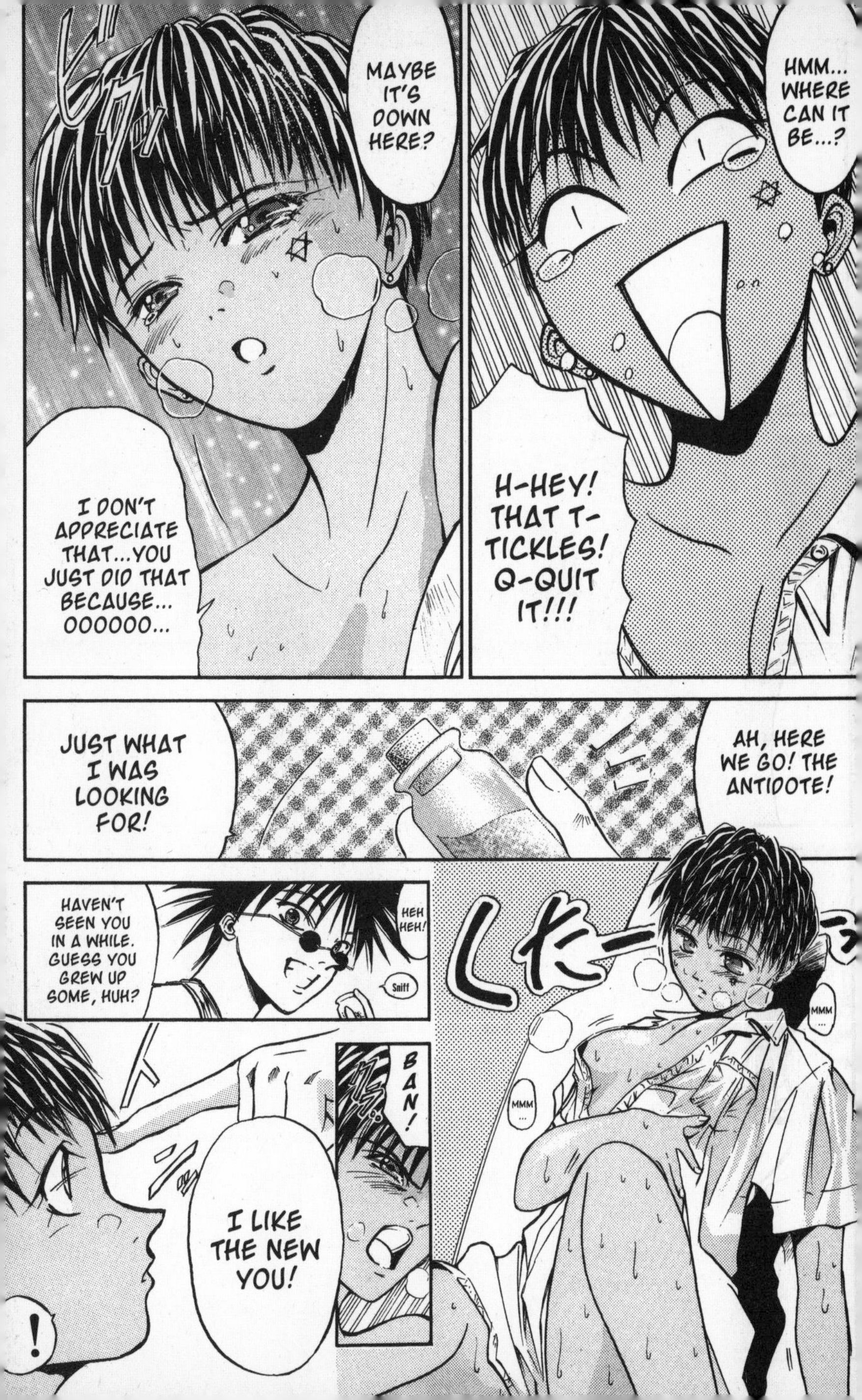
HMM... WHERE CAN IT BE...?
H-HEY! THAT T-TICKLES! Q-QUIT IT!!!
MAYBE IT'S DOWN HERE?
I DON'T APPRECIATE THAT...YOU JUST DID THAT BECAUSE... OOOOOO...
AH, HERE WE GO! THE ANTIDOTE!
JUST WHAT I WAS LOOKING FOR!
MMM ...
MMM ...
HEH HEH!
HAVEN'T SEEN YOU IN A WHILE. GUESS YOU GREW UP SOME, HUH?
Sniff
BAN!
I LIKE THE NEW YOU!
!

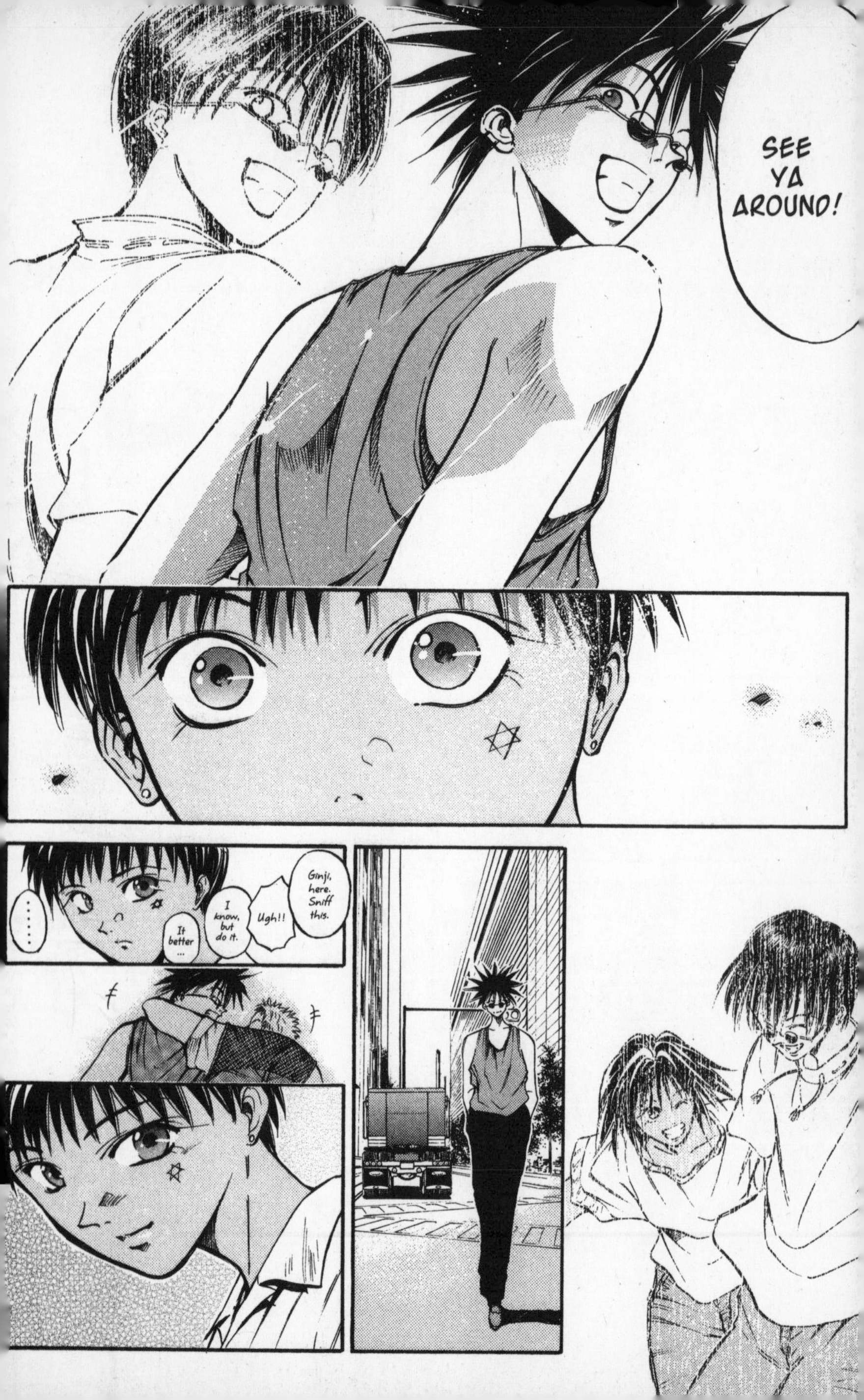
SEE YA AROUND!
Ginji, here. Sniff this.
Ugh!!
I know, but do it.
It better...
......

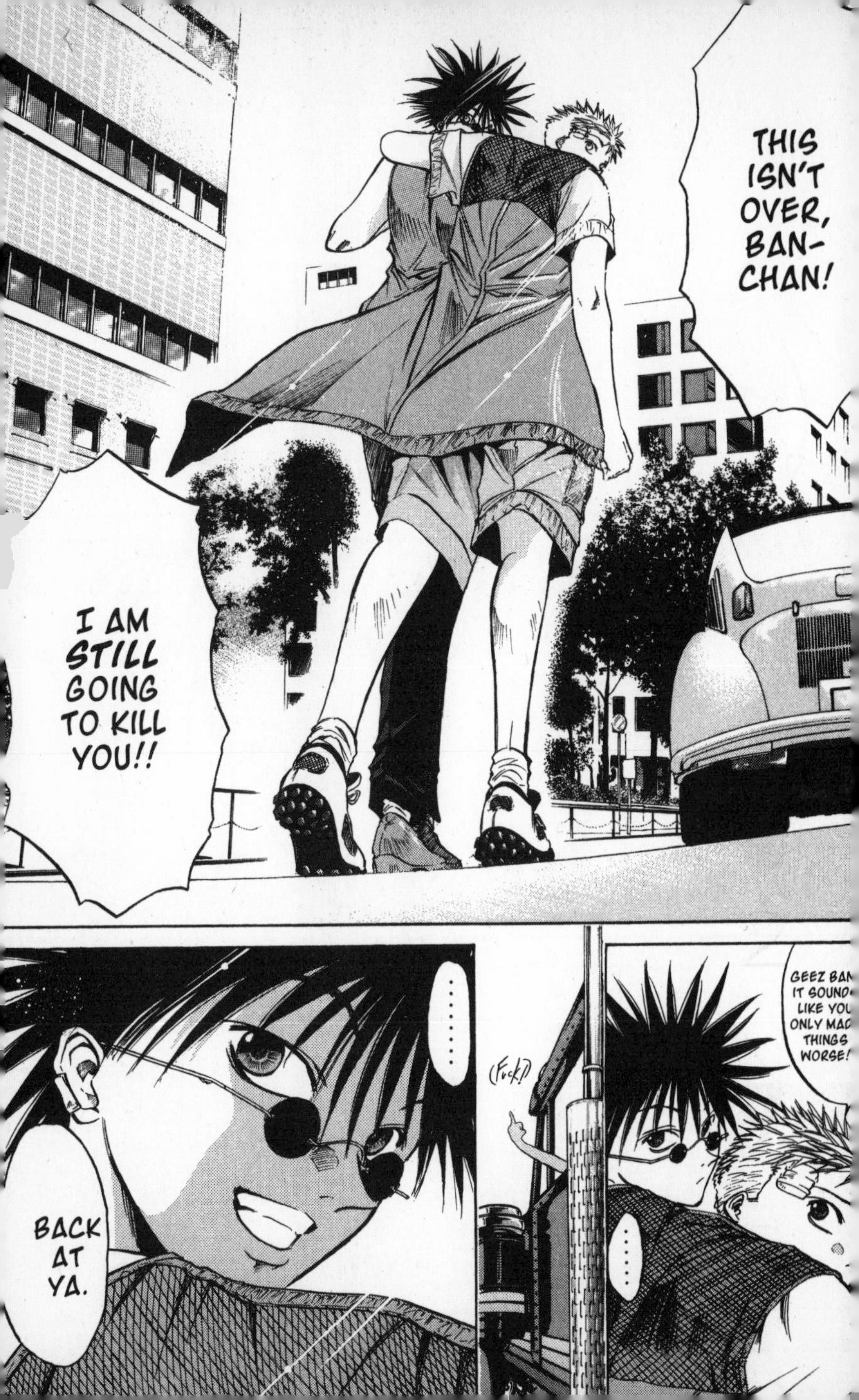
THIS ISN'T OVER, BAN-CHAN!
I AM **STILL** GOING TO KILL YOU!!
GEEZ BAN IT SOUND LIKE YOU ONLY MAD THINGS WORSE!
(Fuck!)
....
......
BACK AT YA.

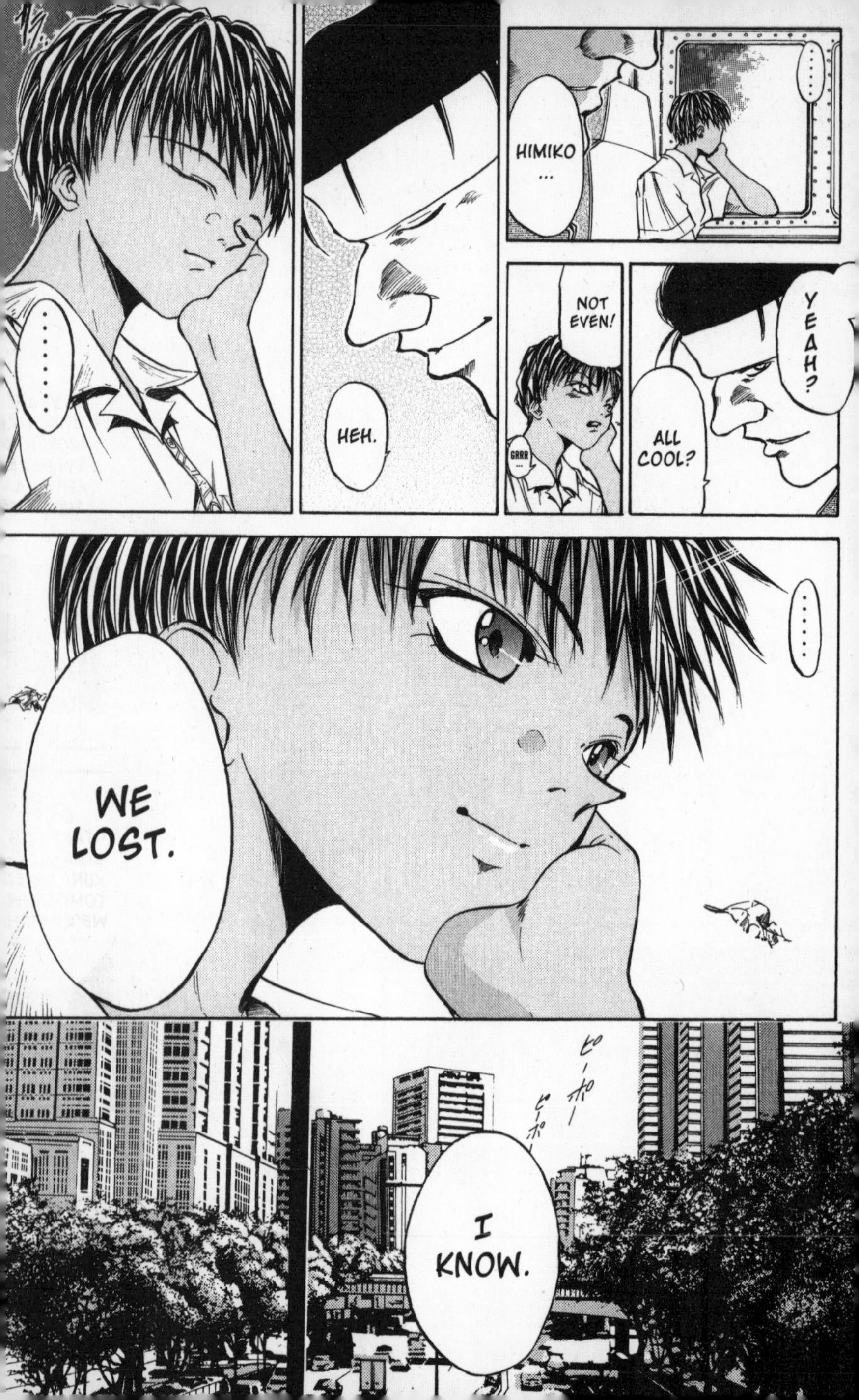
……
HIMIKO …
YEAH?
ALL COOL?
NOT EVEN!
GRRR …
HEH.
……
……
WE LOST.
ピーポー
ピーポ
I KNOW.

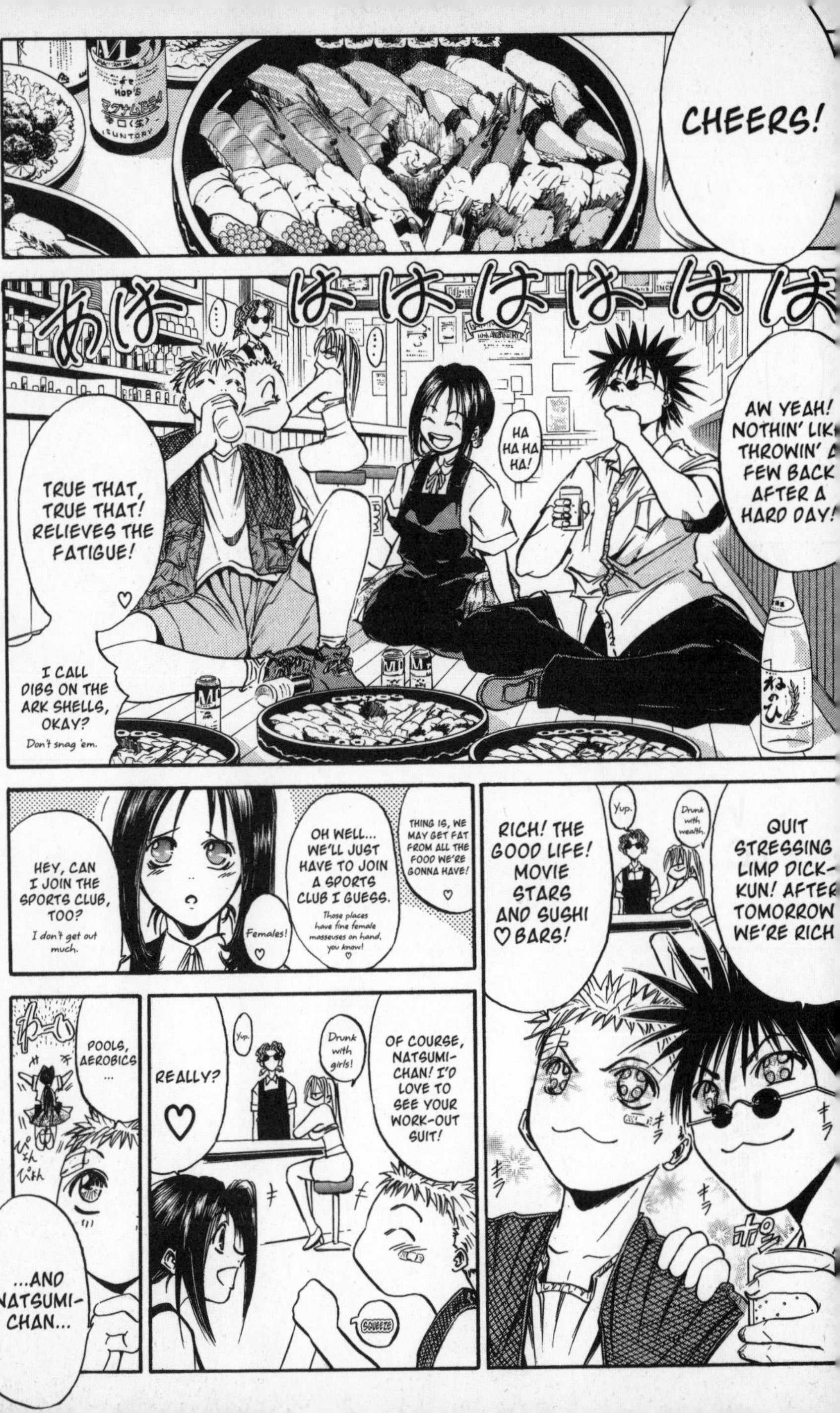
CHEERS!
あは ははははは
AW YEAH! NOTHIN' LIK THROWIN' A FEW BACK AFTER A HARD DAY!
HA HA HA HA HA!
...
TRUE THAT, TRUE THAT! RELIEVES THE FATIGUE! ♡
I CALL DIBS ON THE ARK SHELLS, OKAY?
Don't snag 'em.
QUIT STRESSING LIMP DICK-KUN! AFTER TOMORROW WE'RE RICH
Drunk with wealth.
Yup.
RICH! THE GOOD LIFE! MOVIE STARS AND SUSHI ♡ BARS!
THING IS, WE MAY GET FAT FROM ALL THE FOOD WE'RE GONNA HAVE! ♡
OH WELL... WE'LL JUST HAVE TO JOIN A SPORTS CLUB I GUESS.
Those places have fine female masseuses on hand, you know! ♡
Females! ♡
HEY, CAN I JOIN THE SPORTS CLUB, TOO?
I don't get out much.
Drunk with girls!
Yup.
OF COURSE, NATSUMI-CHAN! I'D LOVE TO SEE YOUR WORK-OUT SUIT!
REALLY? ♡
SQUEEZE
わーい
POOLS, AEROBICS ...
...AND NATSUMI-CHAN...

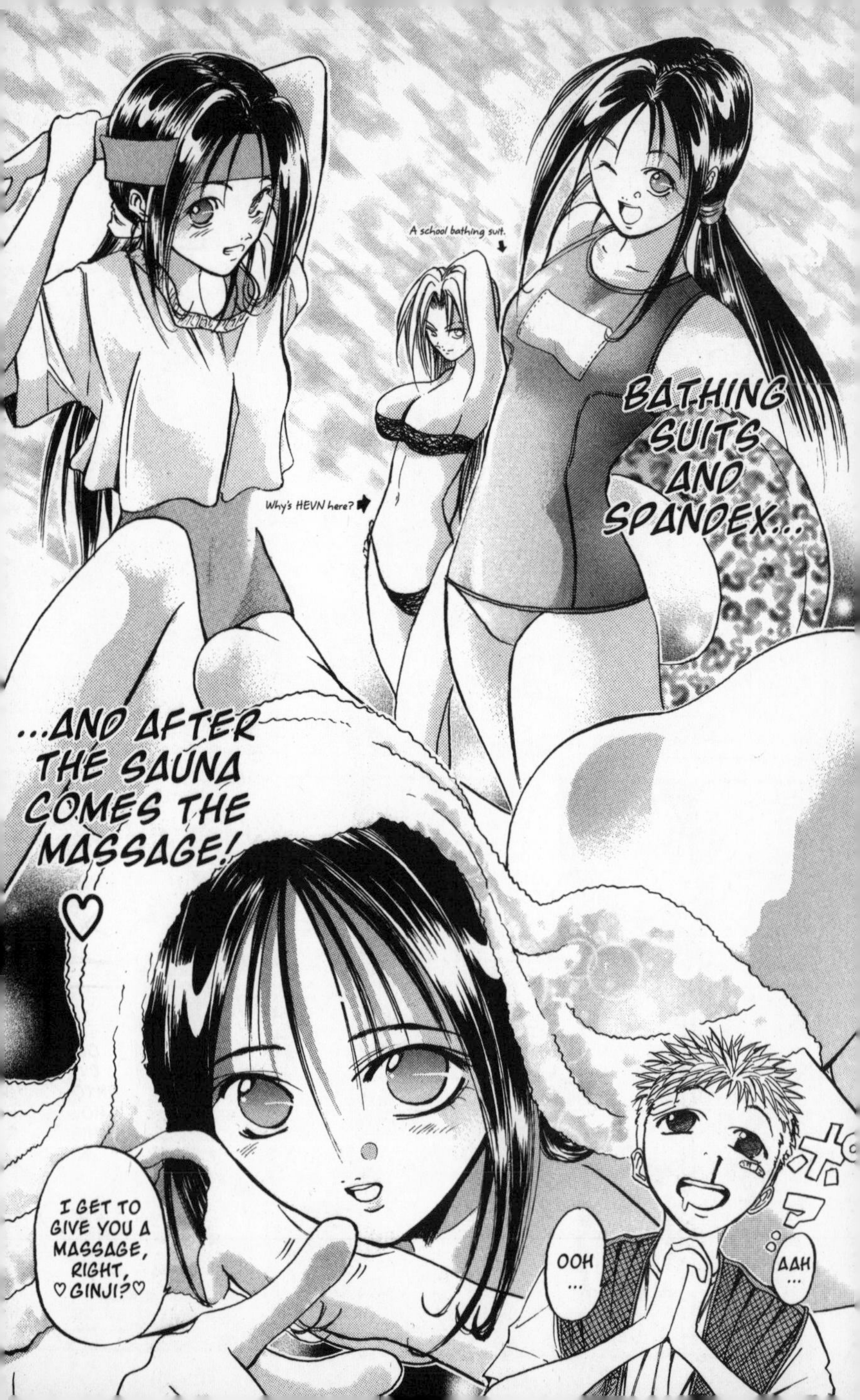
A school bathing suit.
BATHING SUITS AND SPANDEX...
Why's HEVN here?
...AND AFTER THE SAUNA COMES THE MASSAGE! ♡
AAH ...
OOH ...
I GET TO GIVE YOU A MASSAGE, RIGHT, ♡ GINJI?♡

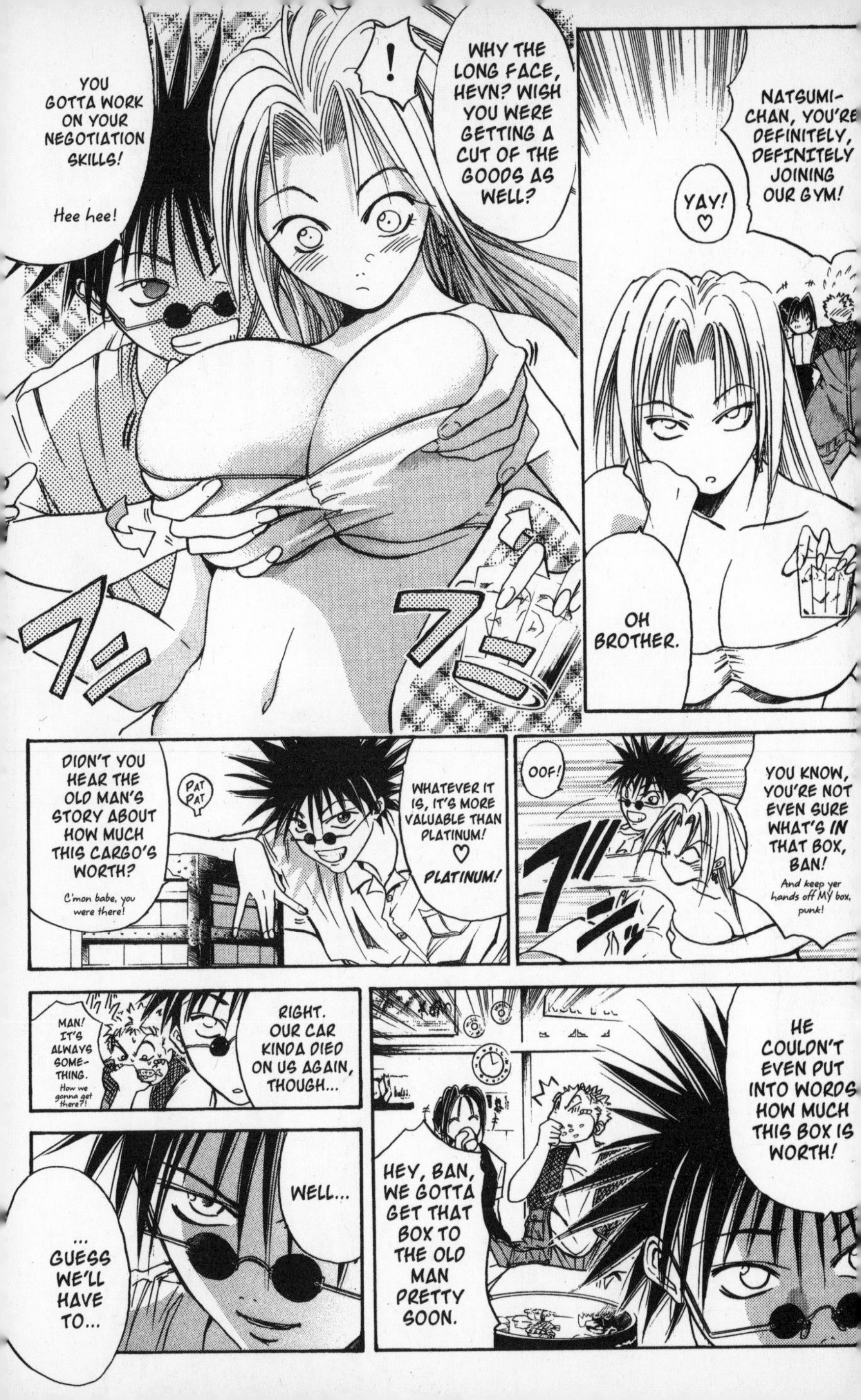
NATSUMI-CHAN, YOU'RE DEFINITELY, DEFINITELY JOINING OUR GYM!
YAY! ♡
OH BROTHER.
!
WHY THE LONG FACE, HEVN? WISH YOU WERE GETTING A CUT OF THE GOODS AS WELL?
YOU GOTTA WORK ON YOUR NEGOTIATION SKILLS!
Hee hee!
OOF!
YOU KNOW, YOU'RE NOT EVEN SURE WHAT'S IN THAT BOX, BAN!
And keep yer hands off MY box, punk!
WHATEVER IT IS, IT'S MORE VALUABLE THAN PLATINUM! ♡
PLATINUM!
PAT PAT
DIDN'T YOU HEAR THE OLD MAN'S STORY ABOUT HOW MUCH THIS CARGO'S WORTH?
C'mon babe, you were there!
HE COULDN'T EVEN PUT INTO WORDS HOW MUCH THIS BOX IS WORTH!
HEY, BAN, WE GOTTA GET THAT BOX TO THE OLD MAN PRETTY SOON.
RIGHT. OUR CAR KINDA DIED ON US AGAIN, THOUGH...
MAN! IT'S ALWAYS SOME-THING.
How we gonna get there?!
WELL...
... GUESS WE'LL HAVE TO...

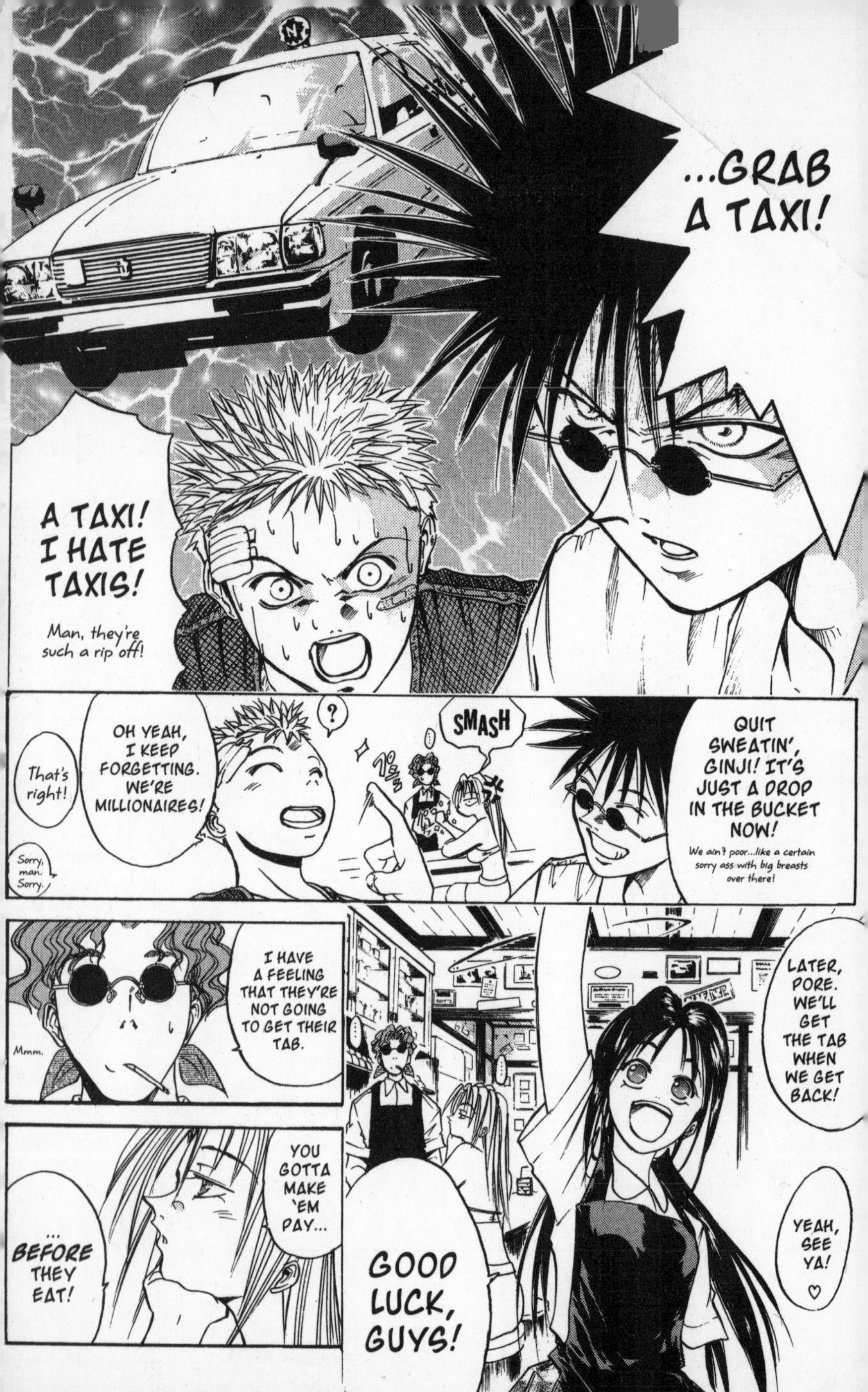
...GRAB A TAXI!
A TAXI! I HATE TAXIS!
Man, they're such a rip off!
QUIT SWEATIN', GINJI! IT'S JUST A DROP IN THE BUCKET NOW!
We ain't poor...like a certain sorry ass with big breasts over there!
SMASH
?
OH YEAH, I KEEP FORGETTING. WE'RE MILLIONAIRES!
That's right!
Sorry, man. Sorry.
LATER, PORE. WE'LL GET THE TAB WHEN WE GET BACK!
YEAH, SEE YA! ♡
GOOD LUCK, GUYS!
I HAVE A FEELING THAT THEY'RE NOT GOING TO GET THEIR TAB.
Mmm.
YOU GOTTA MAKE 'EM PAY...
...BEFORE THEY EAT!

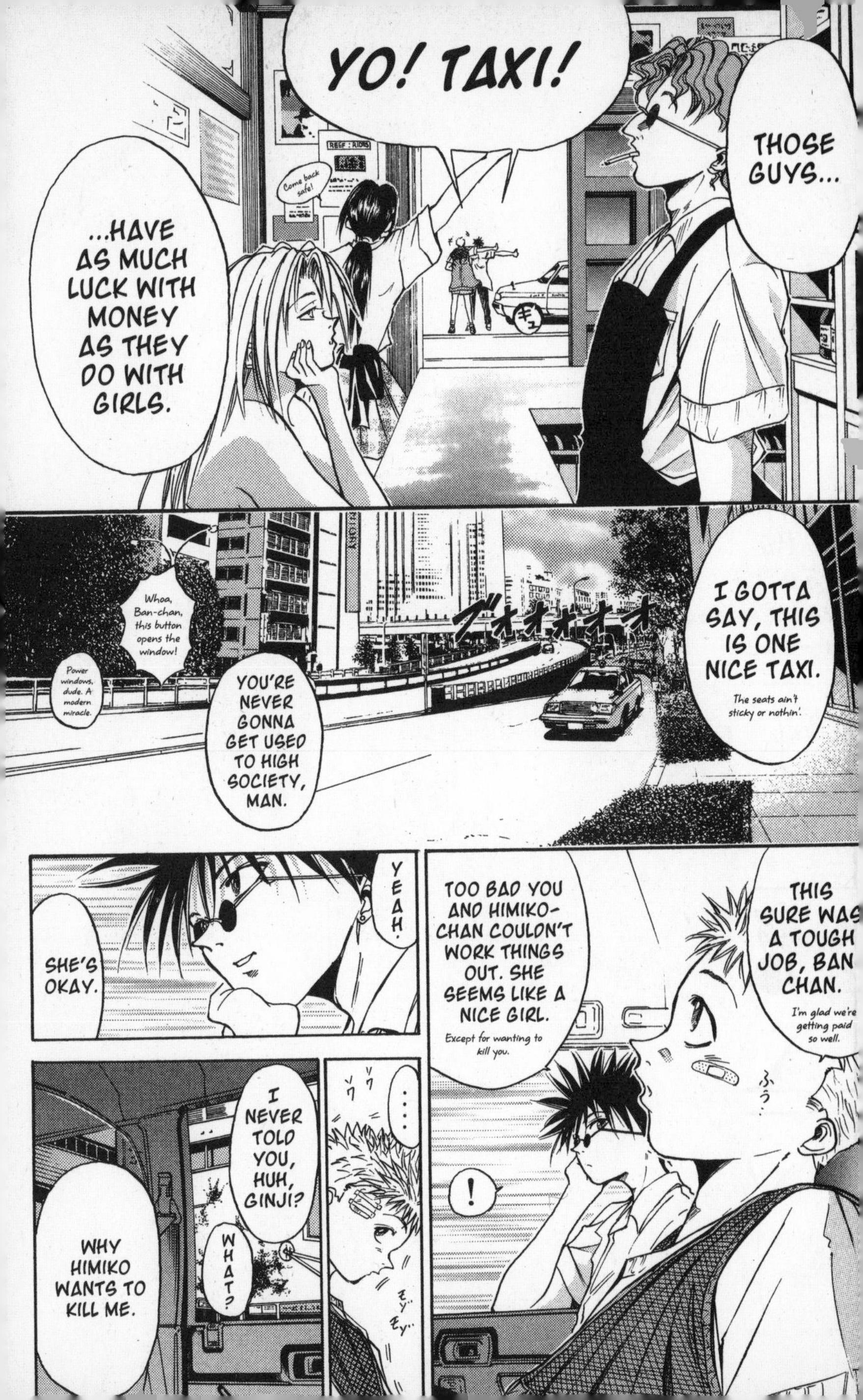
THOSE GUYS...
YO! TAXI!
Come back safe!
...HAVE AS MUCH LUCK WITH MONEY AS THEY DO WITH GIRLS.
I GOTTA SAY, THIS IS ONE NICE TAXI.
The seats ain't sticky or nothin'.
YOU'RE NEVER GONNA GET USED TO HIGH SOCIETY, MAN.
Whoa, Ban-chan, this button opens the window!
Power windows, dude. A modern miracle.
THIS SURE WAS A TOUGH JOB, BAN CHAN.
I'm glad we're getting paid so well.
TOO BAD YOU AND HIMIKO-CHAN COULDN'T WORK THINGS OUT. SHE SEEMS LIKE A NICE GIRL.
Except for wanting to kill you.
YEAH.
SHE'S OKAY.
!
....
I NEVER TOLD YOU, HUH, GINJI?
WHAT?
WHY HIMIKO WANTS TO KILL ME.

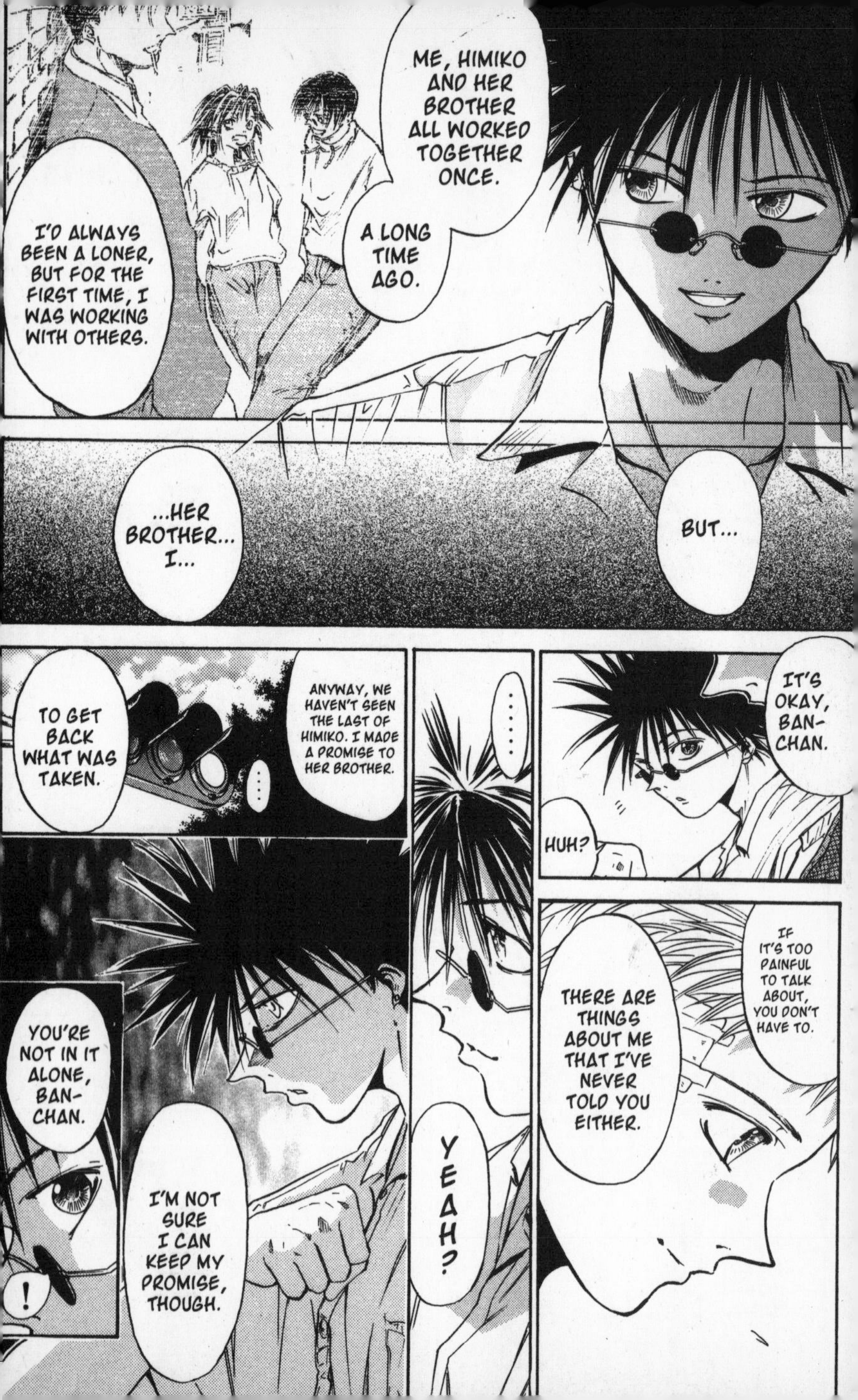
ME, HIMIKO AND HER BROTHER ALL WORKED TOGETHER ONCE.
A LONG TIME AGO.
I'D ALWAYS BEEN A LONER, BUT FOR THE FIRST TIME, I WAS WORKING WITH OTHERS.
BUT...
...HER BROTHER... I...
IT'S OKAY, BAN-CHAN.
HUH?
......
ANYWAY, WE HAVEN'T SEEN THE LAST OF HIMIKO. I MADE A PROMISE TO HER BROTHER.
....
TO GET BACK WHAT WAS TAKEN.
IF IT'S TOO PAINFUL TO TALK ABOUT, YOU DON'T HAVE TO.
THERE ARE THINGS ABOUT ME THAT I'VE NEVER TOLD YOU EITHER.
YEAH?
I'M NOT SURE I CAN KEEP MY PROMISE, THOUGH.
YOU'RE NOT IN IT ALONE, BAN-CHAN.
!

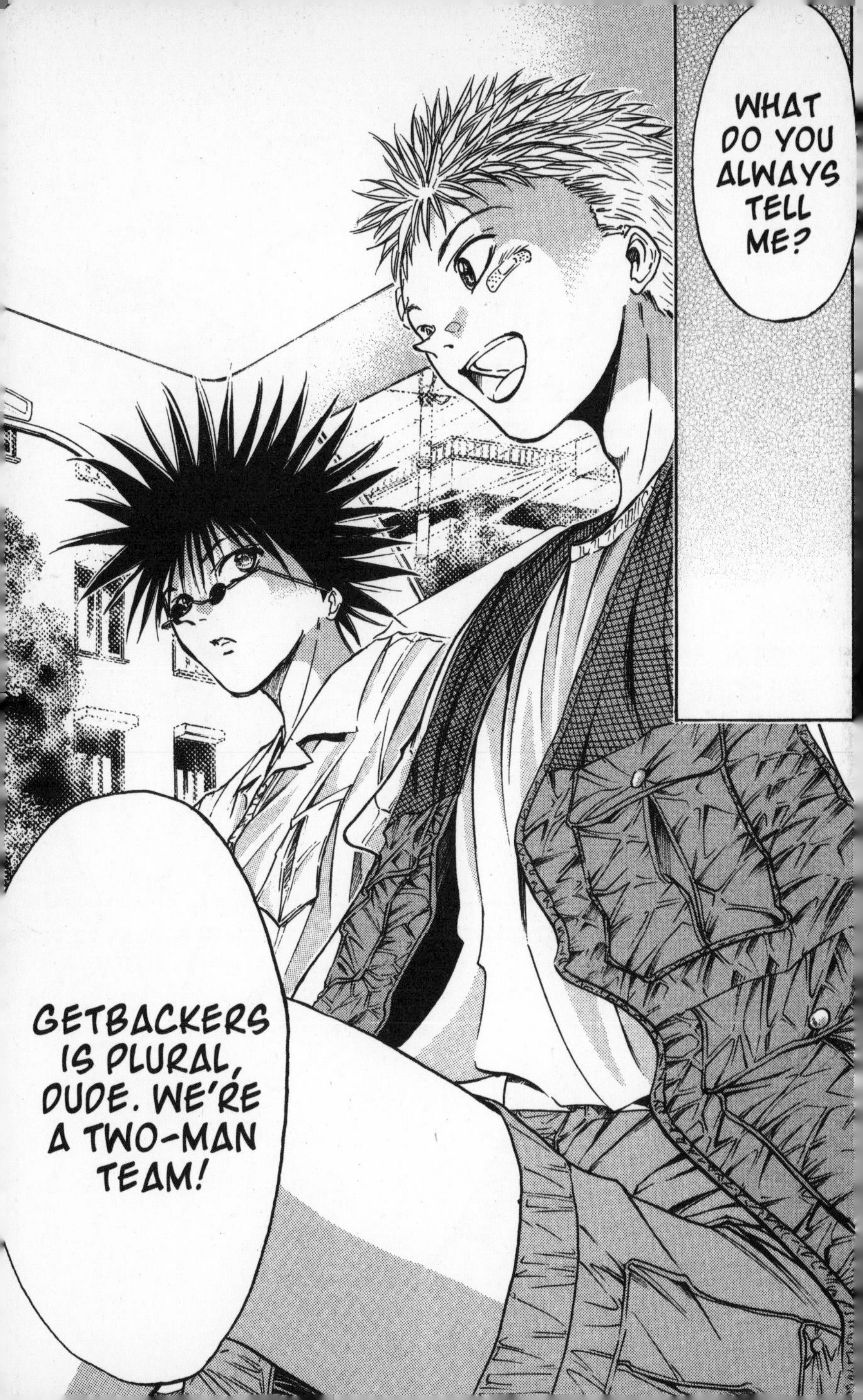
WHAT DO YOU ALWAYS TELL ME?
GETBACKERS IS PLURAL, DUDE. WE'RE A TWO-MAN TEAM!

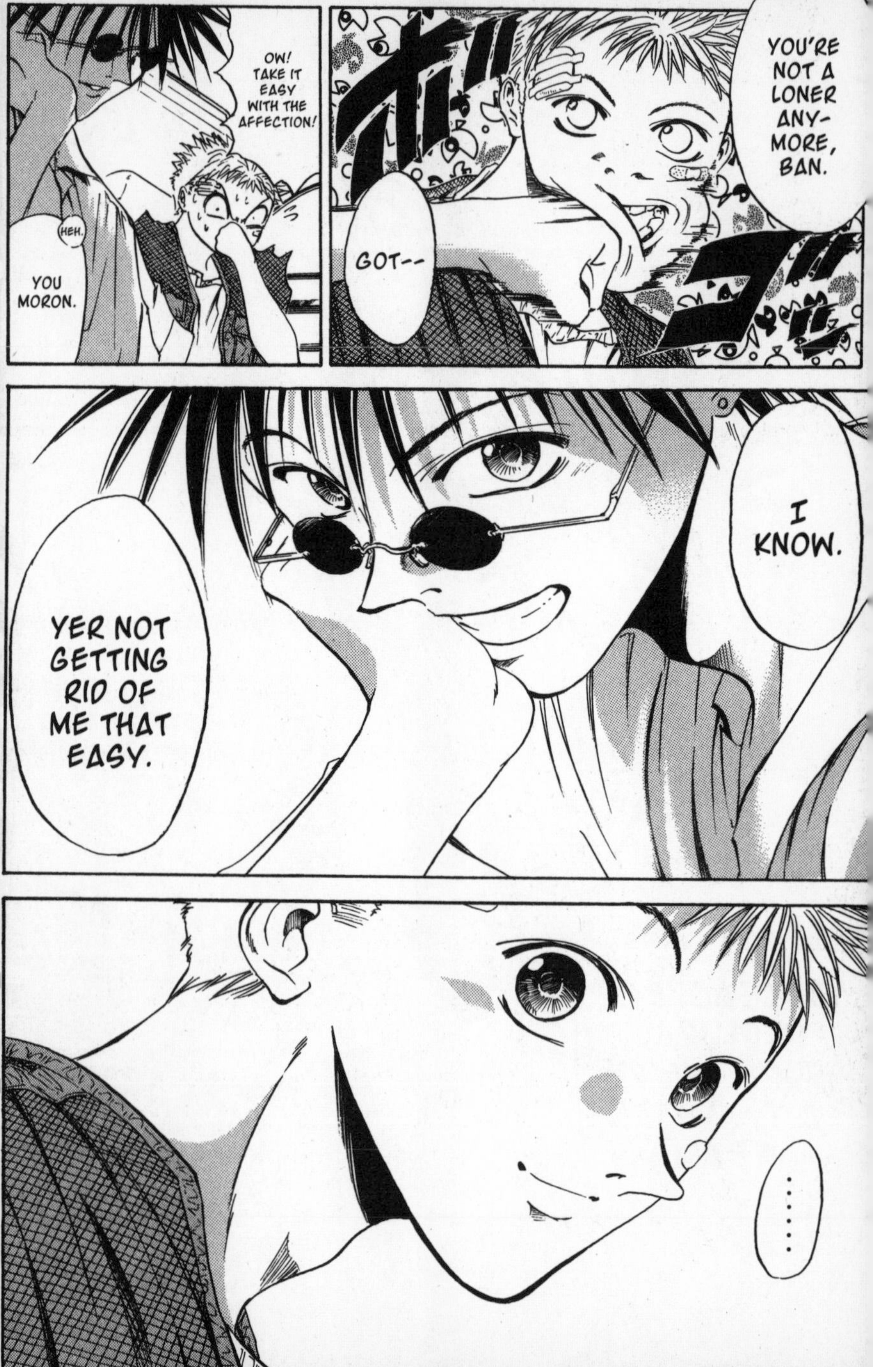
YOU'RE NOT A LONER ANY-MORE, BAN.
GOT--
OW! TAKE IT EASY WITH THE AFFECTION!
HEH.
YOU MORON.
I KNOW.
YER NOT GETTING RID OF ME THAT EASY.
......

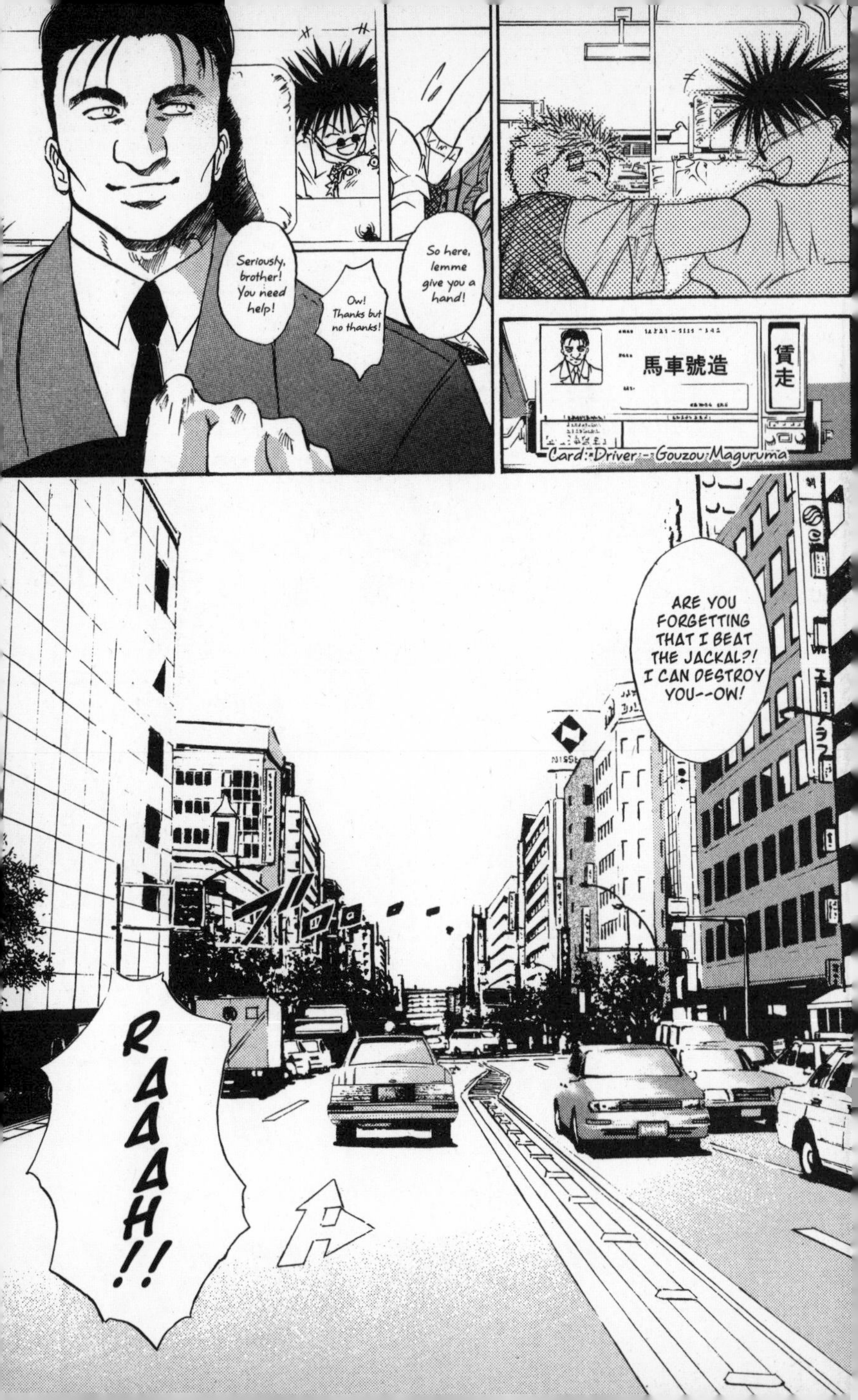

馬車號造
賃走
Card: Driver - Gouzou Maguruma
So here, lemme give you a hand!
Seriously, brother! You need help!
Ow! Thanks but no thanks!
ARE YOU FORGETTING THAT I BEAT THE JACKAL?! I CAN DESTROY YOU--OW!
RAAAAH!!

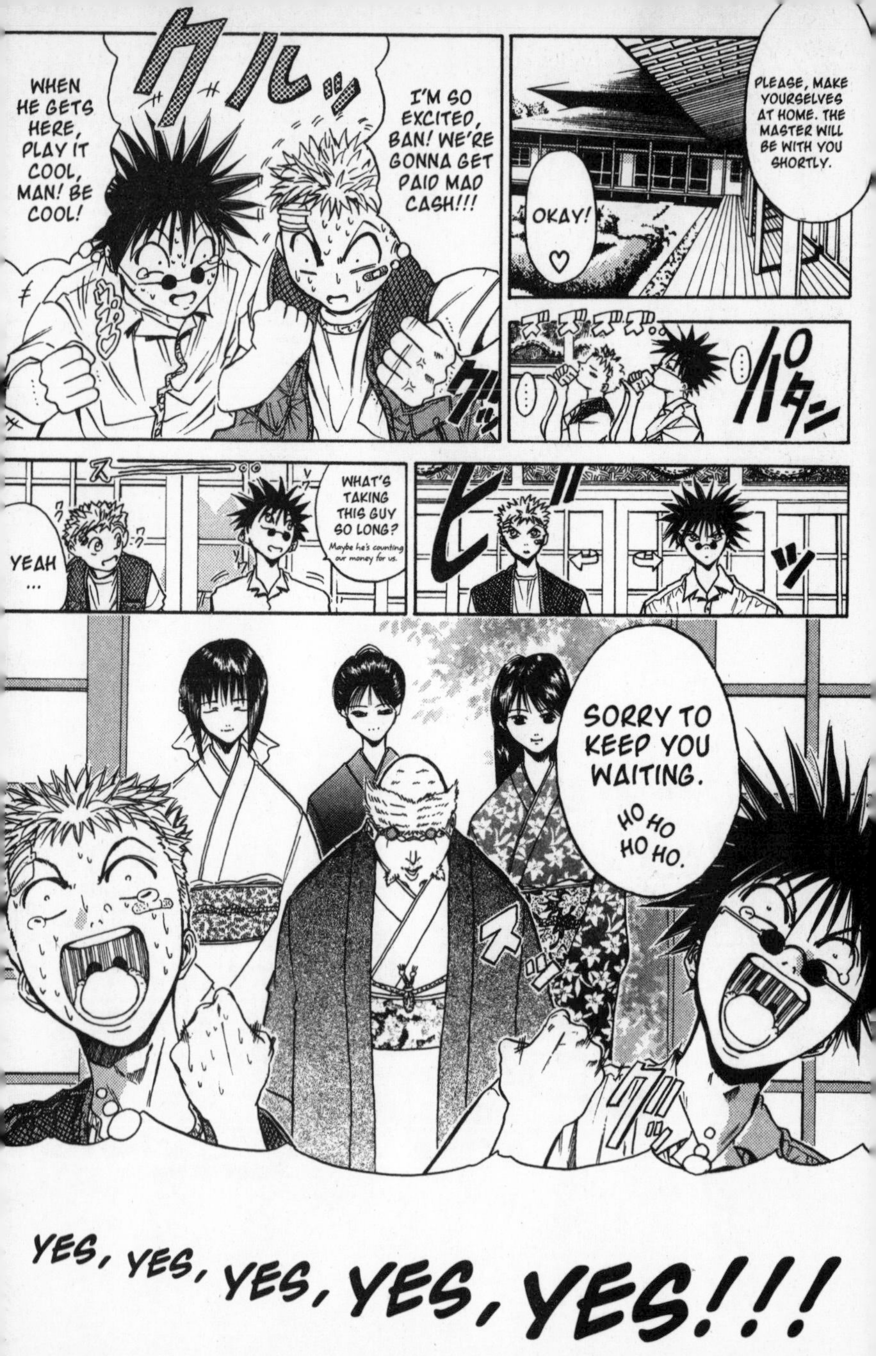
PLEASE, MAKE YOURSELVES AT HOME. THE MASTER WILL BE WITH YOU SHORTLY.
OKAY! ♥
...
...
I'M SO EXCITED, BAN! WE'RE GONNA GET PAID MAD CASH!!!
WHEN HE GETS HERE, PLAY IT COOL, MAN! BE COOL!
WHAT'S TAKING THIS GUY SO LONG?
Maybe he's counting our money for us.
YEAH ...
SORRY TO KEEP YOU WAITING.
HO HO HO HO.
YES, YES, YES, YES, YES!!!
Cha-ching! We're rich!

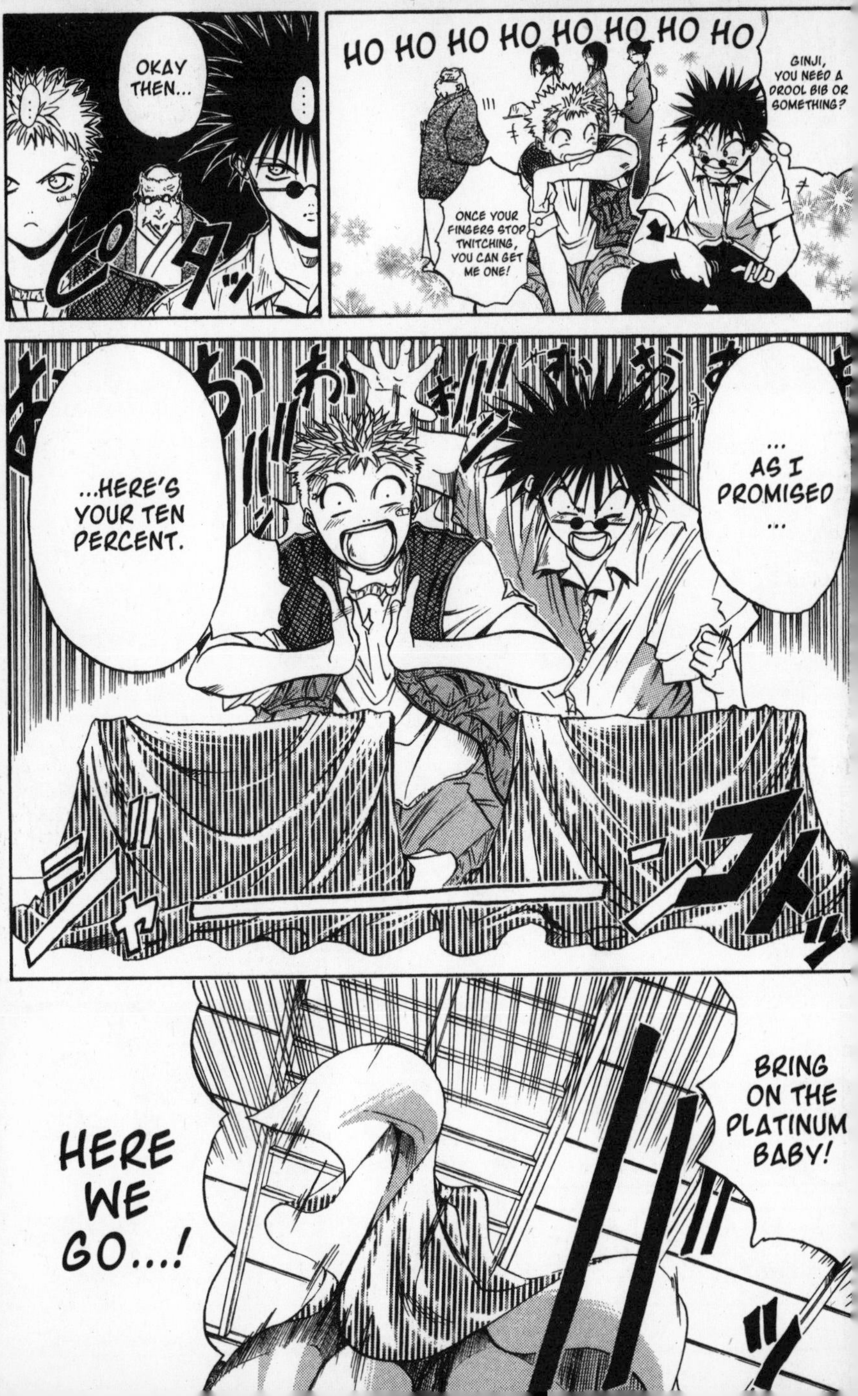
HO HO HO HO HO HO HO HO
GINJI, YOU NEED A DROOL BIB OR SOMETHING?
ONCE YOUR FINGERS STOP TWITCHING, YOU CAN GET ME ONE!
...
OKAY THEN...
...
... AS I PROMISED ...
...HERE'S YOUR TEN PERCENT.
BRING ON THE PLATINUM BABY!
HERE WE GO...!

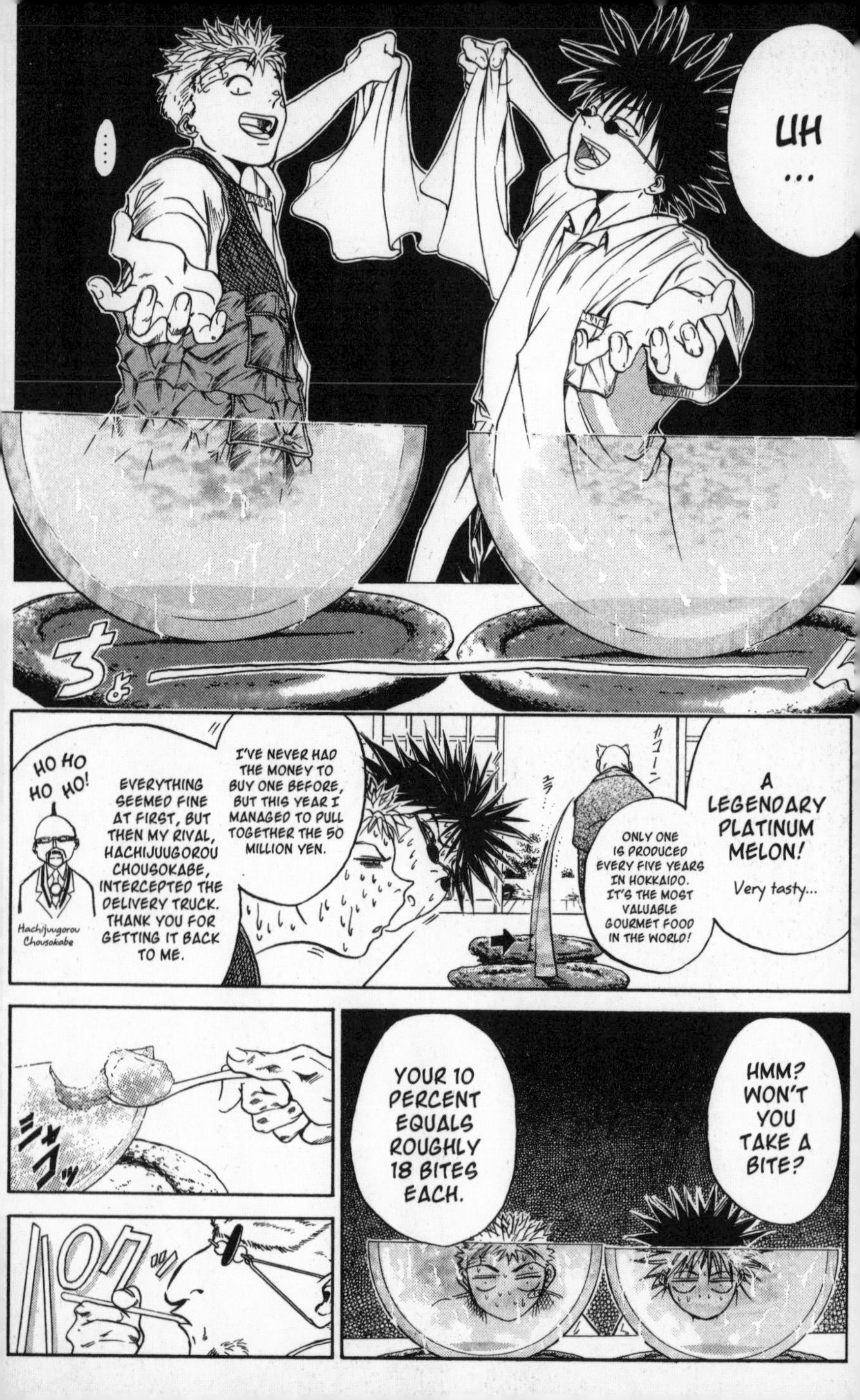
UH ...
...
A LEGENDARY PLATINUM MELON!
Very tasty...
ONLY ONE IS PRODUCED EVERY FIVE YEARS IN HOKKAIDO. IT'S THE MOST VALUABLE GOURMET FOOD IN THE WORLD!
I'VE NEVER HAD THE MONEY TO BUY ONE BEFORE, BUT THIS YEAR I MANAGED TO PULL TOGETHER THE 50 MILLION YEN.
HO HO HO HO!
EVERYTHING SEEMED FINE AT FIRST, BUT THEN MY RIVAL, HACHIJUUGOROU CHOUSOKABE, INTERCEPTED THE DELIVERY TRUCK. THANK YOU FOR GETTING IT BACK TO ME.
Hachijuugorou Chousokabe
HMM? WON'T YOU TAKE A BITE?
YOUR 10 PERCENT EQUALS ROUGHLY 18 BITES EACH.

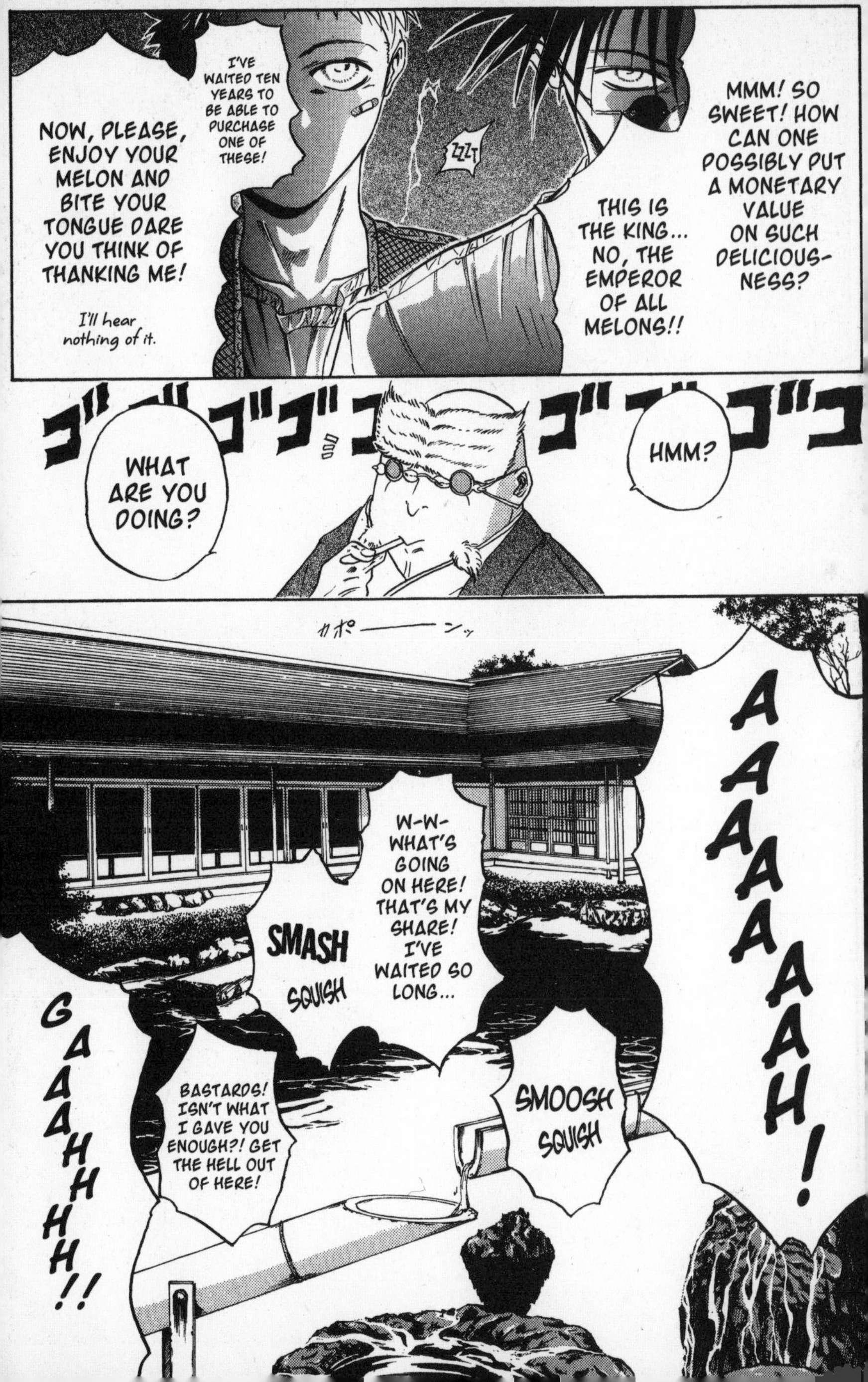
MMM! SO SWEET! HOW CAN ONE POSSIBLY PUT A MONETARY VALUE ON SUCH DELICIOUS-NESS?
THIS IS THE KING... NO, THE EMPEROR OF ALL MELONS!!
ZZZT
I'VE WAITED TEN YEARS TO BE ABLE TO PURCHASE ONE OF THESE!
NOW, PLEASE, ENJOY YOUR MELON AND BITE YOUR TONGUE DARE YOU THINK OF THANKING ME!
I'll hear nothing of it.
HMM?
WHAT ARE YOU DOING?
カポ———ンッ
AAAAAAAH!
W-W-WHAT'S GOING ON HERE! THAT'S MY SHARE! I'VE WAITED SO LONG...
SMASH
SQUISH
SMOOSH
SQUISH
BASTARDS! ISN'T WHAT I GAVE YOU ENOUGH?! GET THE HELL OUT OF HERE!
GAAAHHHH!!

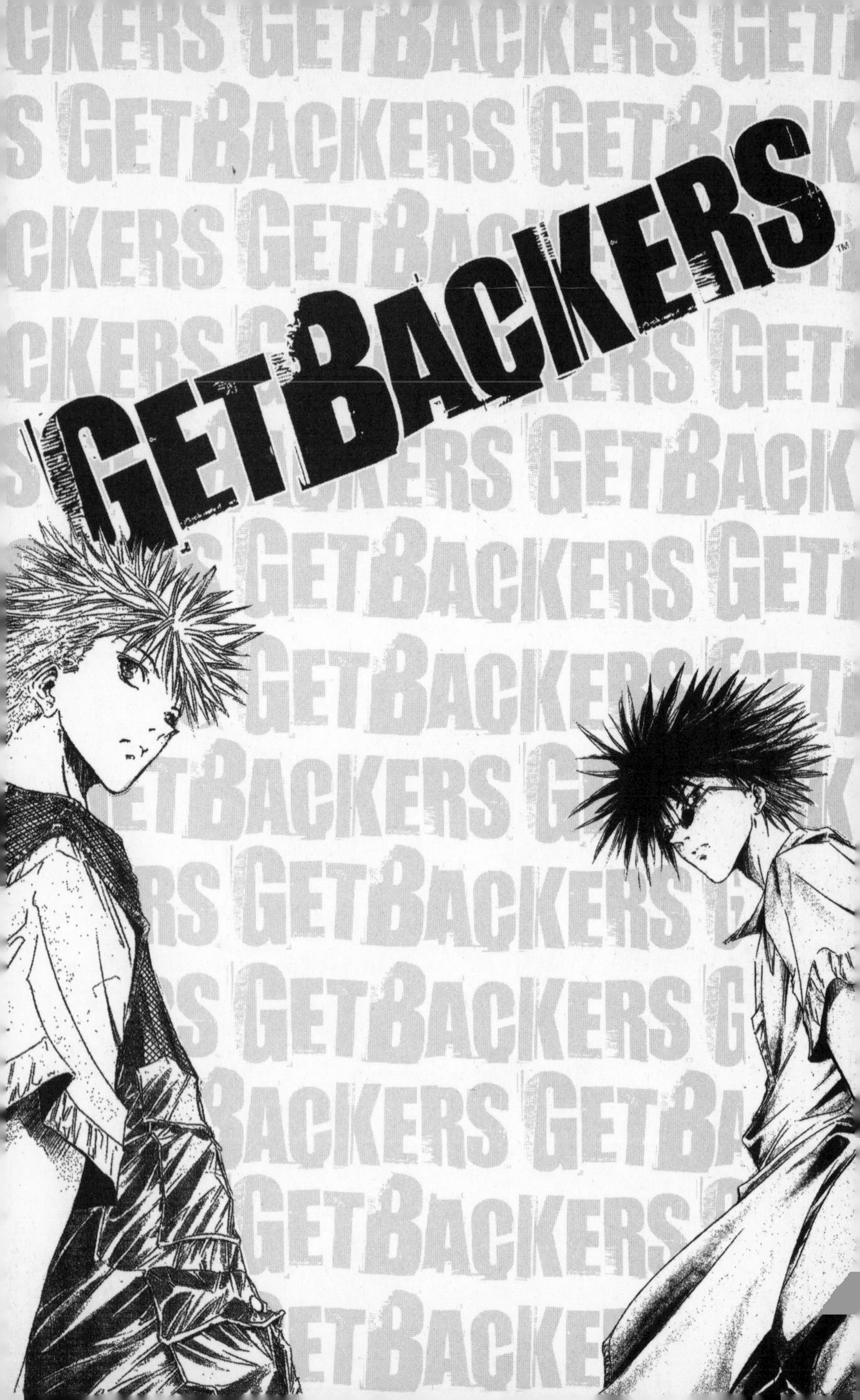
GETBACKERS™

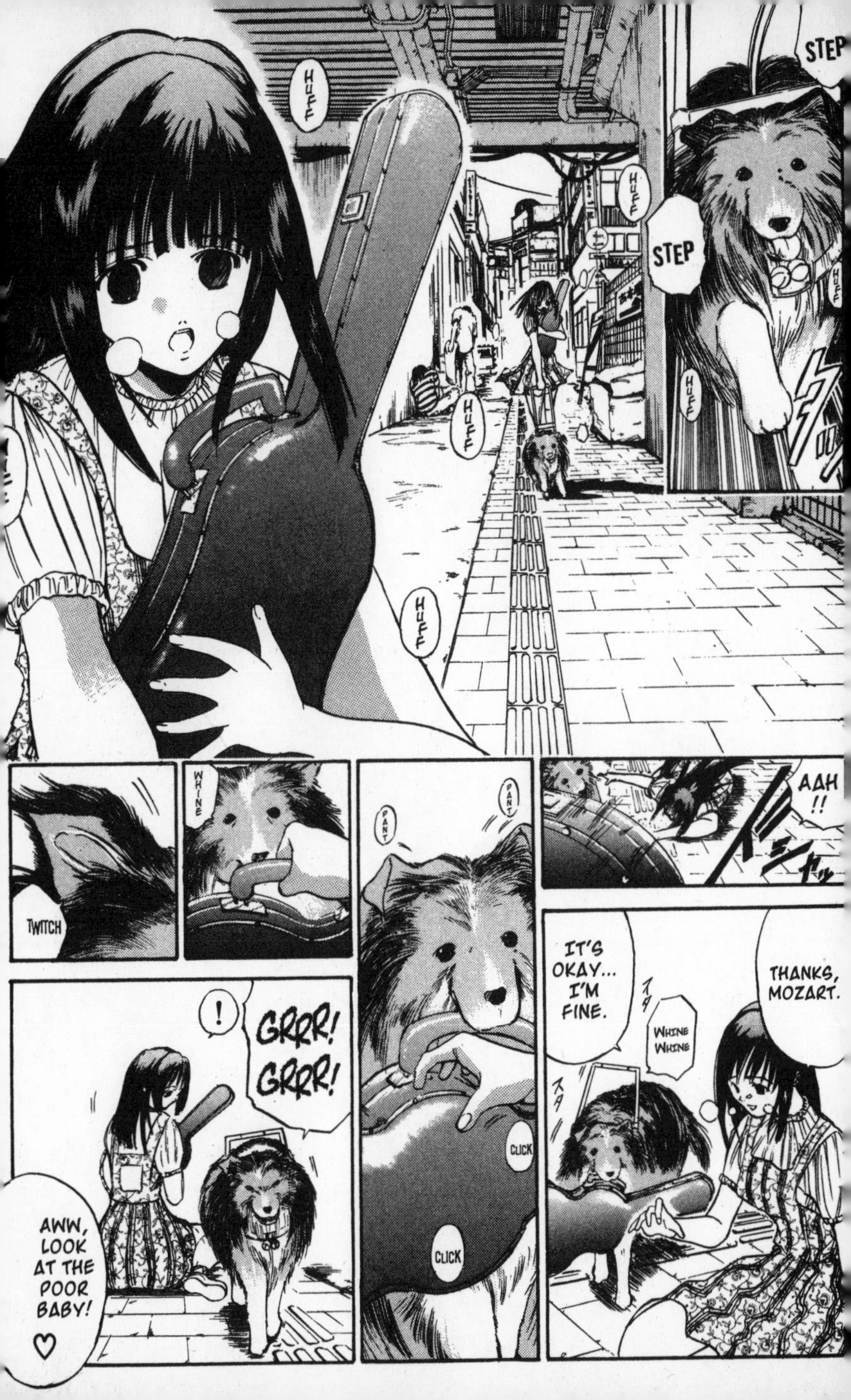
STEP
STEP
HUFF
HUFF
HUFF
HUFF
HUFF
HUFF
AAH!!
THANKS, MOZART.
IT'S OKAY... I'M FINE.
WHINE WHINE
PANT
PANT
CLICK
CLICK
WHINE
TWITCH
!
GRRR! GRRR!
AWW, LOOK AT THE POOR BABY! ♡

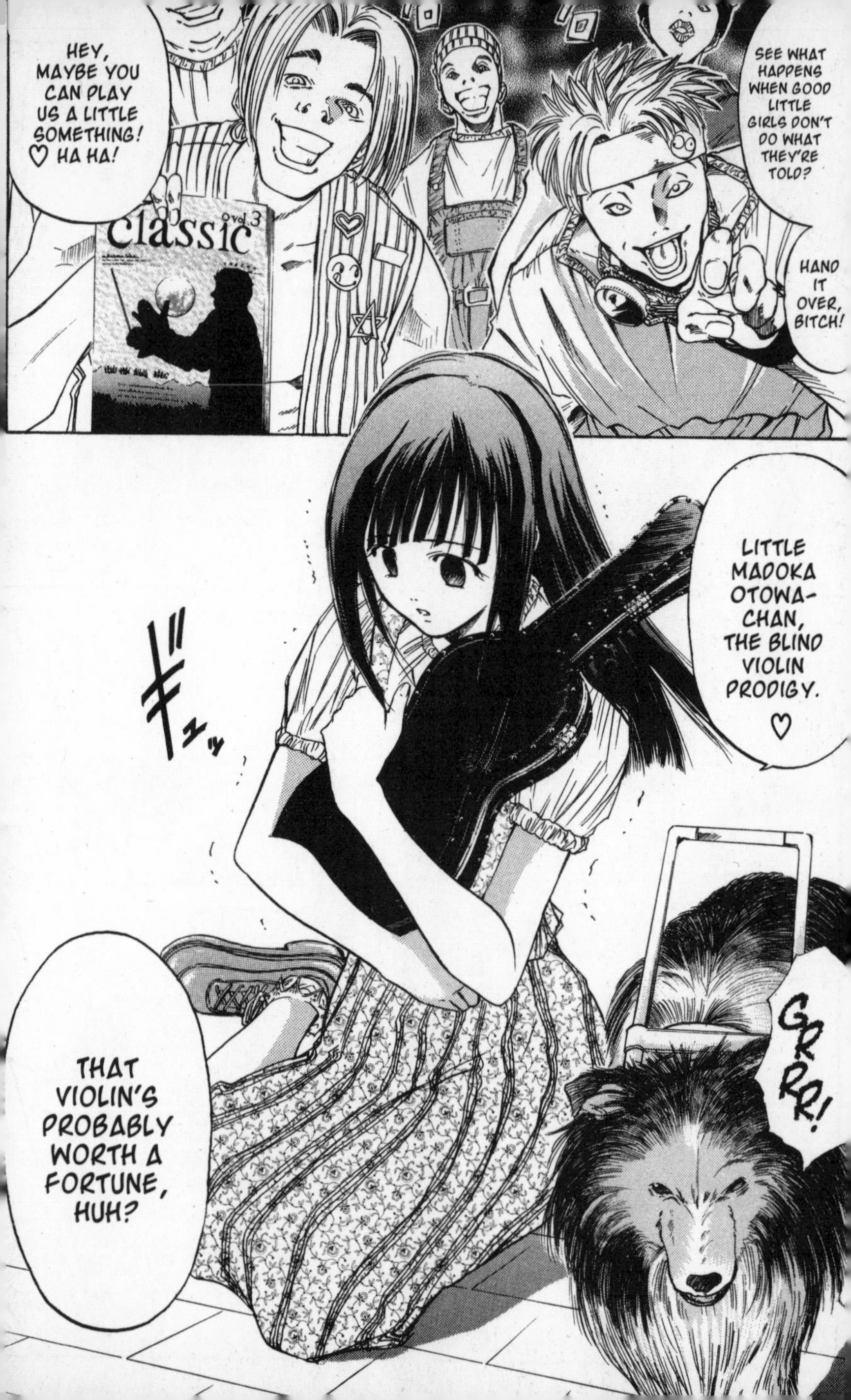
SEE WHAT HAPPENS WHEN GOOD LITTLE GIRLS DON'T DO WHAT THEY'RE TOLD?
HAND IT OVER, BITCH!
HEY, MAYBE YOU CAN PLAY US A LITTLE SOMETHING! ♡ HA HA!
classic vol.3
LITTLE MADOKA OTOWA-CHAN, THE BLIND VIOLIN PRODIGY. ♡
GRRR!
THAT VIOLIN'S PROBABLY WORTH A FORTUNE, HUH?

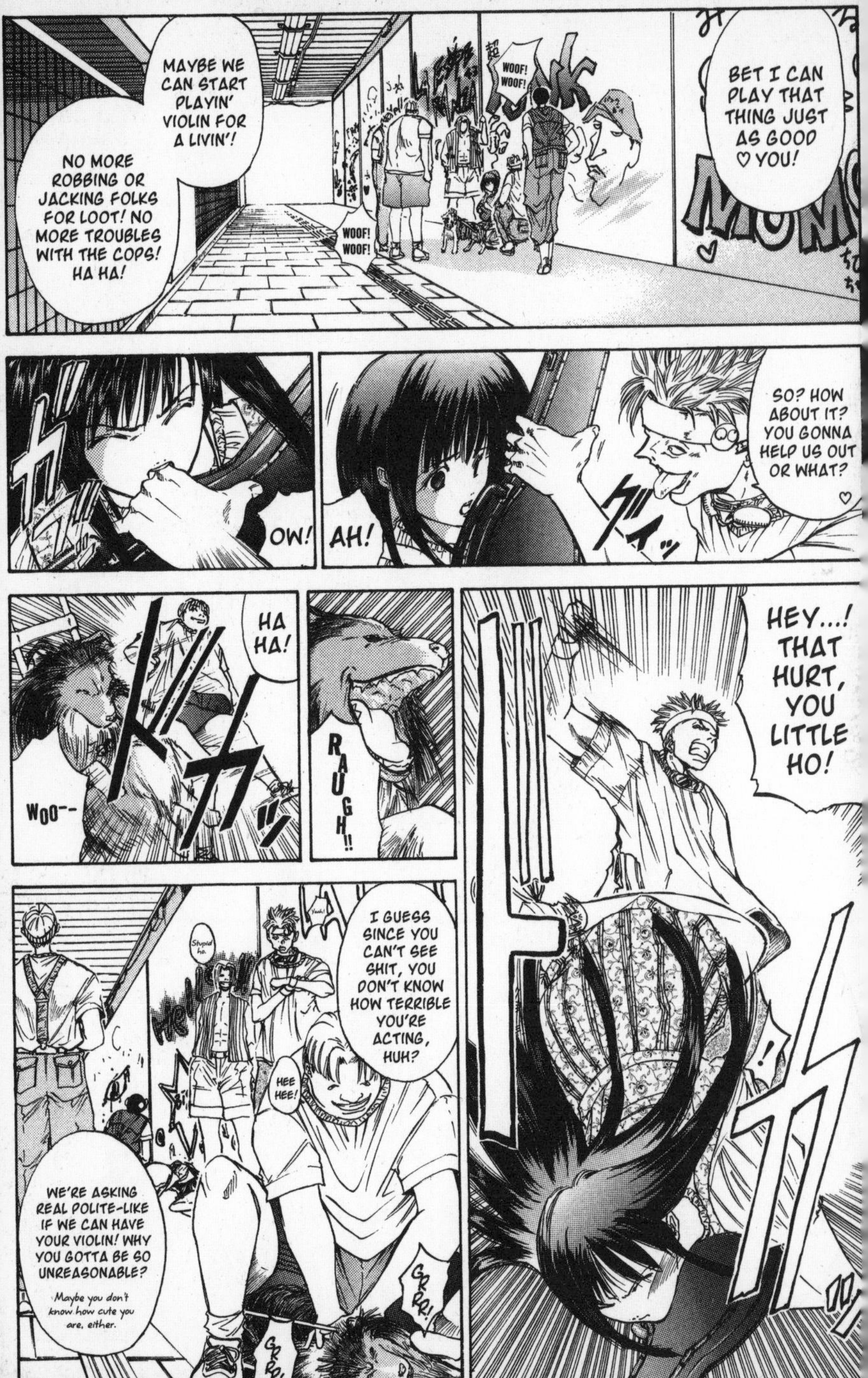
BET I CAN PLAY THAT THING JUST AS GOOD ♡ YOU!
WOOF! WOOF!
MAYBE WE CAN START PLAYIN' VIOLIN FOR A LIVIN'!
NO MORE ROBBING OR JACKING FOLKS FOR LOOT! NO MORE TROUBLES WITH THE COPS! HA HA!
WOOF! WOOF!
SO? HOW ABOUT IT? YOU GONNA HELP US OUT OR WHAT? ♡
AH!
OW!
HEY...! THAT HURT, YOU LITTLE HO!
RAUGH!!
HA HA!
WOO--
I GUESS SINCE YOU CAN'T SEE SHIT, YOU DON'T KNOW HOW TERRIBLE YOU'RE ACTING, HUH?
Yeah!
Stupid ho.
HEE HEE!
WE'RE ASKING REAL POLITE-LIKE IF WE CAN HAVE YOUR VIOLIN! WHY YOU GOTTA BE SO UNREASONABLE?
Maybe you don't know how cute you are, either.
GRRR!
GRRR!

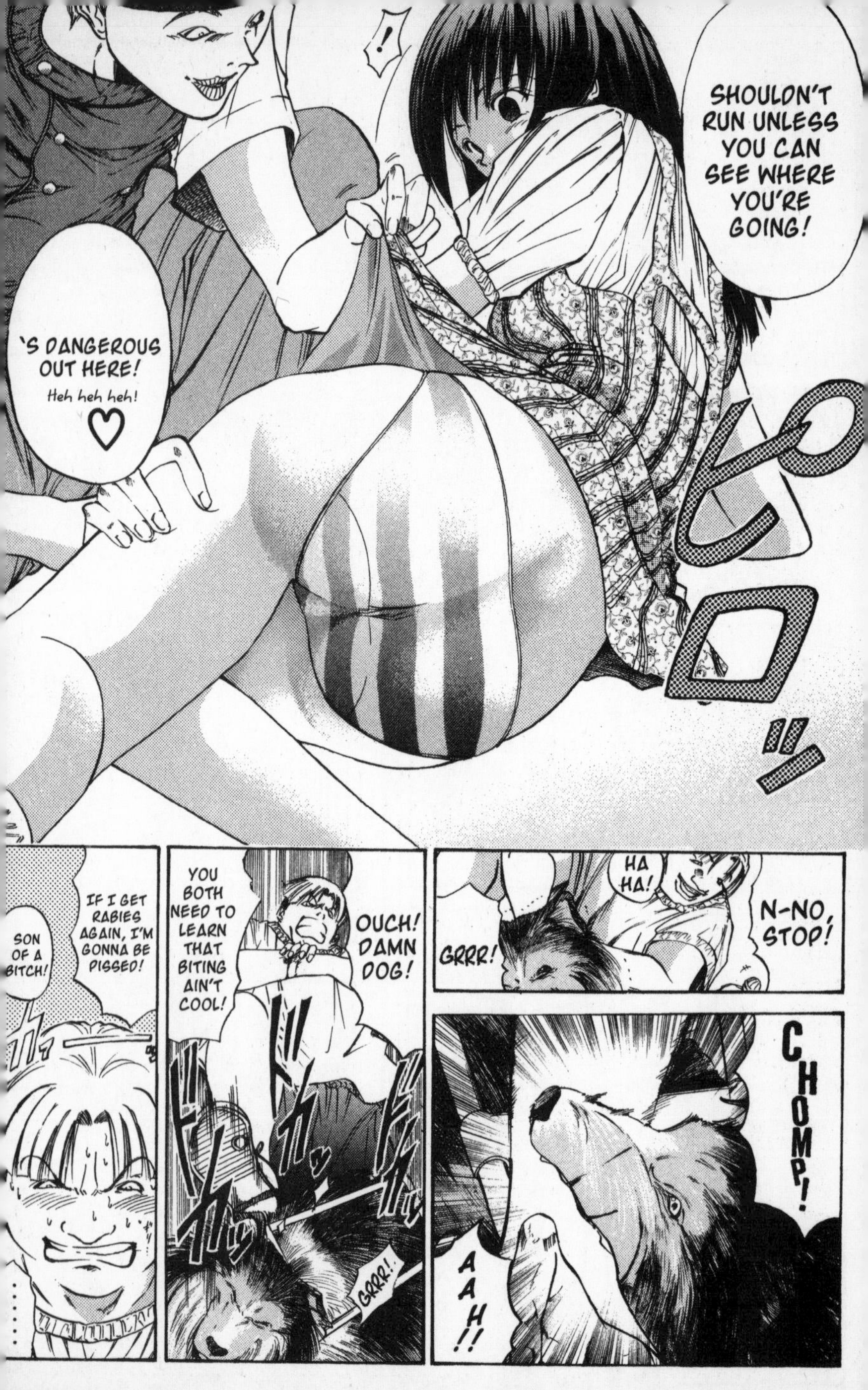
SHOULDN'T RUN UNLESS YOU CAN SEE WHERE YOU'RE GOING!
!
'S DANGEROUS OUT HERE!
Heh heh heh! ♡
HA HA!
N-NO, STOP!
GRRR!
CHOMP!
AAH!!
OUCH! DAMN DOG!
YOU BOTH NEED TO LEARN THAT BITING AIN'T COOL!
GRRR!
IF I GET RABIES AGAIN, I'M GONNA BE PISSED!
SON OF A BITCH!

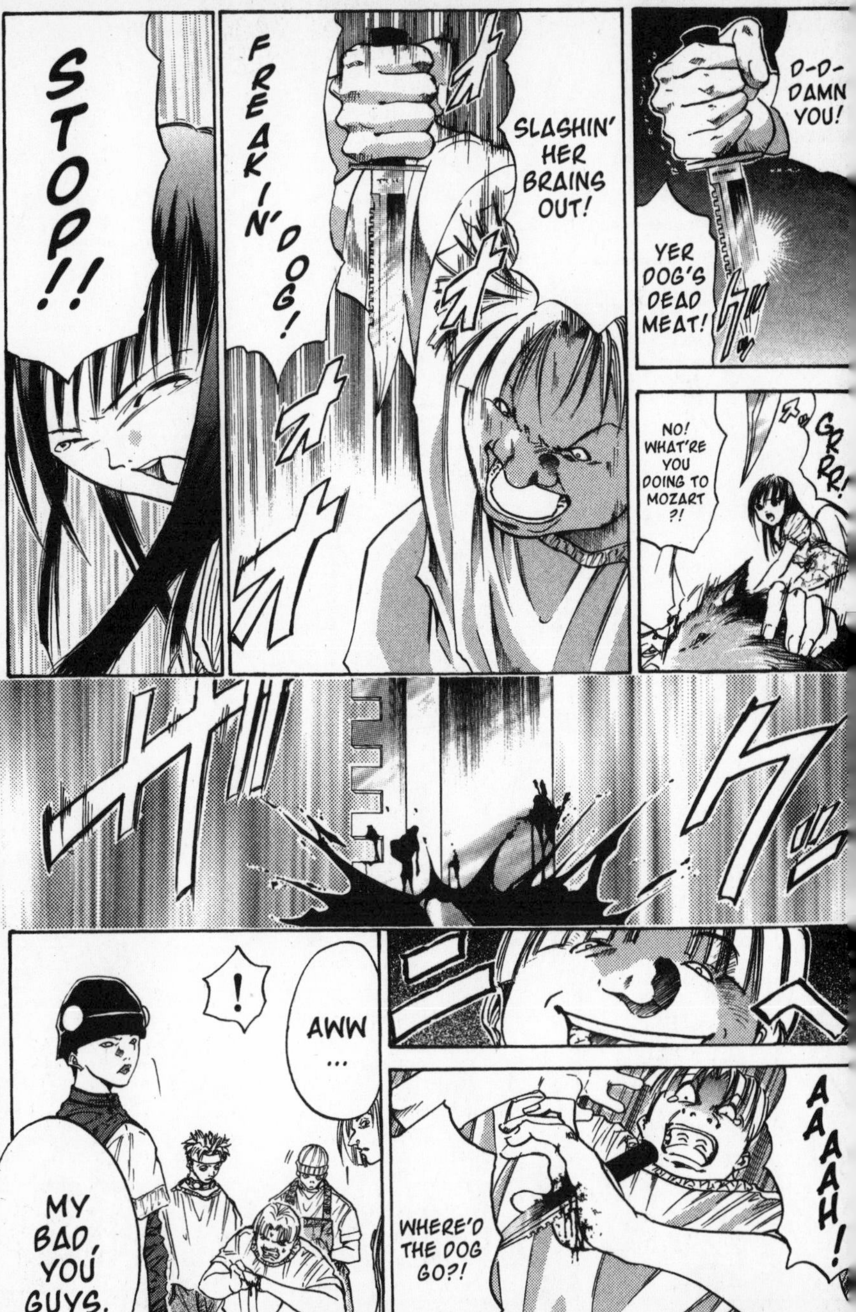
D-D-DAMN YOU!
YER DOG'S DEAD MEAT!
GRRR!
NO! WHAT'RE YOU DOING TO MOZART?!
SLASHIN' HER BRAINS OUT!
FREAKIN' DOG!
STOP!!
AAAAAH!
WHERE'D THE DOG GO?!
AWW ...
!
MY BAD, YOU GUYS.

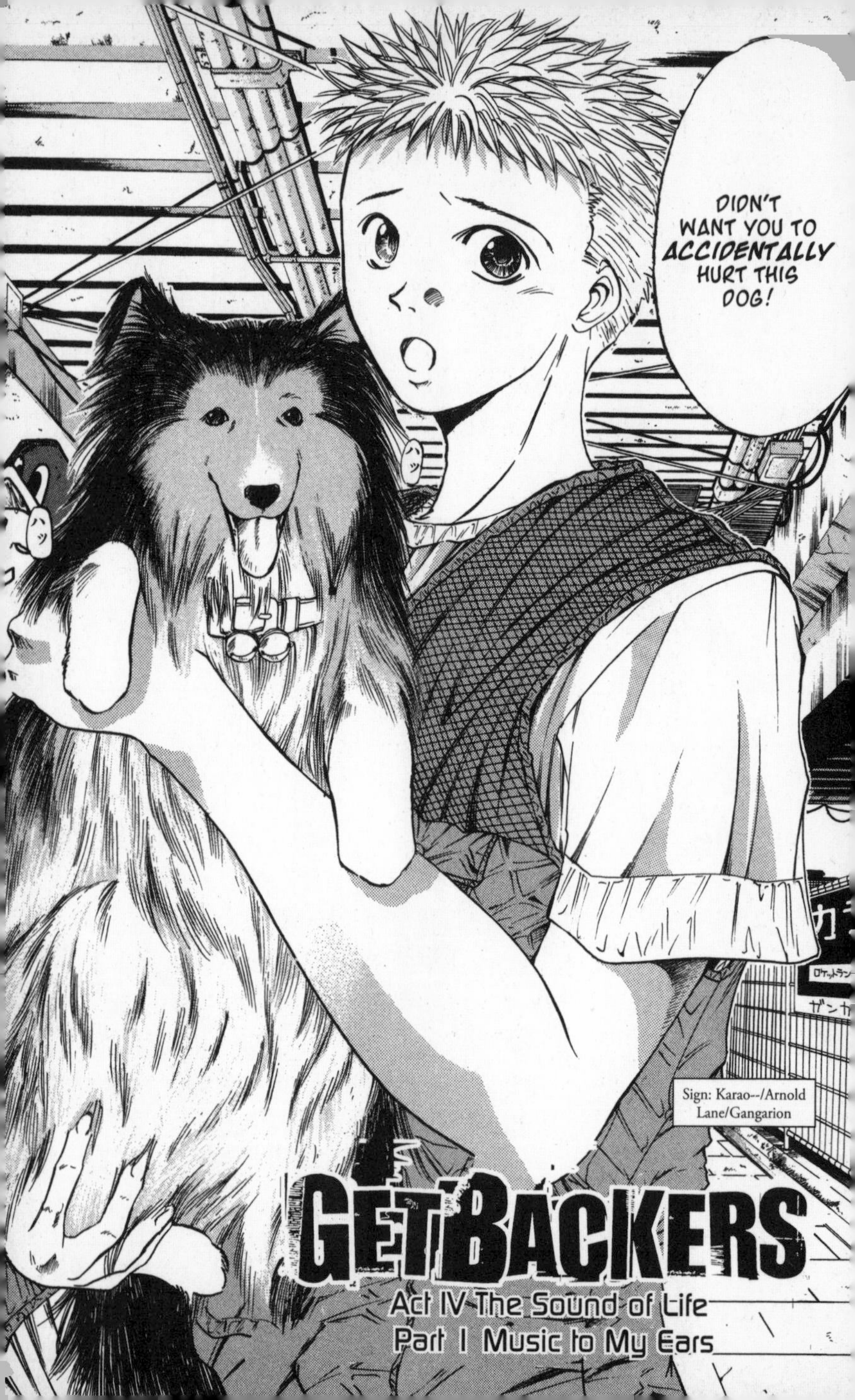
DIDN'T WANT YOU TO ACCIDENTALLY HURT THIS DOG!
ハッ
ハッ
Sign: Karao--/Arnold Lane/Gangarion
GETBACKERS
Act IV The Sound of Life
Part 1 Music to My Ears

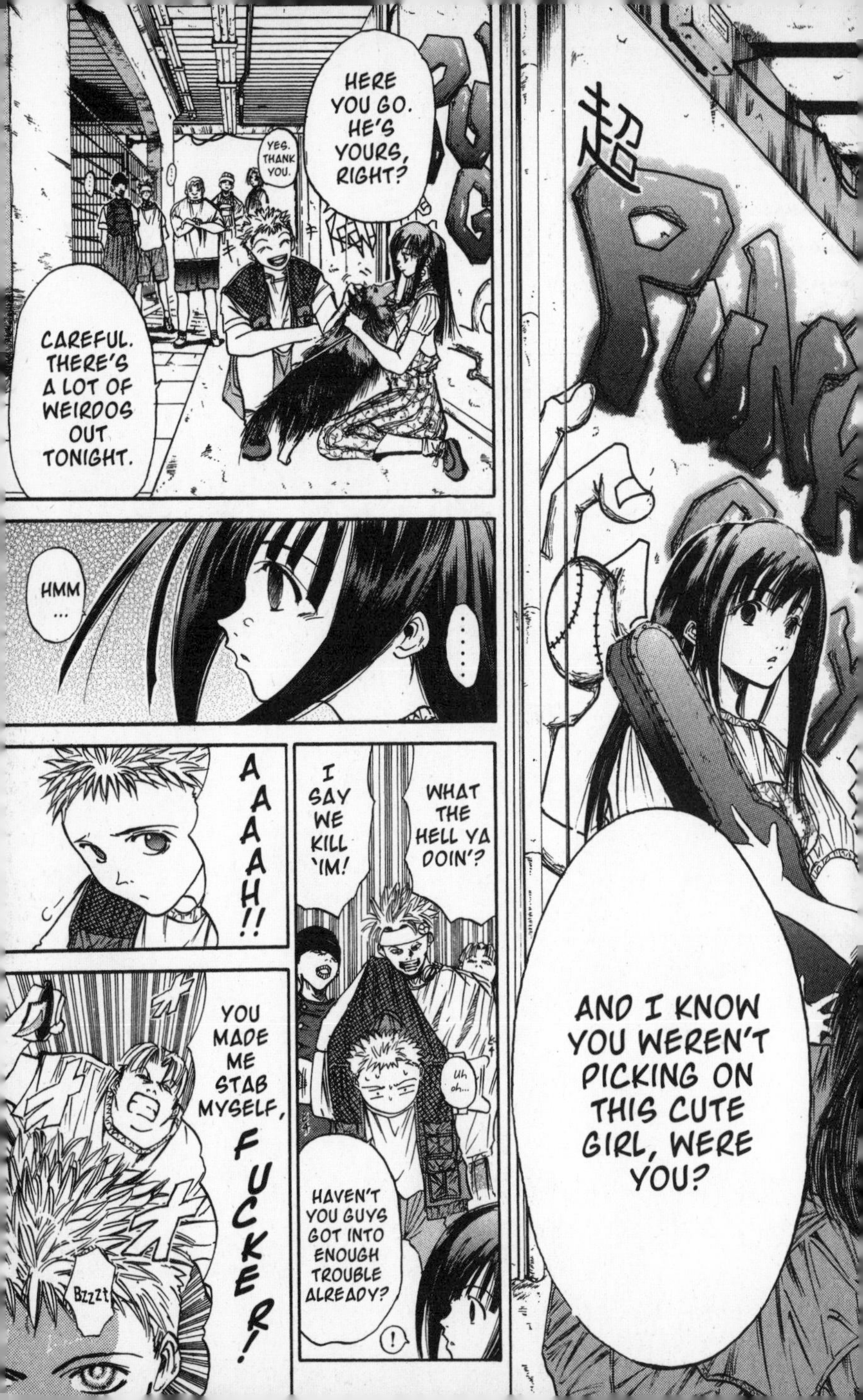
HERE YOU GO. HE'S YOURS, RIGHT?
YES. THANK YOU.
...
...
CAREFUL. THERE'S A LOT OF WEIRDOS OUT TONIGHT.
......
HMM ...
WHAT THE HELL YA DOIN'?
I SAY WE KILL 'IM!
Uh oh...
HAVEN'T YOU GUYS GOT INTO ENOUGH TROUBLE ALREADY?
!
AAAAAH!!
YOU MADE ME STAB MYSELF,
FUCKER!
Bzzzt
超
AND I KNOW YOU WEREN'T PICKING ON THIS CUTE GIRL, WERE YOU?

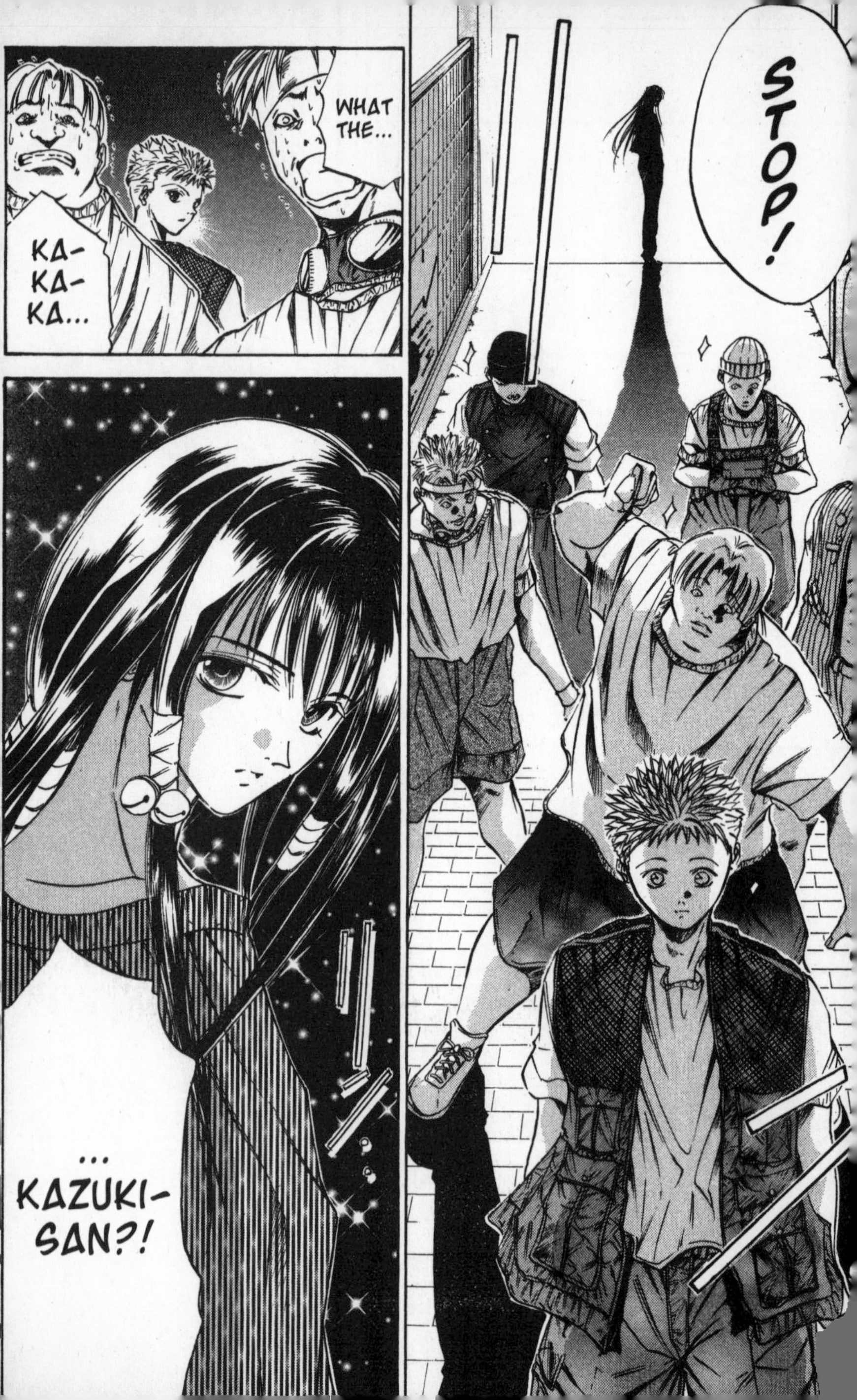
STOP!
WHAT THE...
KA-KA-KA...
...KAZUKI-SAN?!

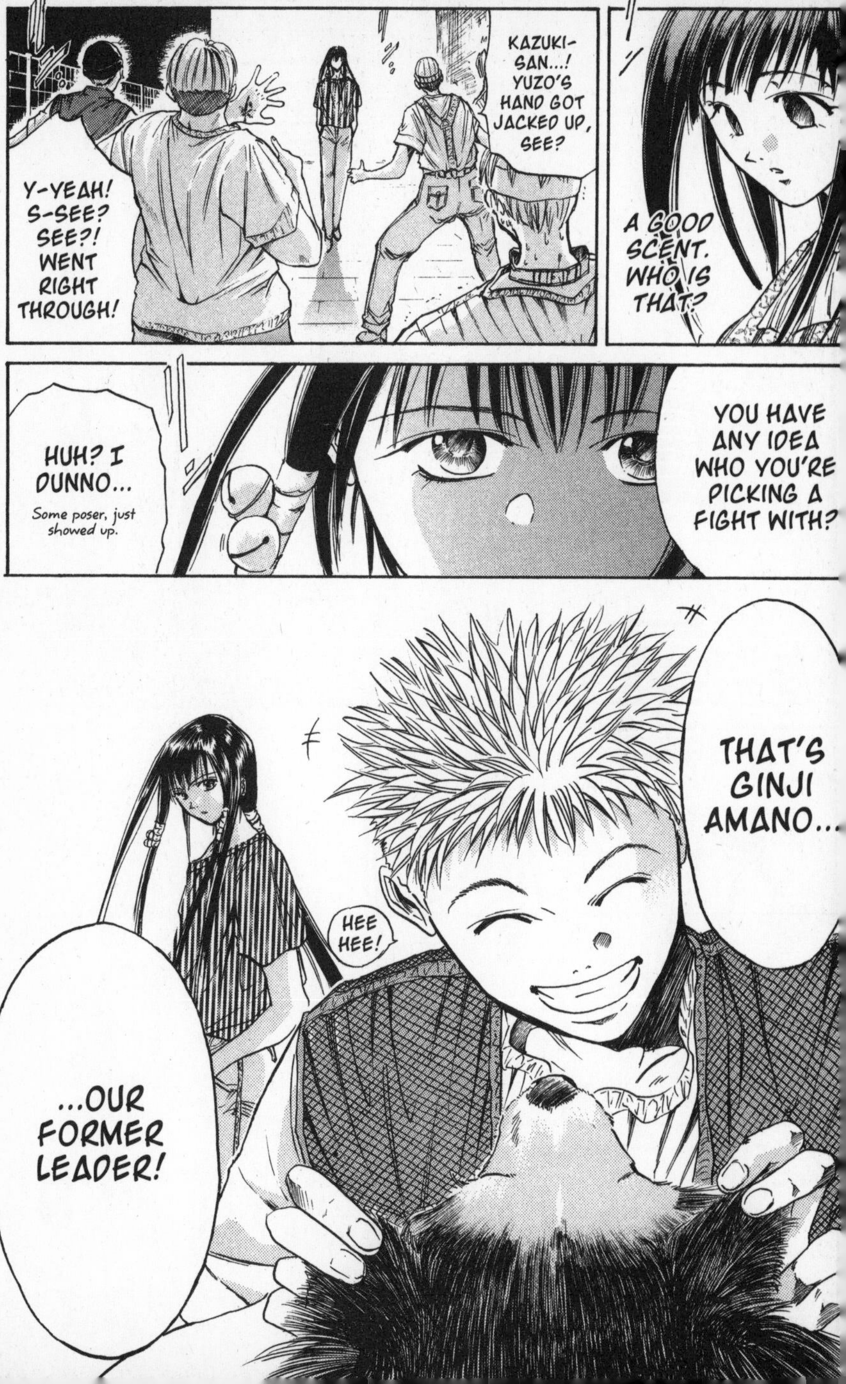
A GOOD SCENT. WHO IS THAT?
KAZUKI-SAN...! YUZO'S HAND GOT JACKED UP, SEE?
Y-YEAH! S-SEE? SEE?! WENT RIGHT THROUGH!
YOU HAVE ANY IDEA WHO YOU'RE PICKING A FIGHT WITH?
HUH? I DUNNO...
Some poser, just showed up.
THAT'S GINJI AMANO...
HEE HEE!
...OUR FORMER LEADER!

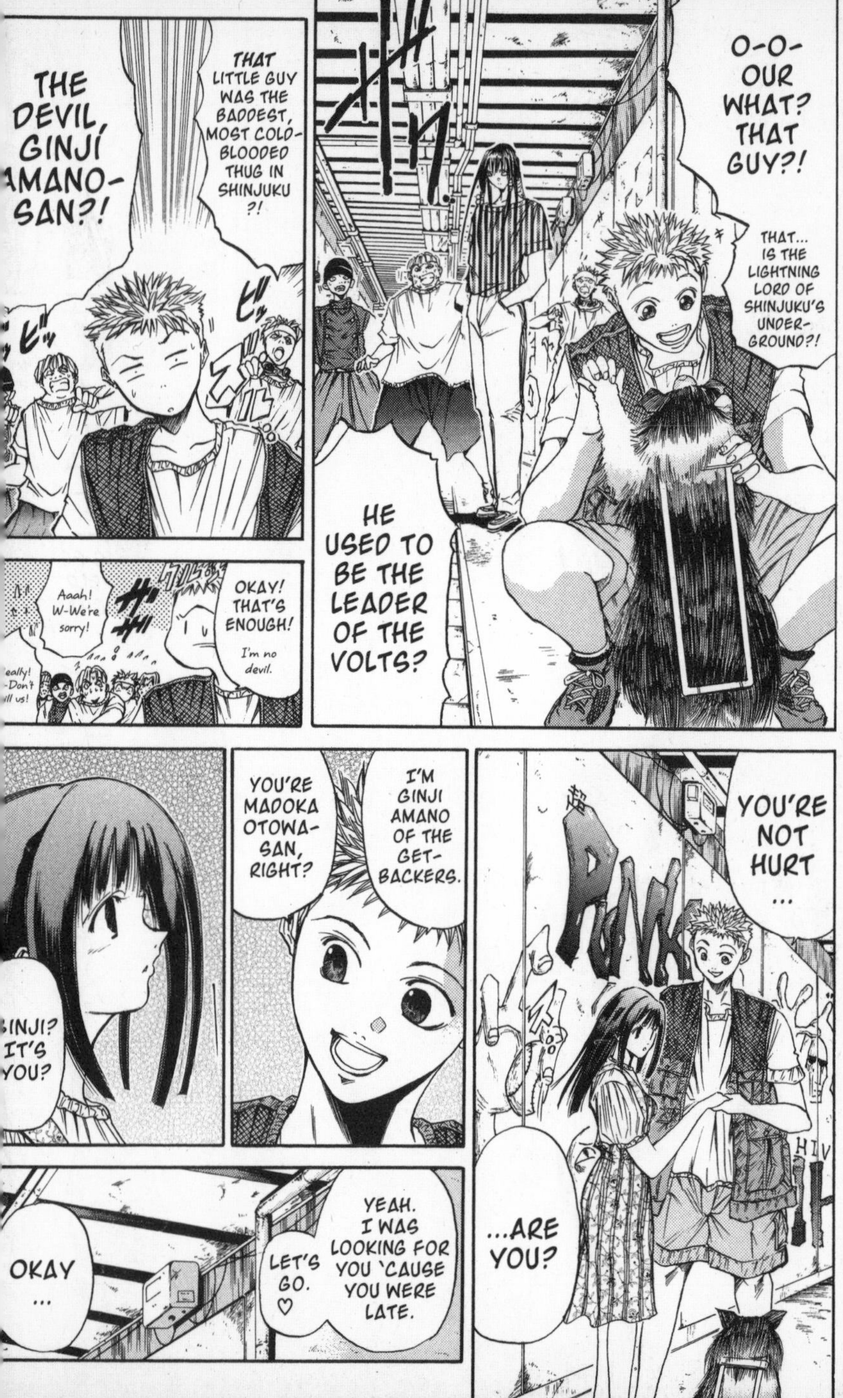
O-O-OUR WHAT? THAT GUY?!
THAT... IS THE LIGHTNING LORD OF SHINJUKU'S UNDERGROUND?!
HE USED TO BE THE LEADER OF THE VOLTS?
THAT LITTLE GUY WAS THE BADDEST, MOST COLD-BLOODED THUG IN SHINJUKU?!
THE DEVIL, GINJI AMANO-SAN?!
OKAY! THAT'S ENOUGH!
I'm no devil.
Aaah! W-We're sorry!
eally! -Don't ill us!
YOU'RE NOT HURT ...
...ARE YOU?
I'M GINJI AMANO OF THE GET-BACKERS.
YOU'RE MADOKA OTOWA-SAN, RIGHT?
INJI? IT'S YOU?
YEAH. I WAS LOOKING FOR YOU 'CAUSE YOU WERE LATE.
LET'S GO. ♡
OKAY ...

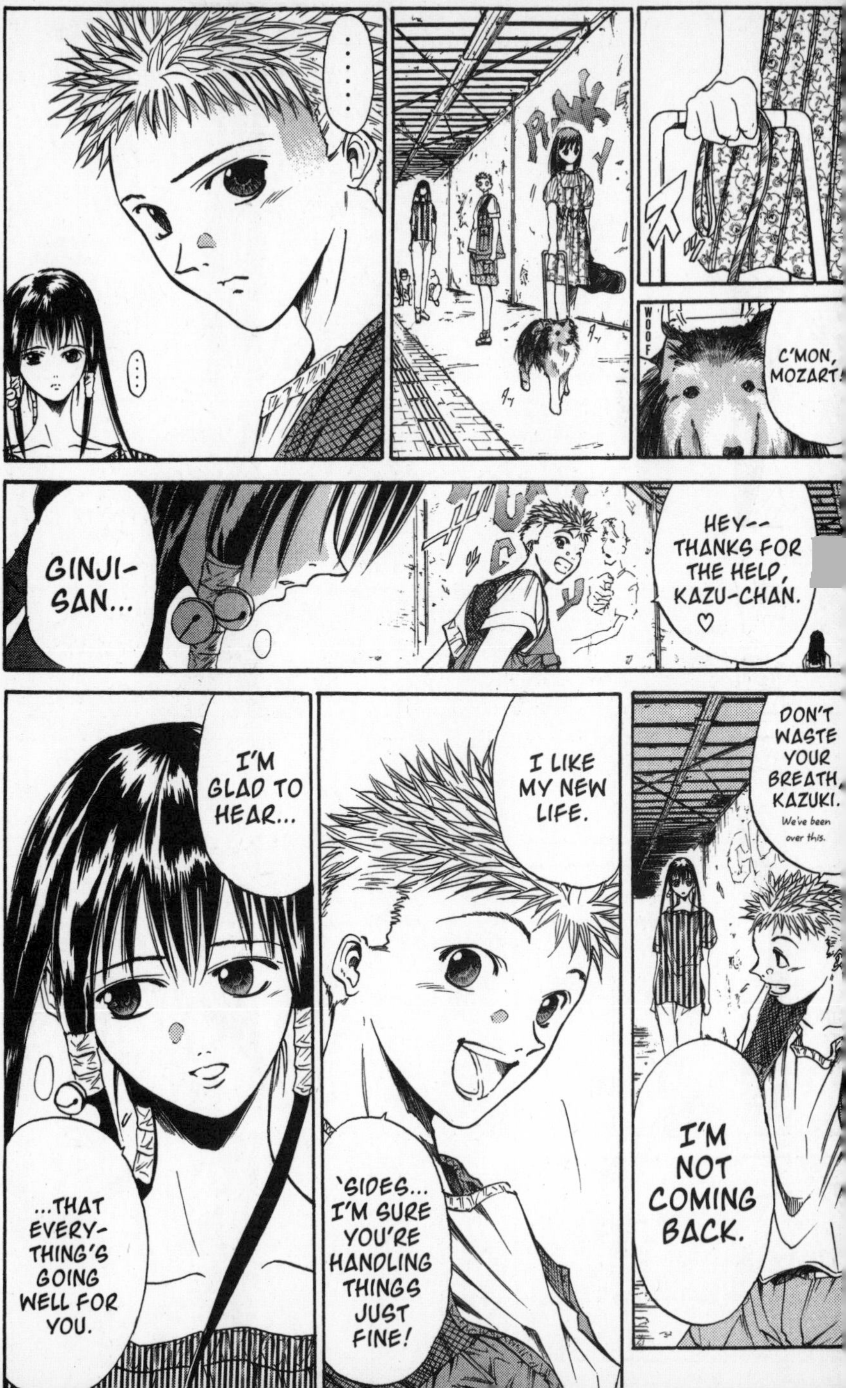
WOOF
C'MON, MOZART!
......
....
HEY-- THANKS FOR THE HELP, KAZU-CHAN. ♡
GINJI-SAN...
DON'T WASTE YOUR BREATH, KAZUKI.
We've been over this.
I'M NOT COMING BACK.
I LIKE MY NEW LIFE.
'SIDES... I'M SURE YOU'RE HANDLING THINGS JUST FINE!
I'M GLAD TO HEAR...
...THAT EVERYTHING'S GOING WELL FOR YOU.

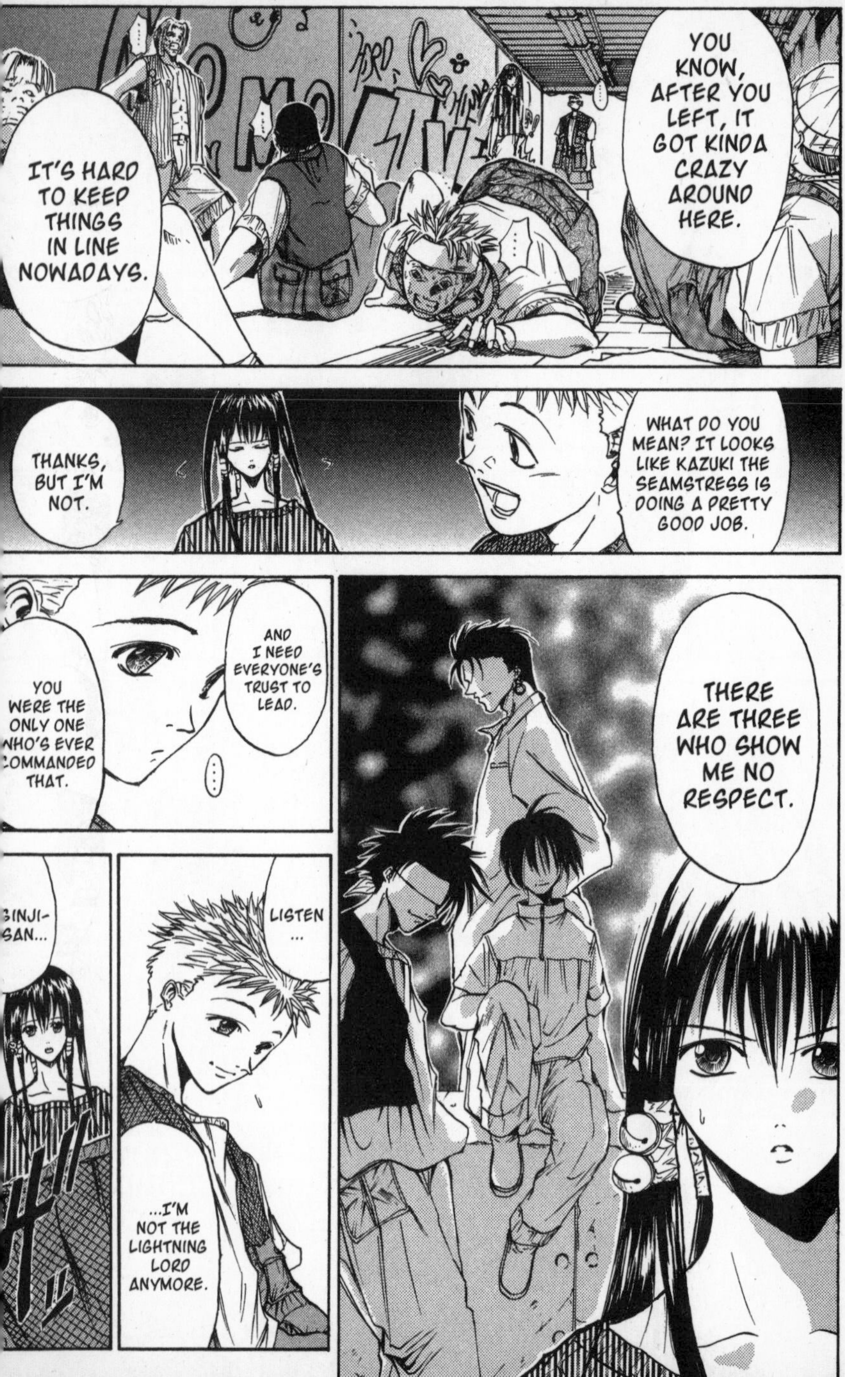
YOU KNOW, AFTER YOU LEFT, IT GOT KINDA CRAZY AROUND HERE.
IT'S HARD TO KEEP THINGS IN LINE NOWADAYS.
WHAT DO YOU MEAN? IT LOOKS LIKE KAZUKI THE SEAMSTRESS IS DOING A PRETTY GOOD JOB.
THANKS, BUT I'M NOT.
THERE ARE THREE WHO SHOW ME NO RESPECT.
AND I NEED EVERYONE'S TRUST TO LEAD.
...
YOU WERE THE ONLY ONE WHO'S EVER COMMANDED THAT.
LISTEN ...
...I'M NOT THE LIGHTNING LORD ANYMORE.
GINJI-SAN...

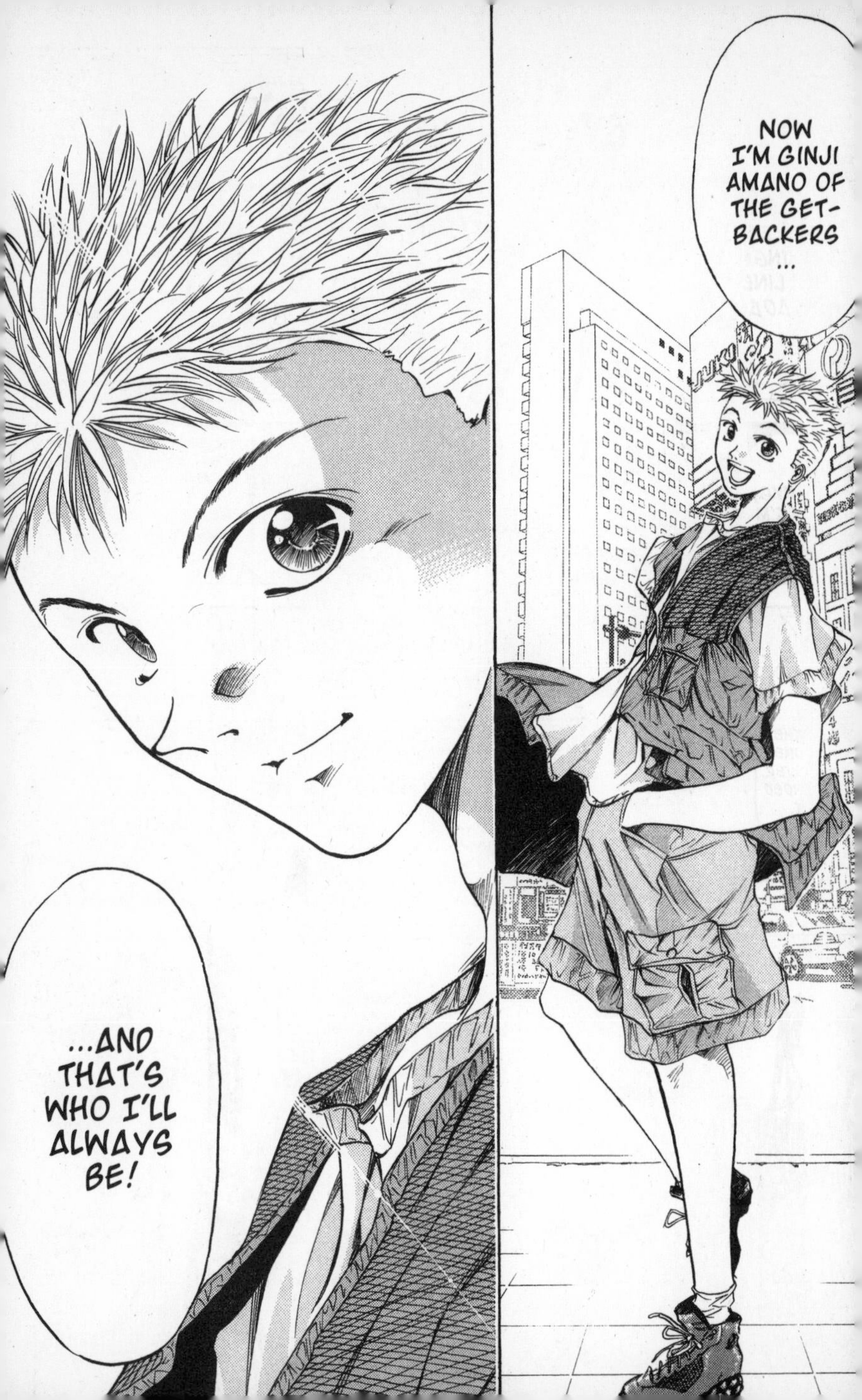
NOW I'M GINJI AMANO OF THE GET-BACKERS ...
...AND THAT'S WHO I'LL ALWAYS BE!

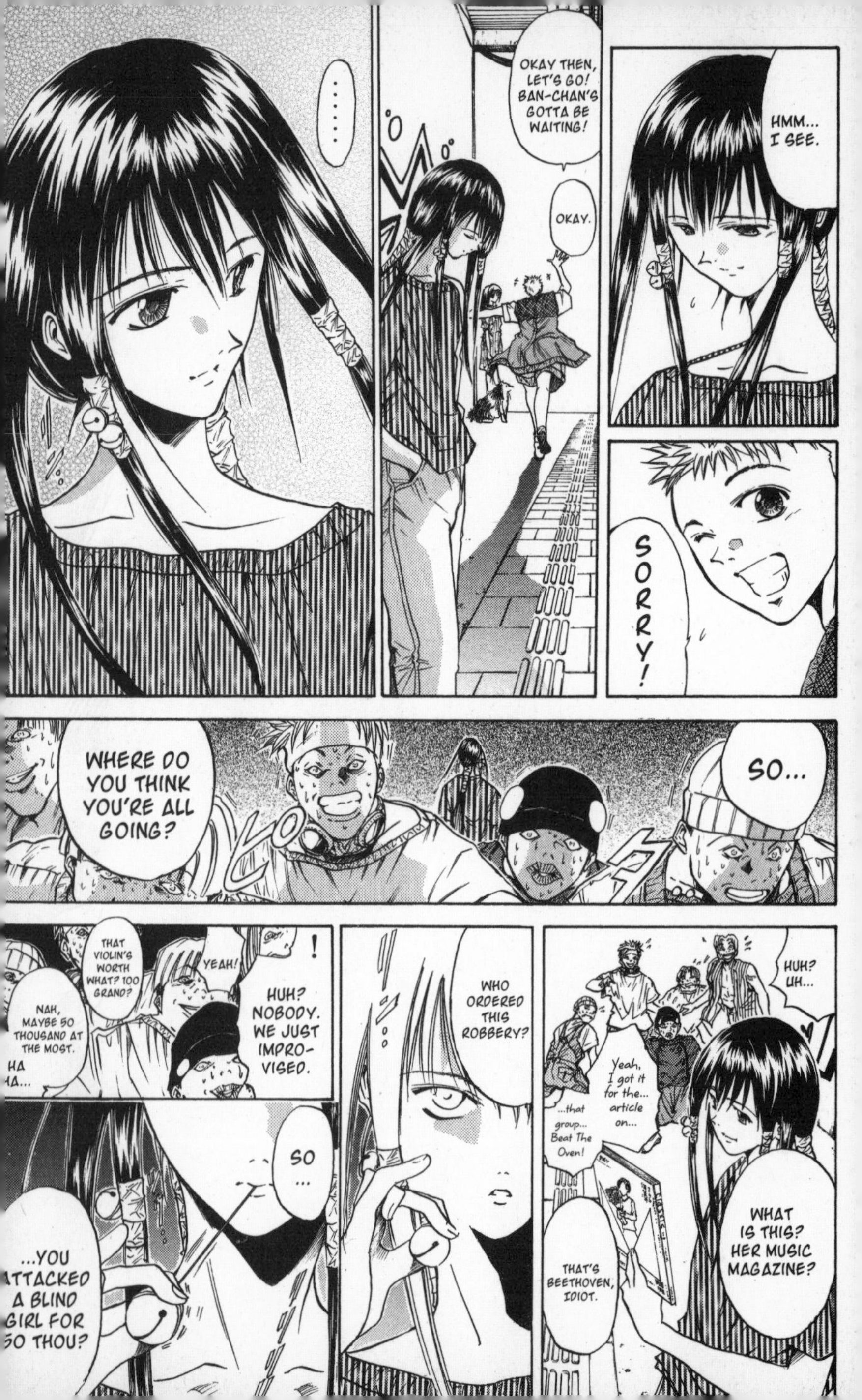
HMM... I SEE.
SORRY!
OKAY THEN, LET'S GO! BAN-CHAN'S GOTTA BE WAITING!
OKAY.
......
SO...
WHERE DO YOU THINK YOU'RE ALL GOING?
HUH? UH...
Yeah, I got it for the... article on...
...that group... Beat The Oven!
WHAT IS THIS? HER MUSIC MAGAZINE?
THAT'S BEETHOVEN, IDIOT.
WHO ORDERED THIS ROBBERY?
!
HUH? NOBODY. WE JUST IMPROVISED.
YEAH!
THAT VIOLIN'S WORTH WHAT? 100 GRAND?
NAH, MAYBE 50 THOUSAND AT THE MOST.
HA HA...
SO ...
...YOU ATTACKED A BLIND GIRL FOR 50 THOU?

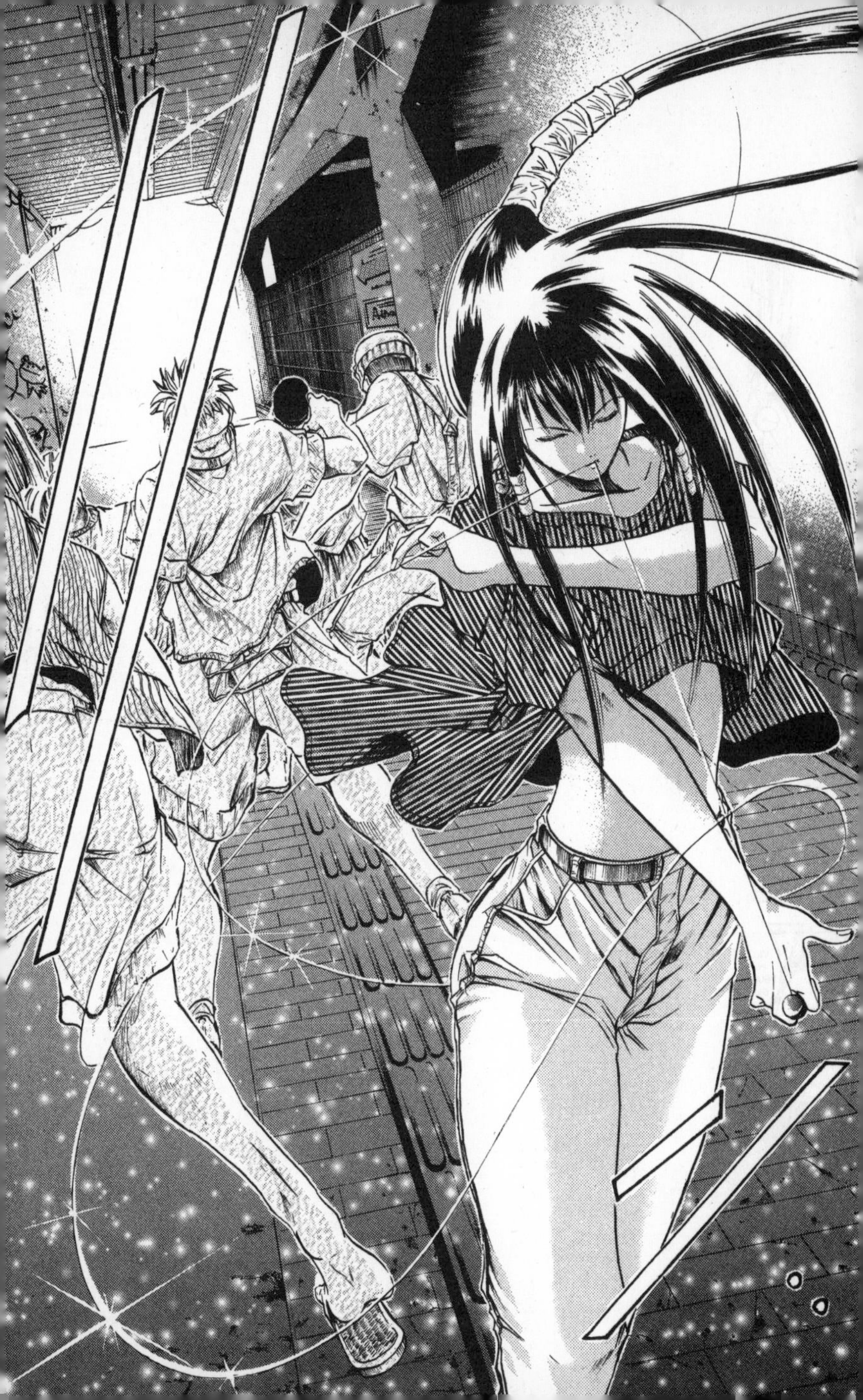

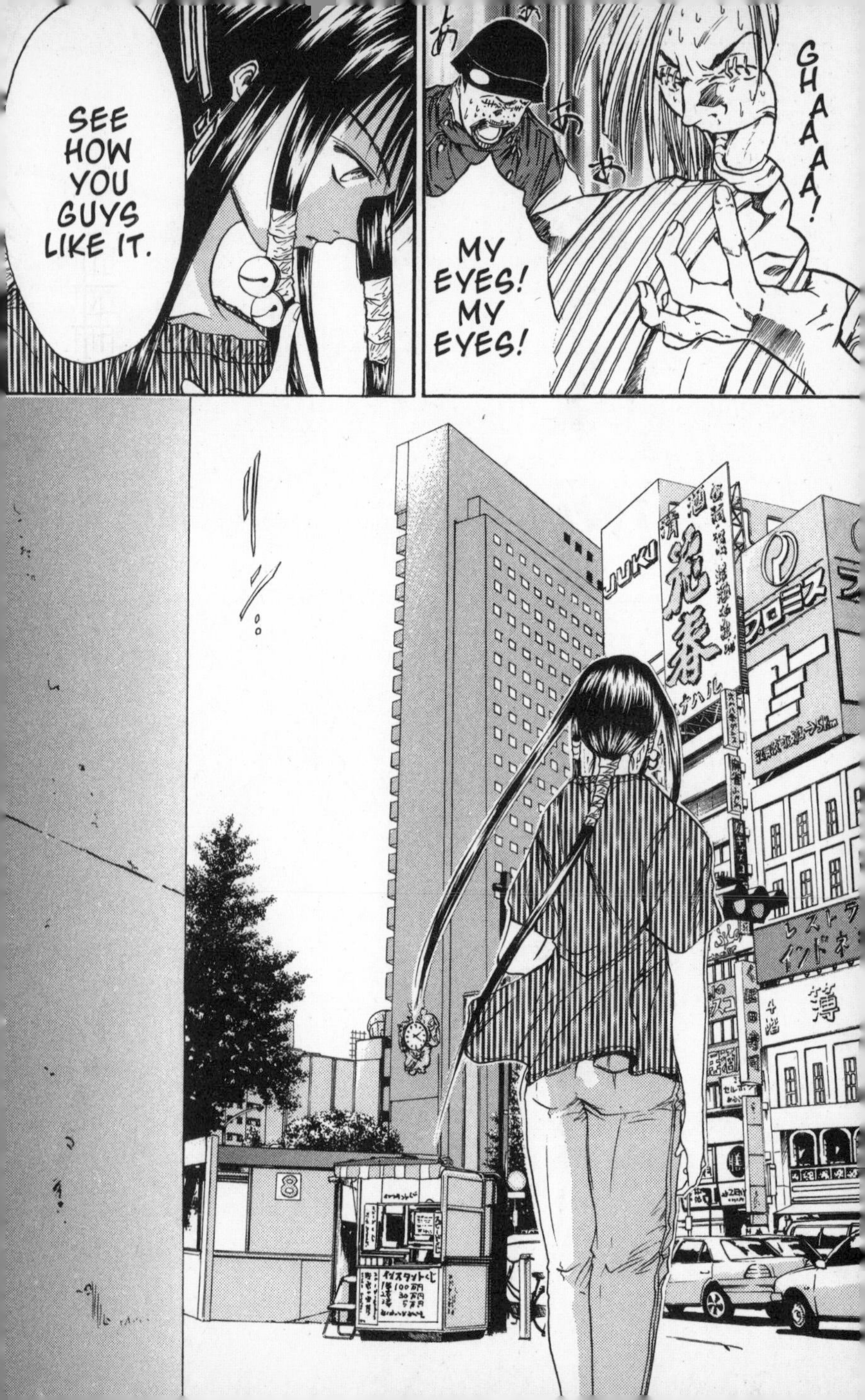
GHAAAA!
MY EYES! MY EYES!
SEE HOW YOU GUYS LIKE IT.
JUKI
花春
プロミス
8

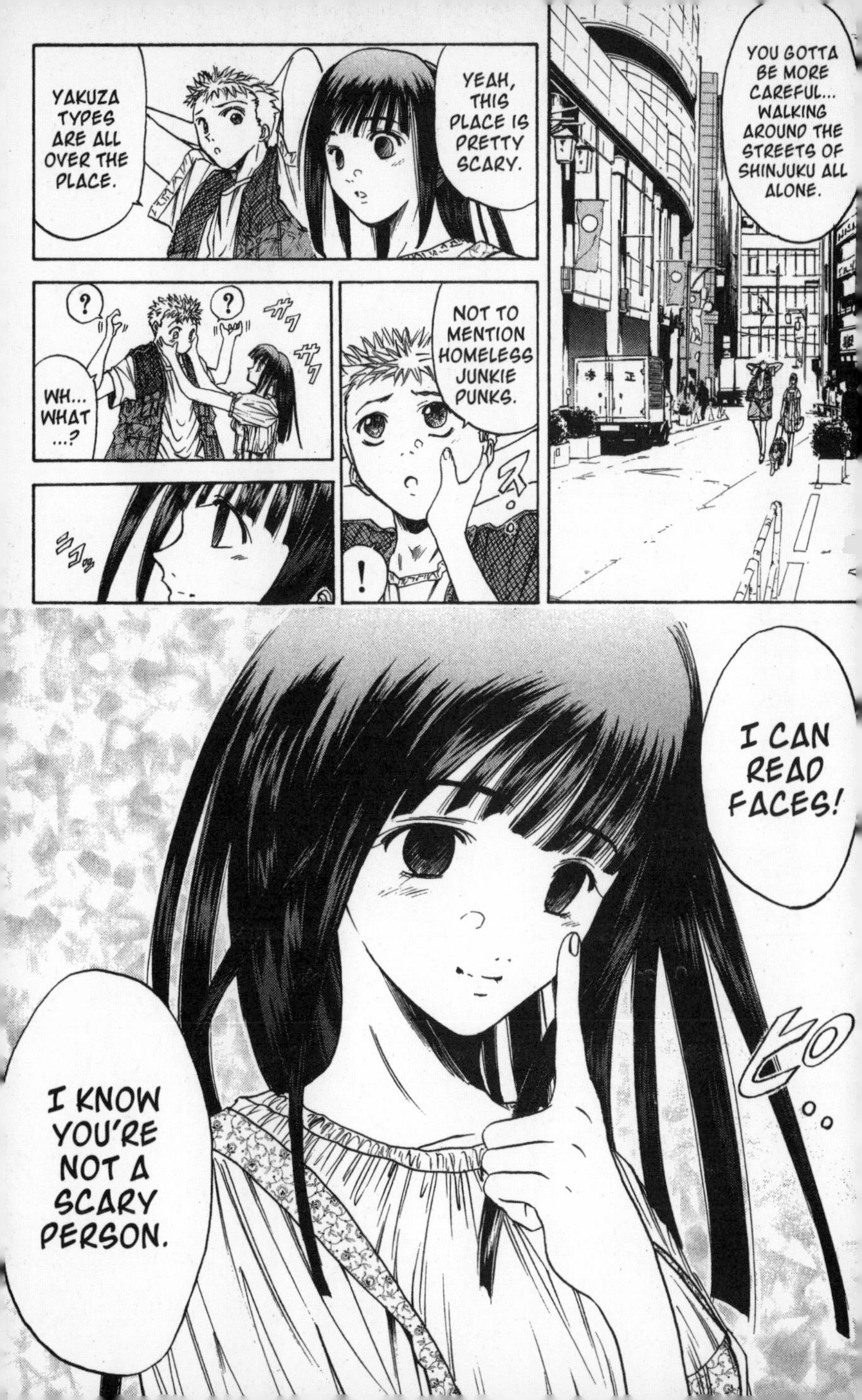
YOU GOTTA BE MORE CAREFUL... WALKING AROUND THE STREETS OF SHINJUKU ALL ALONE.
YAKUZA TYPES ARE ALL OVER THE PLACE.
YEAH, THIS PLACE IS PRETTY SCARY.
NOT TO MENTION HOMELESS JUNKIE PUNKS.
WH... WHAT ...?
I CAN READ FACES!
I KNOW YOU'RE NOT A SCARY PERSON.

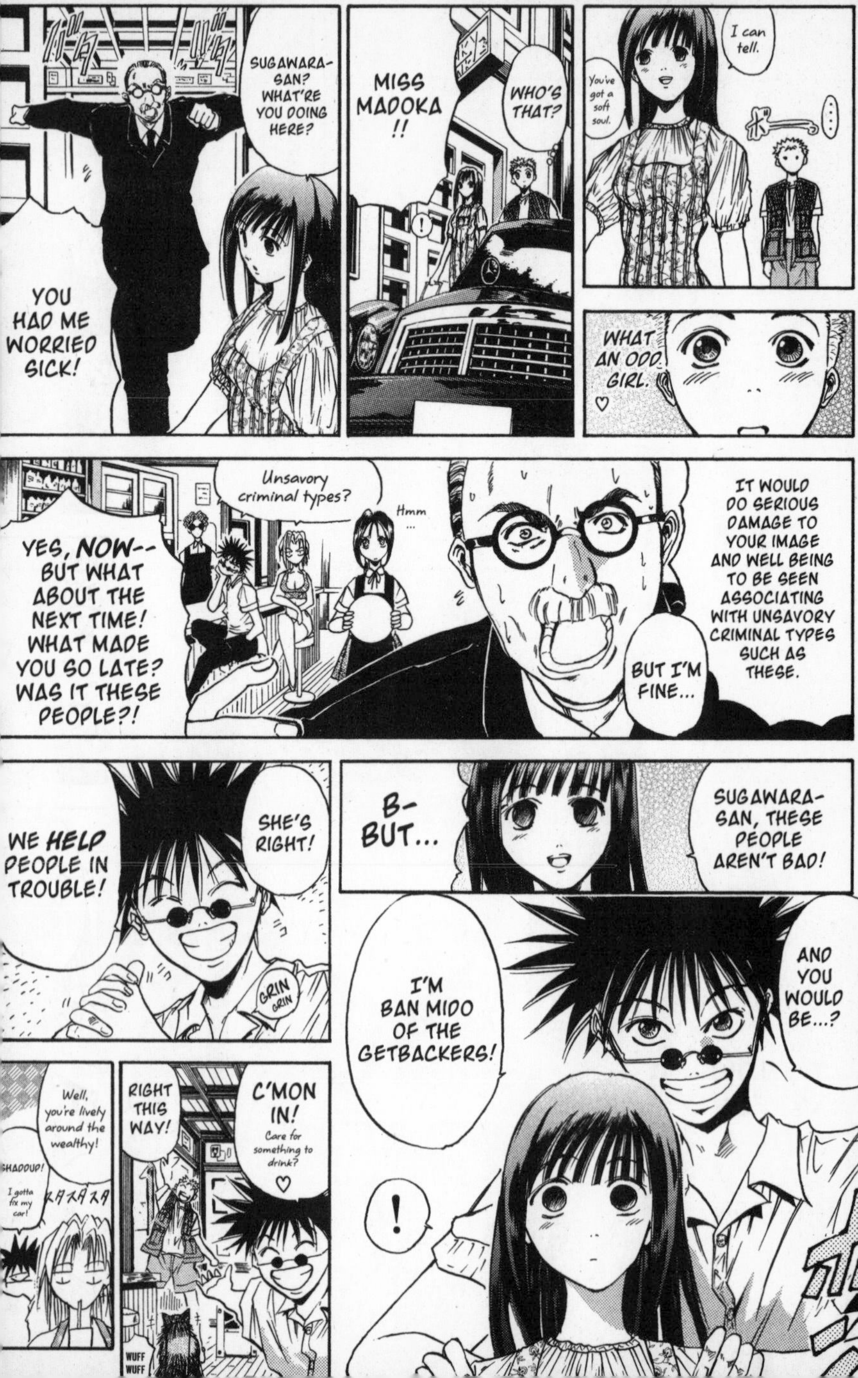
I can tell.
You've got a soft soul.
...
WHAT AN ODD GIRL. ♡
WHO'S THAT?
MISS MADOKA !!
!
SUGAWARA-SAN? WHAT'RE YOU DOING HERE?
YOU HAD ME WORRIED SICK!
IT WOULD DO SERIOUS DAMAGE TO YOUR IMAGE AND WELL BEING TO BE SEEN ASSOCIATING WITH UNSAVORY CRIMINAL TYPES SUCH AS THESE.
BUT I'M FINE...
Hmm ...
Unsavory criminal types?
YES, NOW-- BUT WHAT ABOUT THE NEXT TIME! WHAT MADE YOU SO LATE? WAS IT THESE PEOPLE?!
SUGAWARA-SAN, THESE PEOPLE AREN'T BAD!
B-BUT...
SHE'S RIGHT!
WE HELP PEOPLE IN TROUBLE!
GRIN GRIN
AND YOU WOULD BE...?
I'M BAN MIDO OF THE GETBACKERS!
!
C'MON IN!
Care for something to drink? ♡
RIGHT THIS WAY!
Well, you're lively around the wealthy!
HADDUP!
I gotta fix my car!
スタスタスタ
WUFF WUFF

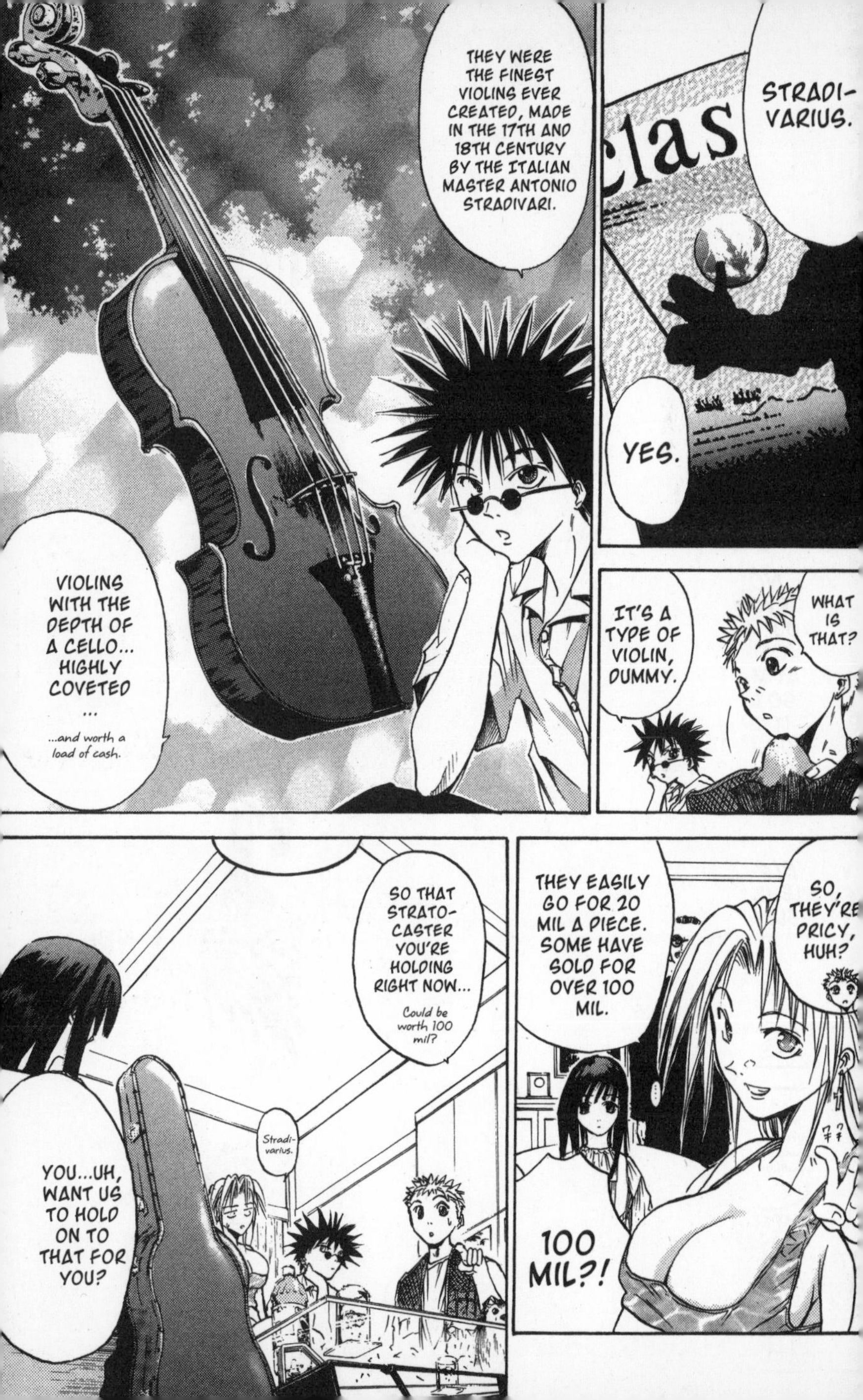

STRADIVARIUS.
YES.
WHAT IS THAT?
IT'S A TYPE OF VIOLIN, DUMMY.
THEY WERE THE FINEST VIOLINS EVER CREATED, MADE IN THE 17TH AND 18TH CENTURY BY THE ITALIAN MASTER ANTONIO STRADIVARI.
VIOLINS WITH THE DEPTH OF A CELLO... HIGHLY COVETED ...
...and worth a load of cash.
SO, THEY'RE PRICY, HUH?
THEY EASILY GO FOR 20 MIL A PIECE. SOME HAVE SOLD FOR OVER 100 MIL.
...
100 MIL?!
SO THAT STRATOCASTER YOU'RE HOLDING RIGHT NOW...
Could be worth 100 mil?
Stradivarius.
YOU...UH, WANT US TO HOLD ON TO THAT FOR YOU?

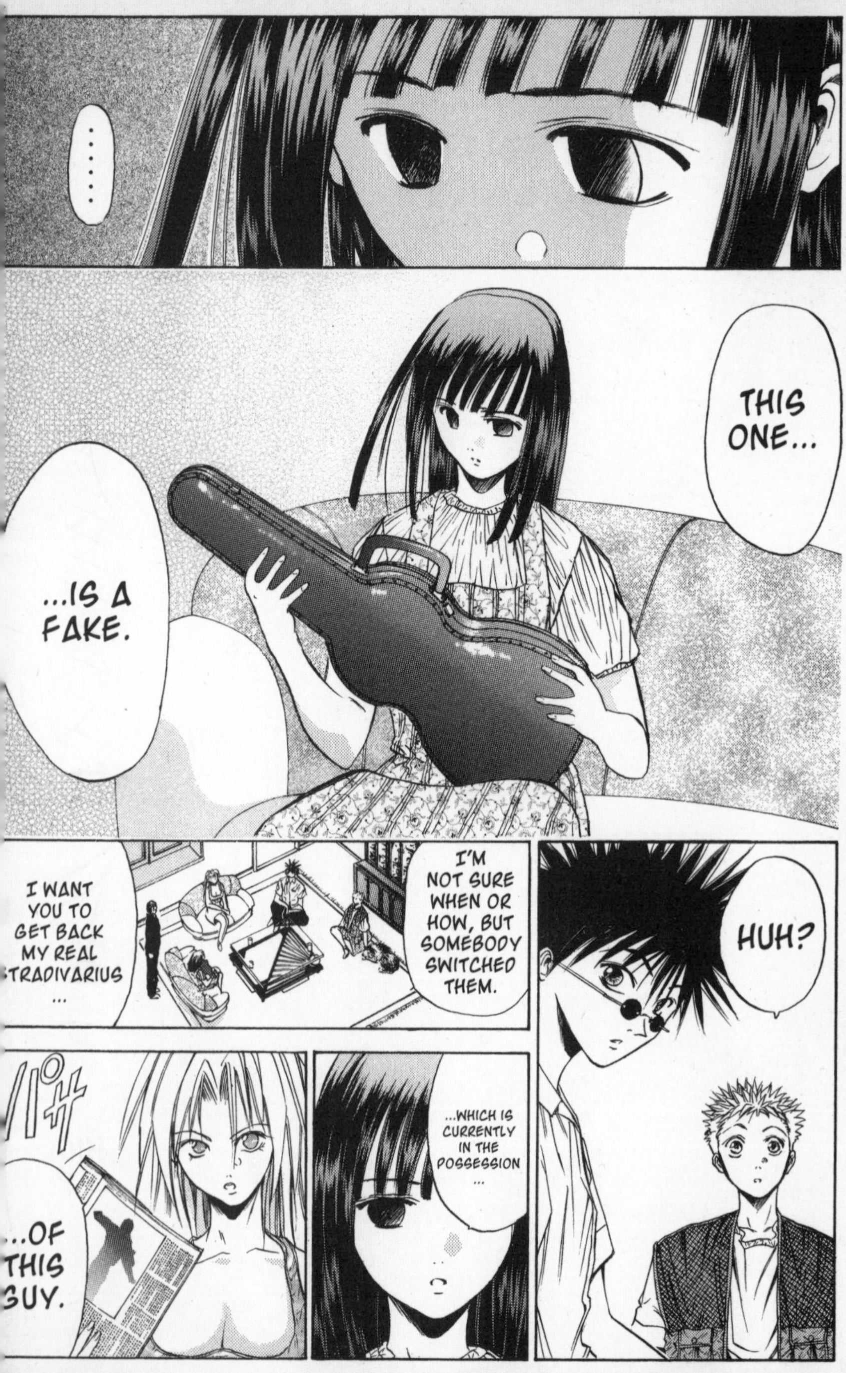
......
THIS ONE...
...IS A FAKE.
HUH?
I'M NOT SURE WHEN OR HOW, BUT SOMEBODY SWITCHED THEM.
I WANT YOU TO GET BACK MY REAL TRADIVARIUS ...
...WHICH IS CURRENTLY IN THE POSSESSION ...
パサ
...OF THIS GUY.

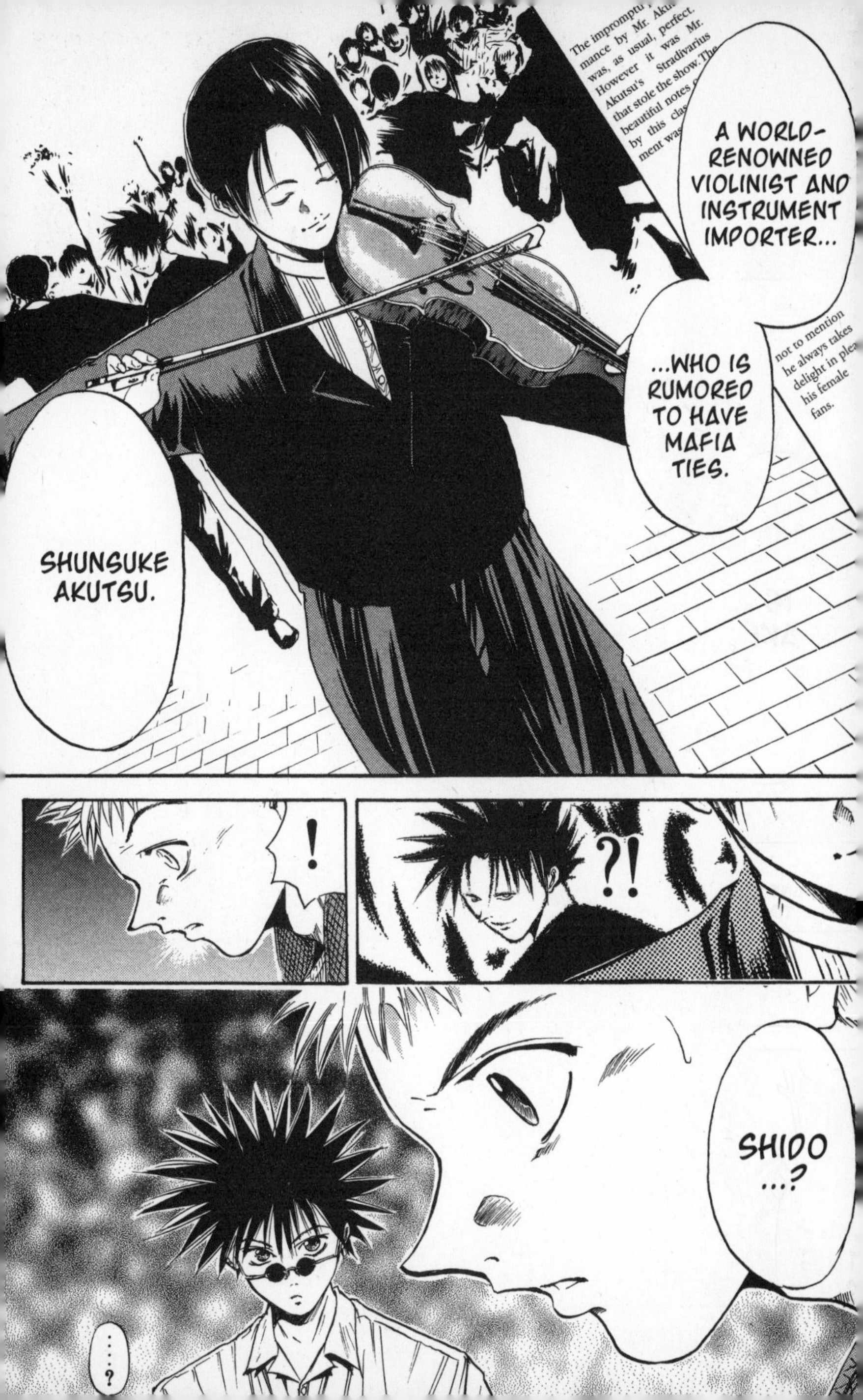
The impromptu
mance by Mr. Aku
was, as usual, perfect.
However it was Mr.
Akutsu's Stradivarius
that stole the show. The
beautiful notes
by this clas
ment was
A WORLD-RENOWNED VIOLINIST AND INSTRUMENT IMPORTER...
...WHO IS RUMORED TO HAVE MAFIA TIES.
not to mention he always takes delight in plea his female fans.
SHUNSUKE AKUTSU.
?!
!
SHIDO ...?
...?

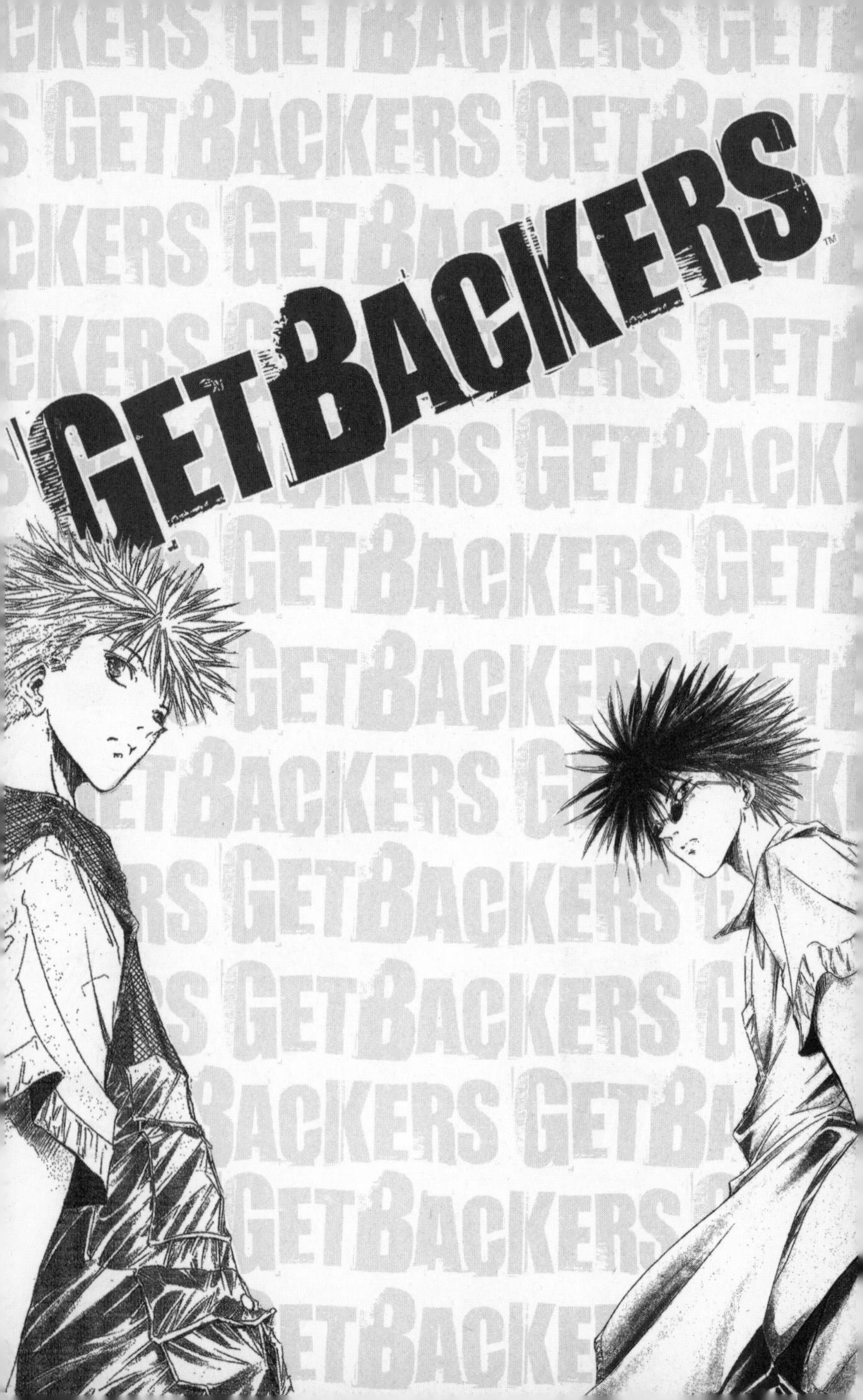
GETBACKERS™

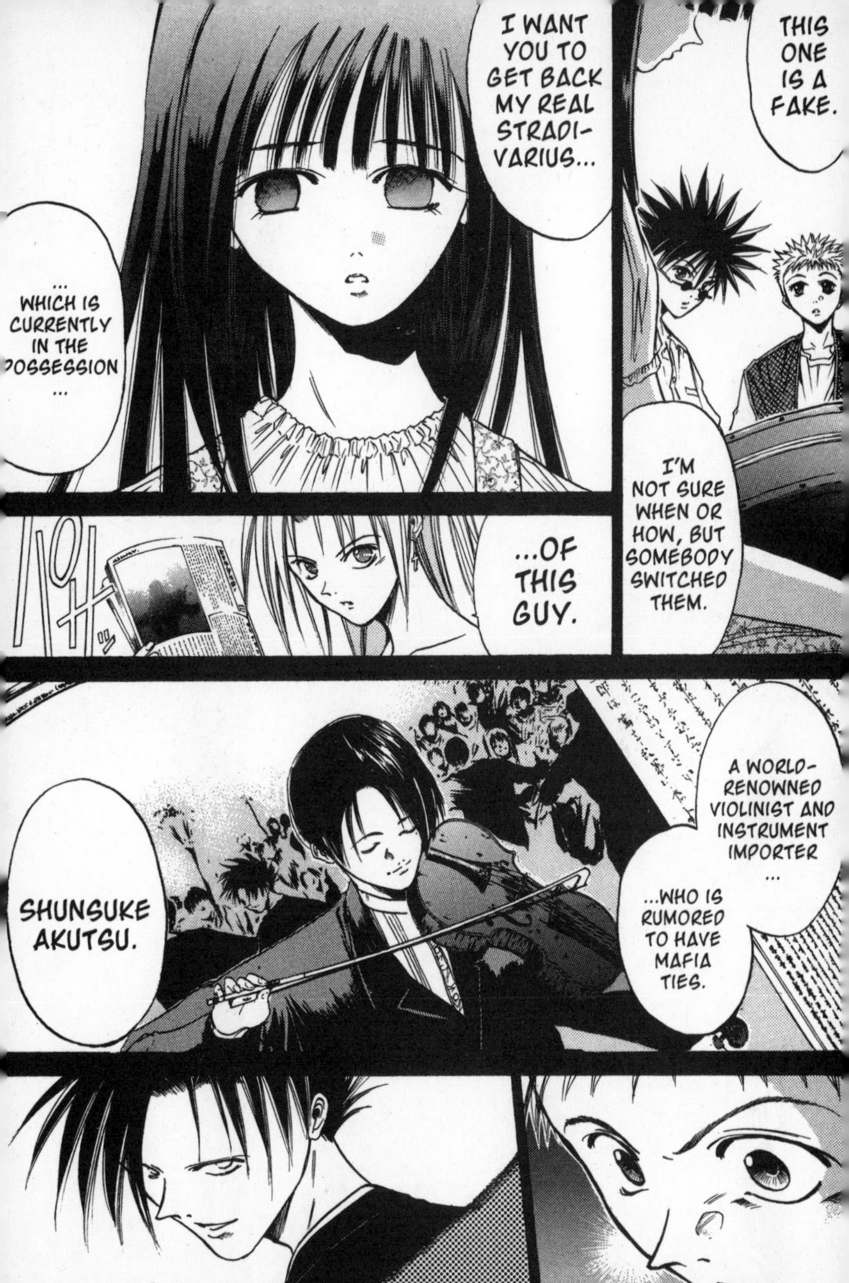
THIS ONE IS A FAKE.
I'M NOT SURE WHEN OR HOW, BUT SOMEBODY SWITCHED THEM.
I WANT YOU TO GET BACK MY REAL STRADI-VARIUS...
...WHICH IS CURRENTLY IN THE POSSESSION...
...OF THIS GUY.
A WORLD-RENOWNED VIOLINIST AND INSTRUMENT IMPORTER...
...WHO IS RUMORED TO HAVE MAFIA TIES.
SHUNSUKE AKUTSU.

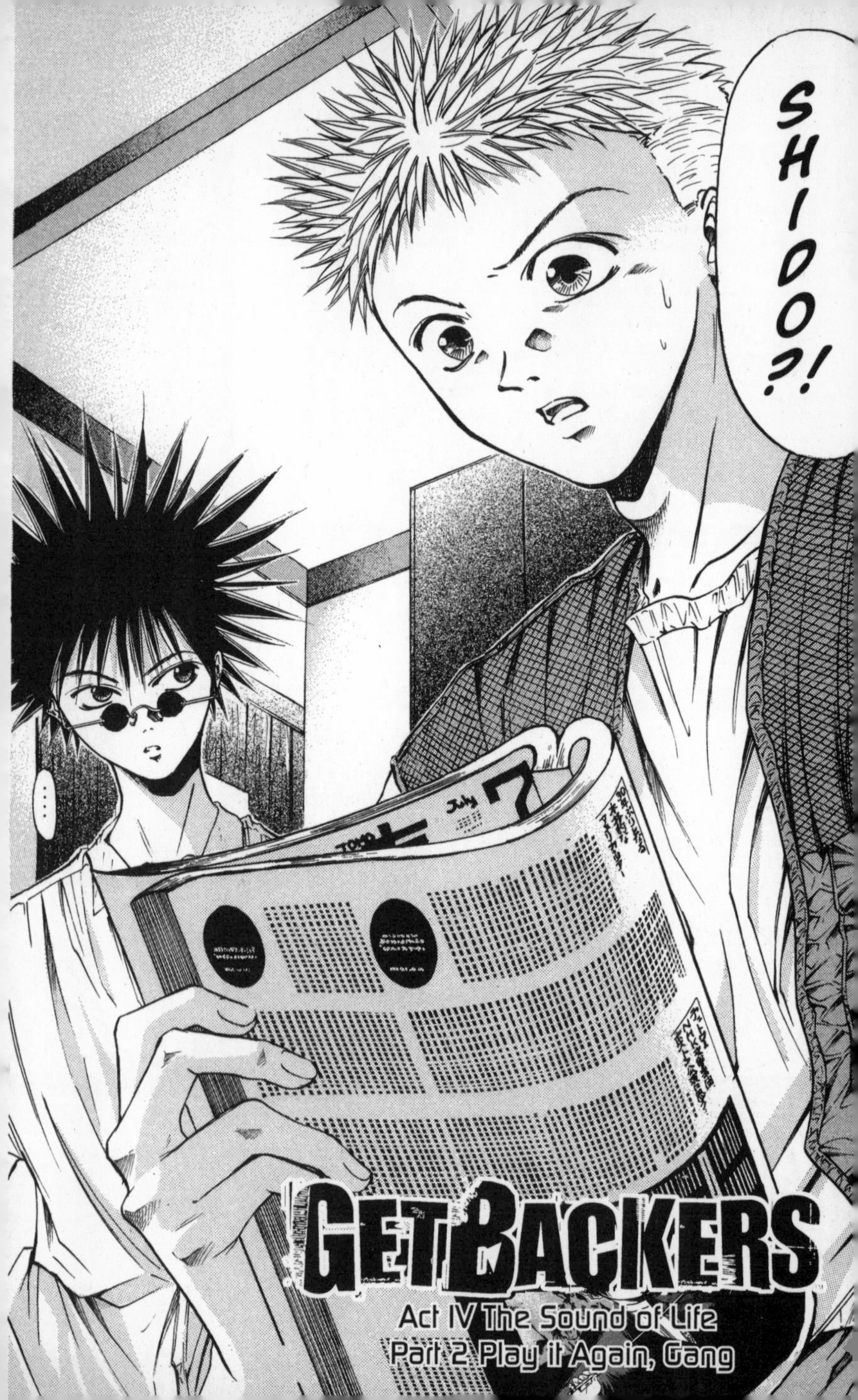
SHIDOO?!
...
GETBACKERS
Act IV The Sound of Life
Part 2 Play it Again, Gang

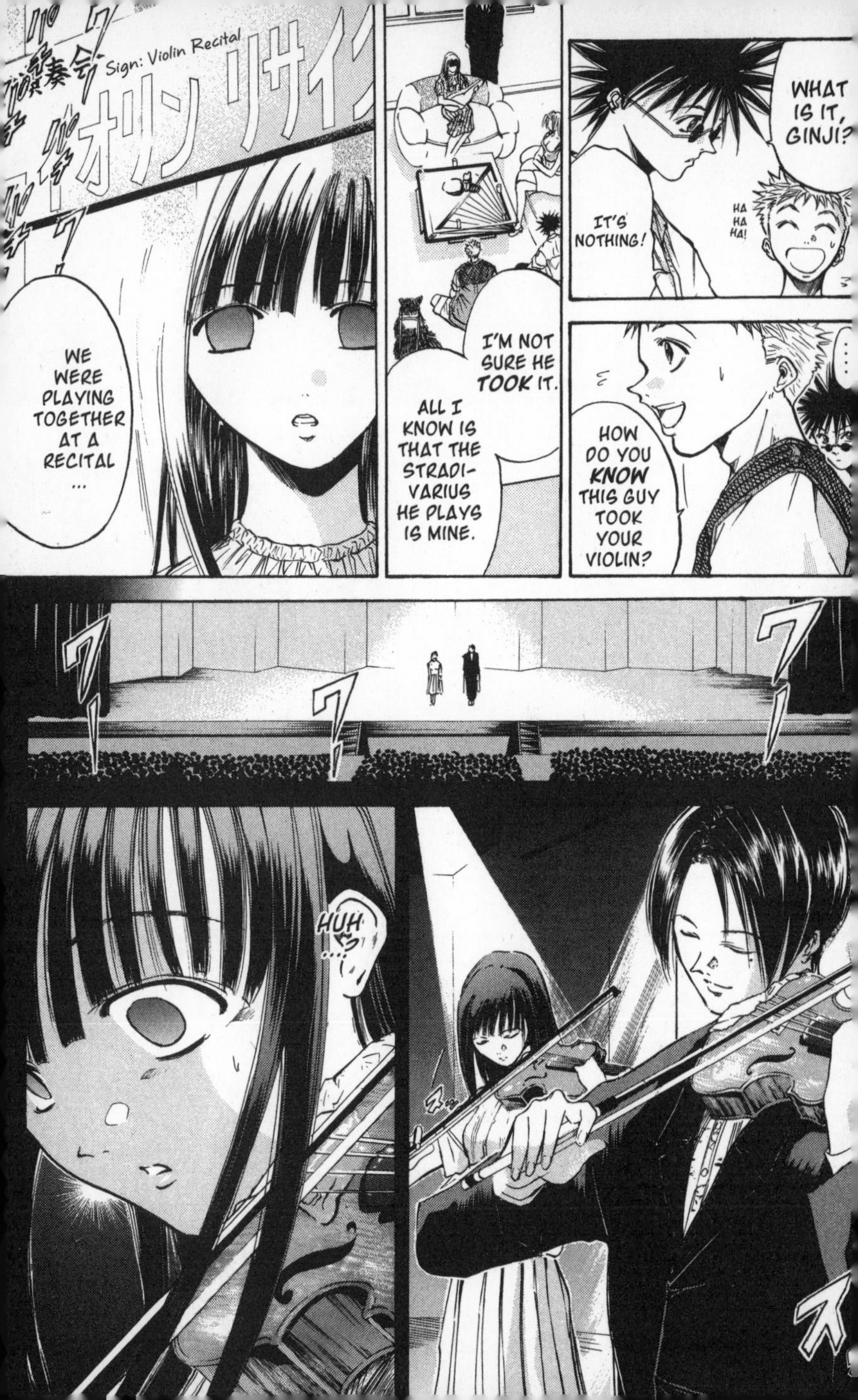
WHAT IS IT, GINJI?
HA HA HA!
IT'S NOTHING!
HOW DO YOU KNOW THIS GUY TOOK YOUR VIOLIN?
I'M NOT SURE HE TOOK IT.
ALL I KNOW IS THAT THE STRADIVARIUS HE PLAYS IS MINE.
Sign: Violin Recital
WE WERE PLAYING TOGETHER AT A RECITAL ...
HUH ...

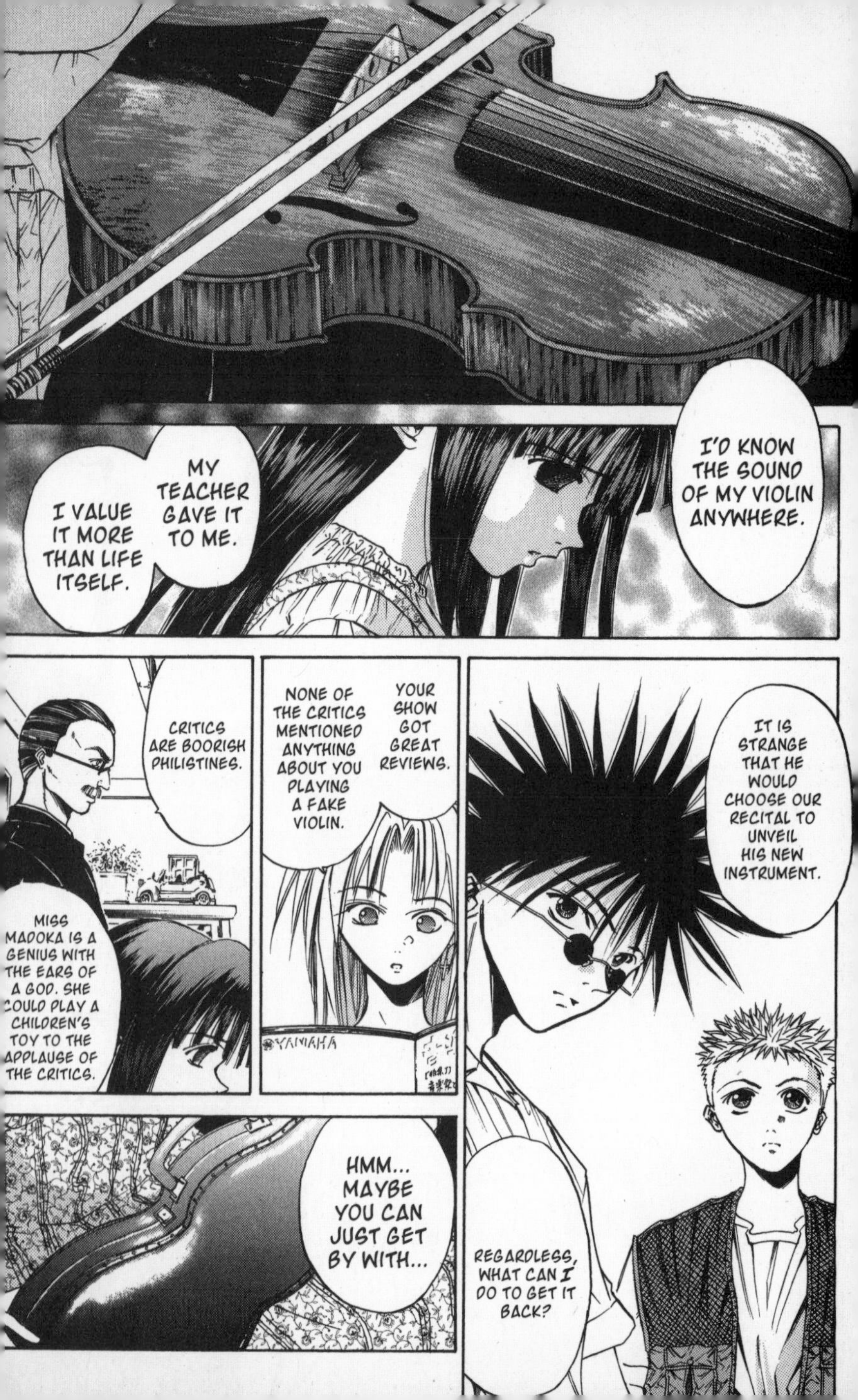
I'D KNOW THE SOUND OF MY VIOLIN ANYWHERE.
MY TEACHER GAVE IT TO ME.
I VALUE IT MORE THAN LIFE ITSELF.
IT IS STRANGE THAT HE WOULD CHOOSE OUR RECITAL TO UNVEIL HIS NEW INSTRUMENT.
REGARDLESS, WHAT CAN I DO TO GET IT BACK?
YOUR SHOW GOT GREAT REVIEWS.
NONE OF THE CRITICS MENTIONED ANYTHING ABOUT YOU PLAYING A FAKE VIOLIN.
YAMAHA
CRITICS ARE BOORISH PHILISTINES.
MISS MADOKA IS A GENIUS WITH THE EARS OF A GOD. SHE COULD PLAY A CHILDREN'S TOY TO THE APPLAUSE OF THE CRITICS.
HMM... MAYBE YOU CAN JUST GET BY WITH...

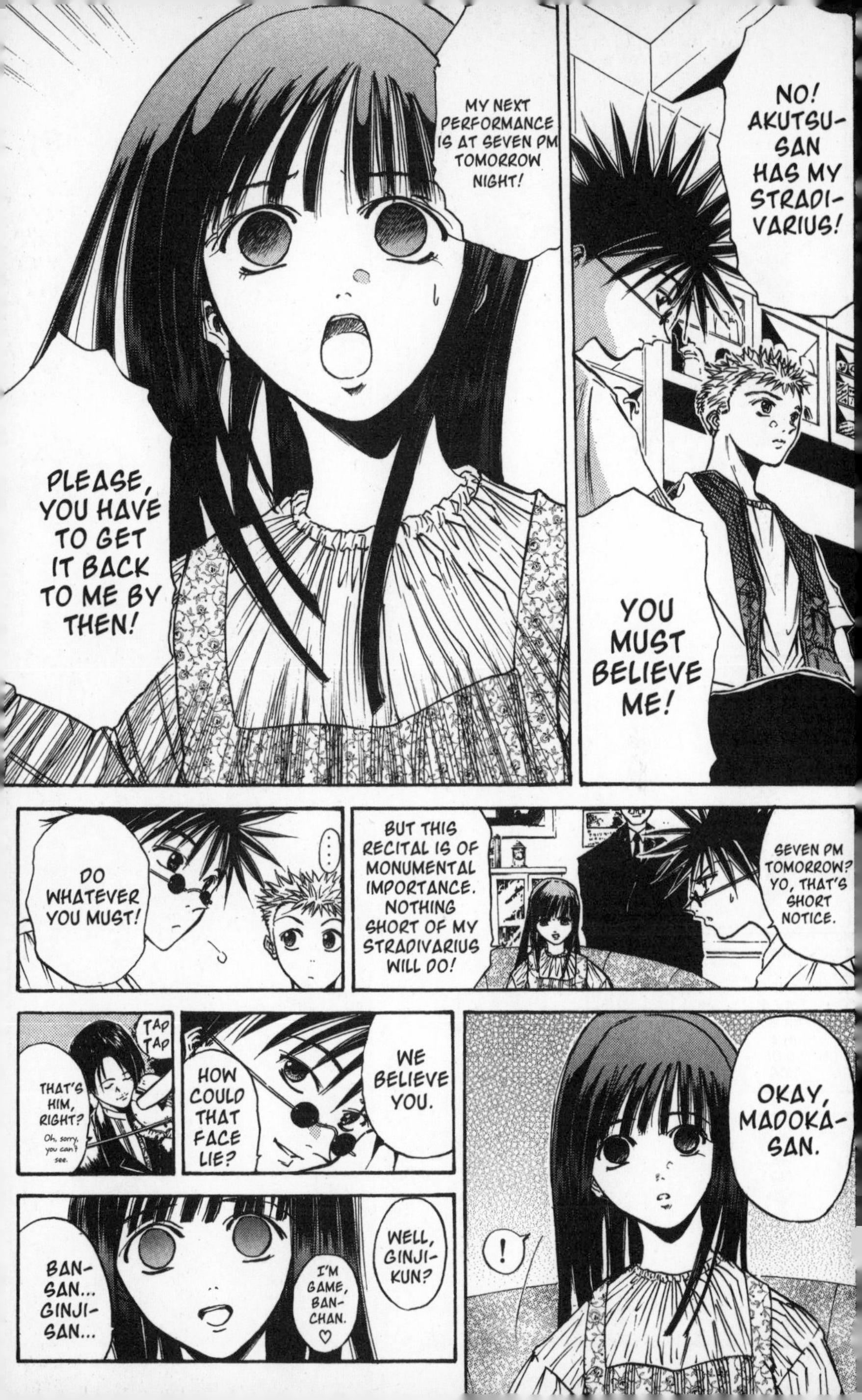

NO! AKUTSU-SAN HAS MY STRADIVARIUS!
YOU MUST BELIEVE ME!
MY NEXT PERFORMANCE IS AT SEVEN PM TOMORROW NIGHT!
PLEASE, YOU HAVE TO GET IT BACK TO ME BY THEN!
SEVEN PM TOMORROW? YO, THAT'S SHORT NOTICE.
BUT THIS RECITAL IS OF MONUMENTAL IMPORTANCE. NOTHING SHORT OF MY STRADIVARIUS WILL DO!
...
DO WHATEVER YOU MUST!
OKAY, MADOKA-SAN.
!
WE BELIEVE YOU.
HOW COULD THAT FACE LIE?
TAP TAP
THAT'S HIM, RIGHT?
Oh, sorry, you can't see.
WELL, GINJI-KUN?
I'M GAME, BAN-CHAN. ♥
BAN-SAN... GINJI-SAN...

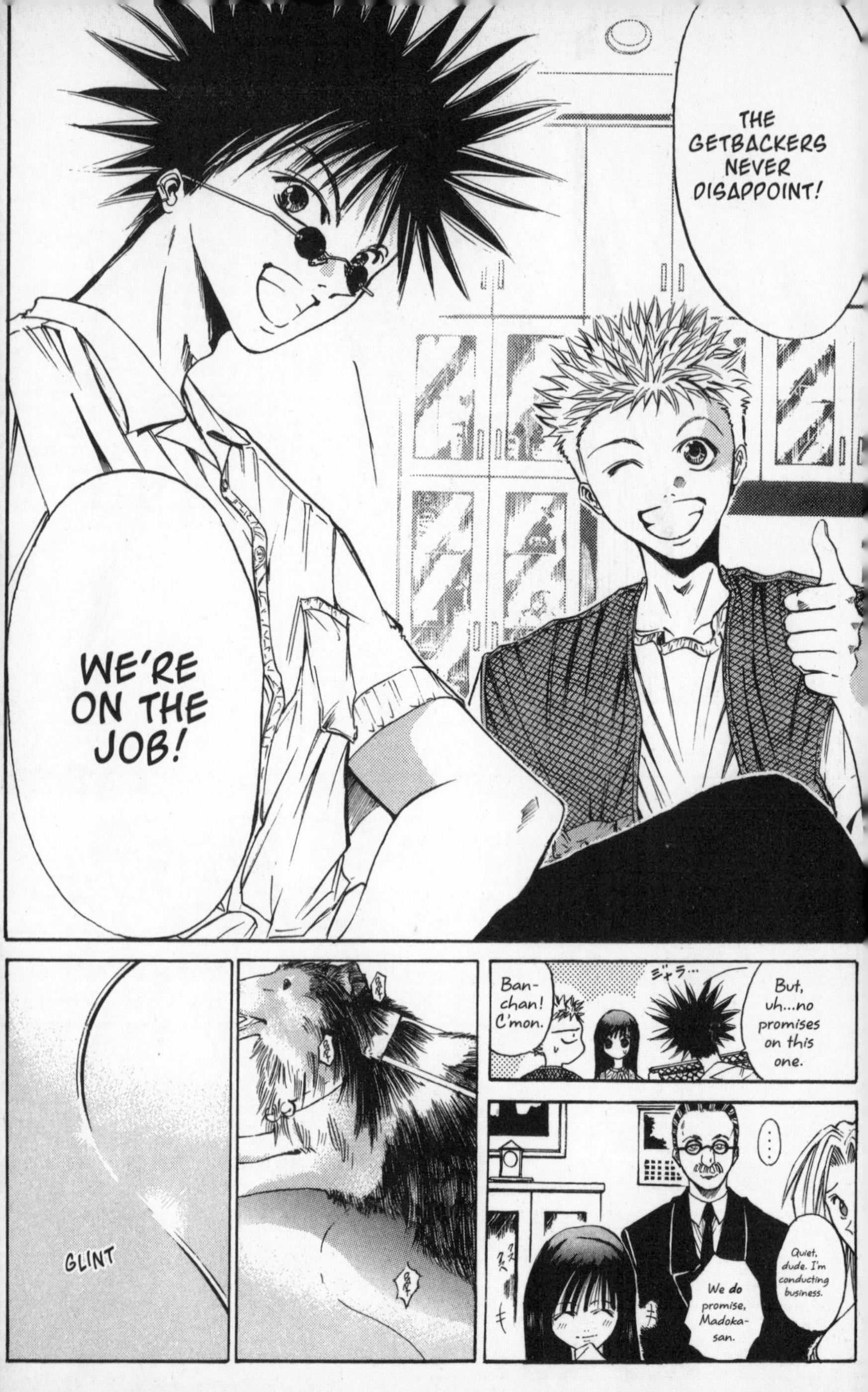
THE GETBACKERS NEVER DISAPPOINT!
WE'RE ON THE JOB!
But, uh...no promises on this one.
ジャラ…
Ban-chan! C'mon.
Quiet, dude. I'm conducting business.
...
We do promise, Madoka-san.
GLINT

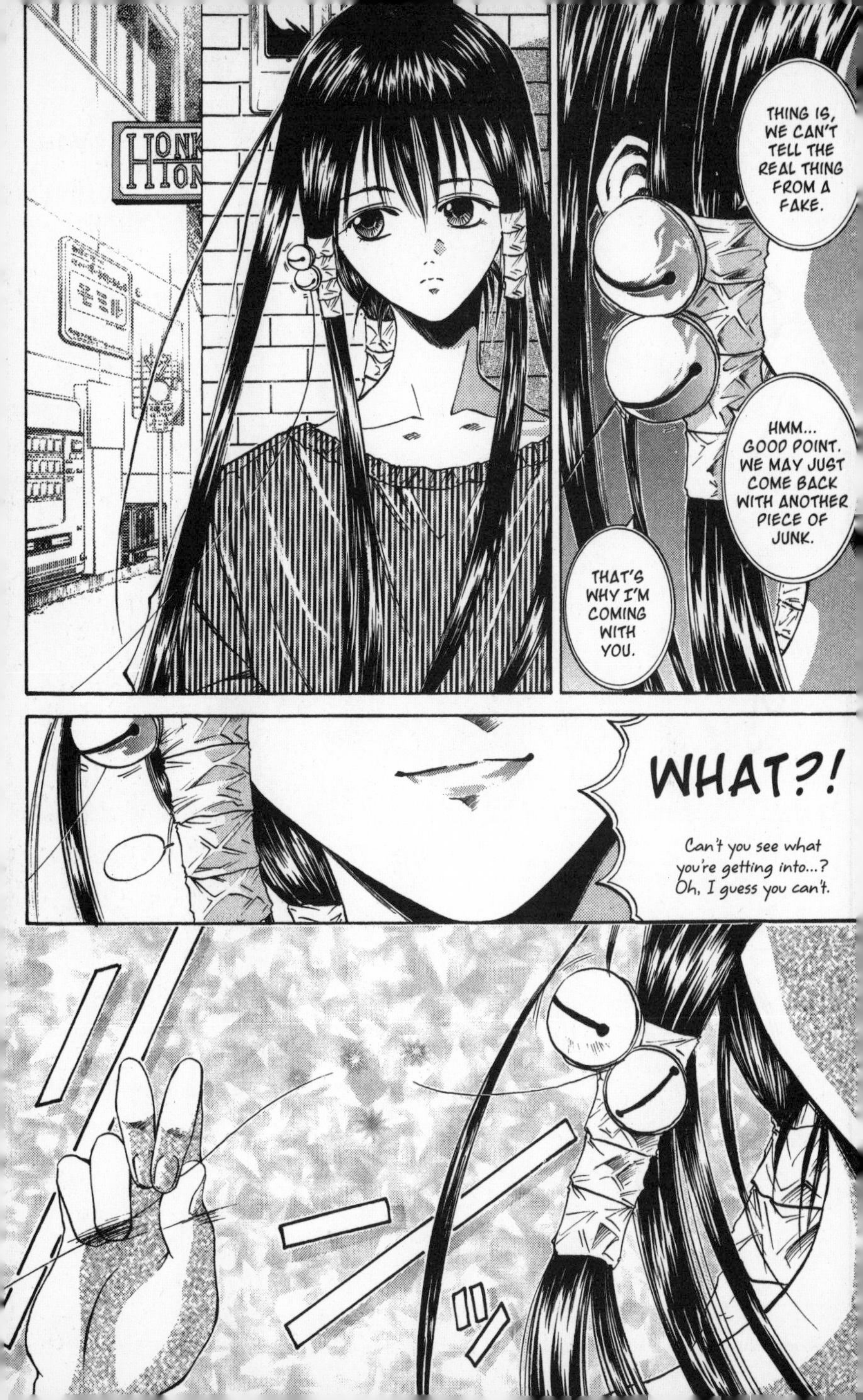
THING IS, WE CAN'T TELL THE REAL THING FROM A FAKE.
HMM... GOOD POINT. WE MAY JUST COME BACK WITH ANOTHER PIECE OF JUNK.
THAT'S WHY I'M COMING WITH YOU.
WHAT?!
Can't you see what you're getting into...? Oh, I guess you can't.

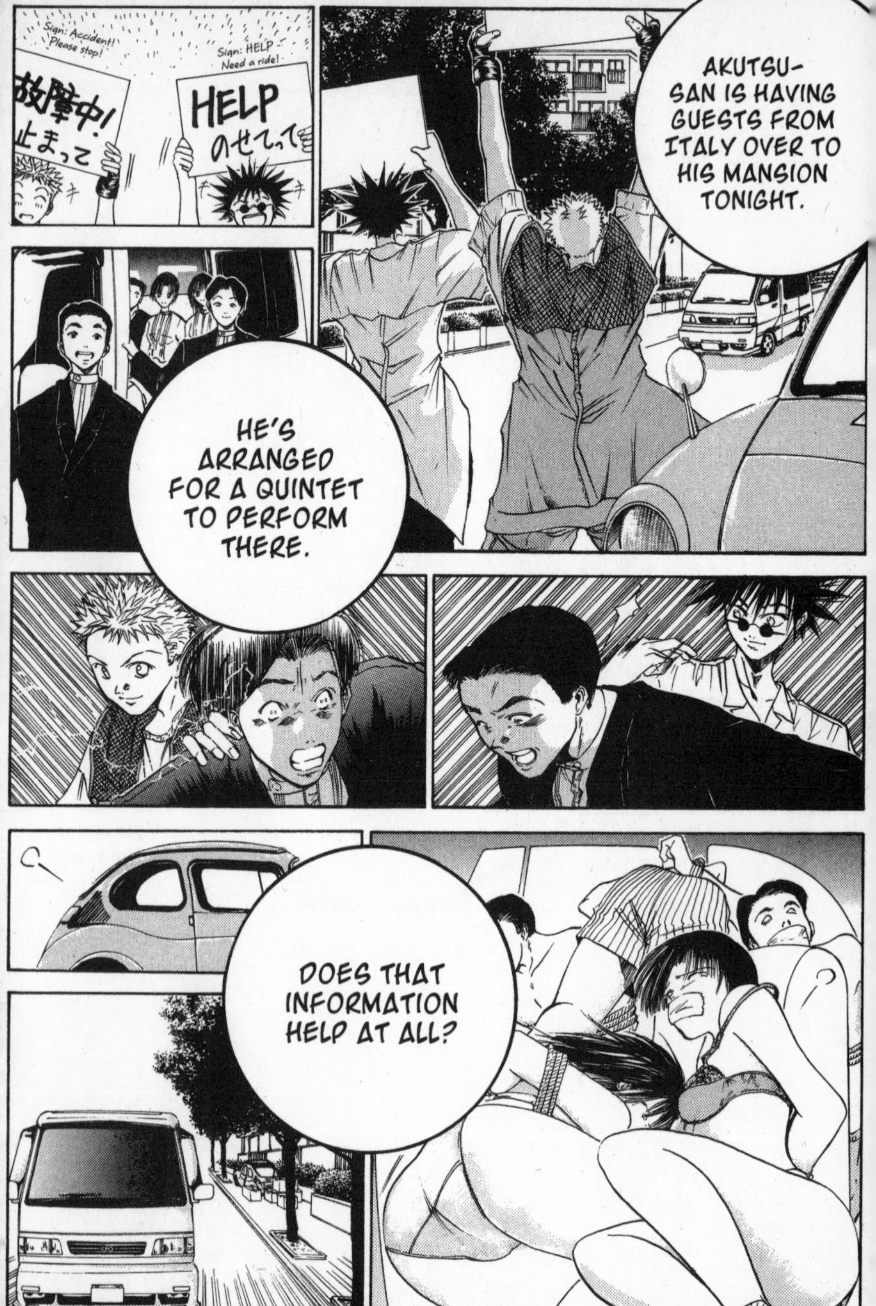

AKUTSU-SAN IS HAVING GUESTS FROM ITALY OVER TO HIS MANSION TONIGHT.
Sign: HELP Need a ride!
HELP のせてって
Sign: Accident! Please stop!
故障中! 止まって
HE'S ARRANGED FOR A QUINTET TO PERFORM THERE.
DOES THAT INFORMATION HELP AT ALL?

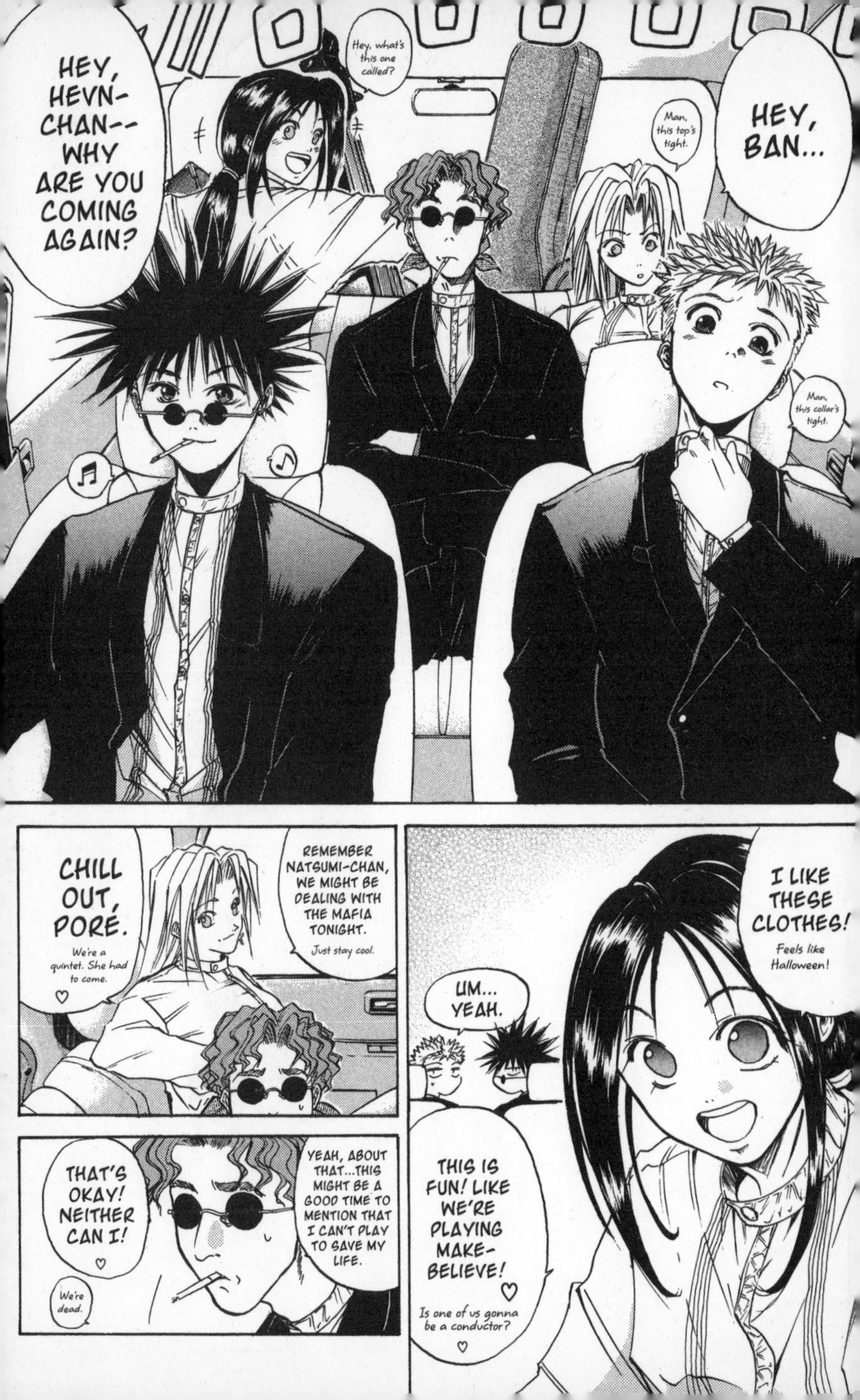
HEY, BAN...
Man, this top's tight.
Hey, what's this one called?
HEY, HEVN-CHAN--WHY ARE YOU COMING AGAIN?
Man, this collar's tight.
I LIKE THESE CLOTHES!
Feels like Halloween!
UM... YEAH.
THIS IS FUN! LIKE WE'RE PLAYING MAKE-BELIEVE! ♡
Is one of us gonna be a conductor? ♡
REMEMBER NATSUMI-CHAN, WE MIGHT BE DEALING WITH THE MAFIA TONIGHT.
Just stay cool.
CHILL OUT, PORÉ.
We're a quintet. She had to come. ♡
YEAH, ABOUT THAT...THIS MIGHT BE A GOOD TIME TO MENTION THAT I CAN'T PLAY TO SAVE MY LIFE.
THAT'S OKAY! NEITHER CAN I! ♡
We're dead.

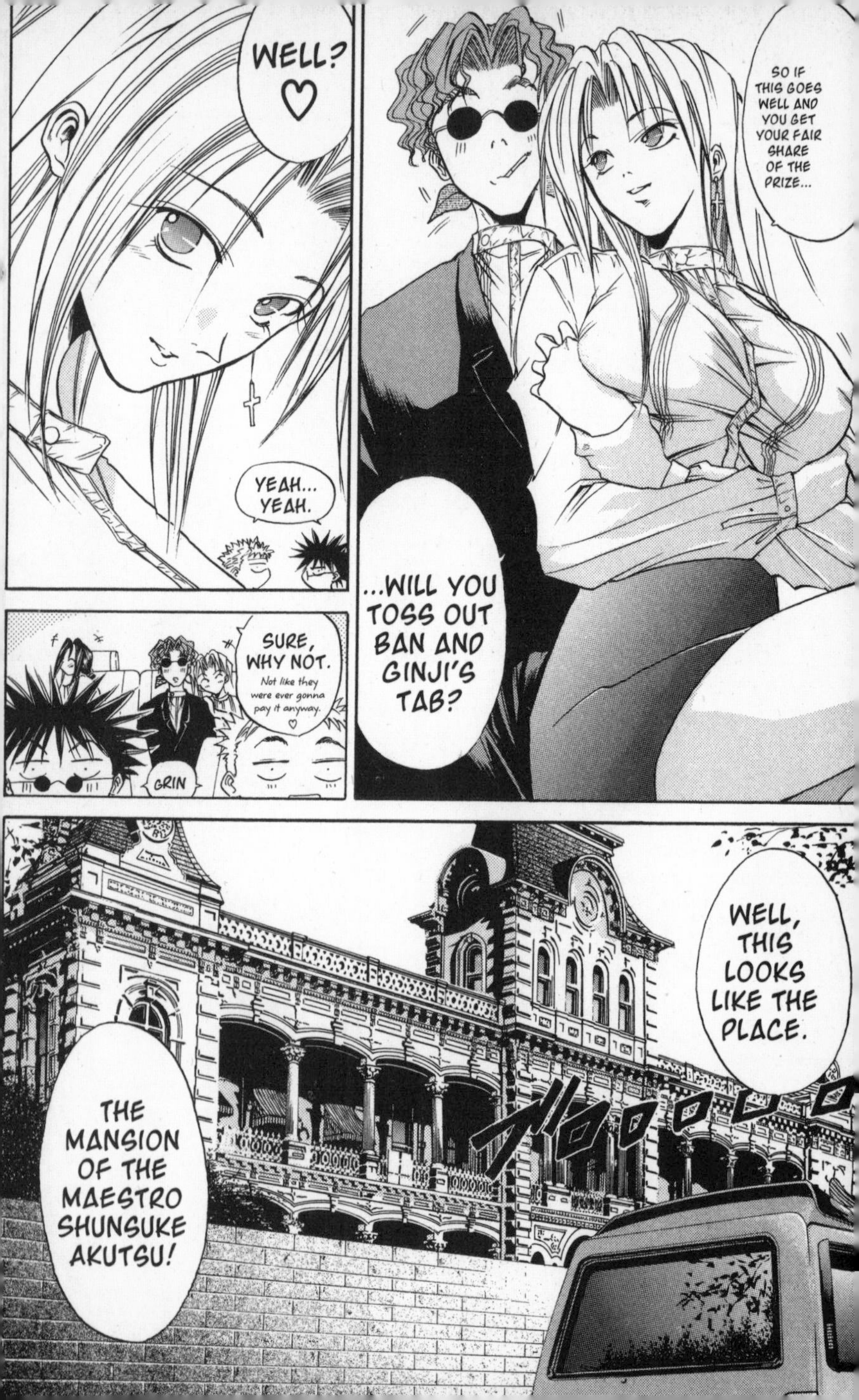
SO IF THIS GOES WELL AND YOU GET YOUR FAIR SHARE OF THE PRIZE...
...WILL YOU TOSS OUT BAN AND GINJI'S TAB?
WELL? ♡
YEAH... YEAH.
SURE, WHY NOT.
Not like they were ever gonna pay it anyway. ♡
GRIN
WELL, THIS LOOKS LIKE THE PLACE.
THE MANSION OF THE MAESTRO SHUNSUKE AKUTSU!

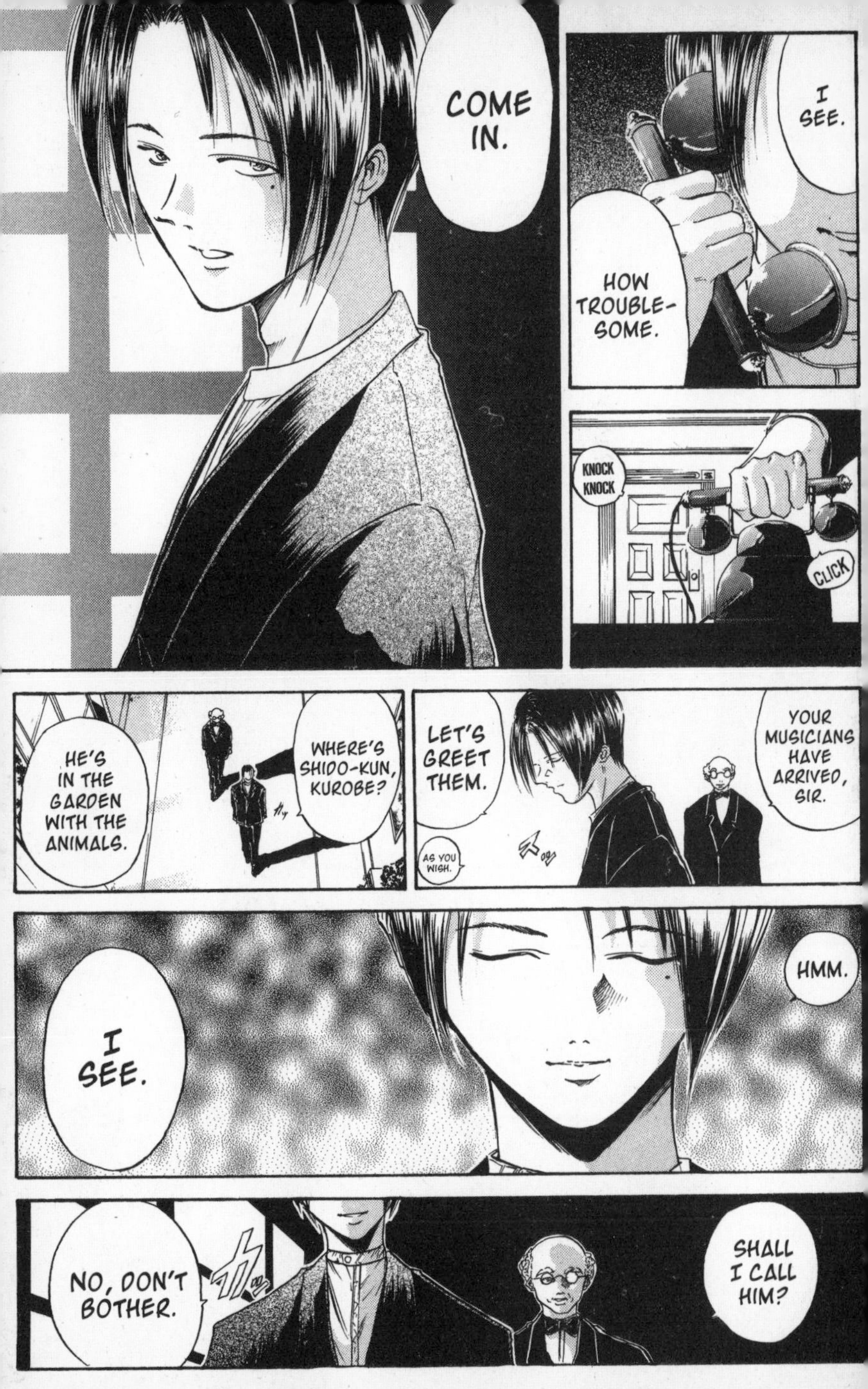
I SEE.
HOW TROUBLE-SOME.
KNOCK KNOCK
CLICK
COME IN.
YOUR MUSICIANS HAVE ARRIVED, SIR.
LET'S GREET THEM.
AS YOU WISH.
WHERE'S SHIDO-KUN, KUROBE?
HE'S IN THE GARDEN WITH THE ANIMALS.
HMM.
I SEE.
SHALL I CALL HIM?
NO, DON'T BOTHER.

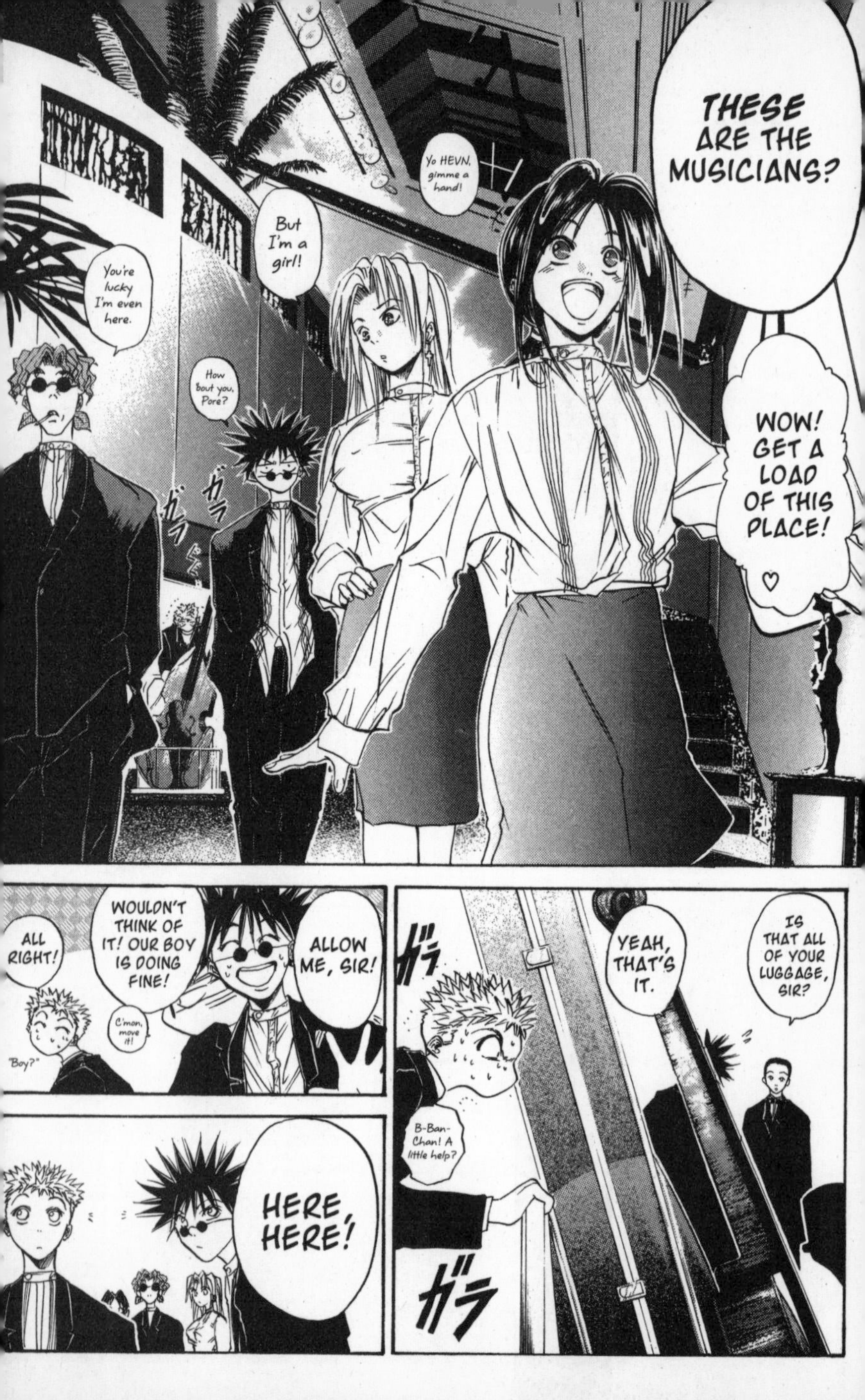
THESE ARE THE MUSICIANS?
WOW! GET A LOAD OF THIS PLACE! ♡
Yo HEVN, gimme a hand!
But I'm a girl!
You're lucky I'm even here.
How bout you, Pore?
ガラ
ガラ
IS THAT ALL OF YOUR LUGGAGE, SIR?
YEAH, THAT'S IT.
ガラ
B-Ban-Chan! A little help?
ガラ
ALLOW ME, SIR!
WOULDN'T THINK OF IT! OUR BOY IS DOING FINE!
C'mon, move it!
ALL RIGHT!
"Boy?"
HERE HERE!

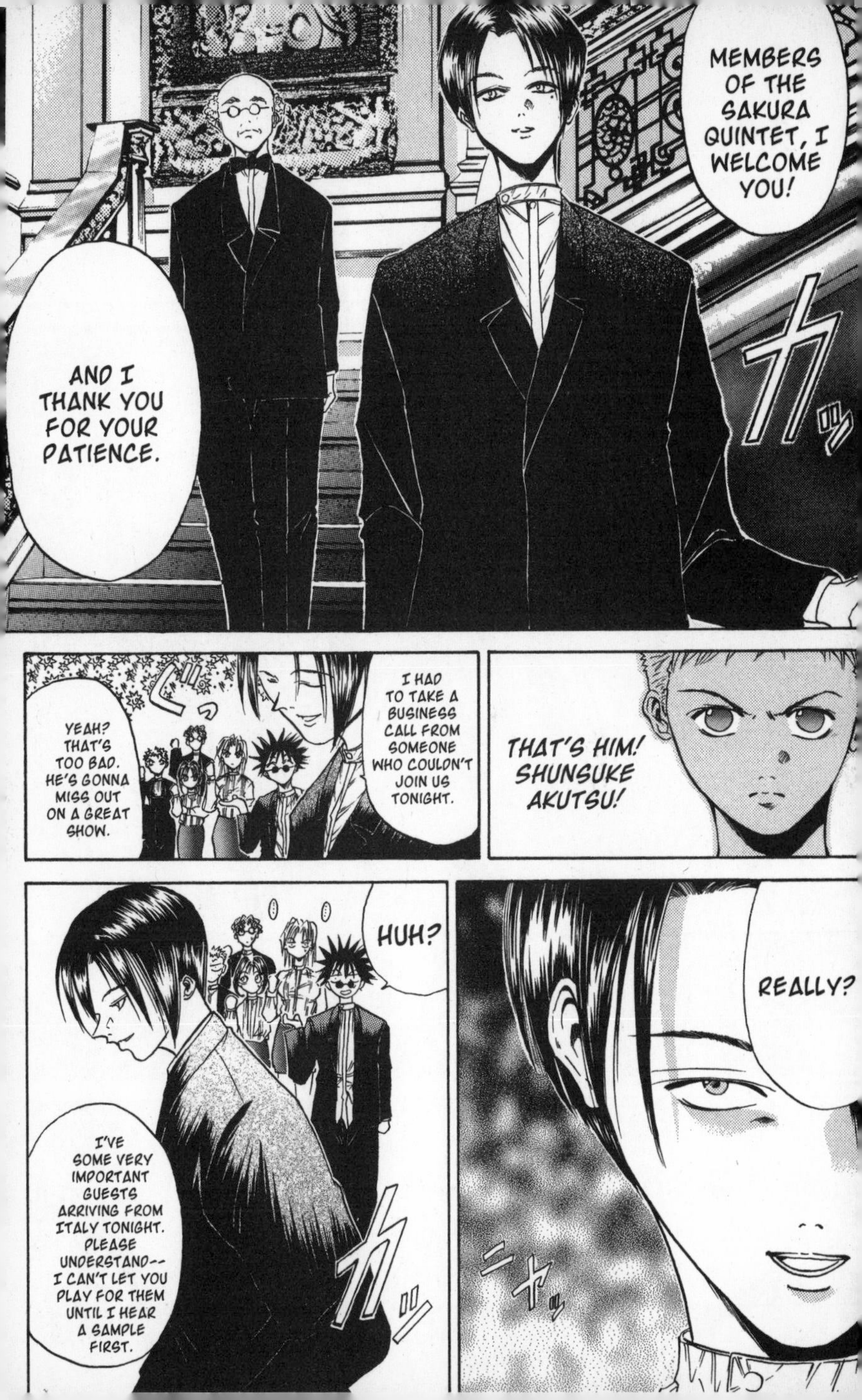
MEMBERS OF THE SAKURA QUINTET, I WELCOME YOU!
AND I THANK YOU FOR YOUR PATIENCE.
カッ
THAT'S HIM! SHUNSUKE AKUTSU!
I HAD TO TAKE A BUSINESS CALL FROM SOMEONE WHO COULDN'T JOIN US TONIGHT.
ぐっ
YEAH? THAT'S TOO BAD. HE'S GONNA MISS OUT ON A GREAT SHOW.
REALLY?
ニヤッ
HUH?
I'VE SOME VERY IMPORTANT GUESTS ARRIVING FROM ITALY TONIGHT. PLEASE UNDERSTAND-- I CAN'T LET YOU PLAY FOR THEM UNTIL I HEAR A SAMPLE FIRST.
カッ

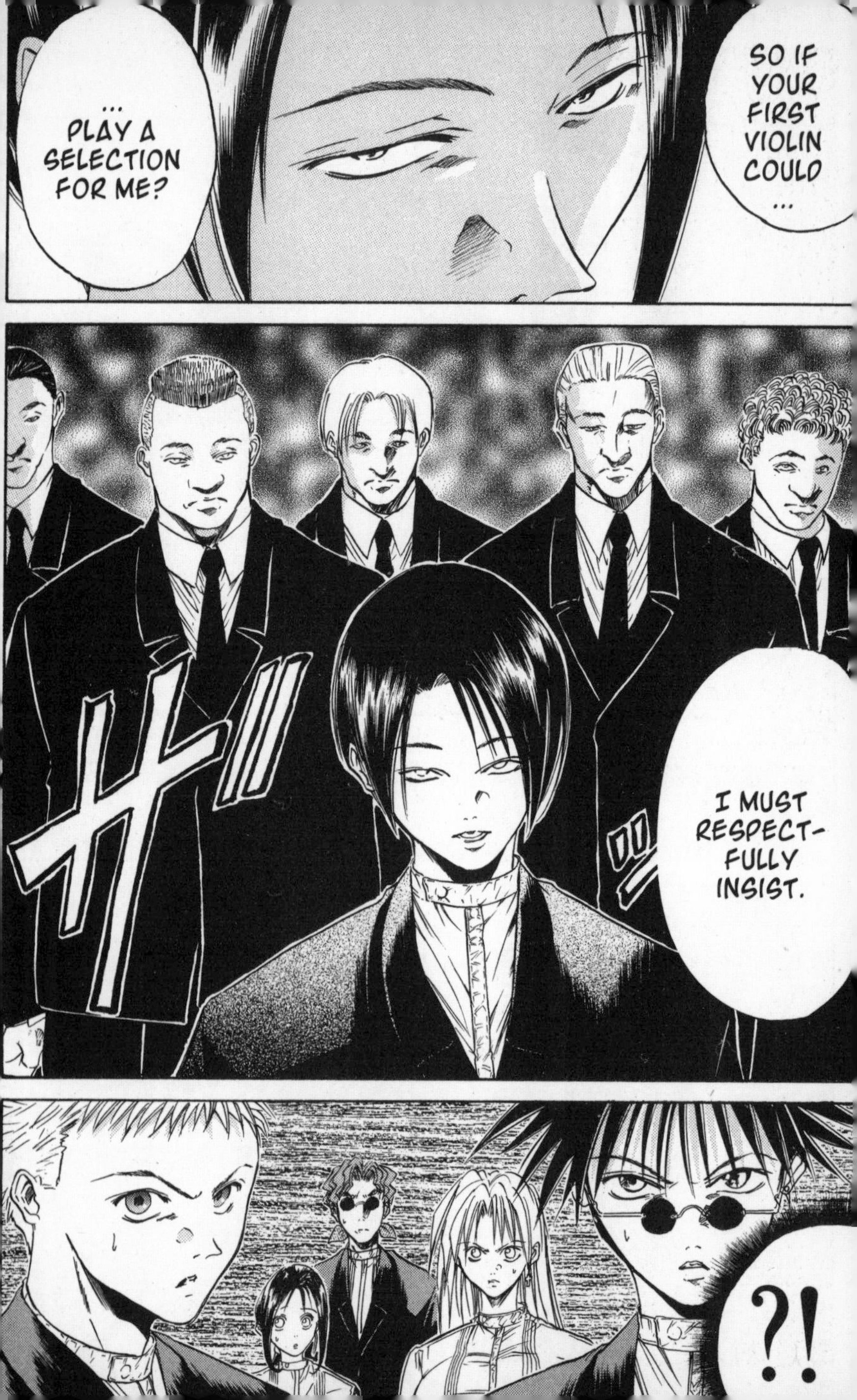
SO IF YOUR FIRST VIOLIN COULD ...
... PLAY A SELECTION FOR ME?
I MUST RESPECT-FULLY INSIST.
?!

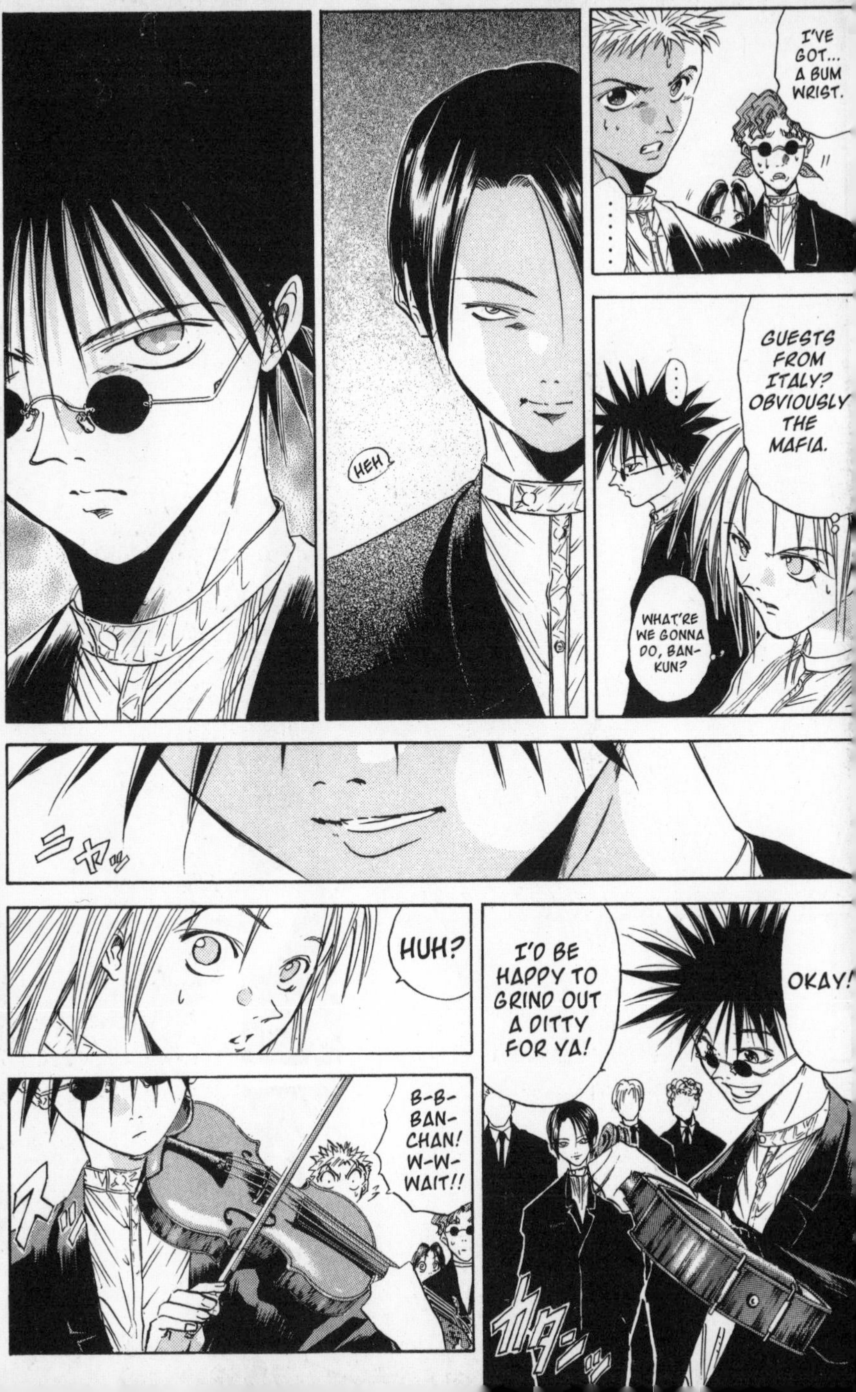
I'VE GOT... A BUM WRIST.
...
GUESTS FROM ITALY? OBVIOUSLY THE MAFIA.
...
WHAT'RE WE GONNA DO, BAN-KUN?
HEH
ニヤッ
OKAY!
I'D BE HAPPY TO GRIND OUT A DITTY FOR YA!
HUH?
B-B-BAN-CHAN! W-W-WAIT!!

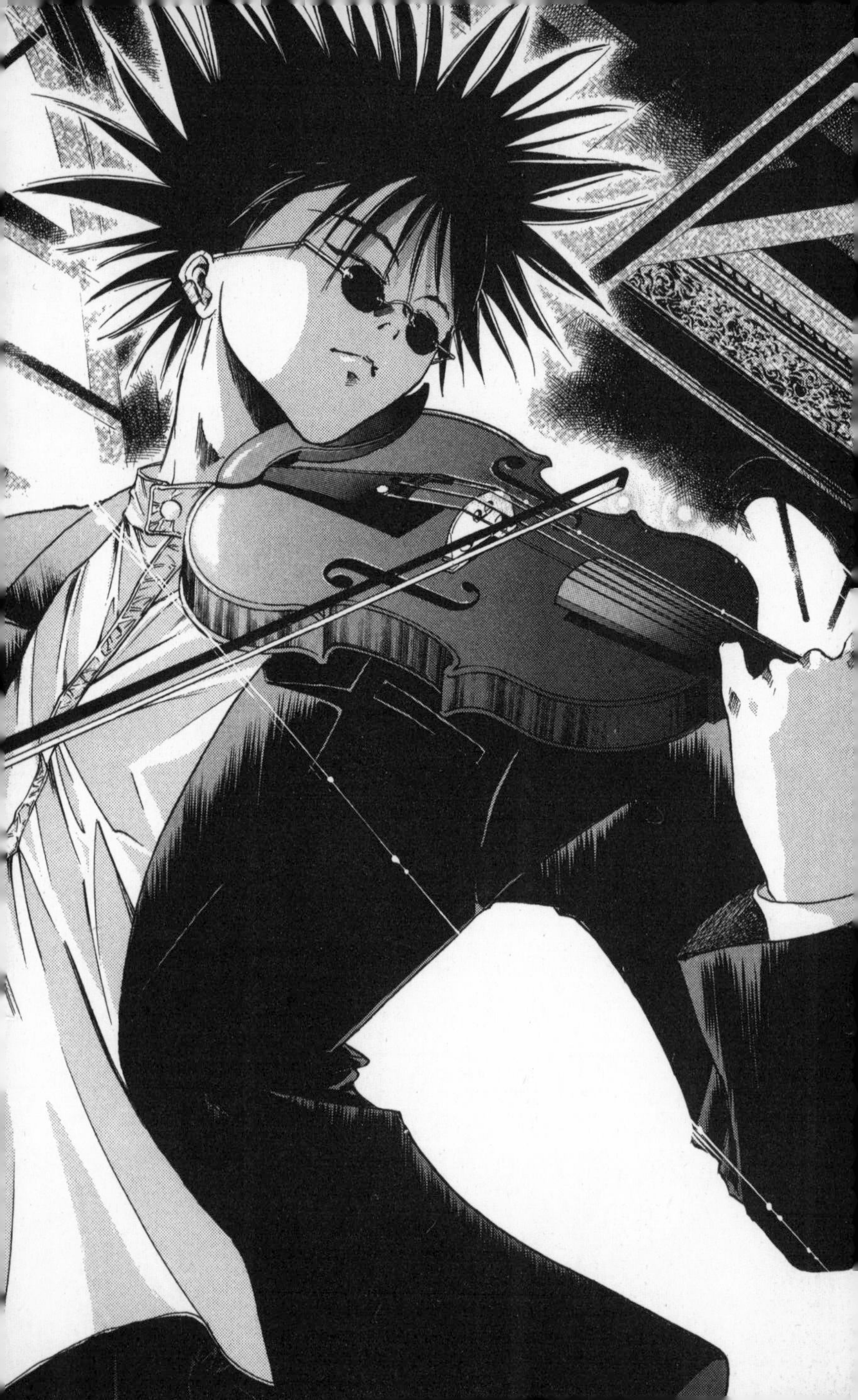

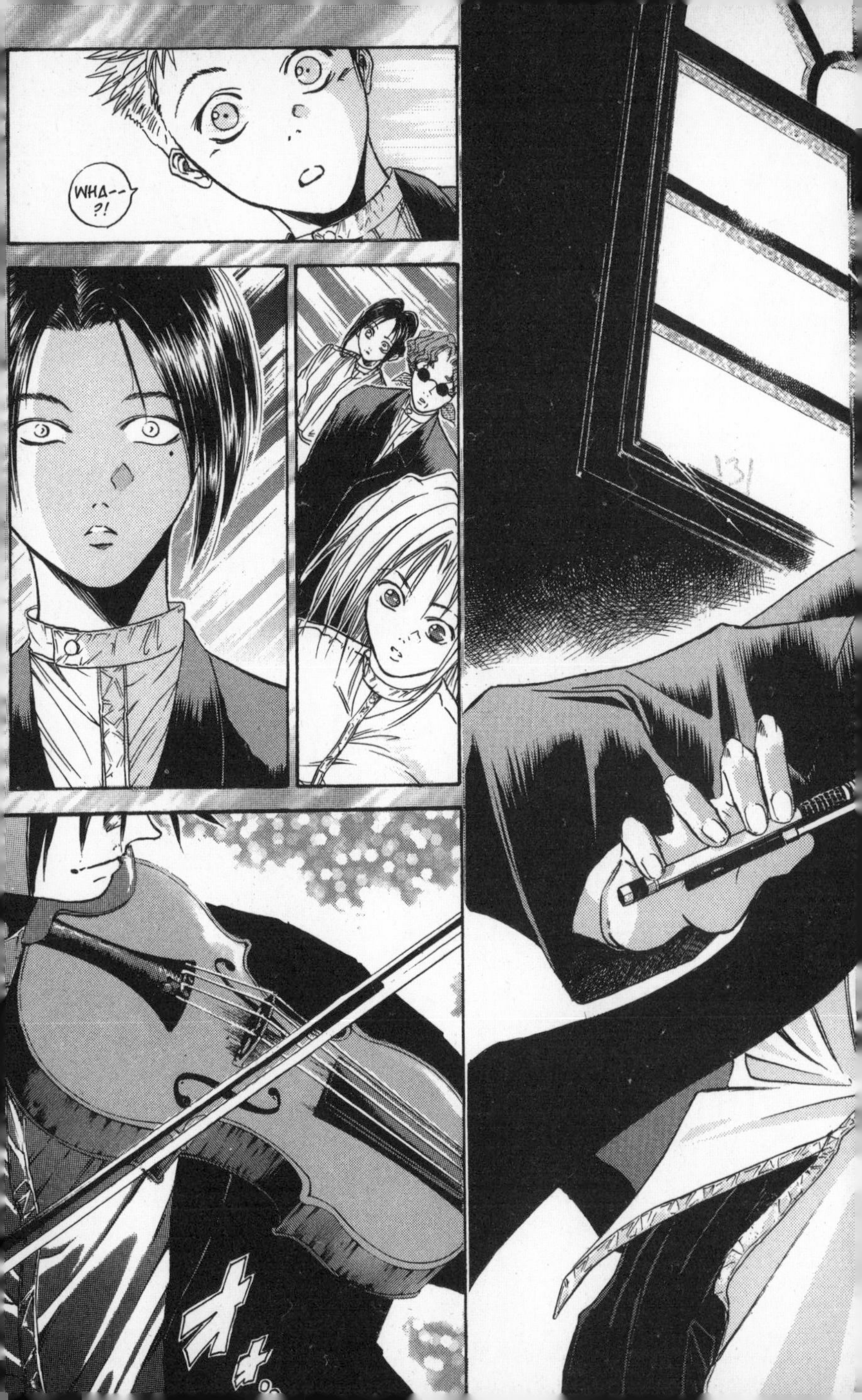
WHA--?!

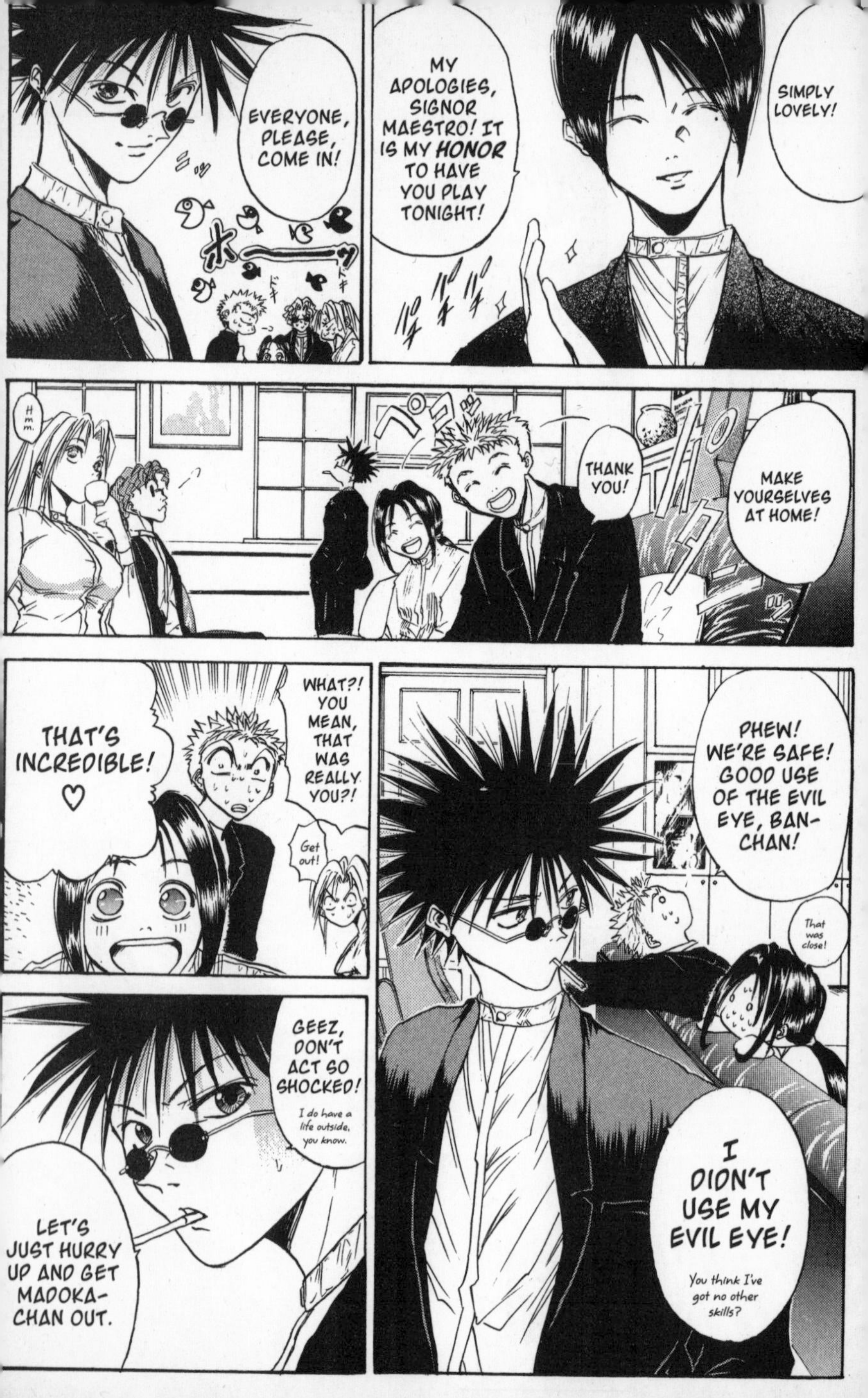
SIMPLY LOVELY!
MY APOLOGIES, SIGNOR MAESTRO! IT IS MY HONOR TO HAVE YOU PLAY TONIGHT!
EVERYONE, PLEASE, COME IN!
MAKE YOURSELVES AT HOME!
THANK YOU!
Hmm.
PHEW! WE'RE SAFE! GOOD USE OF THE EVIL EYE, BAN-CHAN!
That was close!
I DIDN'T USE MY EVIL EYE!
You think I've got no other skills?
WHAT?! YOU MEAN, THAT WAS REALLY YOU?!
Get out!
THAT'S INCREDIBLE! ♡
GEEZ, DON'T ACT SO SHOCKED!
I do have a life outside, you know.
LET'S JUST HURRY UP AND GET MADOKA-CHAN OUT.

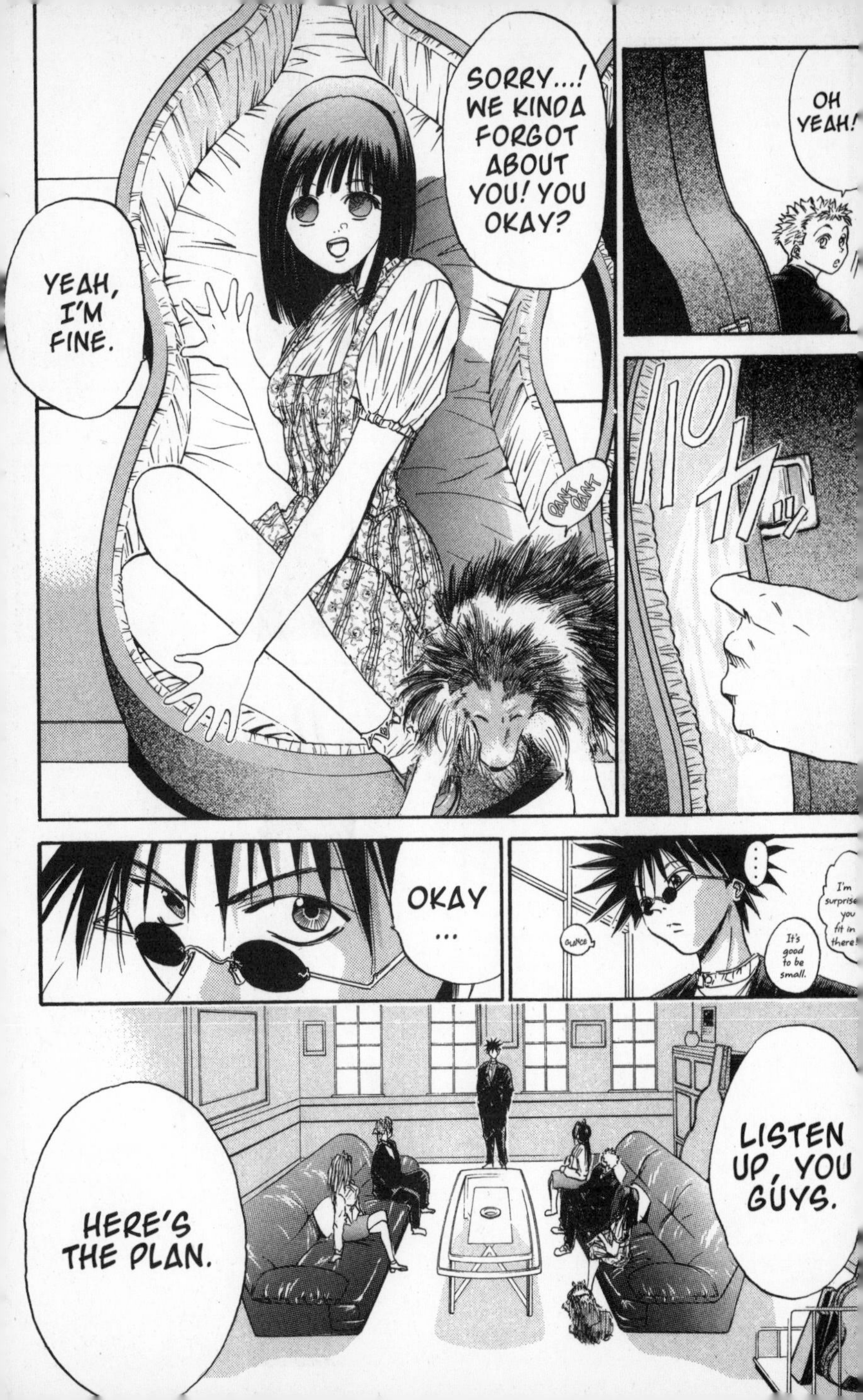
OH YEAH!
SORRY...! WE KINDA FORGOT ABOUT YOU! YOU OKAY?
YEAH, I'M FINE.
PANT PANT
...
I'm surprise you fit in there!
It's good to be small.
GLANCE
OKAY ...
LISTEN UP, YOU GUYS.
HERE'S THE PLAN.

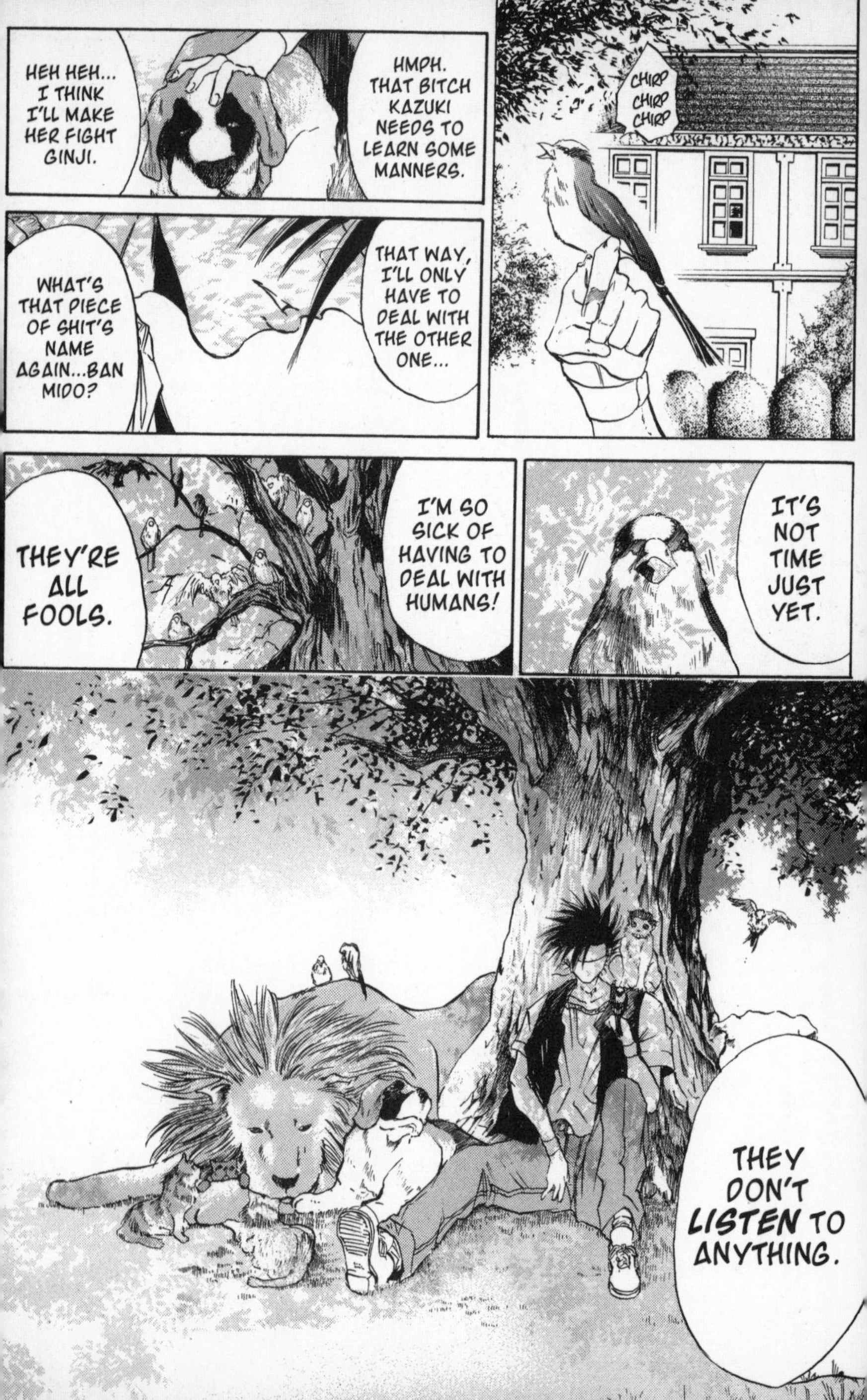
CHIRP CHIRP CHIRP
HMPH. THAT BITCH KAZUKI NEEDS TO LEARN SOME MANNERS.
HEH HEH... I THINK I'LL MAKE HER FIGHT GINJI.
THAT WAY, I'LL ONLY HAVE TO DEAL WITH THE OTHER ONE...
WHAT'S THAT PIECE OF SHIT'S NAME AGAIN...BAN MIDO?
IT'S NOT TIME JUST YET.
I'M SO SICK OF HAVING TO DEAL WITH HUMANS!
THEY'RE ALL FOOLS.
THEY DON'T LISTEN TO ANYTHING.

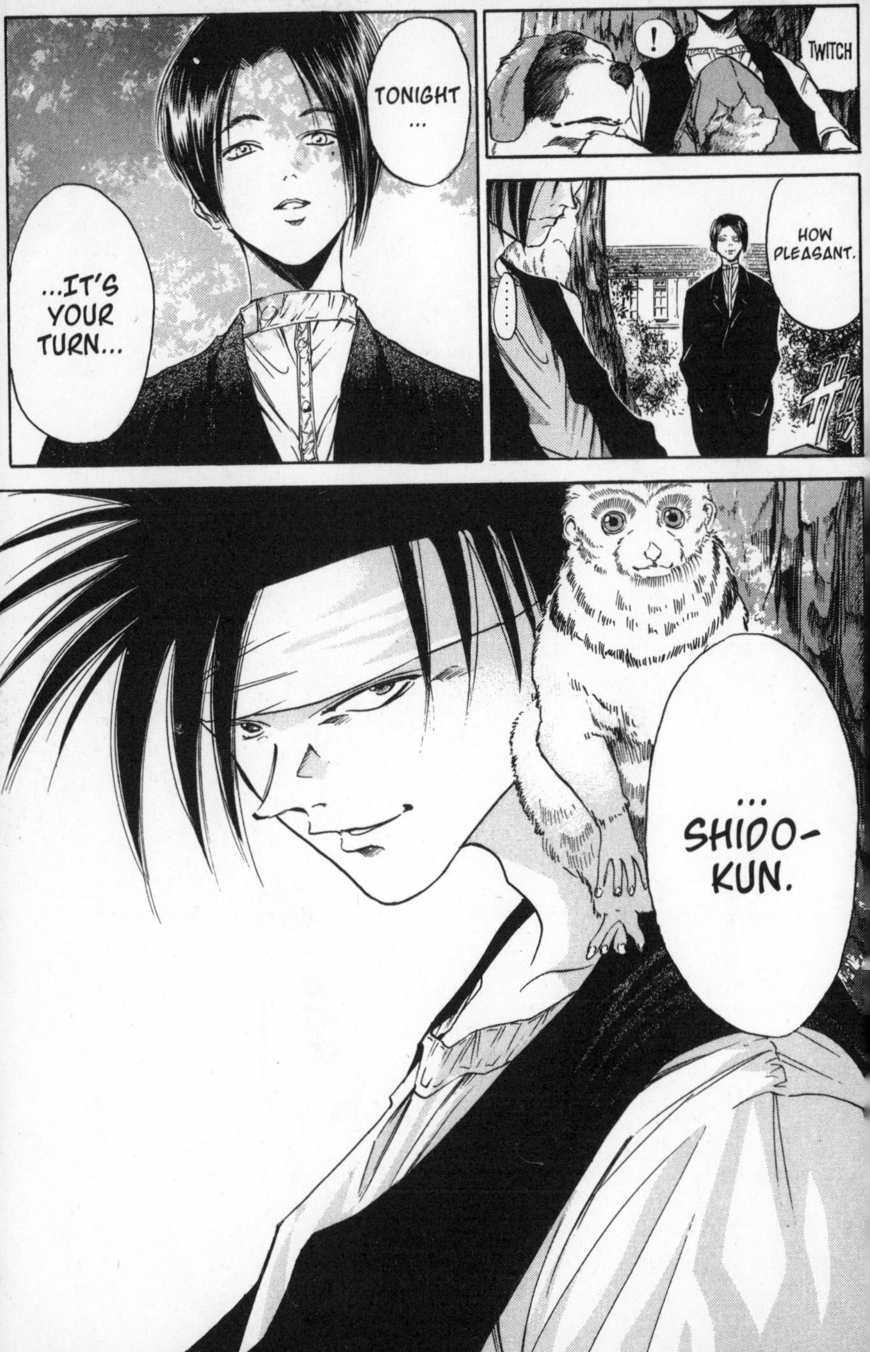
!
TWITCH
HOW PLEASANT.
.....
TONIGHT ...
...IT'S YOUR TURN...
... SHIDO-KUN.

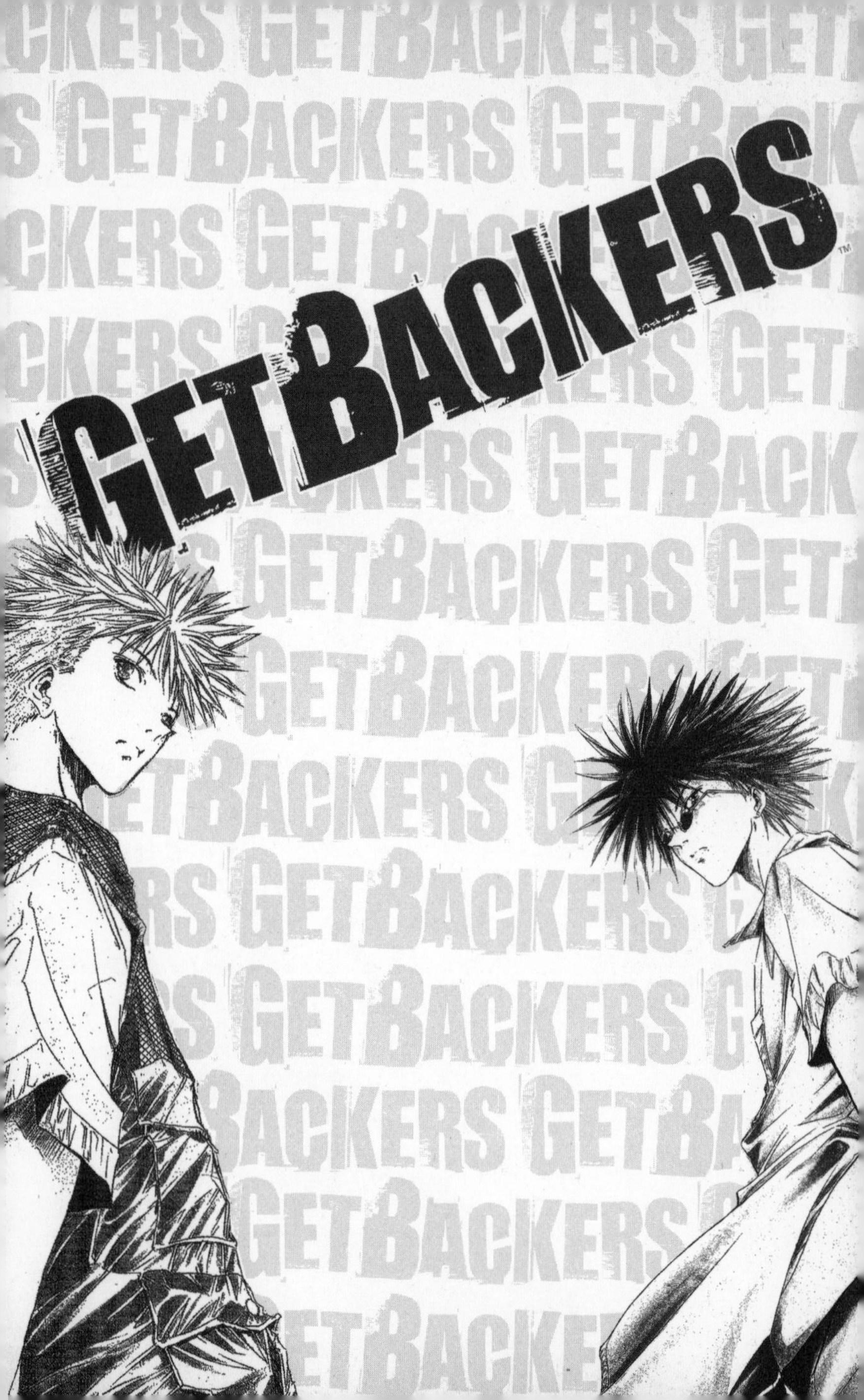
GETBACKERS™

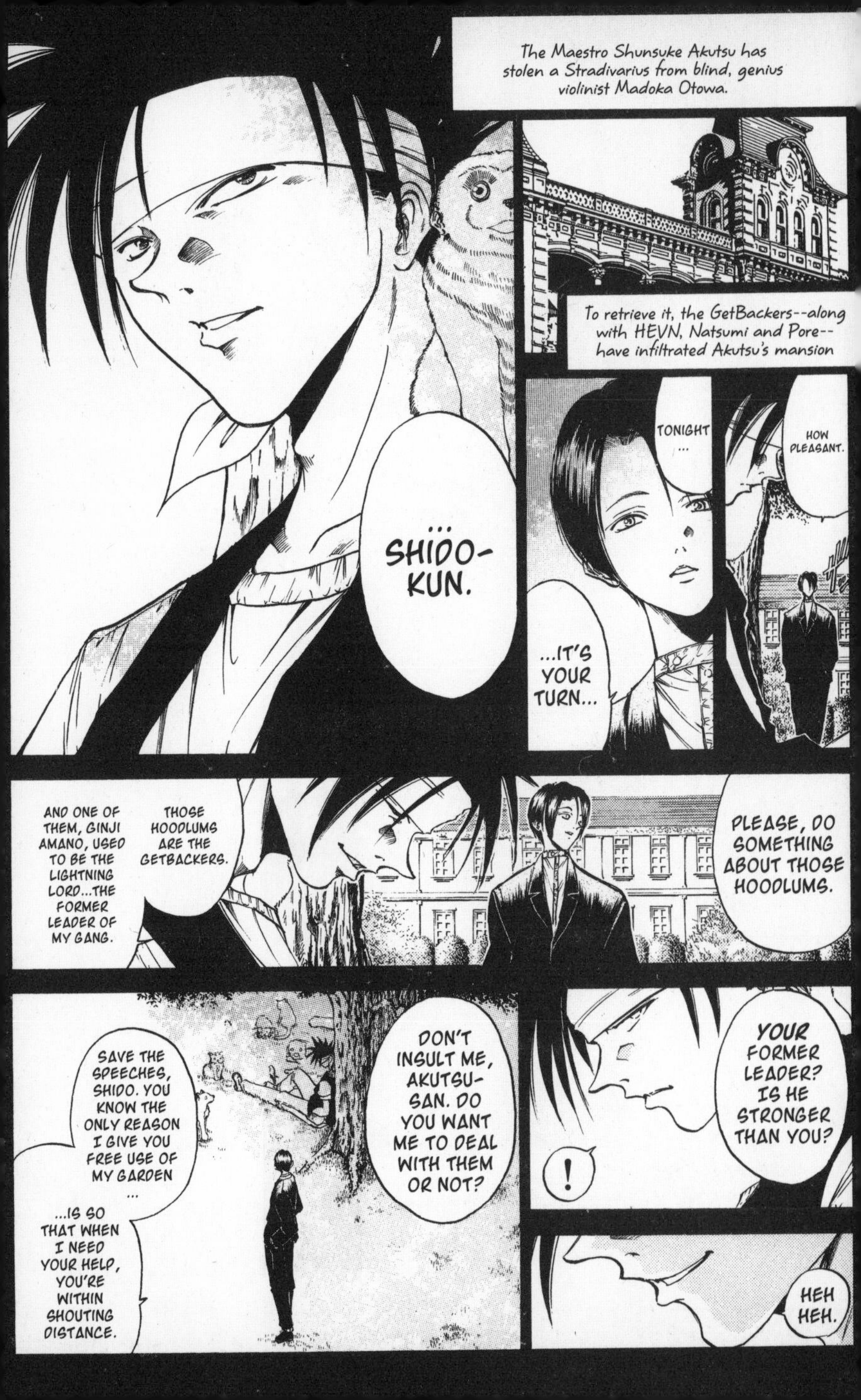
The Maestro Shunsuke Akutsu has stolen a Stradivarius from blind, genius violinist Madoka Otowa.
To retrieve it, the GetBackers--along with HEVN, Natsumi and Pore--have infiltrated Akutsu's mansion
HOW PLEASANT.
TONIGHT...
...IT'S YOUR TURN...
...SHIDO-KUN.
PLEASE, DO SOMETHING ABOUT THOSE HOODLUMS.
THOSE HOODLUMS ARE THE GETBACKERS.
AND ONE OF THEM, GINJI AMANO, USED TO BE THE LIGHTNING LORD...THE FORMER LEADER OF MY GANG.
YOUR FORMER LEADER? IS HE STRONGER THAN YOU?
!
HEH HEH.
DON'T INSULT ME, AKUTSU-SAN. DO YOU WANT ME TO DEAL WITH THEM OR NOT?
SAVE THE SPEECHES, SHIDO. YOU KNOW THE ONLY REASON I GIVE YOU FREE USE OF MY GARDEN...
...IS SO THAT WHEN I NEED YOUR HELP, YOU'RE WITHIN SHOUTING DISTANCE.

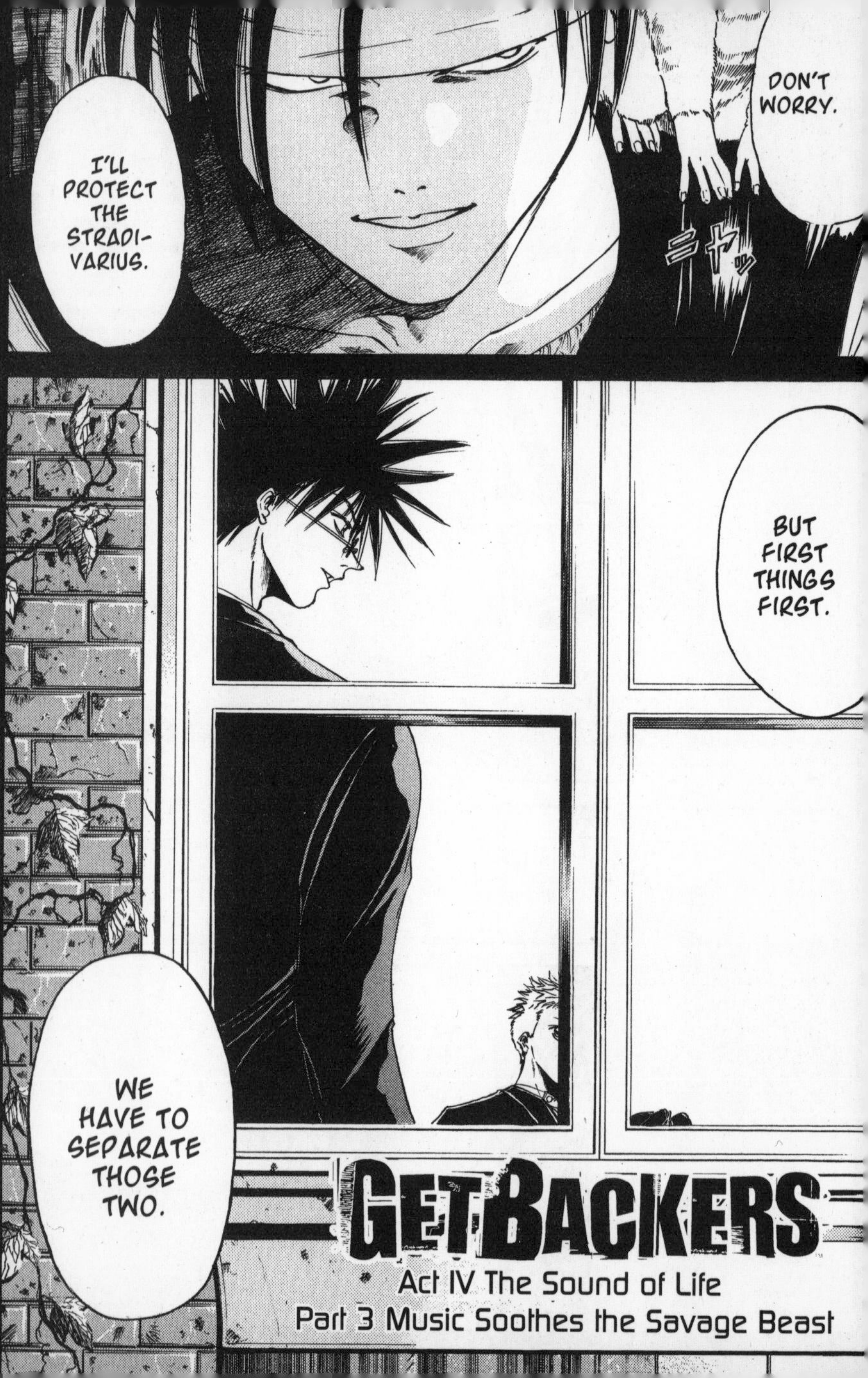
DON'T WORRY.
I'LL PROTECT THE STRADI-VARIUS.
ニヤッ
BUT FIRST THINGS FIRST.
WE HAVE TO SEPARATE THOSE TWO.
GETBACKERS
Act IV The Sound of Life
Part 3 Music Soothes the Savage Beast

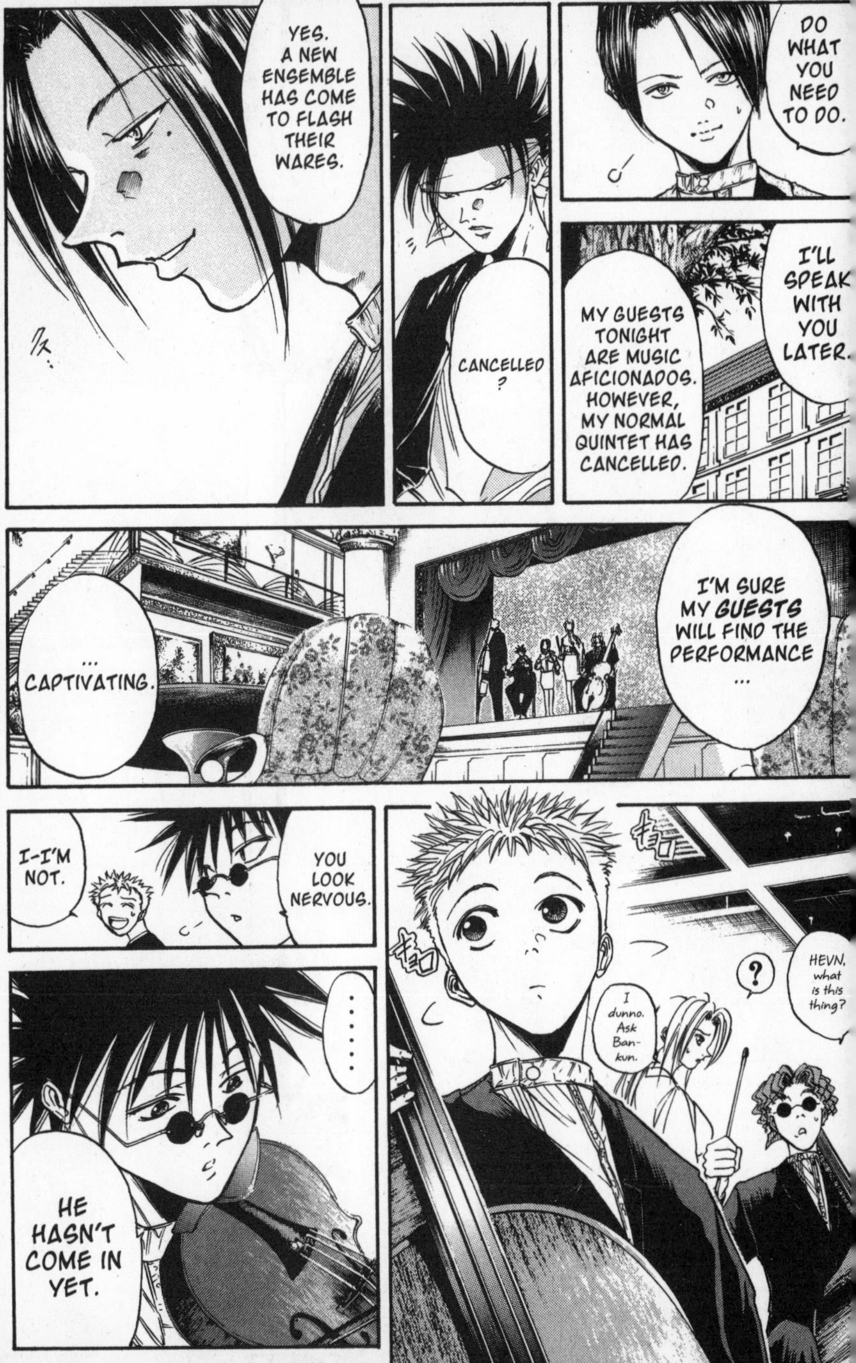
DO WHAT YOU NEED TO DO.
I'LL SPEAK WITH YOU LATER.
MY GUESTS TONIGHT ARE MUSIC AFICIONADOS. HOWEVER, MY NORMAL QUINTET HAS CANCELLED.
CANCELLED?
YES. A NEW ENSEMBLE HAS COME TO FLASH THEIR WARES.
I'M SURE MY **GUESTS** WILL FIND THE PERFORMANCE ...
... CAPTIVATING.
HEVN, what is this thing?
?
I dunno. Ask Ban-kun.
YOU LOOK NERVOUS.
I-I'M NOT.
......
HE HASN'T COME IN YET.

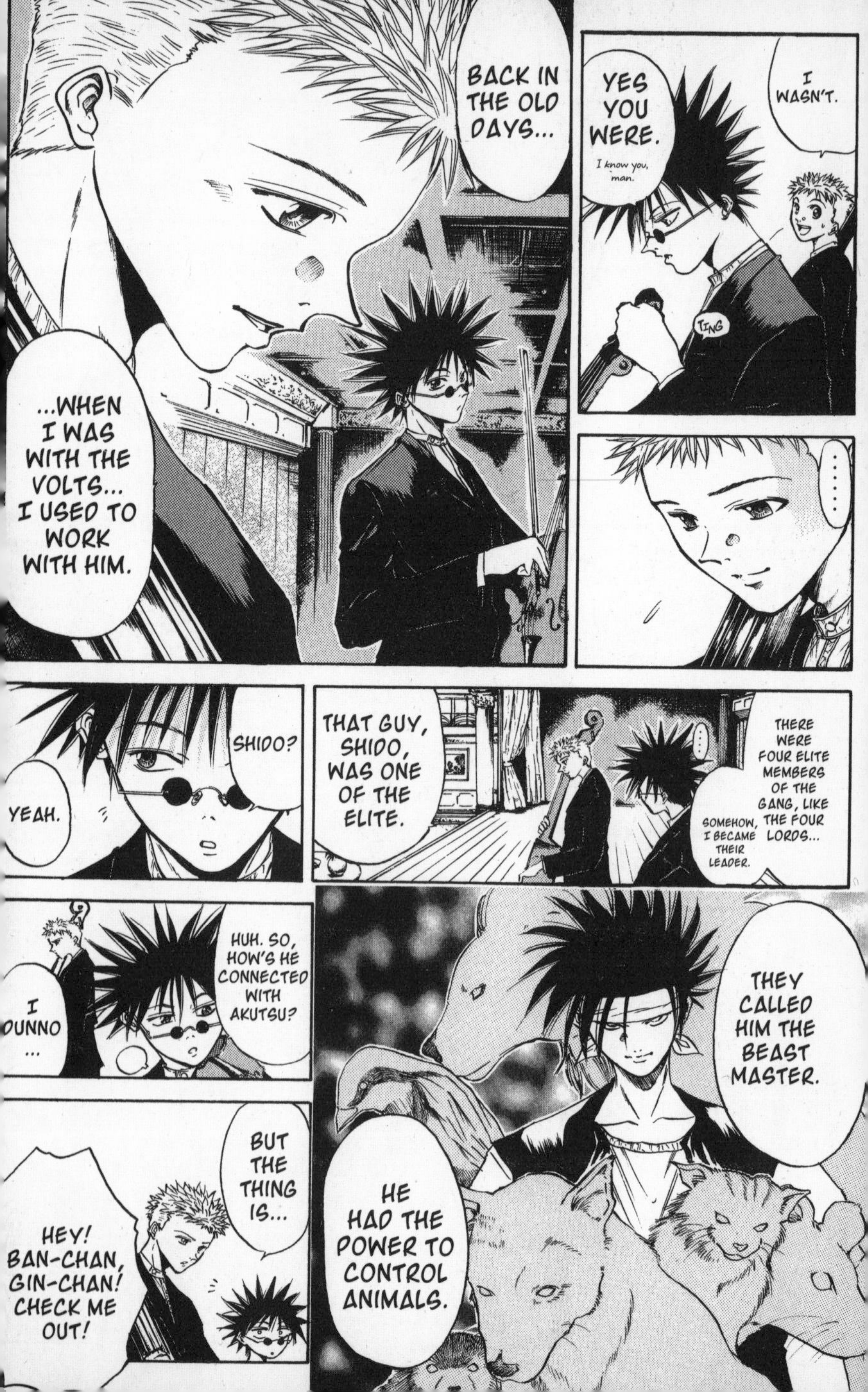
I WASN'T.
YES YOU WERE.
I know you, man.
TING
......
BACK IN THE OLD DAYS...
...WHEN I WAS WITH THE VOLTS... I USED TO WORK WITH HIM.
...
THERE WERE FOUR ELITE MEMBERS OF THE GANG, LIKE THE FOUR LORDS...
SOMEHOW, I BECAME THEIR LEADER.
THAT GUY, SHIDO, WAS ONE OF THE ELITE.
SHIDO?
YEAH.
THEY CALLED HIM THE BEAST MASTER.
HE HAD THE POWER TO CONTROL ANIMALS.
HUH. SO, HOW'S HE CONNECTED WITH AKUTSU?
I DUNNO ...
BUT THE THING IS...
HEY! BAN-CHAN, GIN-CHAN! CHECK ME OUT!

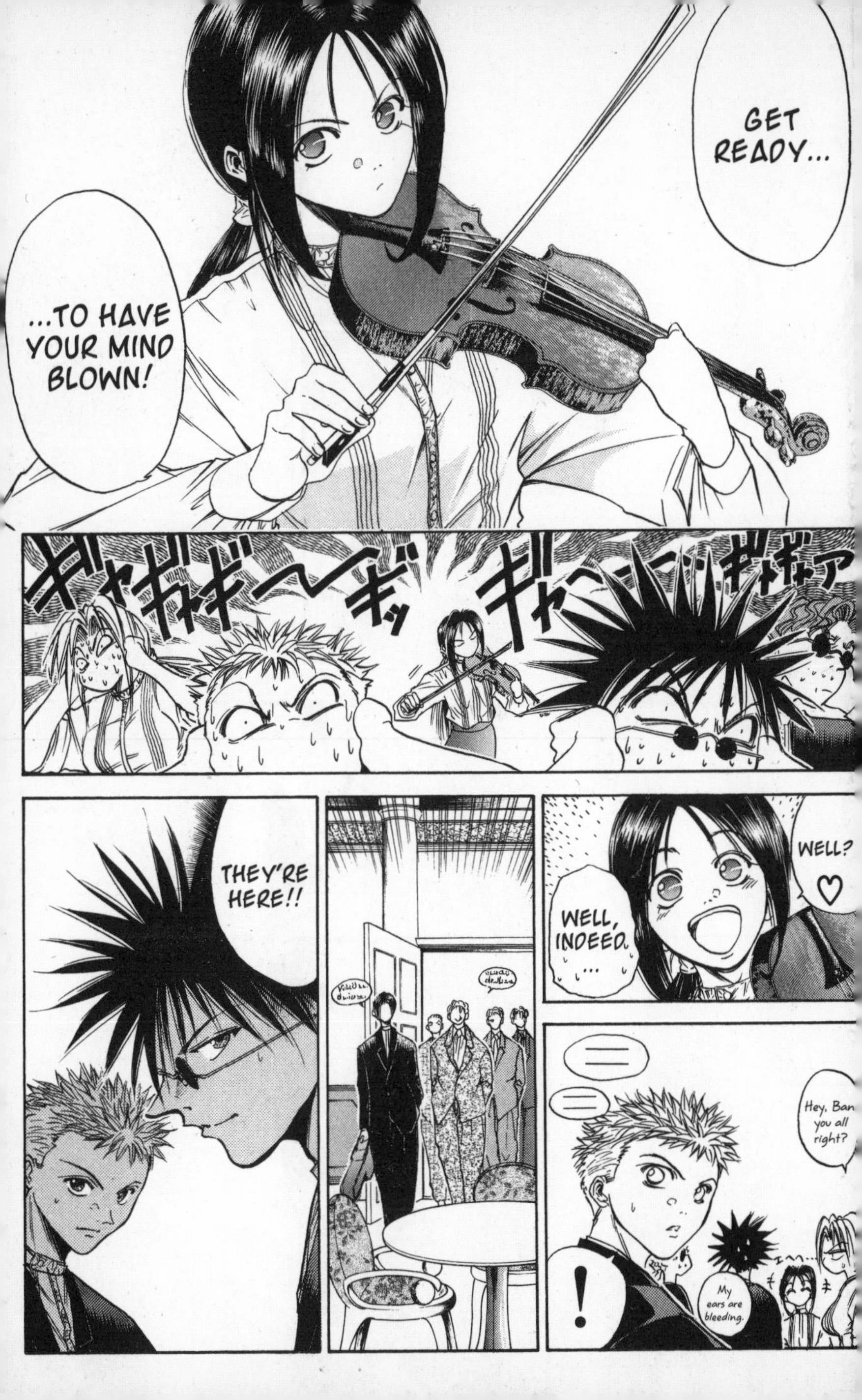
GET READY...
...TO HAVE YOUR MIND BLOWN!
WELL? ♥
WELL, INDEED...
Hey, Ban you all right?
!
My ears are bleeding.
エへ…
THEY'RE HERE!!

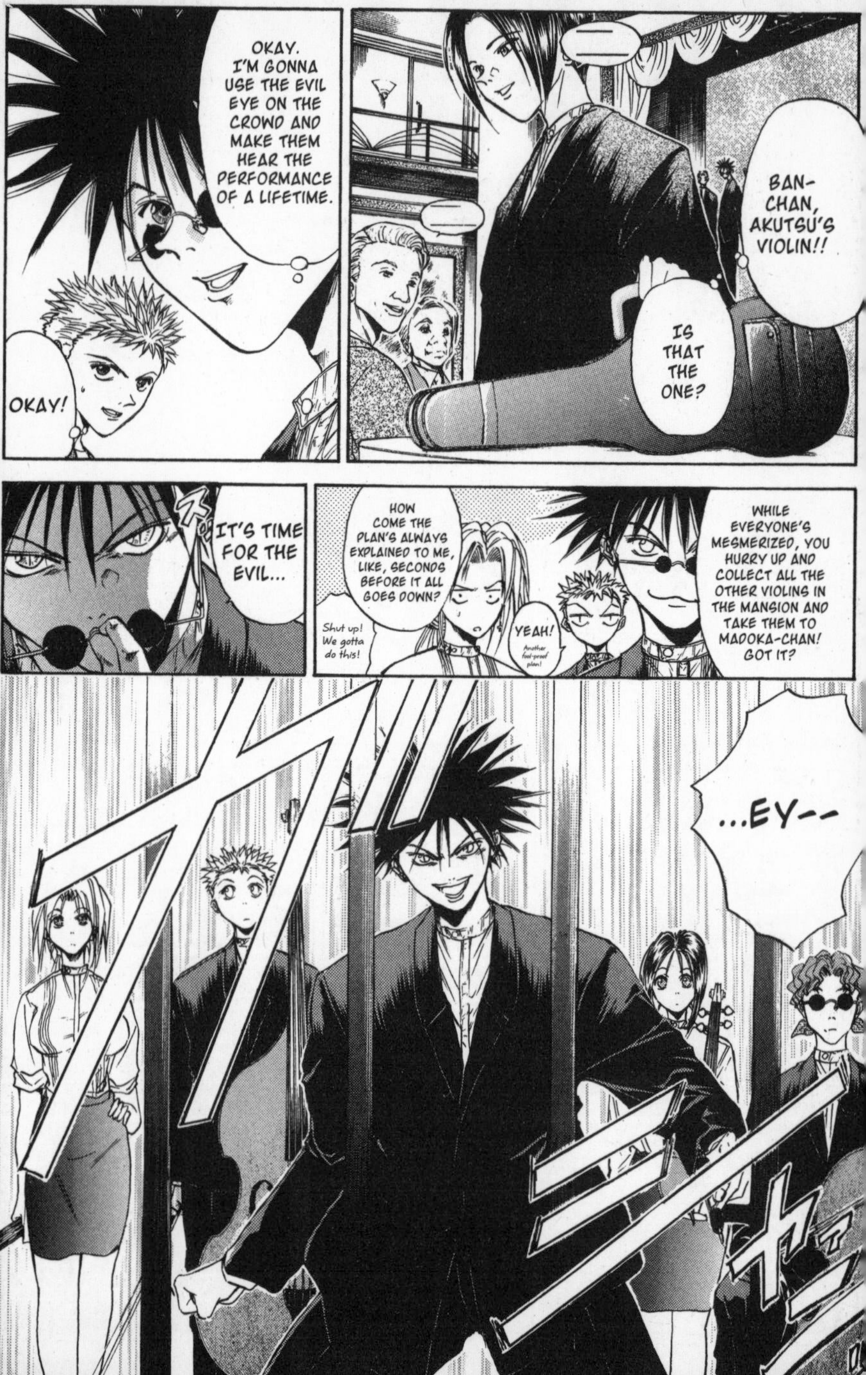
BAN-CHAN, AKUTSU'S VIOLIN!!
IS THAT THE ONE?
OKAY. I'M GONNA USE THE EVIL EYE ON THE CROWD AND MAKE THEM HEAR THE PERFORMANCE OF A LIFETIME.
OKAY!
WHILE EVERYONE'S MESMERIZED, YOU HURRY UP AND COLLECT ALL THE OTHER VIOLINS IN THE MANSION AND TAKE THEM TO MADOKA-CHAN! GOT IT?
HOW COME THE PLAN'S ALWAYS EXPLAINED TO ME, LIKE, SECONDS BEFORE IT ALL GOES DOWN?
YEAH!
Another fool-proof plan!
Shut up! We gotta do this!
IT'S TIME FOR THE EVIL...
...EY--

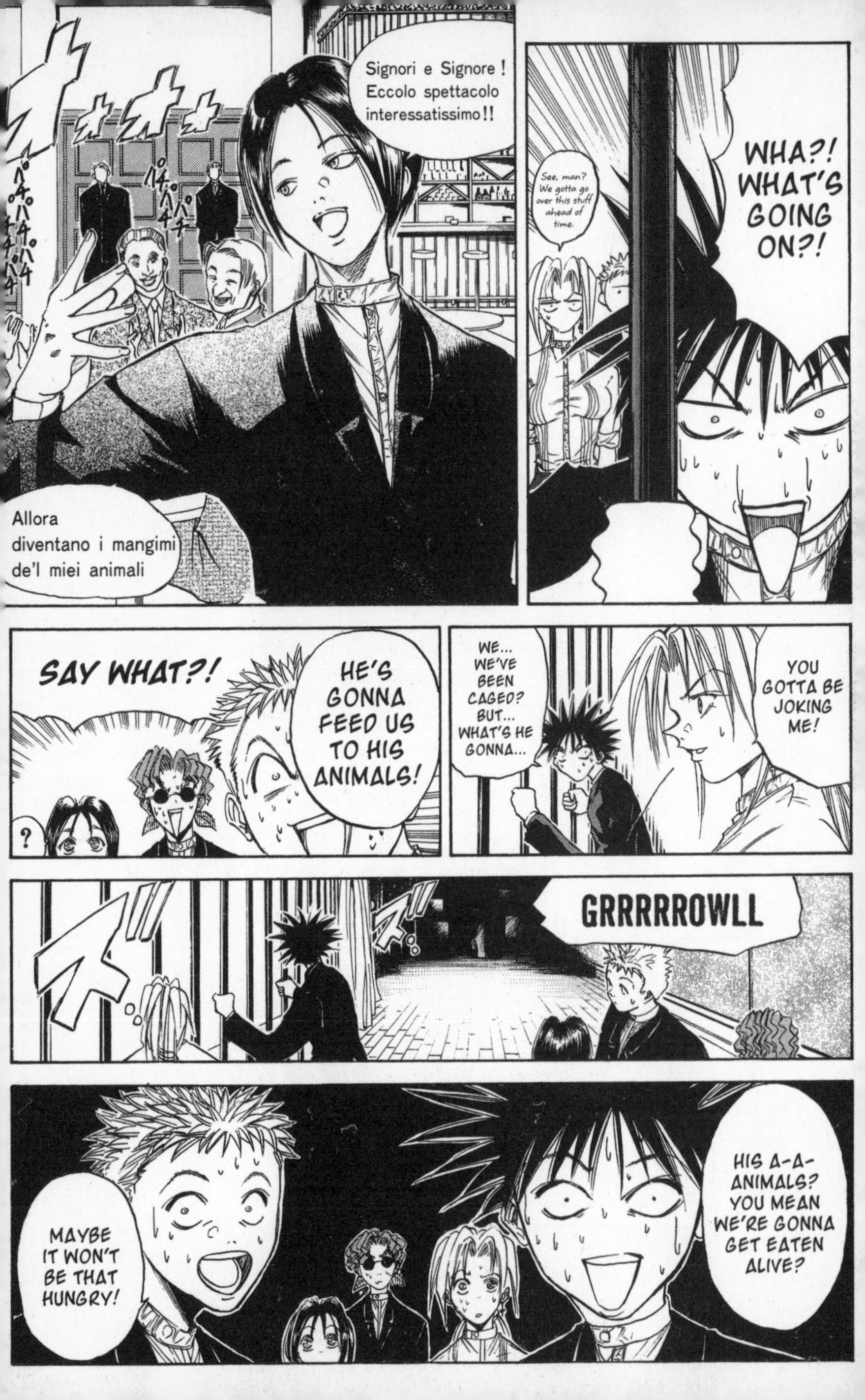
WHA?! WHAT'S GOING ON?!
See, man? We gotta go over this stuff ahead of time.
Signori e Signore! Eccolo spettacolo interessatissimo!!
Allora diventano i mangimi de'l miei animali
YOU GOTTA BE JOKING ME!
WE... WE'VE BEEN CAGED? BUT... WHAT'S HE GONNA...
HE'S GONNA FEED US TO HIS ANIMALS!
SAY WHAT?!
?
GRRRRROWLL
HIS A-A-ANIMALS? YOU MEAN WE'RE GONNA GET EATEN ALIVE?
MAYBE IT WON'T BE THAT HUNGRY!

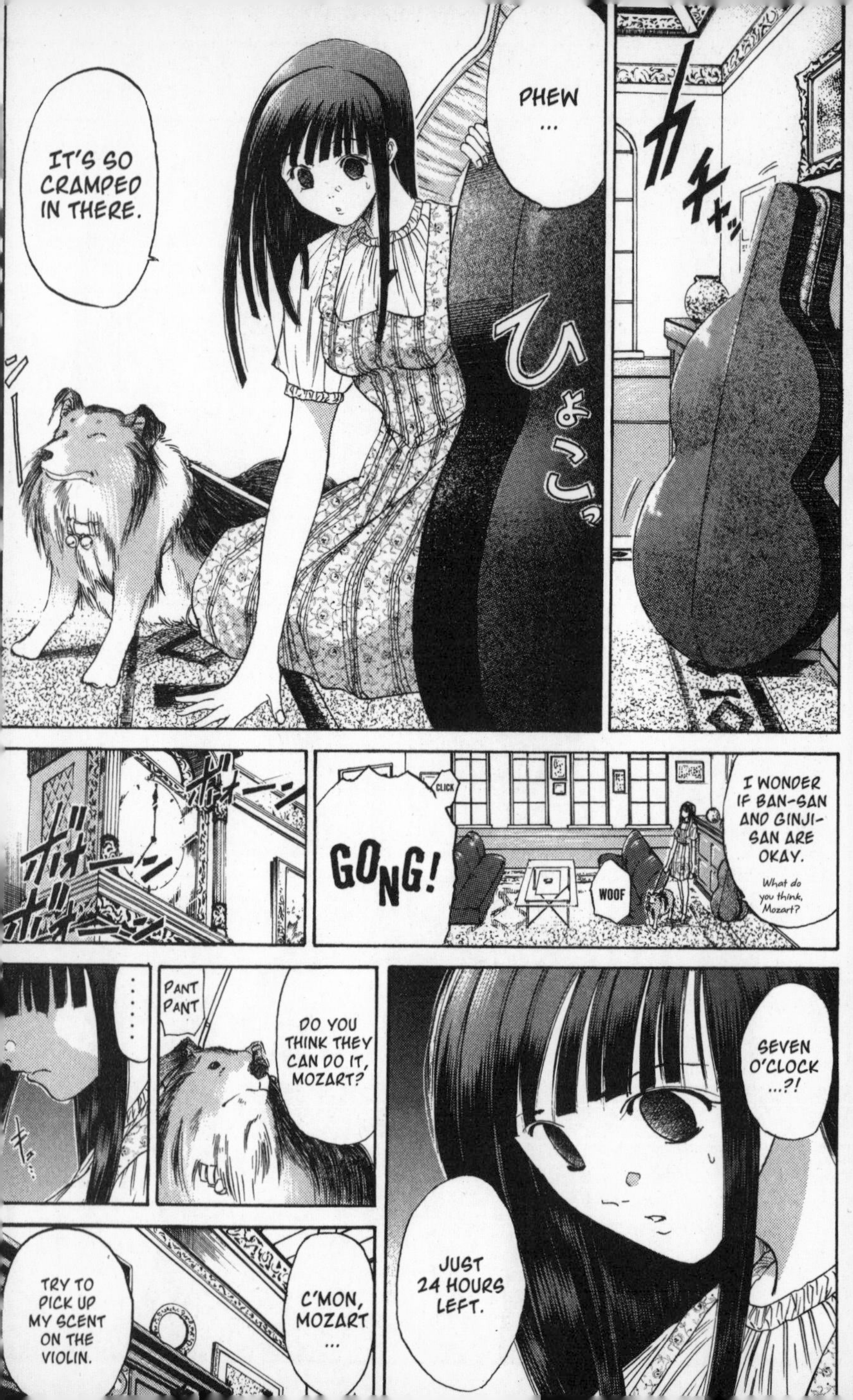
カチャッ
PHEW ...
IT'S SO CRAMPED IN THERE.
ひょこっ
I WONDER IF BAN-SAN AND GINJI-SAN ARE OKAY.
What do you think, Mozart?
WOOF
CLICK
GONG!
SEVEN O'CLOCK ...?!
JUST 24 HOURS LEFT.
DO YOU THINK THEY CAN DO IT, MOZART?
PANT PANT
......
C'MON, MOZART ...
TRY TO PICK UP MY SCENT ON THE VIOLIN.

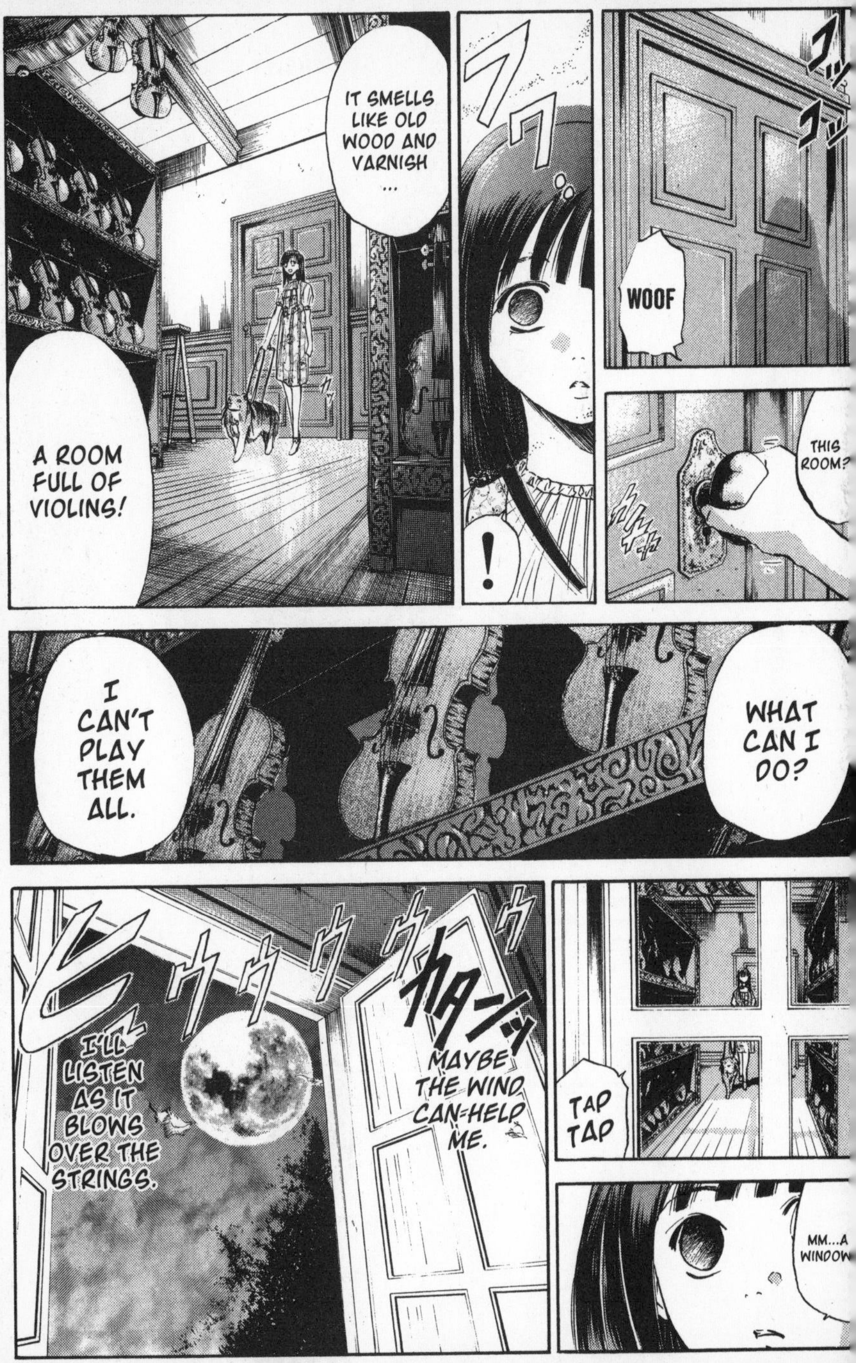
WOOF
THIS ROOM?
!
IT SMELLS LIKE OLD WOOD AND VARNISH ...
A ROOM FULL OF VIOLINS!
WHAT CAN I DO?
I CAN'T PLAY THEM ALL.
TAP TAP
MM...A WINDOW
MAYBE THE WIND CAN HELP ME.
I'LL LISTEN AS IT BLOWS OVER THE STRINGS.

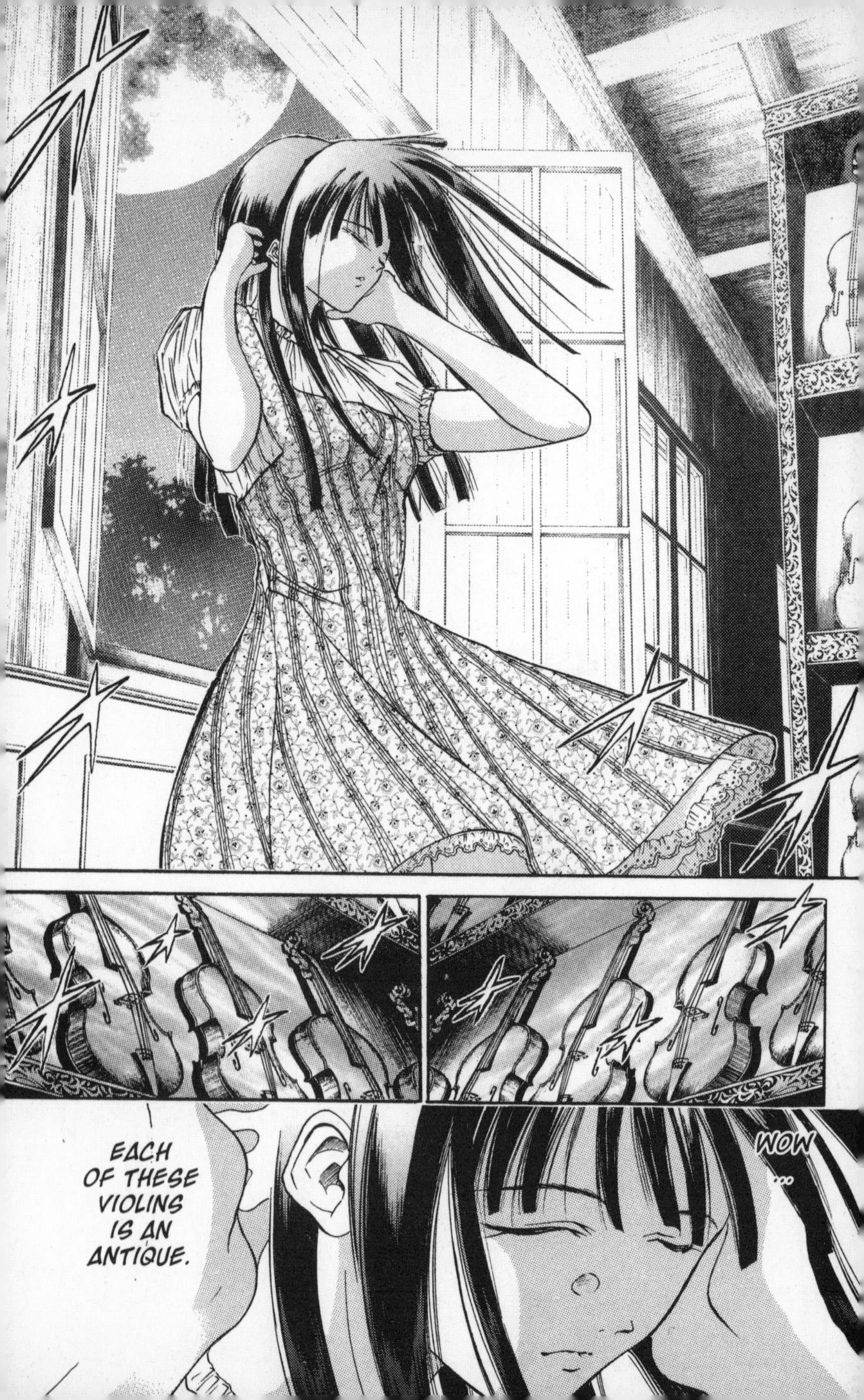
WOW ...
EACH OF THESE VIOLINS IS AN ANTIQUE.

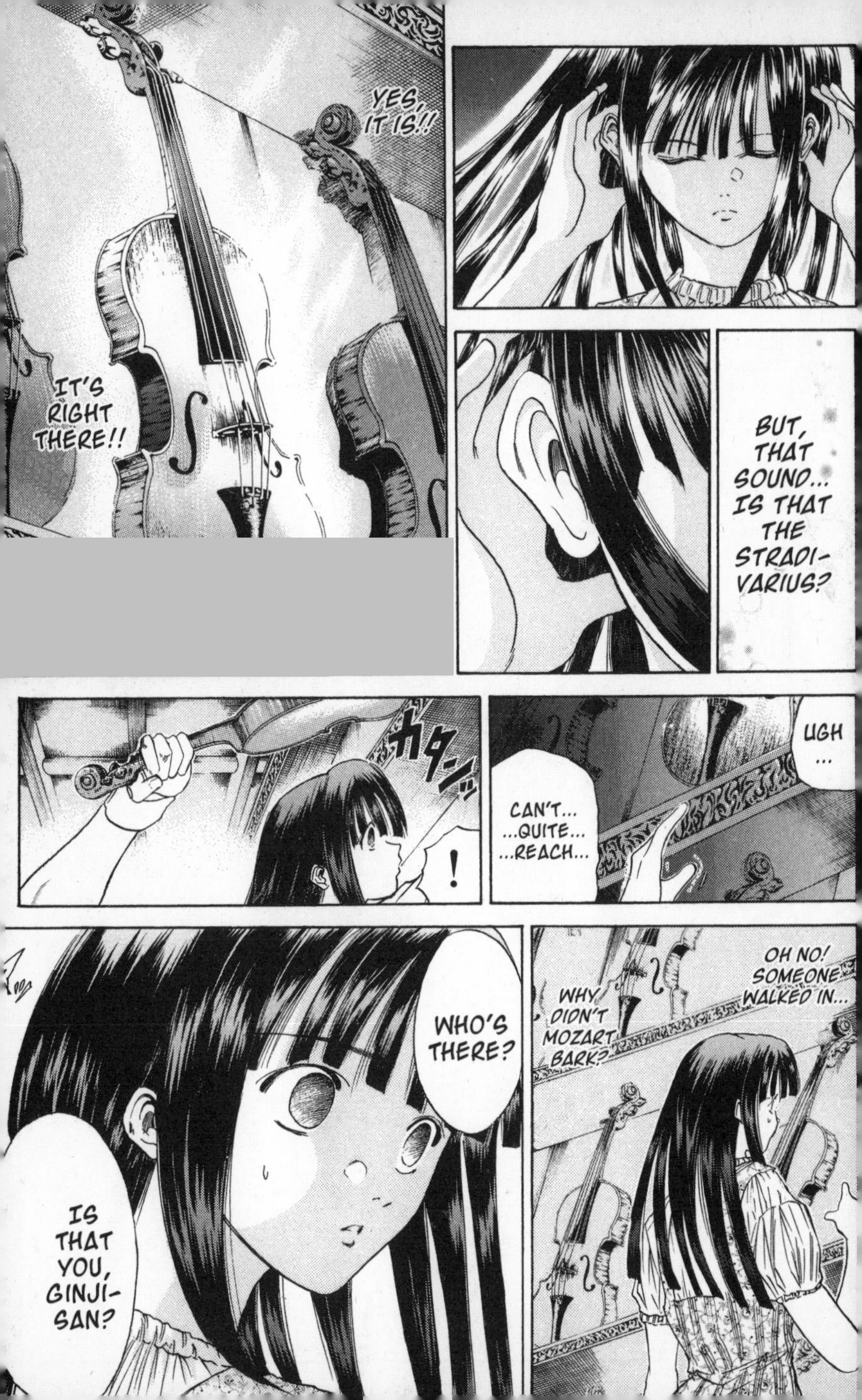
BUT, THAT SOUND... IS THAT THE STRADIVARIUS?
YES, IT IS!!
IT'S RIGHT THERE!!
UGH ...
CAN'T... ...QUITE... ...REACH...
カターンッ
!
OH NO! SOMEONE WALKED IN...
WHY DIDN'T MOZART BARK?
WHO'S THERE?
IS THAT YOU, GINJI-SAN?

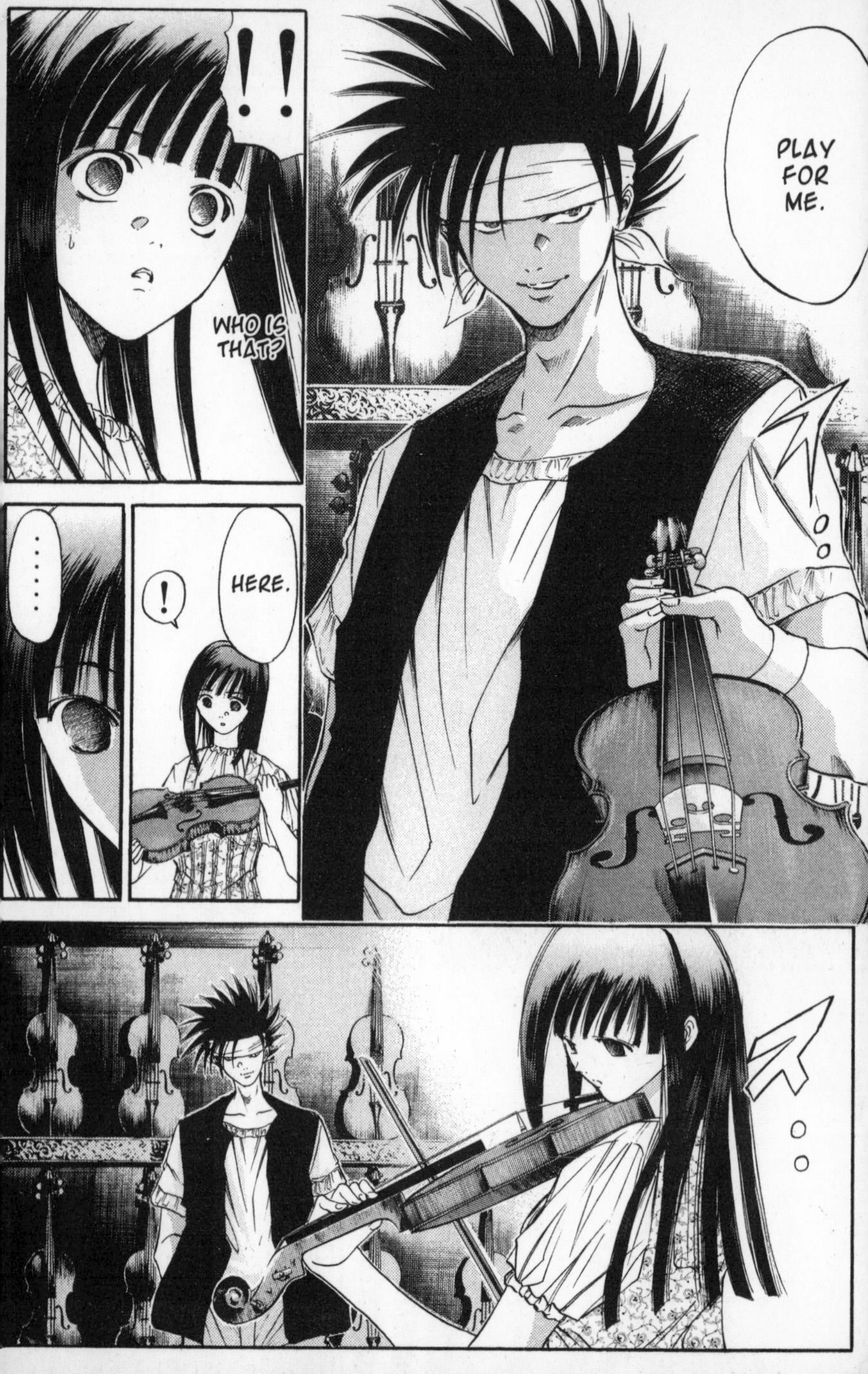
PLAY FOR ME.
!!
WHO IS THAT?
HERE.
!
......

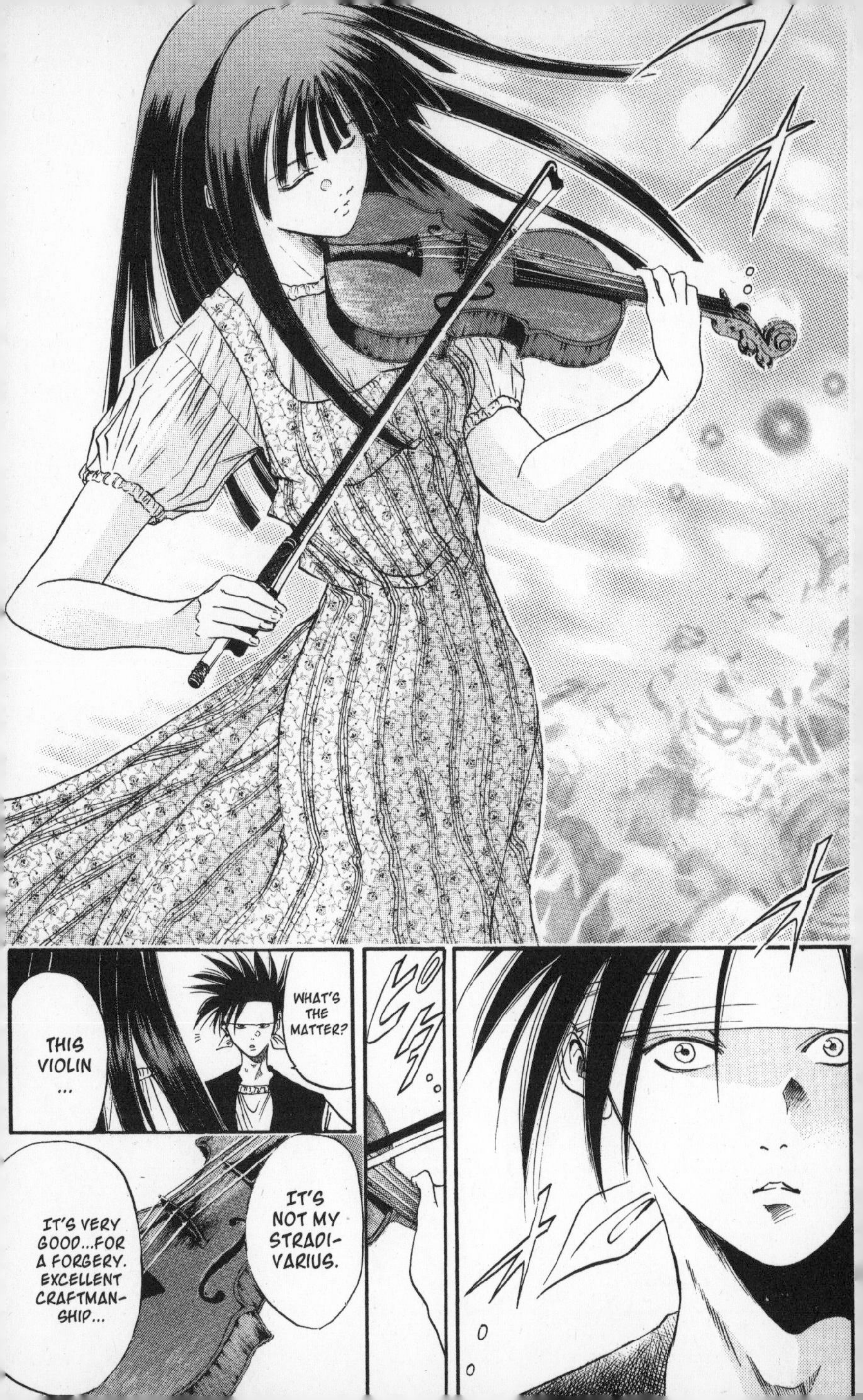
WHAT'S THE MATTER?
THIS VIOLIN ...
IT'S NOT MY STRADIVARIUS.
IT'S VERY GOOD...FOR A FORGERY. EXCELLENT CRAFTMANSHIP...

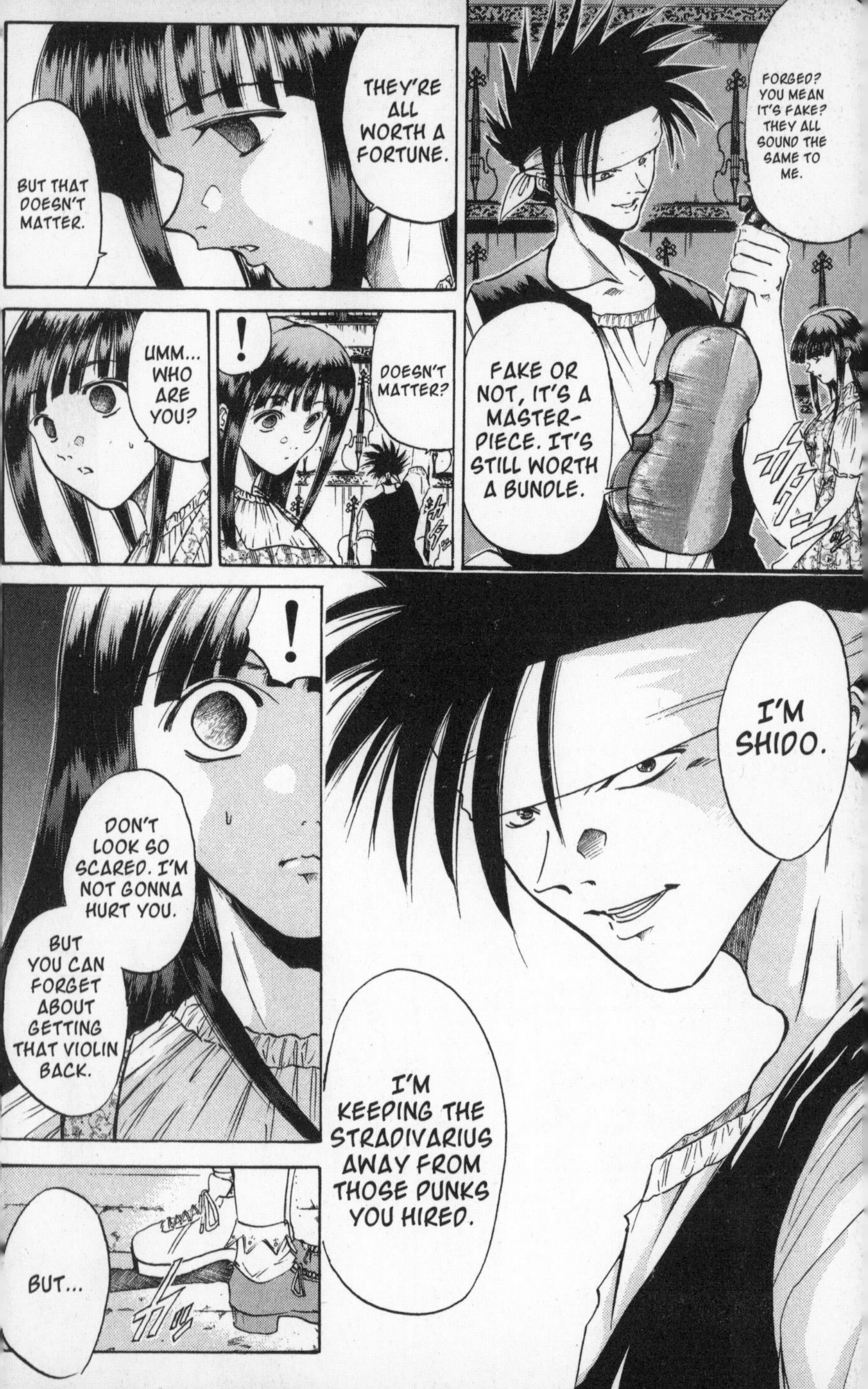
FORGED? YOU MEAN IT'S FAKE? THEY ALL SOUND THE SAME TO ME.
FAKE OR NOT, IT'S A MASTER-PIECE. IT'S STILL WORTH A BUNDLE.
THEY'RE ALL WORTH A FORTUNE.
BUT THAT DOESN'T MATTER.
!
DOESN'T MATTER?
UMM... WHO ARE YOU?
I'M SHIDO.
!
DON'T LOOK SO SCARED. I'M NOT GONNA HURT YOU.
BUT YOU CAN FORGET ABOUT GETTING THAT VIOLIN BACK.
I'M KEEPING THE STRADIVARIUS AWAY FROM THOSE PUNKS YOU HIRED.
BUT...

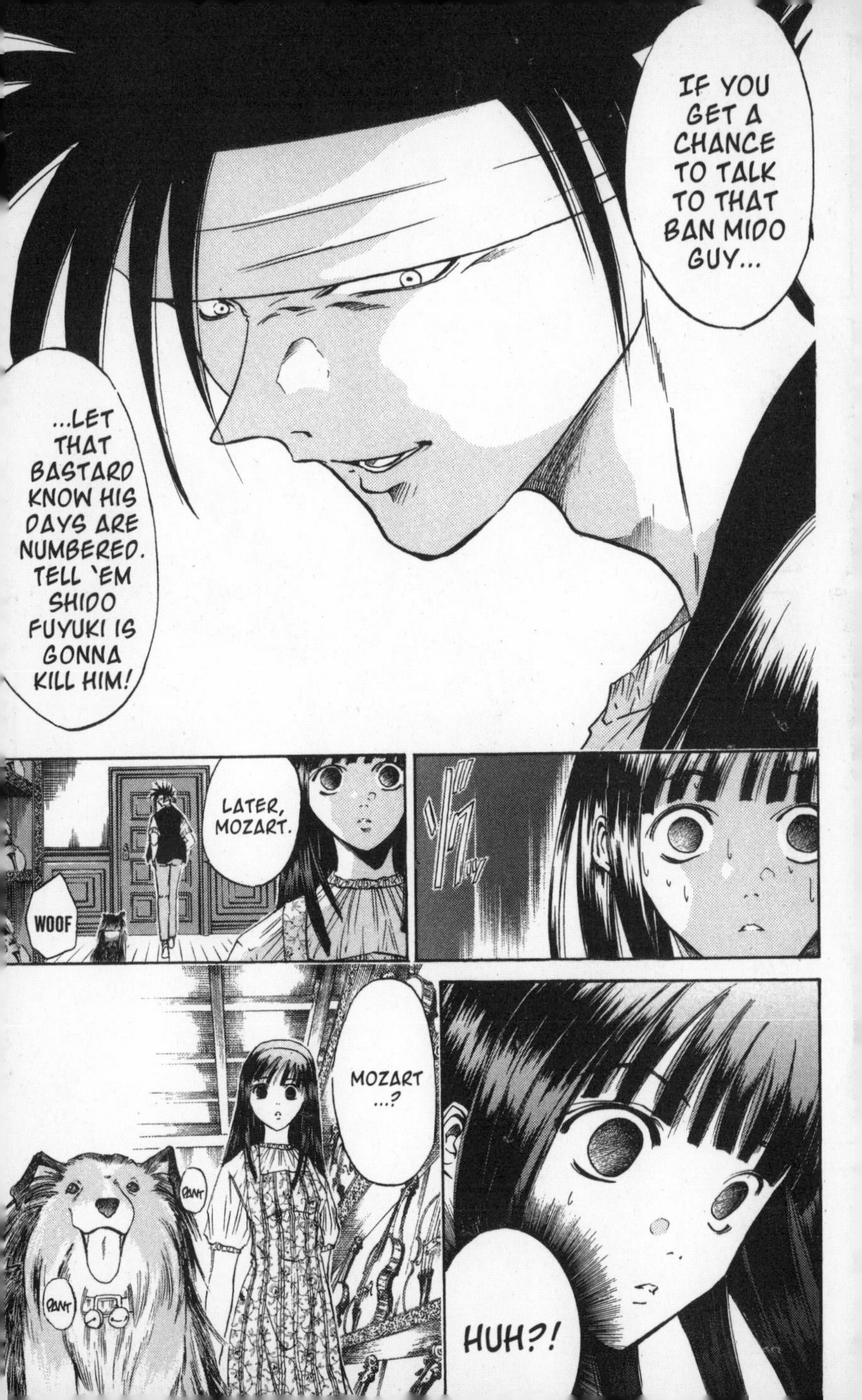
IF YOU GET A CHANCE TO TALK TO THAT BAN MIDO GUY...
...LET THAT BASTARD KNOW HIS DAYS ARE NUMBERED. TELL 'EM SHIDO FUYUKI IS GONNA KILL HIM!
LATER, MOZART.
WOOF
HUH?!
MOZART ...?
PANT
PANT

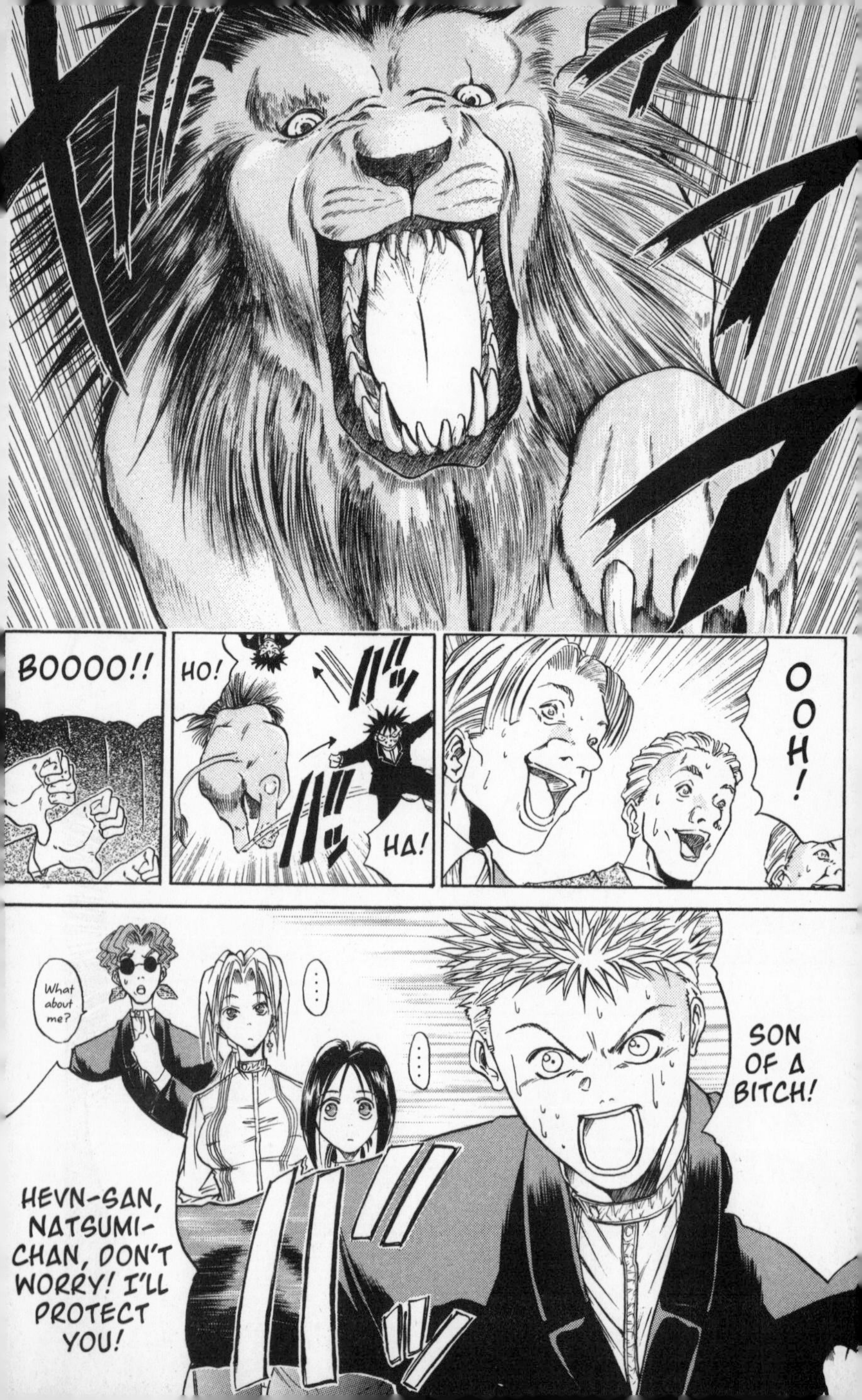
OOH!
HO!
HA!
BOOOO!!
SON OF A BITCH!
HEVN-SAN, NATSUMI-CHAN, DON'T WORRY! I'LL PROTECT YOU!
...
...
What about me?

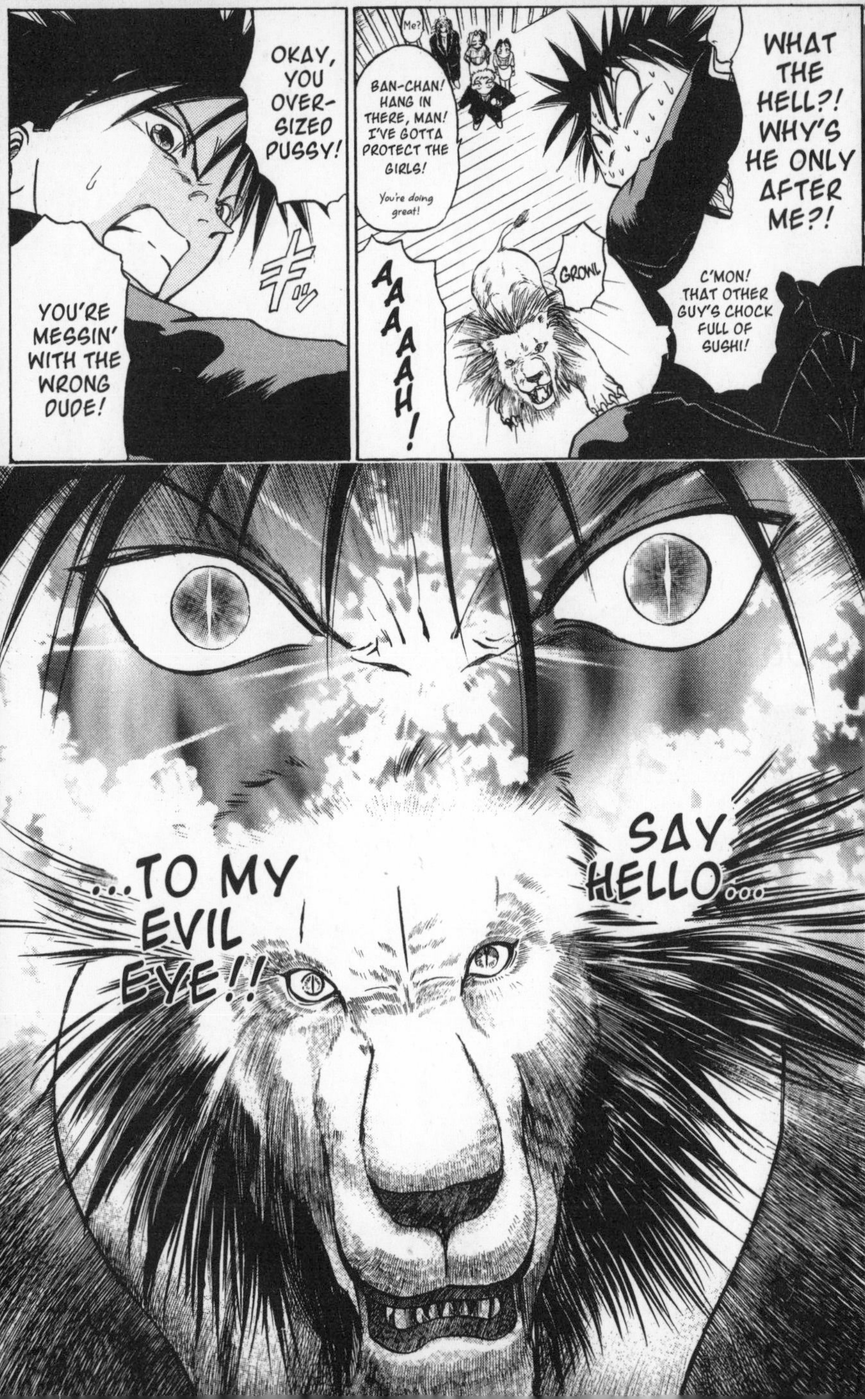
WHAT THE HELL?! WHY'S HE ONLY AFTER ME?!
Me?
BAN-CHAN! HANG IN THERE, MAN! I'VE GOTTA PROTECT THE GIRLS!
You're doing great!
C'MON! THAT OTHER GUY'S CHOCK FULL OF SUSHI!
GROWL
AAAAAAH!
OKAY, YOU OVER-SIZED PUSSY!
ギッ
YOU'RE MESSIN' WITH THE WRONG DUDE!
SAY HELLO...
...TO MY EVIL EYE!!

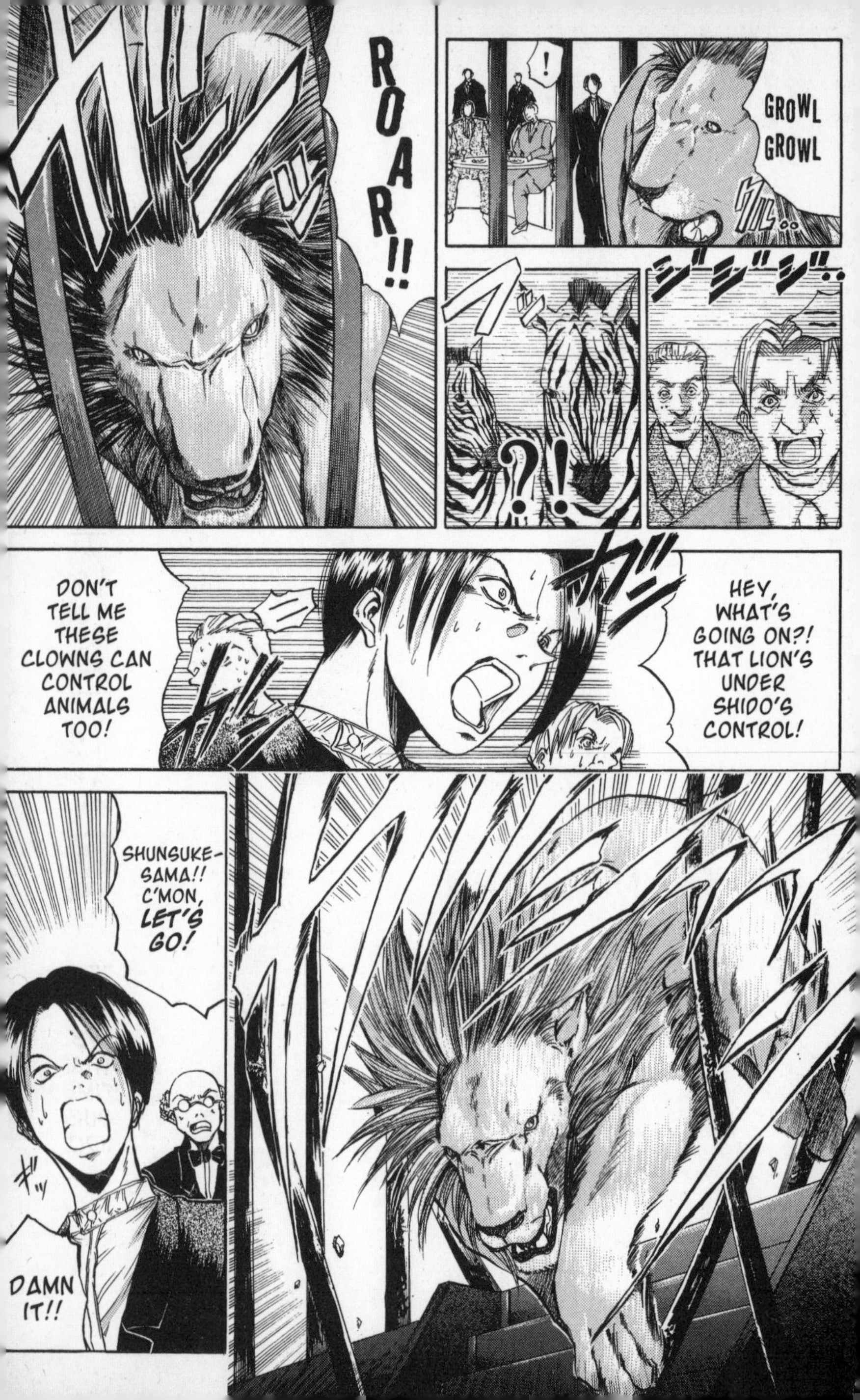
!
GROWL GROWL
?!
!
ROAR!!
HEY, WHAT'S GOING ON?! THAT LION'S UNDER SHIDO'S CONTROL!
DON'T TELL ME THESE CLOWNS CAN CONTROL ANIMALS TOO!
SHUNSUKE-SAMA!! C'MON, LET'S GO!
DAMN IT!!

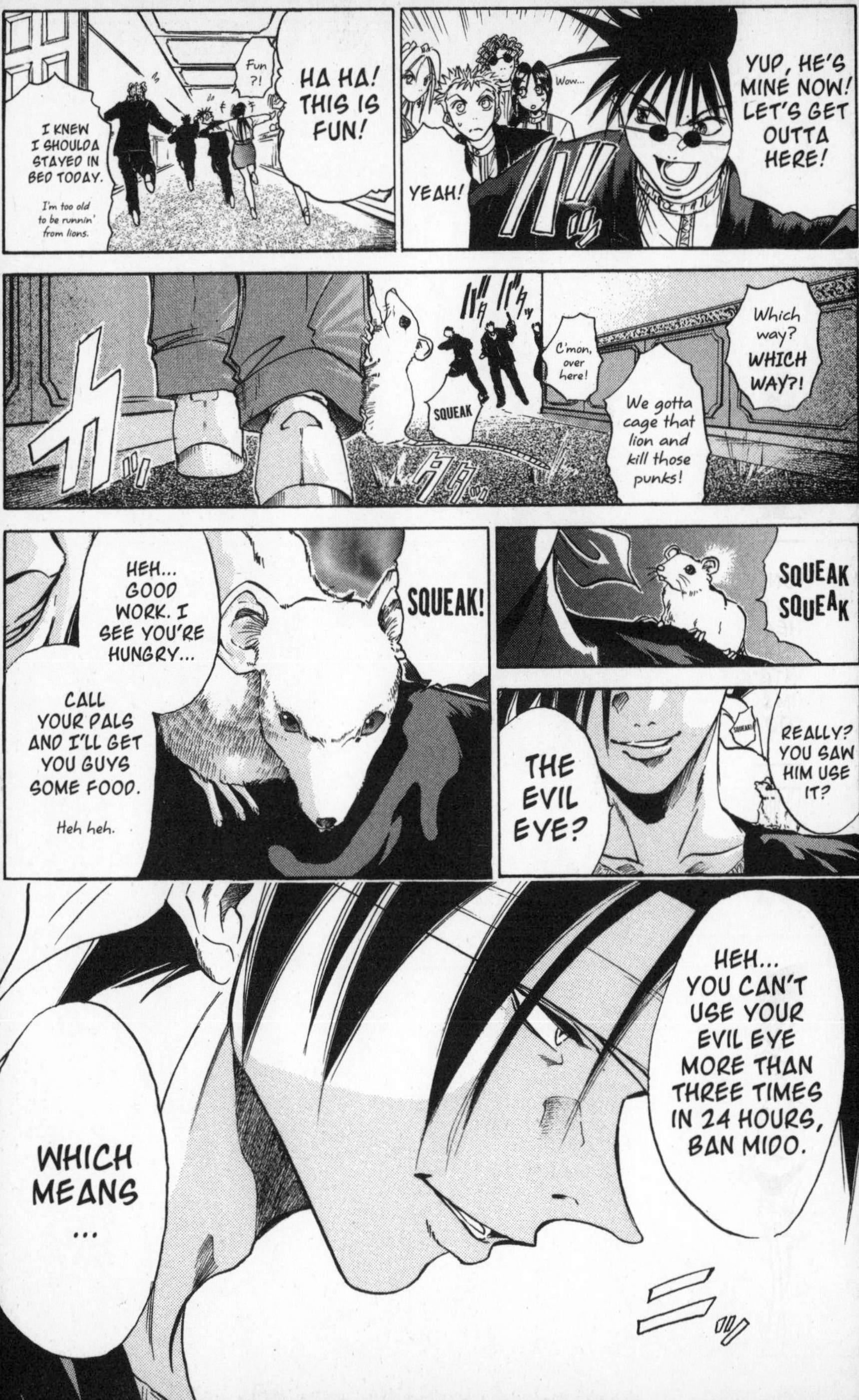
YUP, HE'S MINE NOW! LET'S GET OUTTA HERE!
Wow...
YEAH!
HA HA! THIS IS FUN!
Fun ?!
I KNEW I SHOULDA STAYED IN BED TODAY.
I'm too old to be runnin' from lions.
Which way? WHICH WAY?!
C'mon, over here!
We gotta cage that lion and kill those punks!
SQUEAK
SQUEAK SQUEAK
REALLY? YOU SAW HIM USE IT?
THE EVIL EYE?
SQUEAK!
HEH... GOOD WORK. I SEE YOU'RE HUNGRY...
CALL YOUR PALS AND I'LL GET YOU GUYS SOME FOOD.
Heh heh.
HEH... YOU CAN'T USE YOUR EVIL EYE MORE THAN THREE TIMES IN 24 HOURS, BAN MIDO.
WHICH MEANS ...

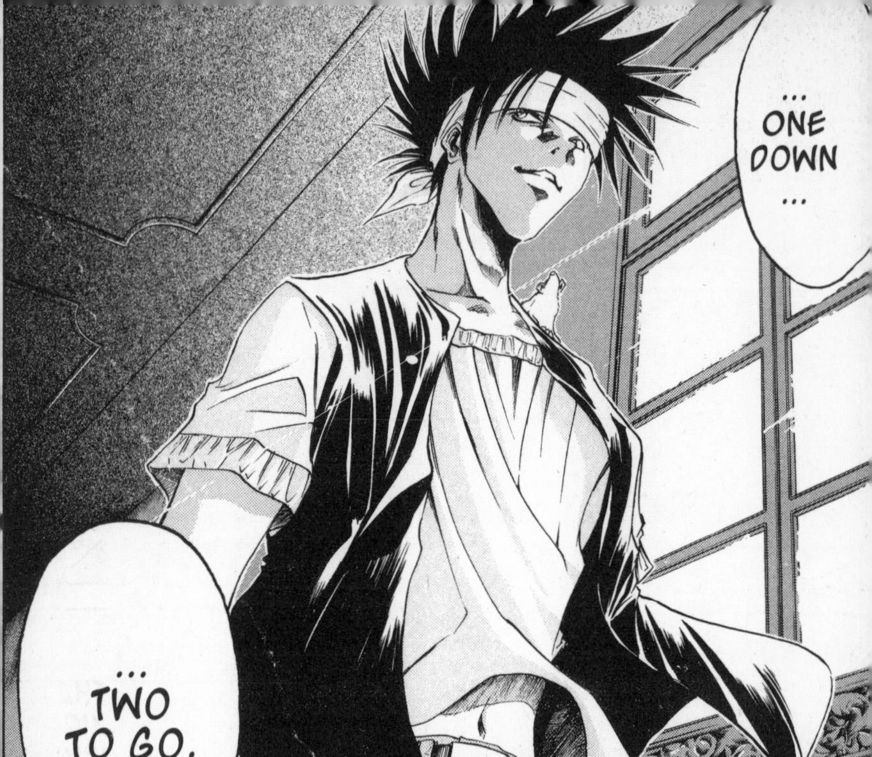
... ONE DOWN ...
... TWO TO GO.
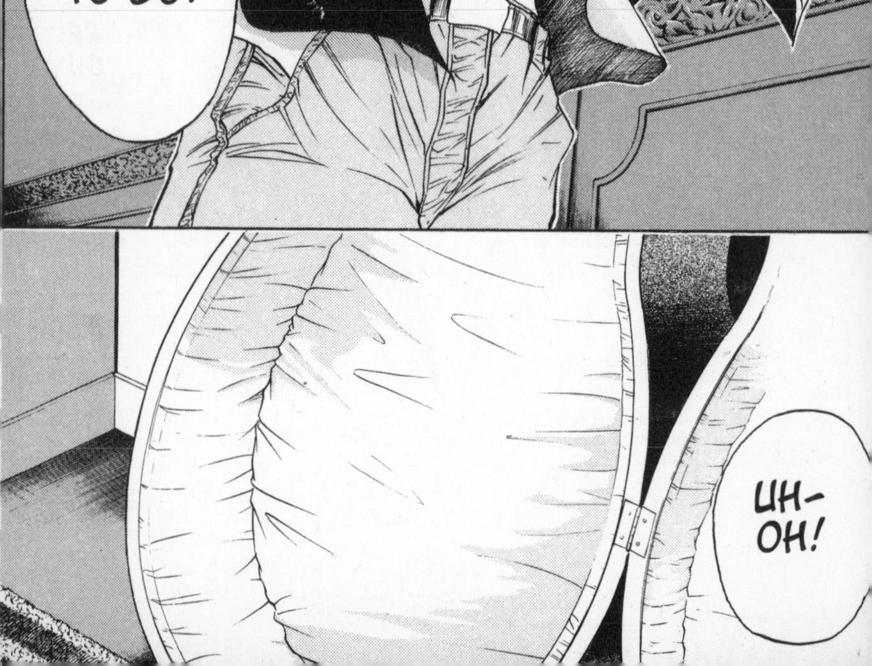
UH-OH!

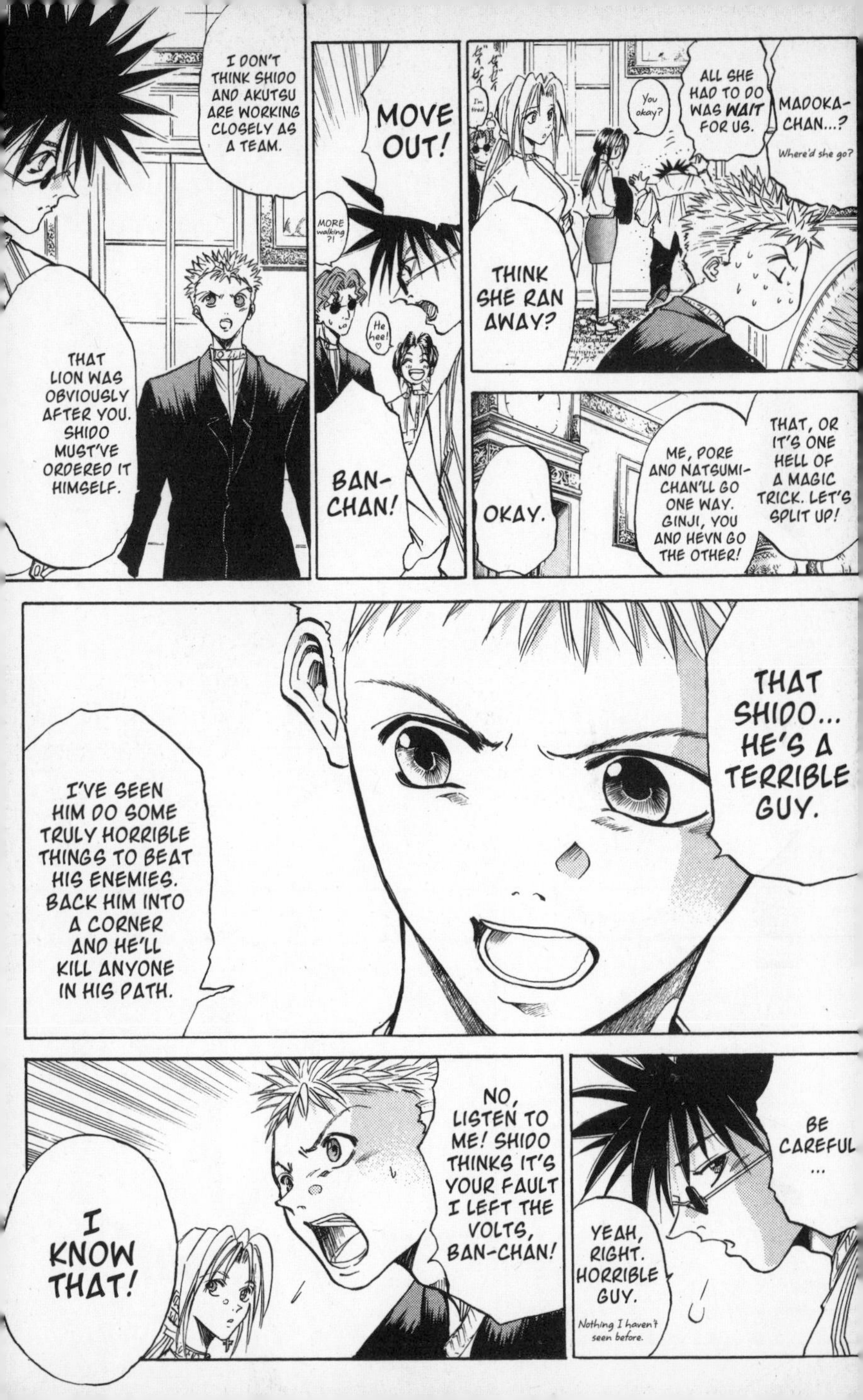

MADOKA-CHAN...?
Where'd she go?
ALL SHE HAD TO DO WAS WAIT FOR US.
You okay?
I'm tired.
THINK SHE RAN AWAY?
THAT, OR IT'S ONE HELL OF A MAGIC TRICK. LET'S SPLIT UP!
ME, PORE AND NATSUMI-CHAN'LL GO ONE WAY. GINJI, YOU AND HEVN GO THE OTHER!
OKAY.
MOVE OUT!
MORE walking?!
He hee!
BAN-CHAN!
I DON'T THINK SHIDO AND AKUTSU ARE WORKING CLOSELY AS A TEAM.
THAT LION WAS OBVIOUSLY AFTER YOU. SHIDO MUST'VE ORDERED IT HIMSELF.
THAT SHIDO... HE'S A TERRIBLE GUY.
I'VE SEEN HIM DO SOME TRULY HORRIBLE THINGS TO BEAT HIS ENEMIES. BACK HIM INTO A CORNER AND HE'LL KILL ANYONE IN HIS PATH.
BE CAREFUL...
YEAH, RIGHT. HORRIBLE GUY.
Nothing I haven't seen before.
NO, LISTEN TO ME! SHIDO THINKS IT'S YOUR FAULT I LEFT THE VOLTS, BAN-CHAN!
I KNOW THAT!

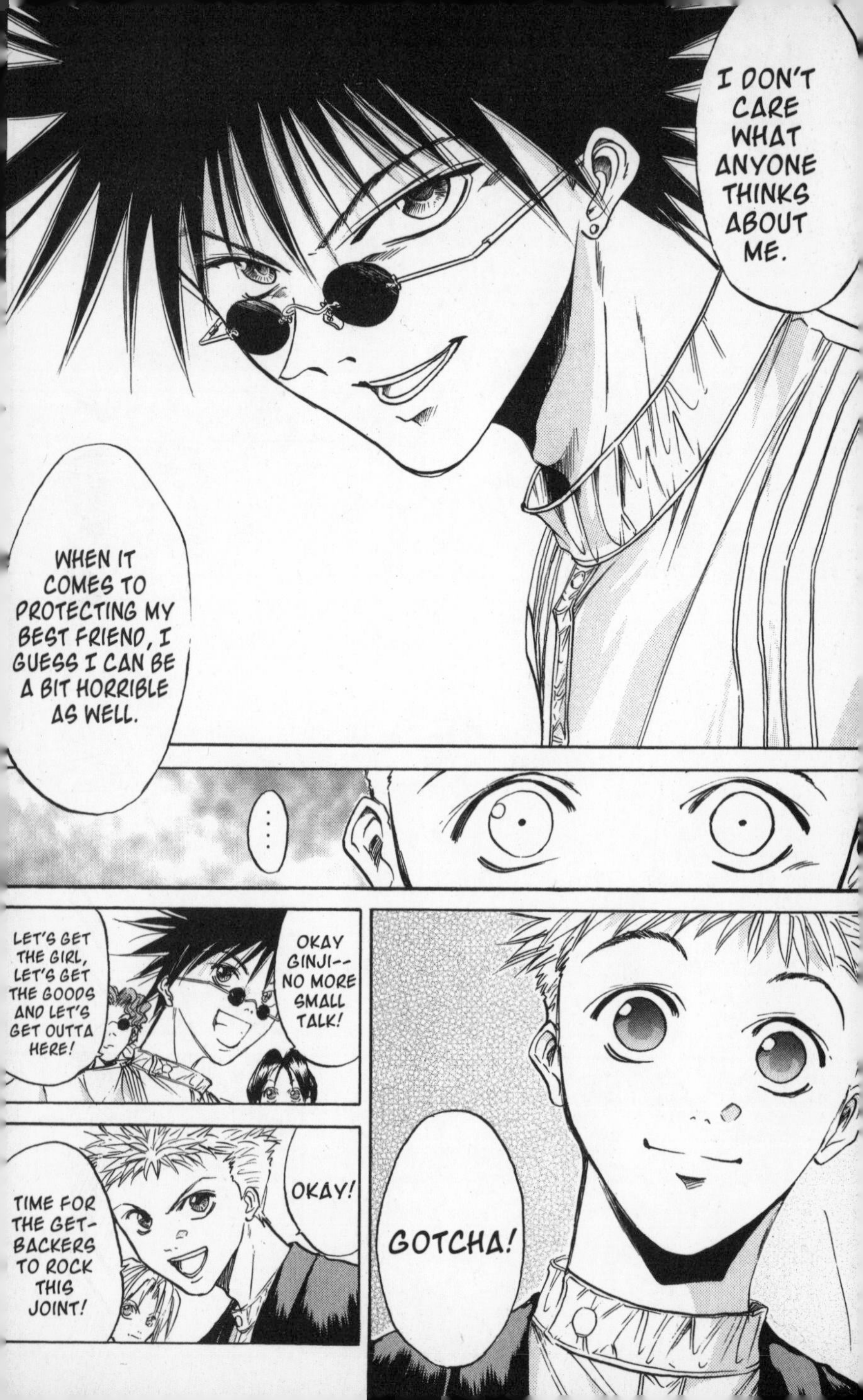
I DON'T CARE WHAT ANYONE THINKS ABOUT ME.
WHEN IT COMES TO PROTECTING MY BEST FRIEND, I GUESS I CAN BE A BIT HORRIBLE AS WELL.
....
GOTCHA!
OKAY GINJI-- NO MORE SMALL TALK!
LET'S GET THE GIRL, LET'S GET THE GOODS AND LET'S GET OUTTA HERE!
OKAY!
TIME FOR THE GET-BACKERS TO ROCK THIS JOINT!

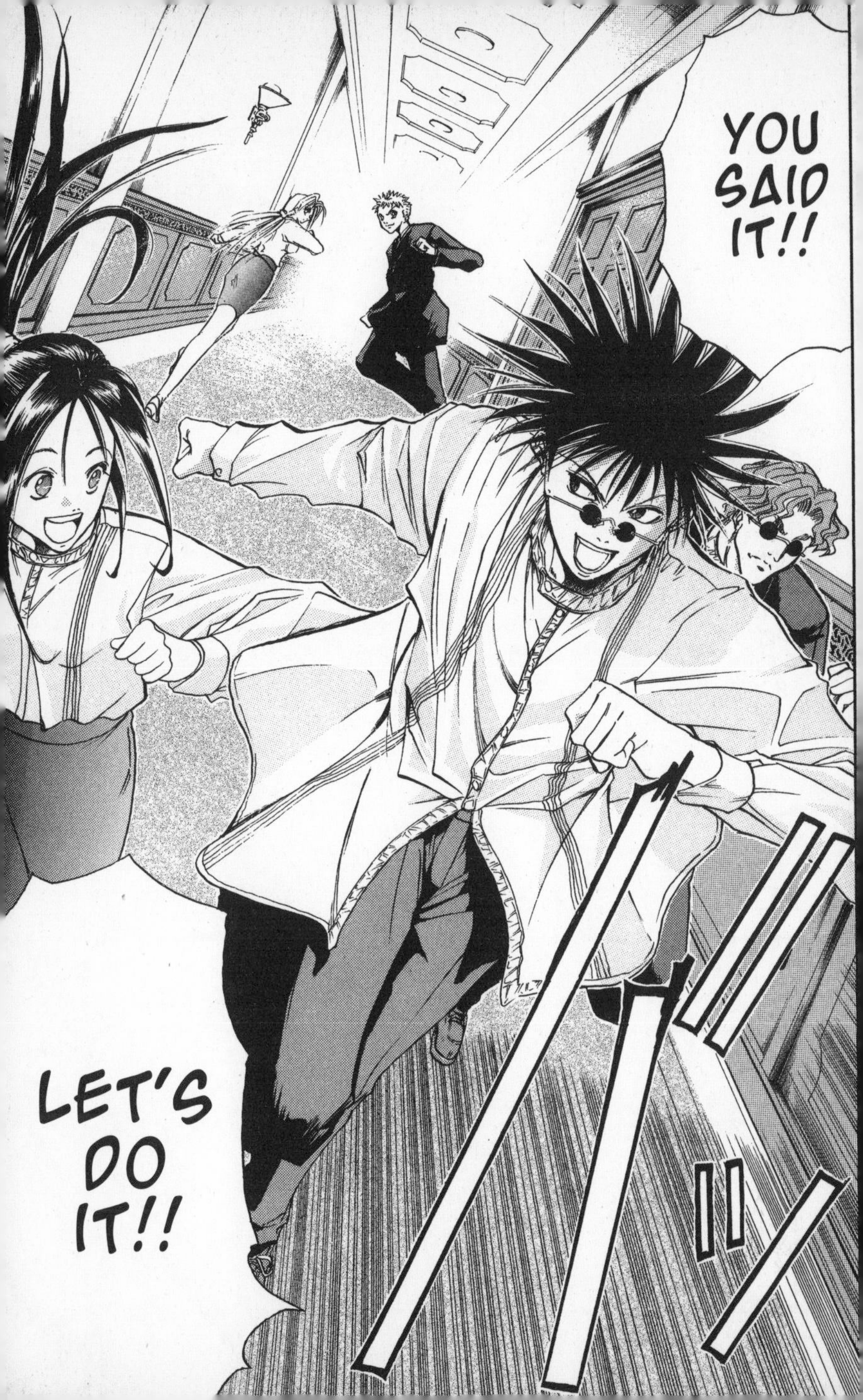
YOU SAID IT!!
LET'S DO IT!!

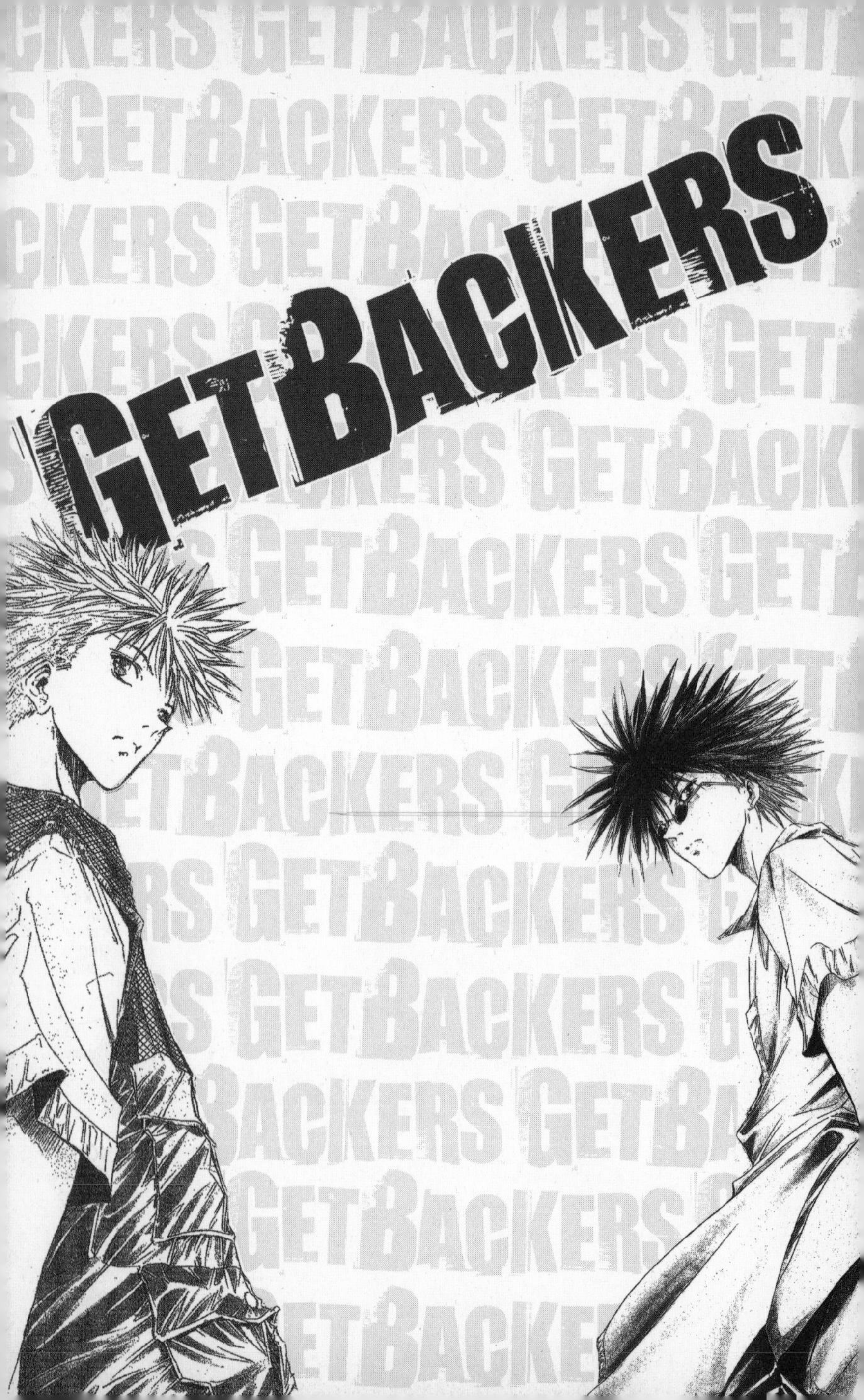
GETBACKERS™

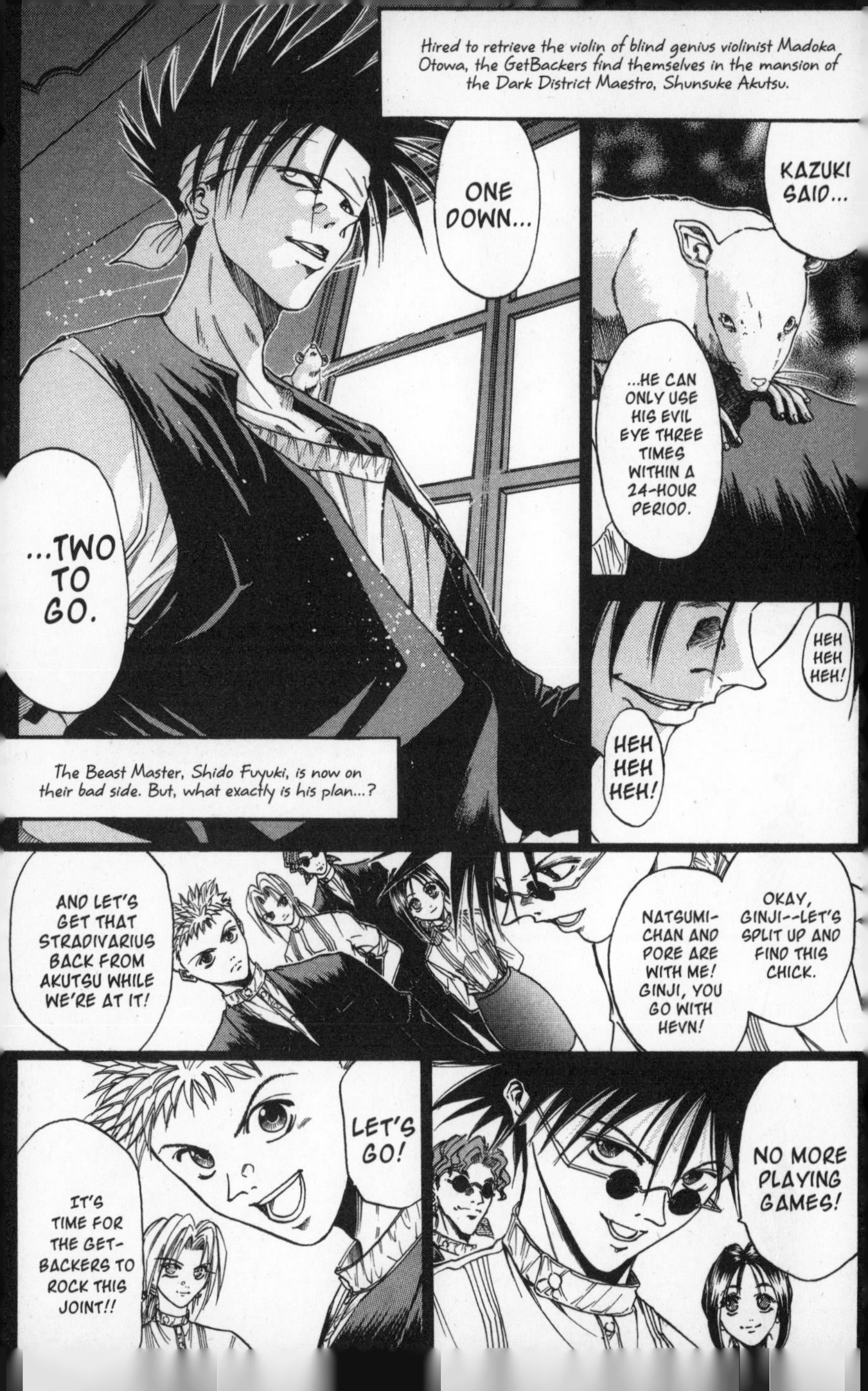
Hired to retrieve the violin of blind genius violinist Madoka Otowa, the GetBackers find themselves in the mansion of the Dark District Maestro, Shunsuke Akutsu.
KAZUKI SAID...
...HE CAN ONLY USE HIS EVIL EYE THREE TIMES WITHIN A 24-HOUR PERIOD.
HEH HEH HEH!
HEH HEH HEH!
ONE DOWN...
...TWO TO GO.
The Beast Master, Shido Fuyuki, is now on their bad side. But, what exactly is his plan...?
OKAY, GINJI--LET'S SPLIT UP AND FIND THIS CHICK.
NATSUMI-CHAN AND PORE ARE WITH ME! GINJI, YOU GO WITH HEVN!
AND LET'S GET THAT STRADIVARIUS BACK FROM AKUTSU WHILE WE'RE AT IT!
NO MORE PLAYING GAMES!
LET'S GO!
IT'S TIME FOR THE GET-BACKERS TO ROCK THIS JOINT!!

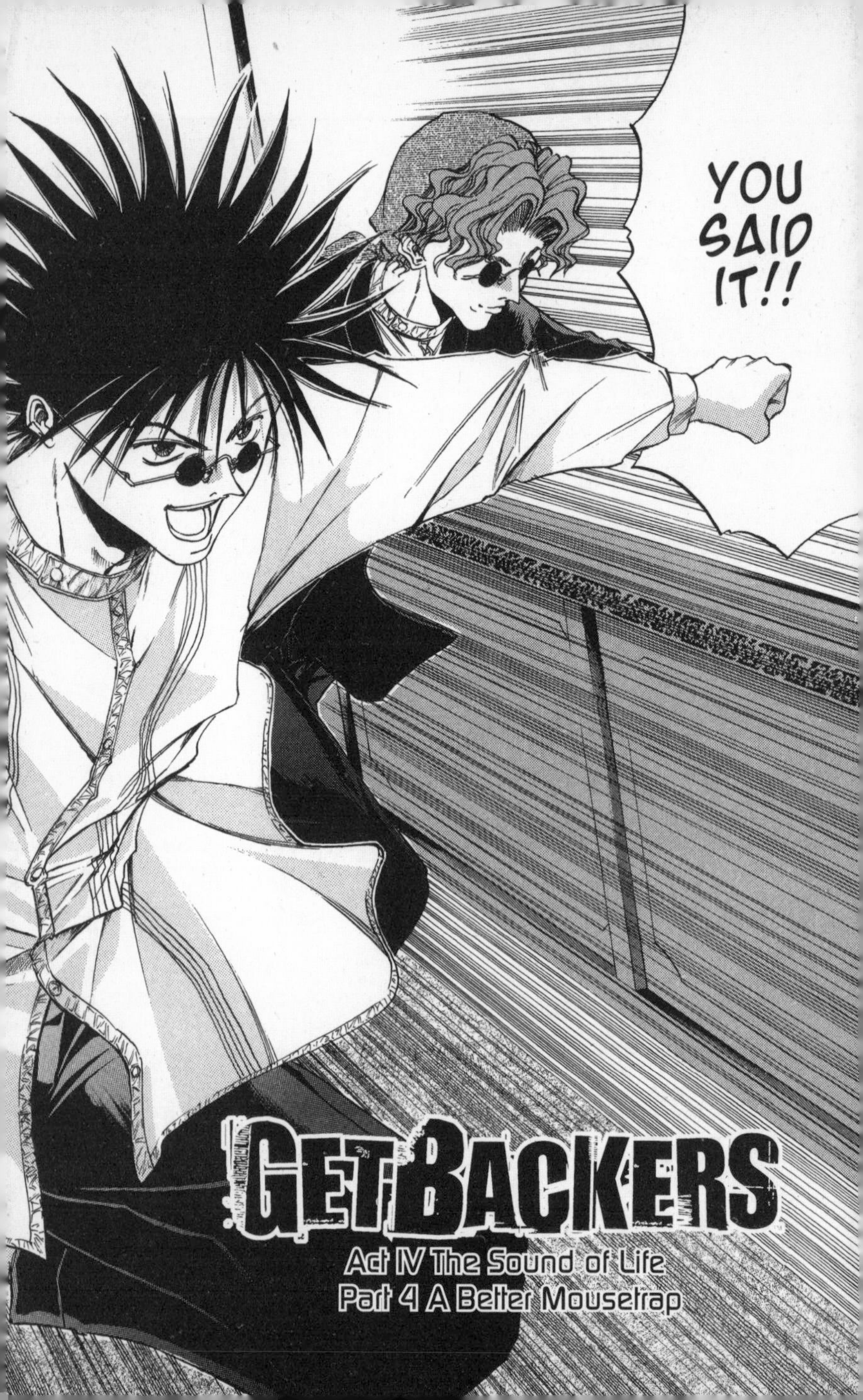
YOU SAID IT!!
GETBACKERS
Act IV The Sound of Life
Part 4 A Better Mousetrap

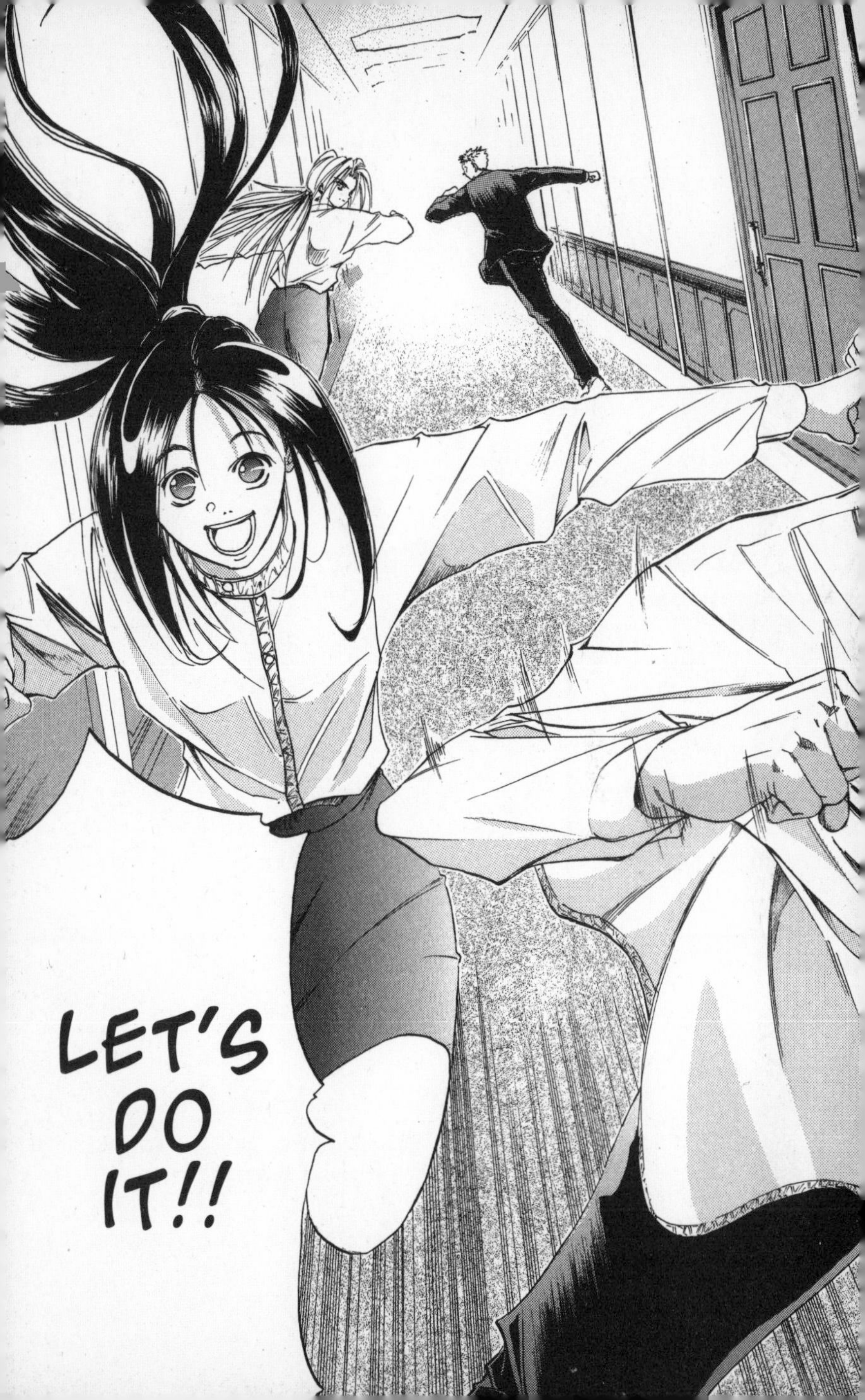
LET'S DO IT!!

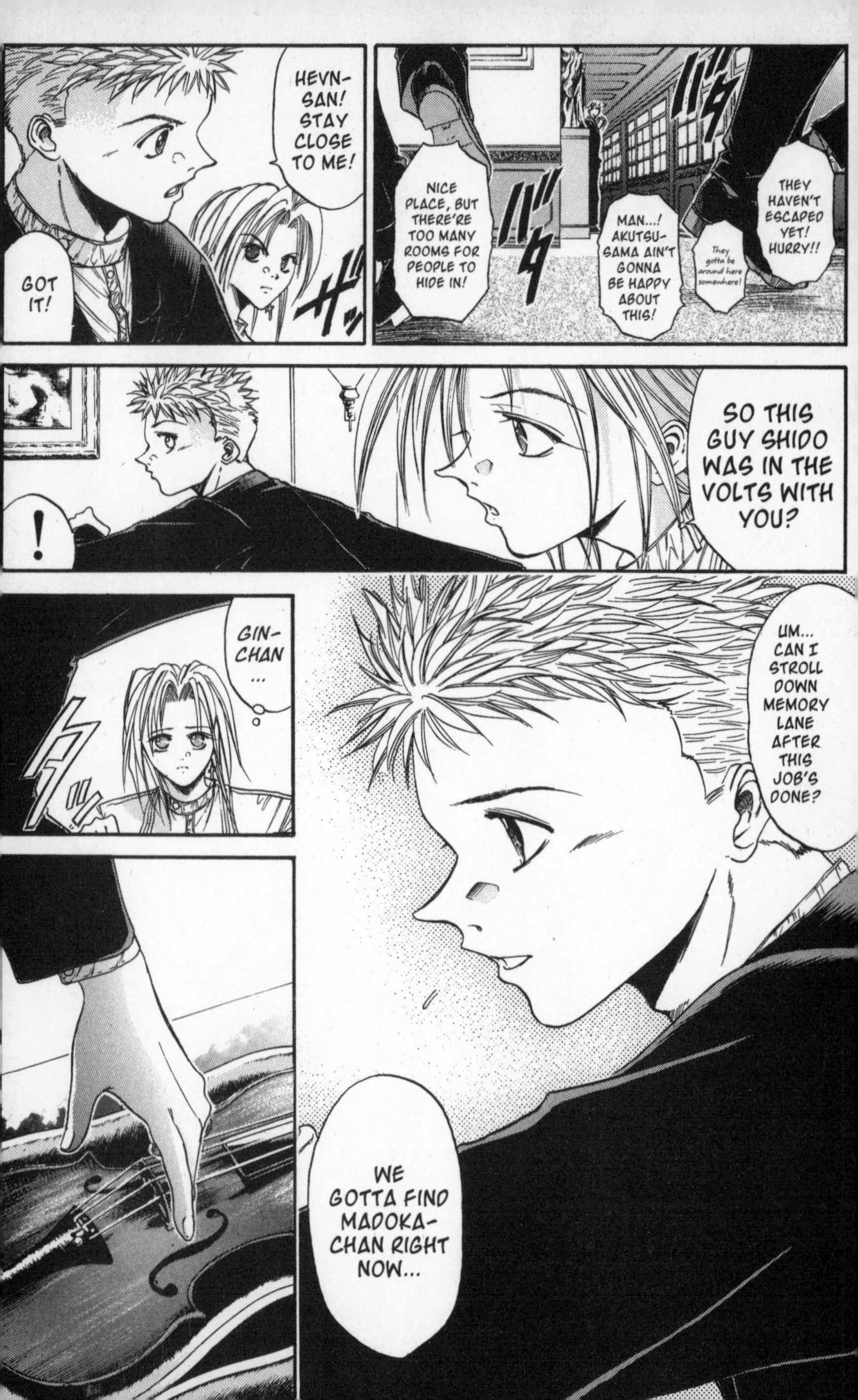

THEY HAVEN'T ESCAPED YET! HURRY!!
They gotta be around here somewhere!
MAN...! AKUTSU-SAMA AIN'T GONNA BE HAPPY ABOUT THIS!
NICE PLACE, BUT THERE'RE TOO MANY ROOMS FOR PEOPLE TO HIDE IN!
HEVN-SAN! STAY CLOSE TO ME!
GOT IT!
SO THIS GUY SHIDO WAS IN THE VOLTS WITH YOU?
!
UM... CAN I STROLL DOWN MEMORY LANE AFTER THIS JOB'S DONE?
WE GOTTA FIND MADOKA-CHAN RIGHT NOW...
GIN-CHAN ...

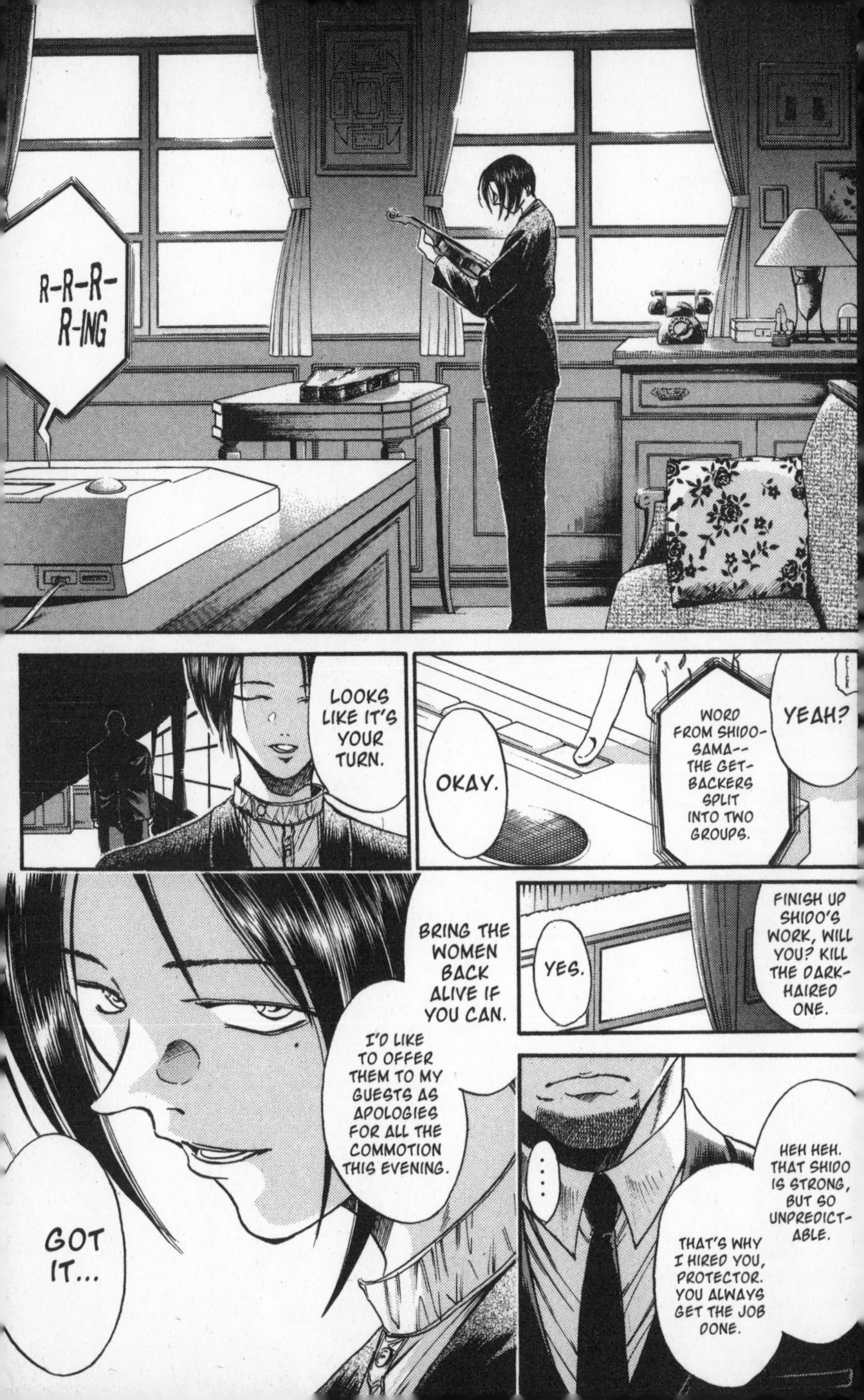
R-R-R-R-ING
CLICK
YEAH?
WORD FROM SHIDO-SAMA-- THE GET-BACKERS SPLIT INTO TWO GROUPS.
OKAY.
LOOKS LIKE IT'S YOUR TURN.
FINISH UP SHIDO'S WORK, WILL YOU? KILL THE DARK-HAIRED ONE.
YES.
HEH HEH. THAT SHIDO IS STRONG, BUT SO UNPREDICT-ABLE.
THAT'S WHY I HIRED YOU, PROTECTOR. YOU ALWAYS GET THE JOB DONE.
...
BRING THE WOMEN BACK ALIVE IF YOU CAN.
I'D LIKE TO OFFER THEM TO MY GUESTS AS APOLOGIES FOR ALL THE COMMOTION THIS EVENING.
GOT IT...

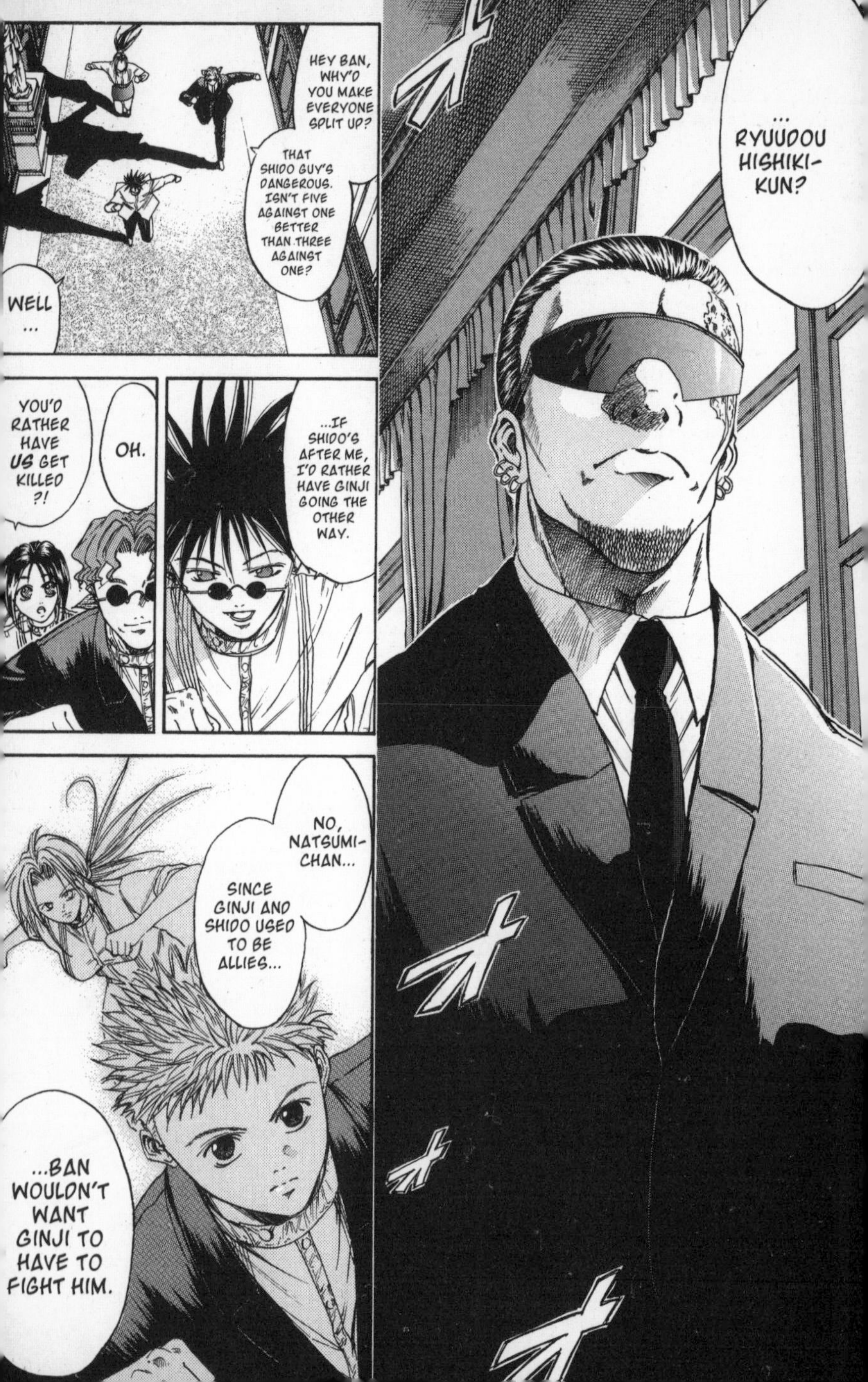
... RYUUDOU HISHIKI-KUN?
HEY BAN, WHY'D YOU MAKE EVERYONE SPLIT UP?
THAT SHIDO GUY'S DANGEROUS. ISN'T FIVE AGAINST ONE BETTER THAN THREE AGAINST ONE?
WELL ...
...IF SHIDO'S AFTER ME, I'D RATHER HAVE GINJI GOING THE OTHER WAY.
OH.
YOU'D RATHER HAVE US GET KILLED ?!
NO, NATSUMI-CHAN...
SINCE GINJI AND SHIDO USED TO BE ALLIES...
...BAN WOULDN'T WANT GINJI TO HAVE TO FIGHT HIM.

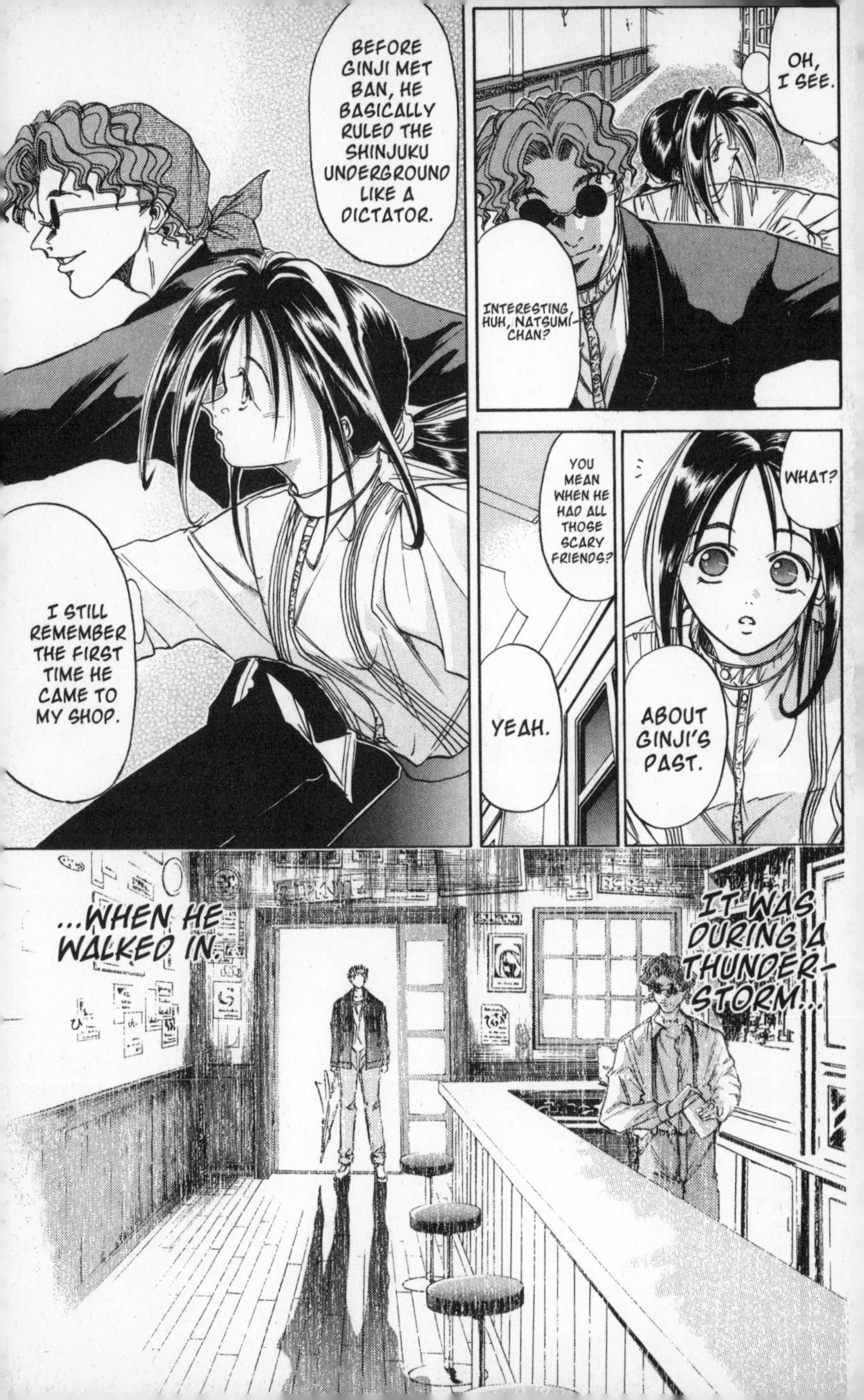
OH, I SEE.
INTERESTING, HUH, NATSUMI-CHAN?
WHAT?
ABOUT GINJI'S PAST.
YOU MEAN WHEN HE HAD ALL THOSE SCARY FRIENDS?
YEAH.
BEFORE GINJI MET BAN, HE BASICALLY RULED THE SHINJUKU UNDERGROUND LIKE A DICTATOR.
I STILL REMEMBER THE FIRST TIME HE CAME TO MY SHOP.
IT WAS DURING A THUNDER-STORM...
...WHEN HE WALKED IN.

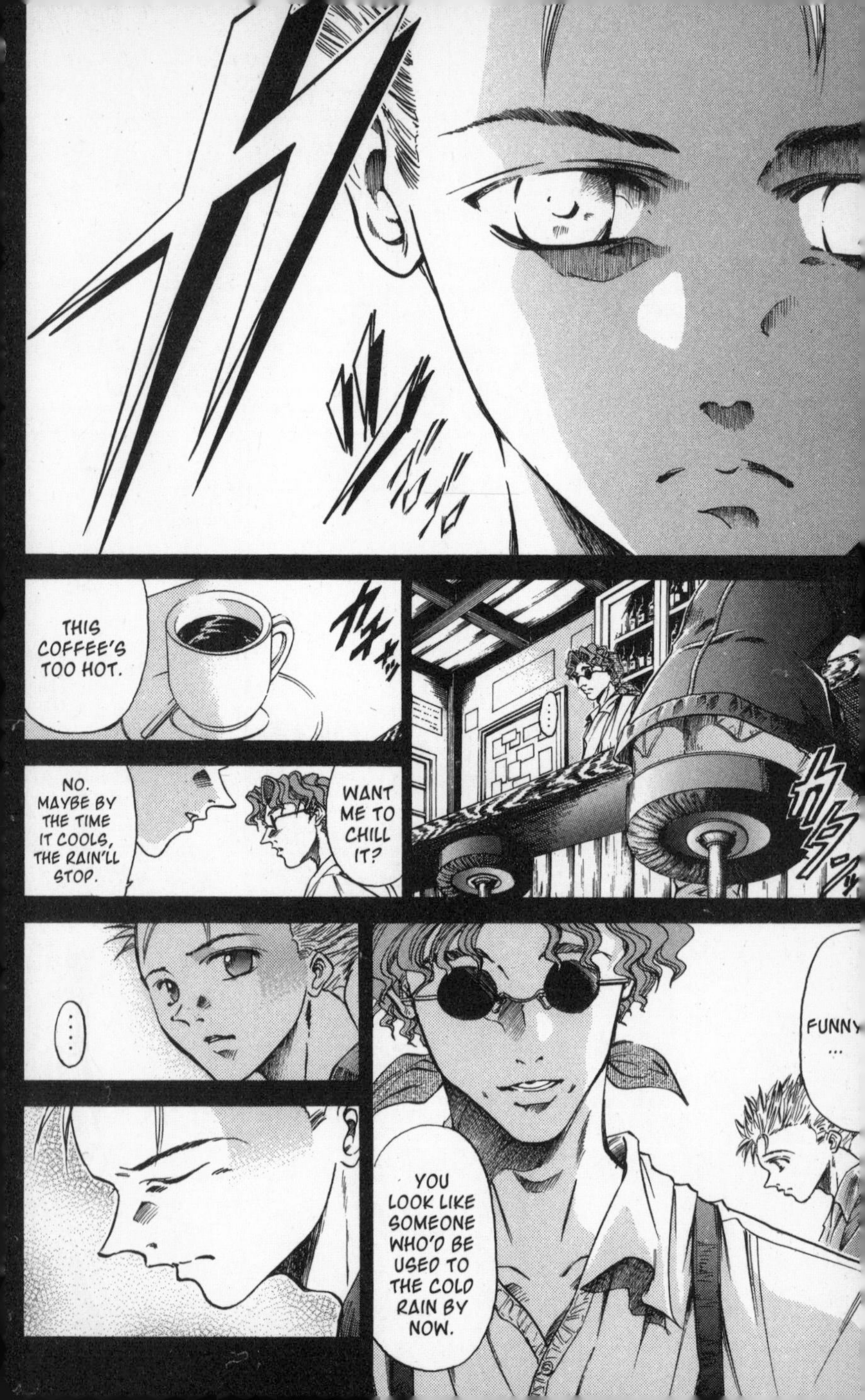
...
THIS COFFEE'S TOO HOT.
WANT ME TO CHILL IT?
NO. MAYBE BY THE TIME IT COOLS, THE RAIN'LL STOP.
FUNNY...
YOU LOOK LIKE SOMEONE WHO'D BE USED TO THE COLD RAIN BY NOW.
...

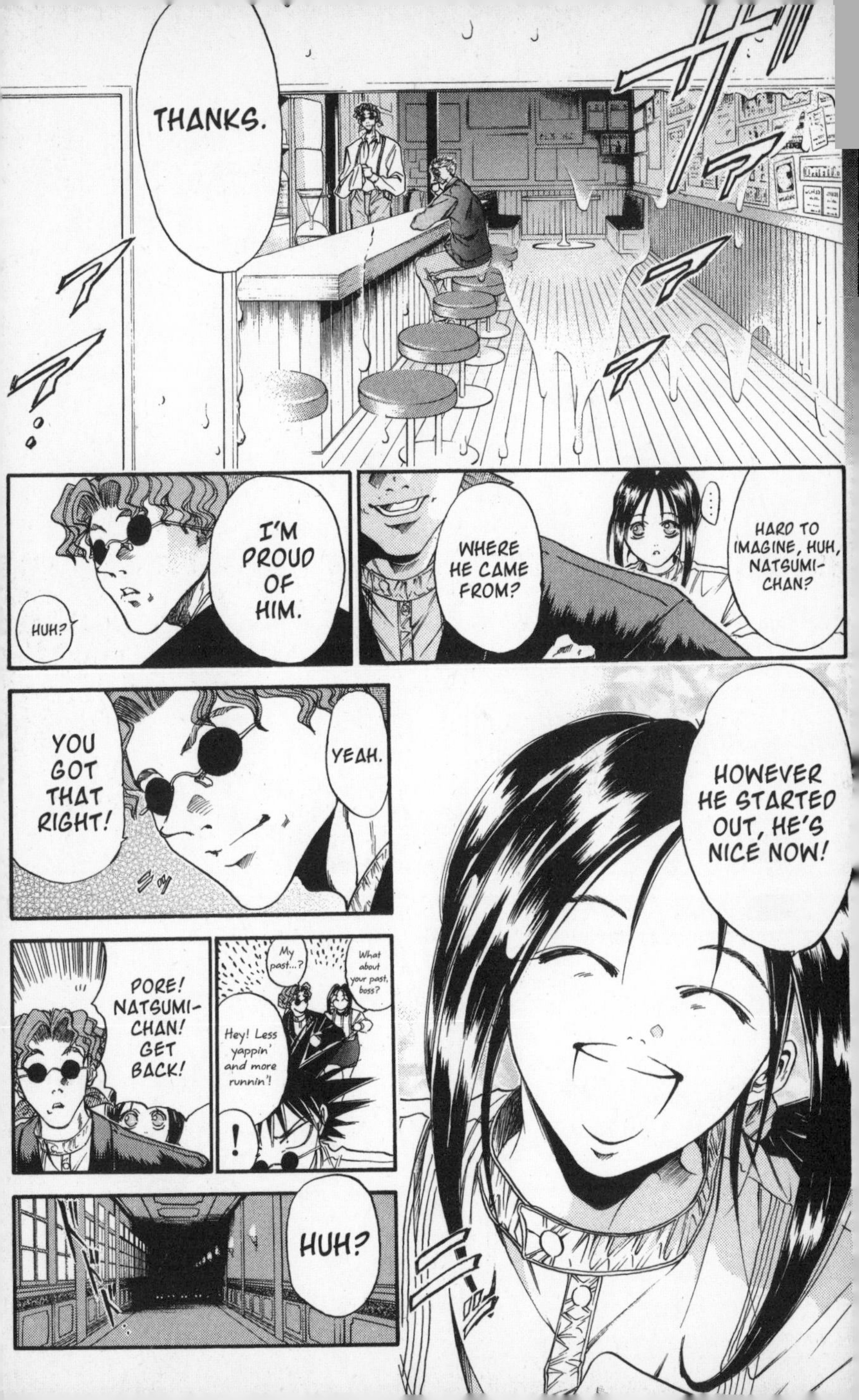
THANKS.
...
HARD TO IMAGINE, HUH, NATSUMI-CHAN?
WHERE HE CAME FROM?
I'M PROUD OF HIM.
HUH?
HOWEVER HE STARTED OUT, HE'S NICE NOW!
YEAH.
YOU GOT THAT RIGHT!
What about your past, boss?
My past...?
Hey! Less yappin' and more runnin'!
!
PORE! NATSUMI-CHAN! GET BACK!
HUH?

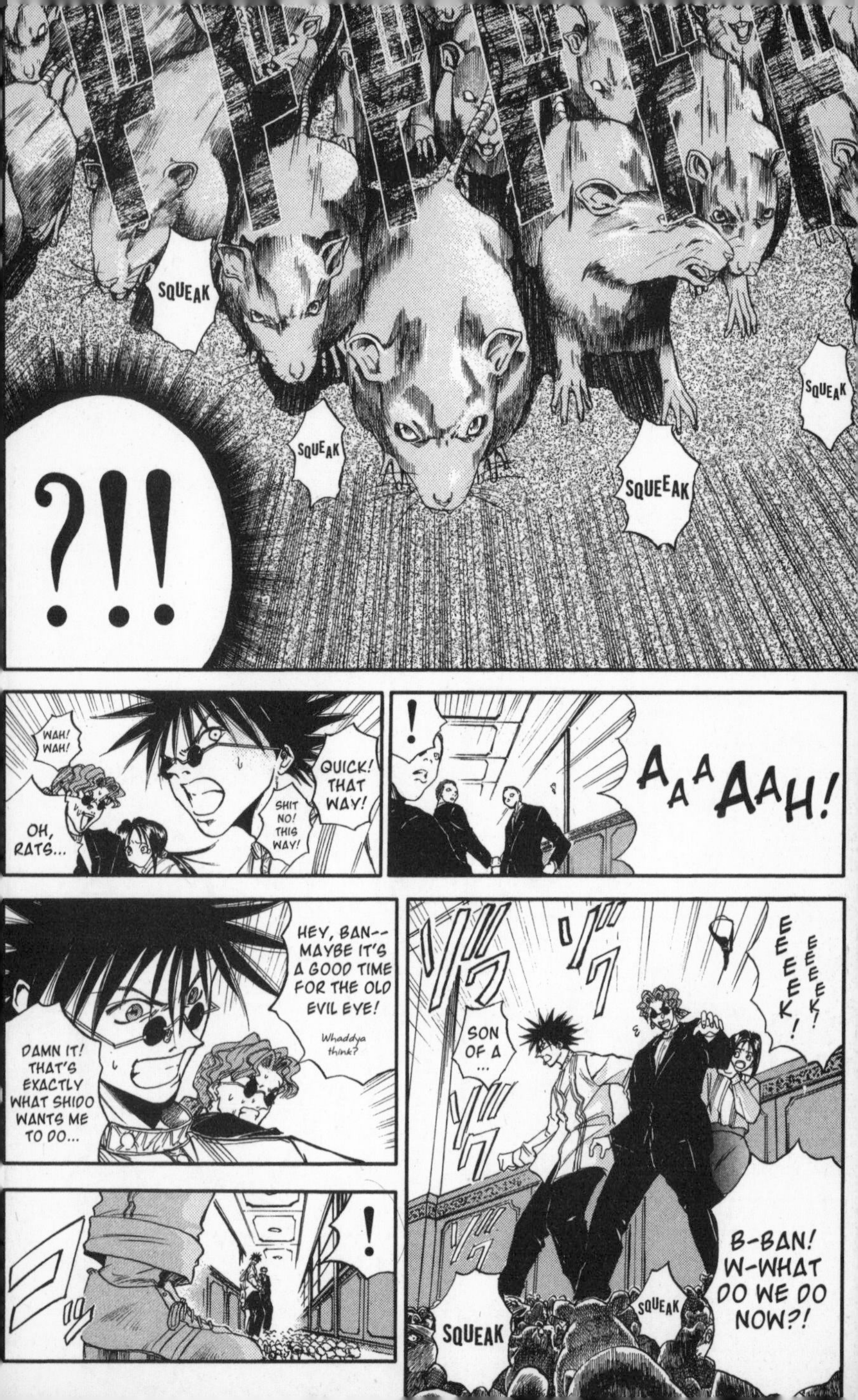
SQUEAK
SQUEAK
SQUEAK
SQUEEAK
?!!
!
AAAAAH!
QUICK! THAT WAY!
SHIT NO! THIS WAY!
WAH! WAH!
OH, RATS...
EEEEK!
EEEEK!
SON OF A ...
B-BAN! W-WHAT DO WE DO NOW?!
SQUEAK
SQUEAK
HEY, BAN-- MAYBE IT'S A GOOD TIME FOR THE OLD EVIL EYE!
Whaddya think?
DAMN IT! THAT'S EXACTLY WHAT SHIDO WANTS ME TO DO...
!

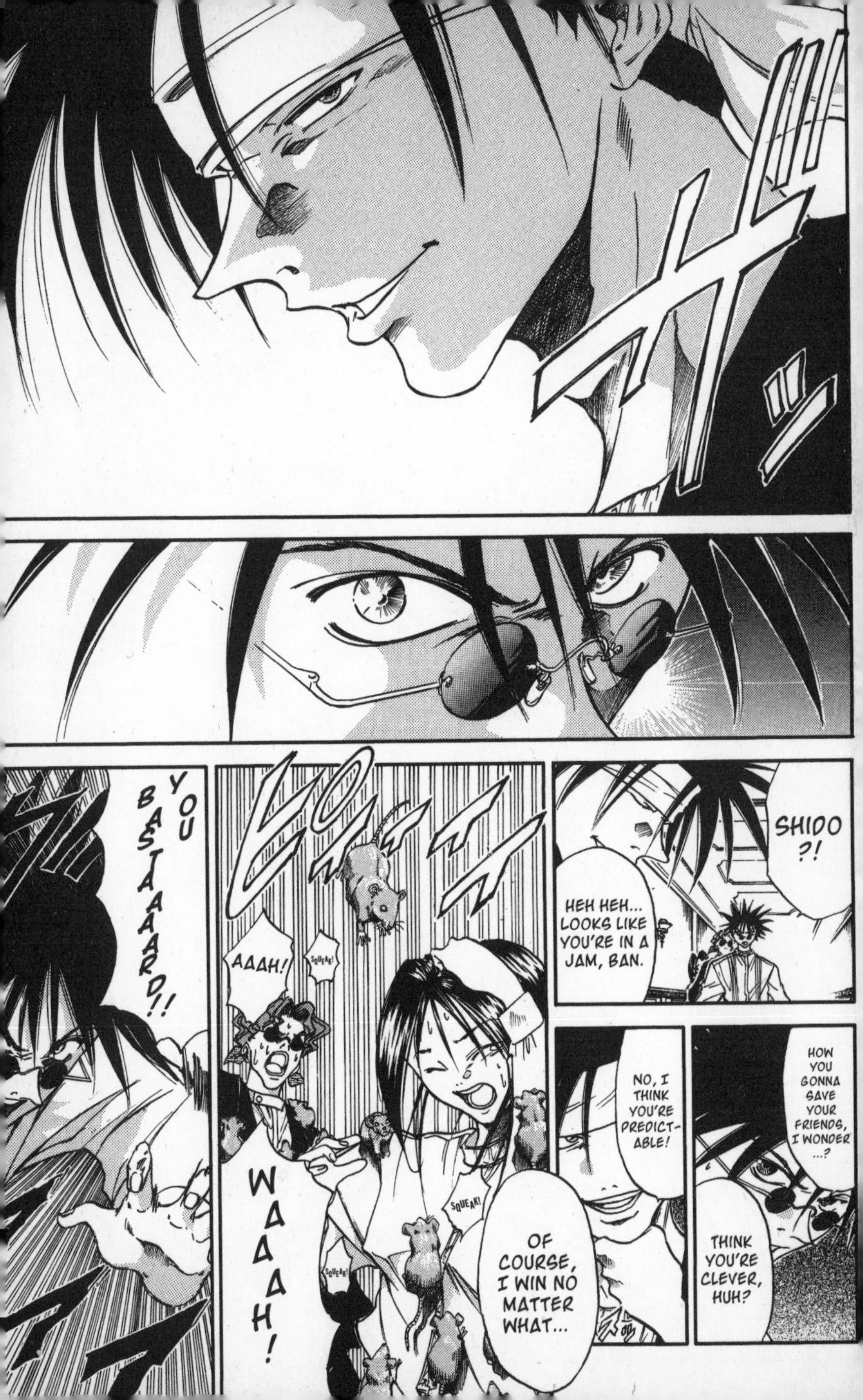
SHIDO?!
HEH HEH... LOOKS LIKE YOU'RE IN A JAM, BAN.
HOW YOU GONNA SAVE YOUR FRIENDS, I WONDER...?
THINK YOU'RE CLEVER, HUH?
NO, I THINK YOU'RE PREDICT-ABLE!
OF COURSE, I WIN NO MATTER WHAT...
AAAH!
SQUEAK!
WAAAAH!
SQUEAK!
SQUEAK!
YOU BASTAAAARD!!

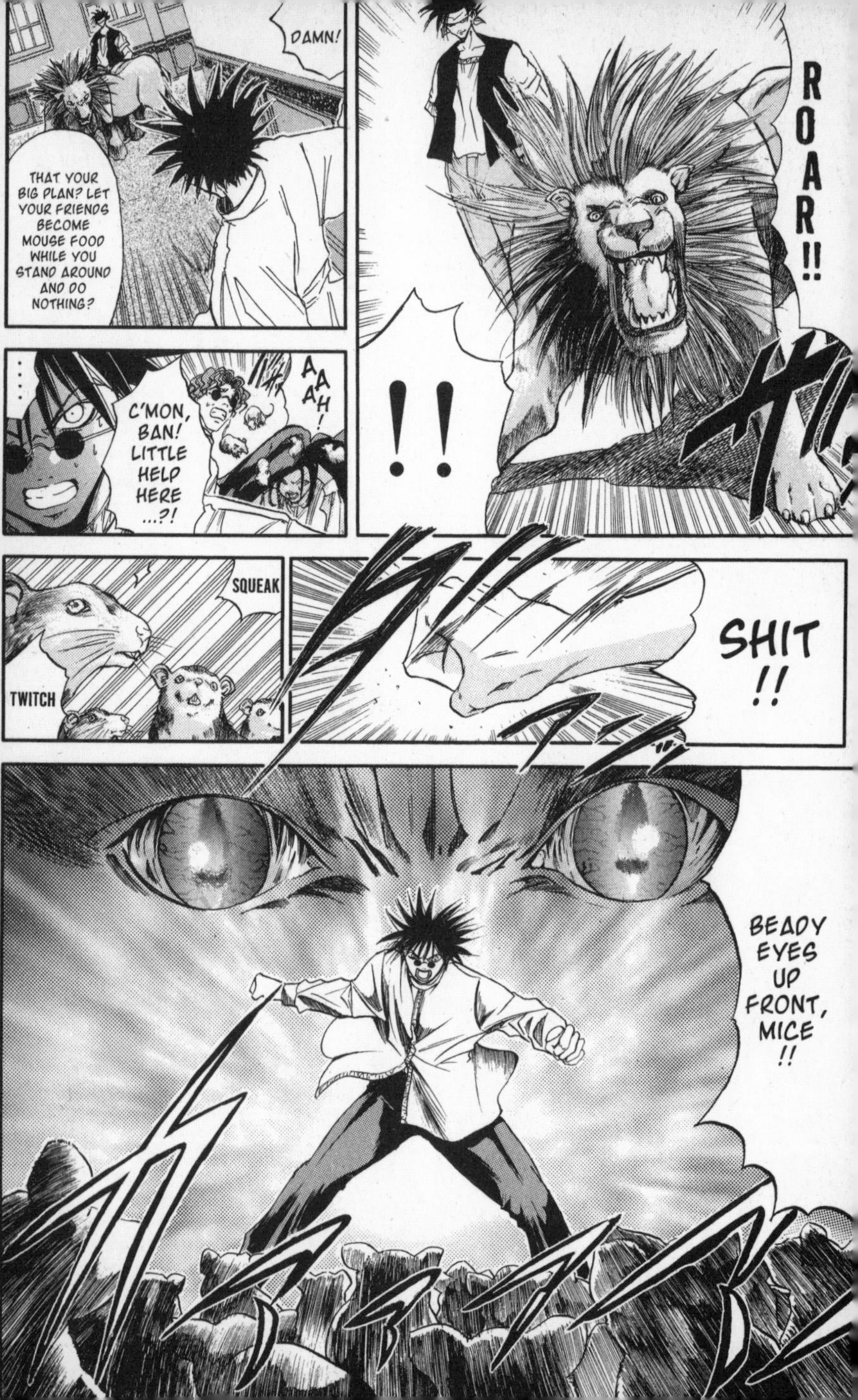
ROAR!!
!!
DAMN!
THAT YOUR BIG PLAN? LET YOUR FRIENDS BECOME MOUSE FOOD WHILE YOU STAND AROUND AND DO NOTHING?
AAAH!
C'MON, BAN! LITTLE HELP HERE ...?!
....
SHIT !!
SQUEAK
TWITCH
BEADY EYES UP FRONT, MICE !!

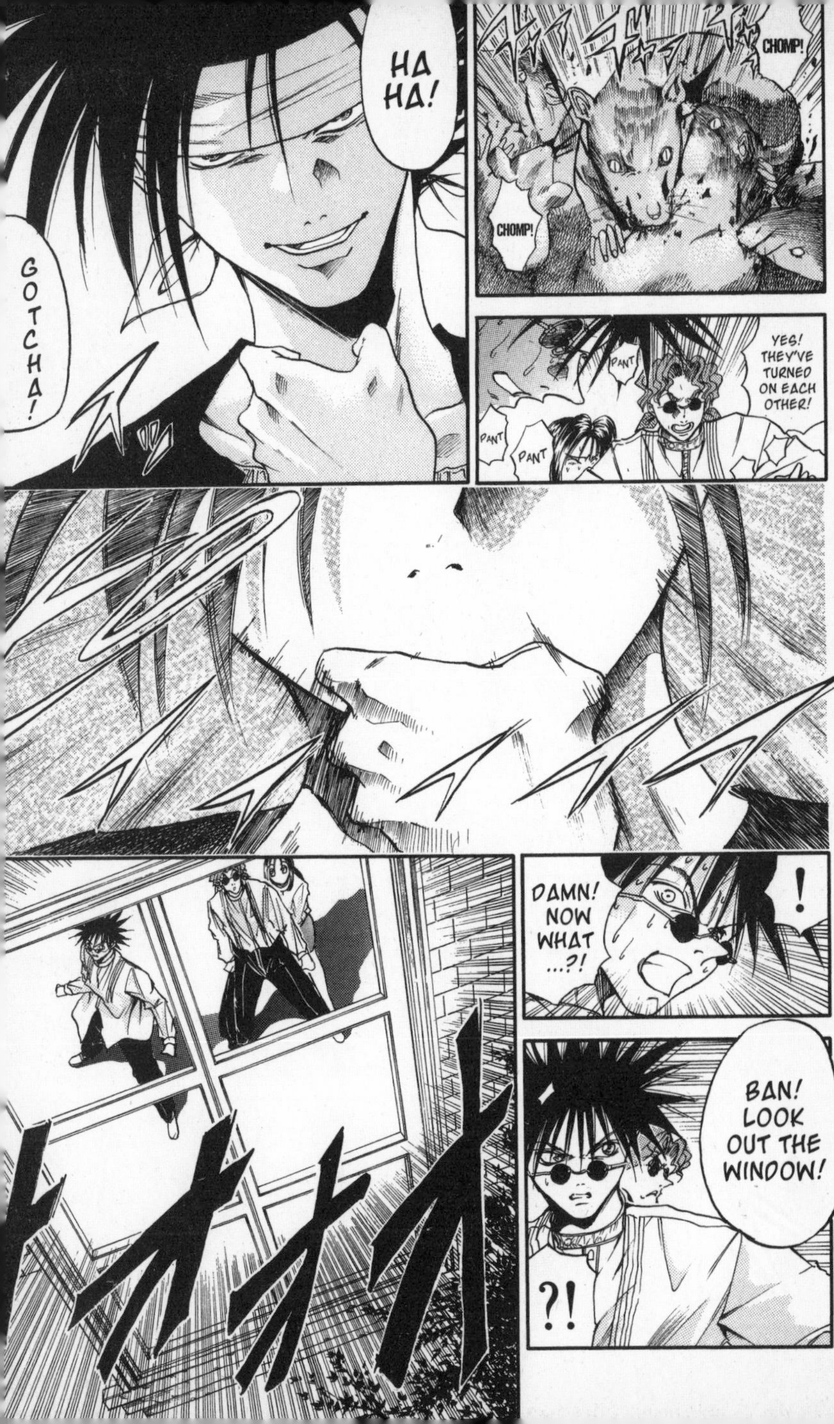
CHOMP!
CHOMP!
YES! THEY'VE TURNED ON EACH OTHER!
PANT
PANT
PANT
HA HA!
GOTCHA!
!
DAMN! NOW WHAT ...?!
BAN! LOOK OUT THE WINDOW!
?!

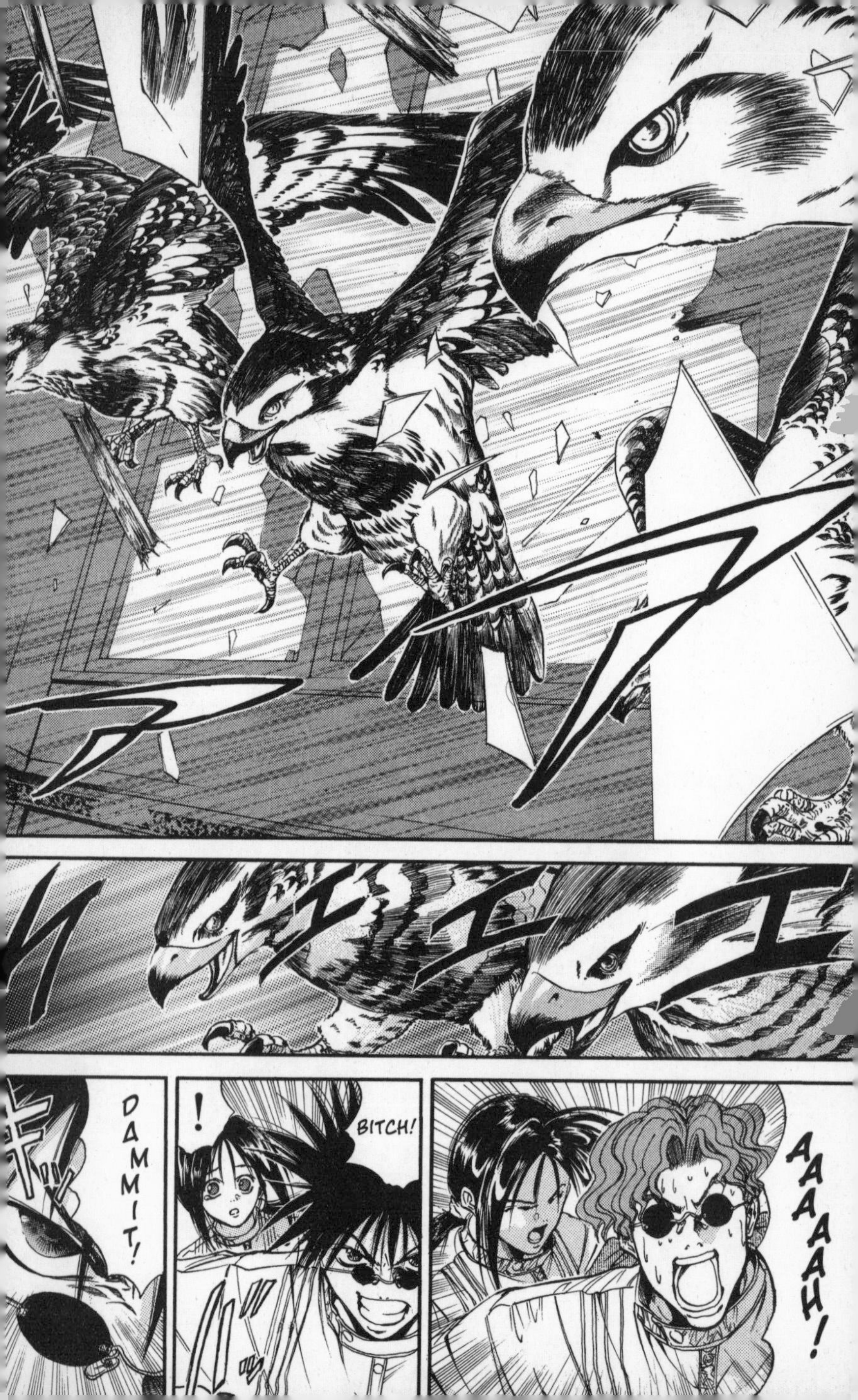
AAAAAH!
BITCH!
!
DAMMIT!

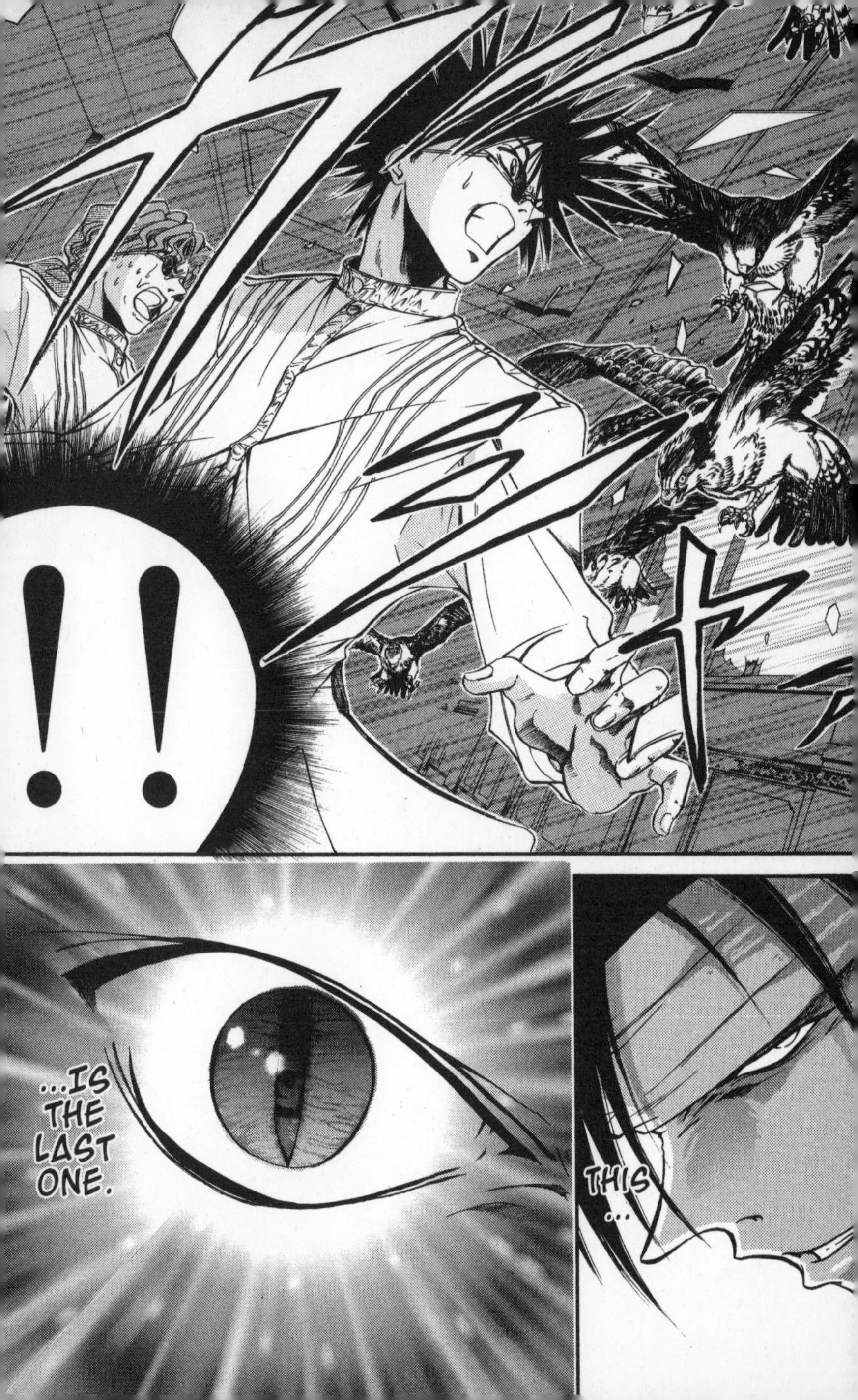
!!
THIS ...
...IS THE LAST ONE.

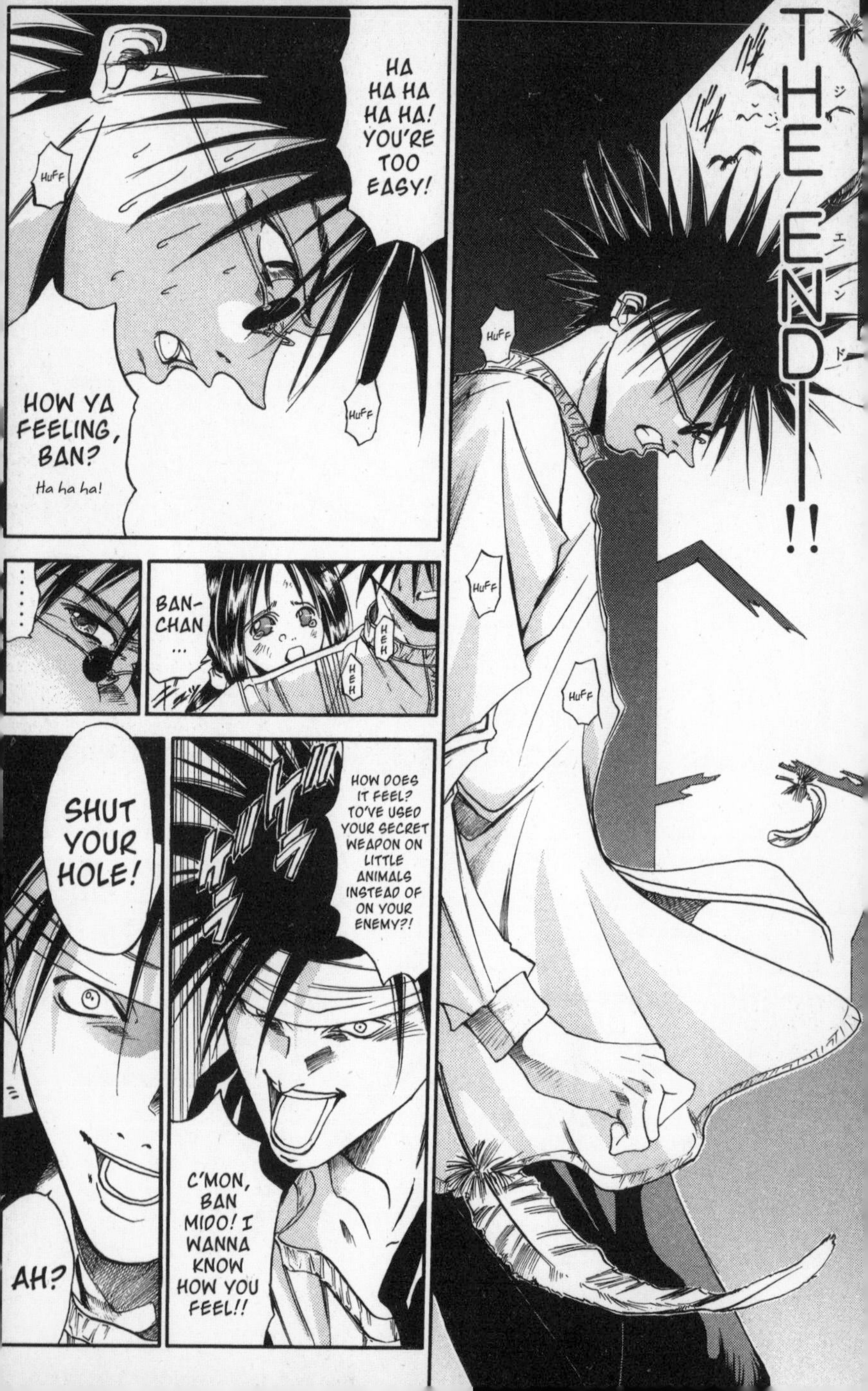
THE END!!
ジ エン ド
HUFF
HUFF
HUFF
HUFF
HA HA HA HA HA! YOU'RE TOO EASY!
HUFF
HUFF
HOW YA FEELING, BAN?
Ha ha ha!
BAN-CHAN ...
HEH
HEH
......
HOW DOES IT FEEL? TO'VE USED YOUR SECRET WEAPON ON LITTLE ANIMALS INSTEAD OF ON YOUR ENEMY?!
C'MON, BAN MIDO! I WANNA KNOW HOW YOU FEEL!!
SHUT YOUR HOLE!
AH?

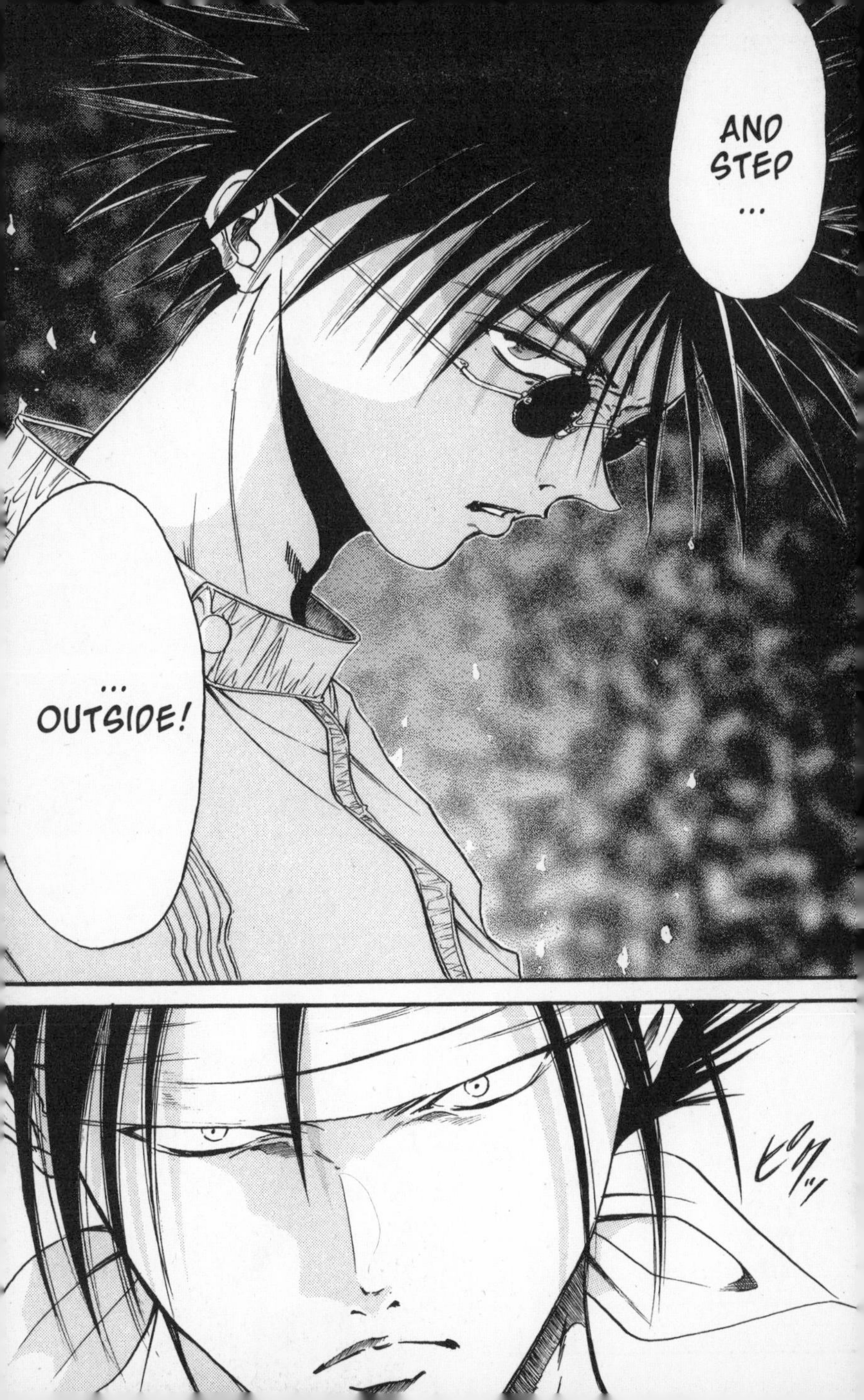
AND STEP ...
... OUTSIDE!
ピクッ

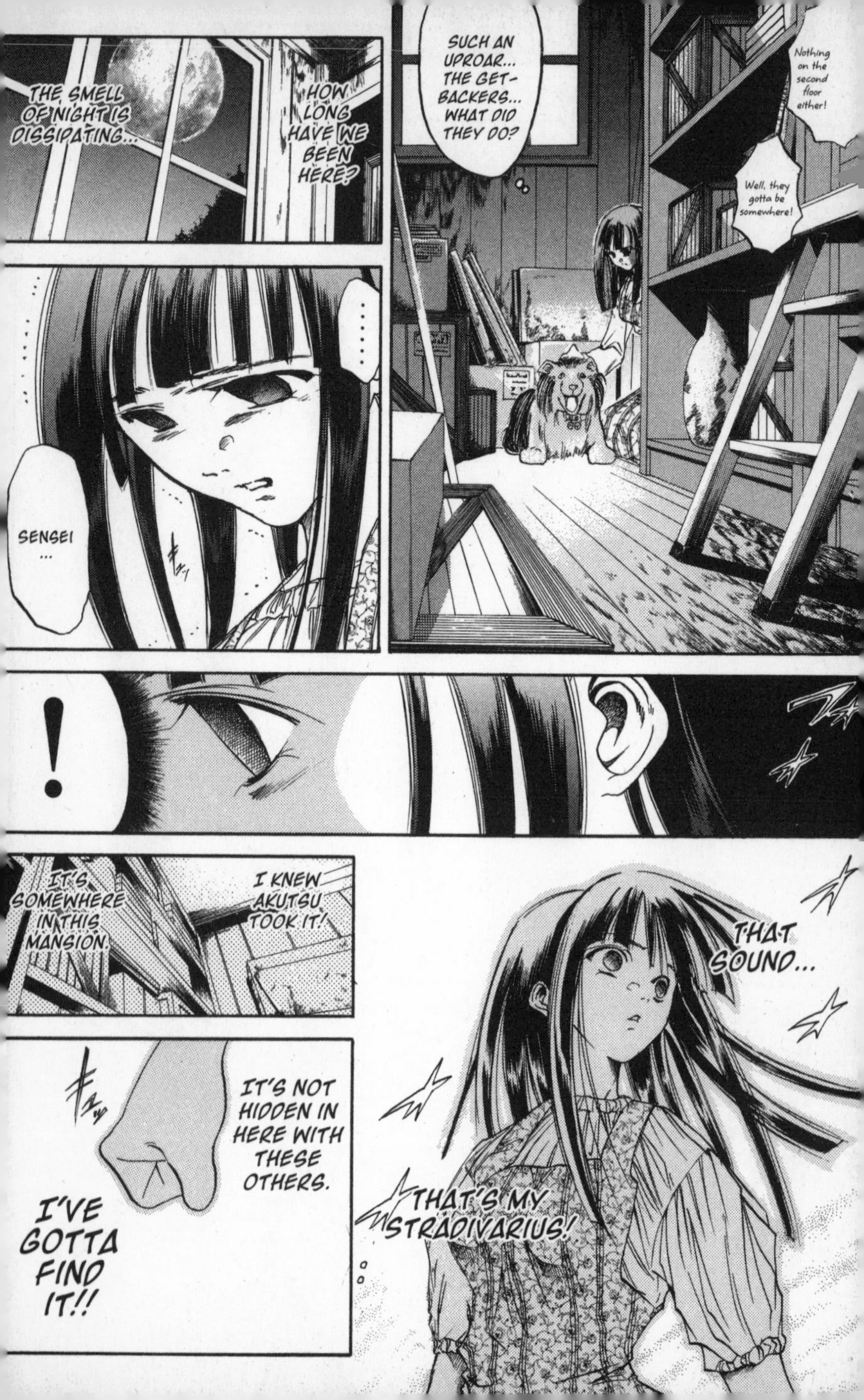
Nothing on the second floor either!
Well, they gotta be somewhere!
SUCH AN UPROAR... THE GET-BACKERS... WHAT DID THEY DO?
HOW LONG HAVE WE BEEN HERE?
THE SMELL OF NIGHT IS DISSIPATING...
....
....
SENSEI ...
!
THAT SOUND...
THAT'S MY STRADIVARIUS!
I KNEW AKUTSU TOOK IT!
IT'S SOMEWHERE IN THIS MANSION.
IT'S NOT HIDDEN IN HERE WITH THESE OTHERS.
I'VE GOTTA FIND IT!!

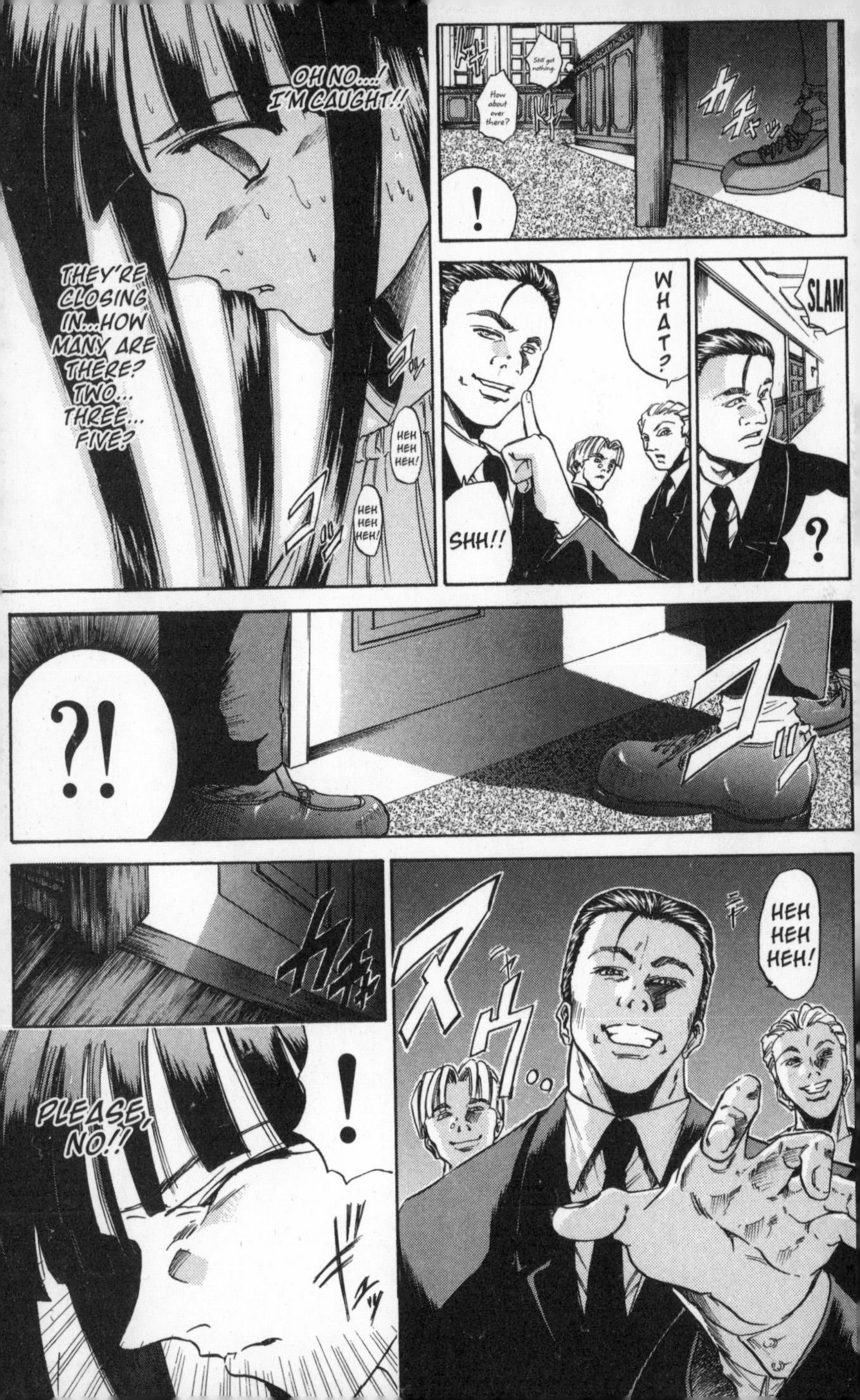
Still got nothing.
How about over there?
!
SLAM
?
WHAT?
SHH!!
OH NO...! I'M CAUGHT!!
THEY'RE CLOSING IN...HOW MANY ARE THERE? TWO... THREE... FIVE?
HEH HEH HEH!
HEH HEH HEH!
?!
HEH HEH HEH!
PLEASE, NO!!
!

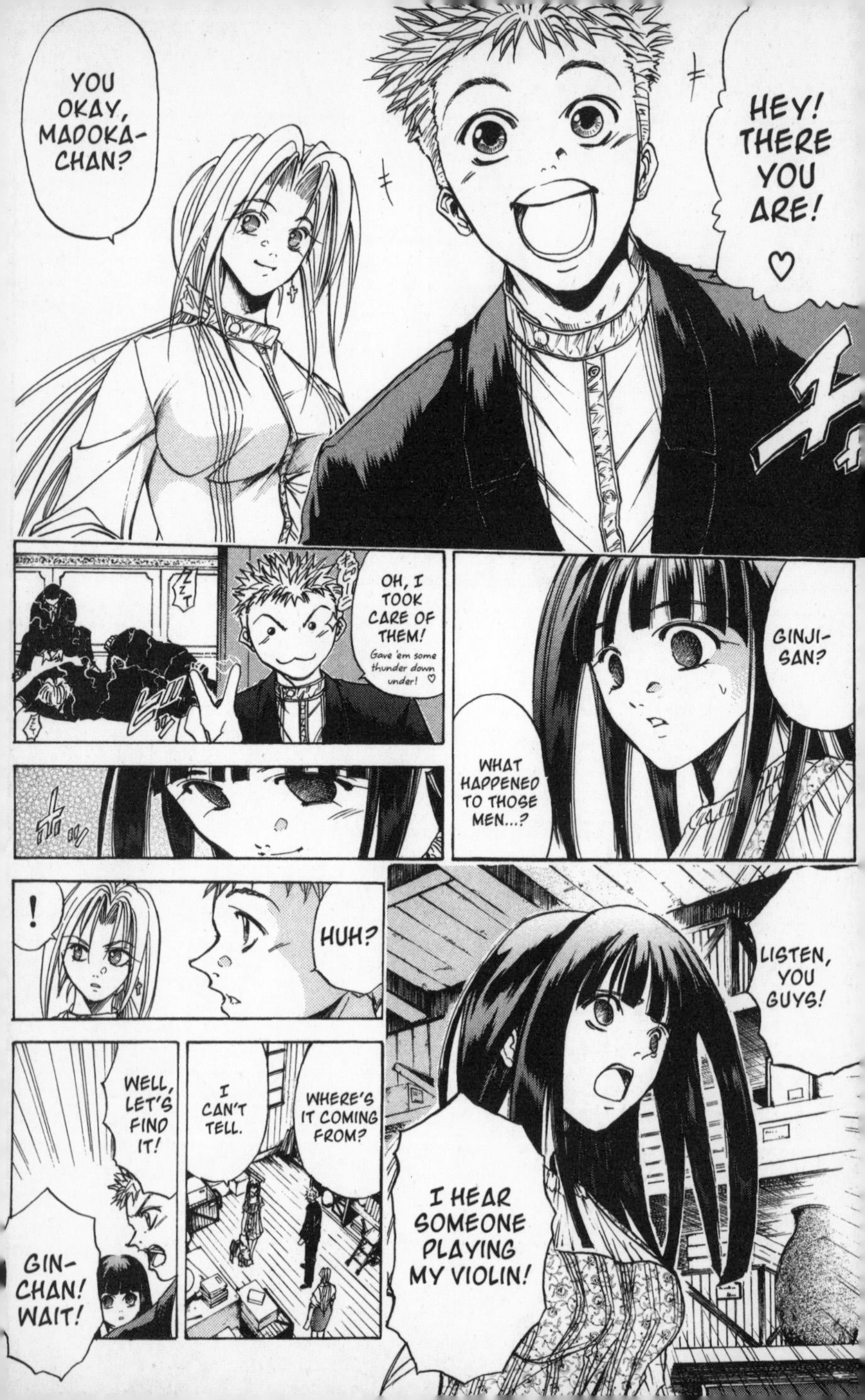
HEY! THERE YOU ARE! ♡
YOU OKAY, MADOKA-CHAN?
GINJI-SAN?
WHAT HAPPENED TO THOSE MEN...?
OH, I TOOK CARE OF THEM!
Gave 'em some thunder down under! ♡
LISTEN, YOU GUYS!
I HEAR SOMEONE PLAYING MY VIOLIN!
HUH?
!
WHERE'S IT COMING FROM?
I CAN'T TELL.
WELL, LET'S FIND IT!
GIN-CHAN! WAIT!

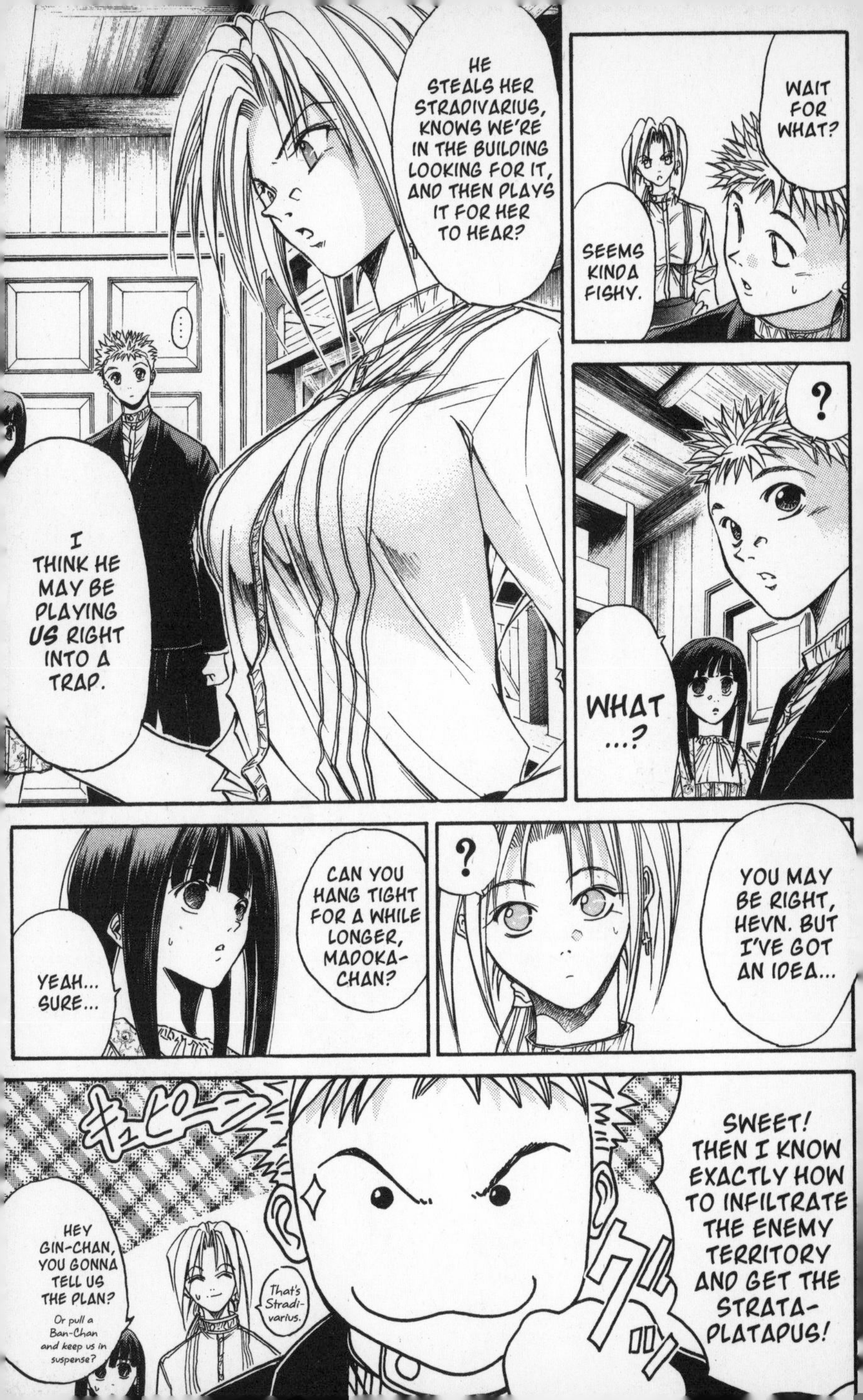
WAIT FOR WHAT?
SEEMS KINDA FISHY.
?
WHAT ...?
HE STEALS HER STRADIVARIUS, KNOWS WE'RE IN THE BUILDING LOOKING FOR IT, AND THEN PLAYS IT FOR HER TO HEAR?
...
I THINK HE MAY BE PLAYING US RIGHT INTO A TRAP.
YOU MAY BE RIGHT, HEVN. BUT I'VE GOT AN IDEA...
?
CAN YOU HANG TIGHT FOR A WHILE LONGER, MADOKA-CHAN?
YEAH... SURE...
SWEET! THEN I KNOW EXACTLY HOW TO INFILTRATE THE ENEMY TERRITORY AND GET THE STRATA-PLATAPUS!
That's Stradivarius.
HEY GIN-CHAN, YOU GONNA TELL US THE PLAN?
Or pull a Ban-Chan and keep us in suspense?

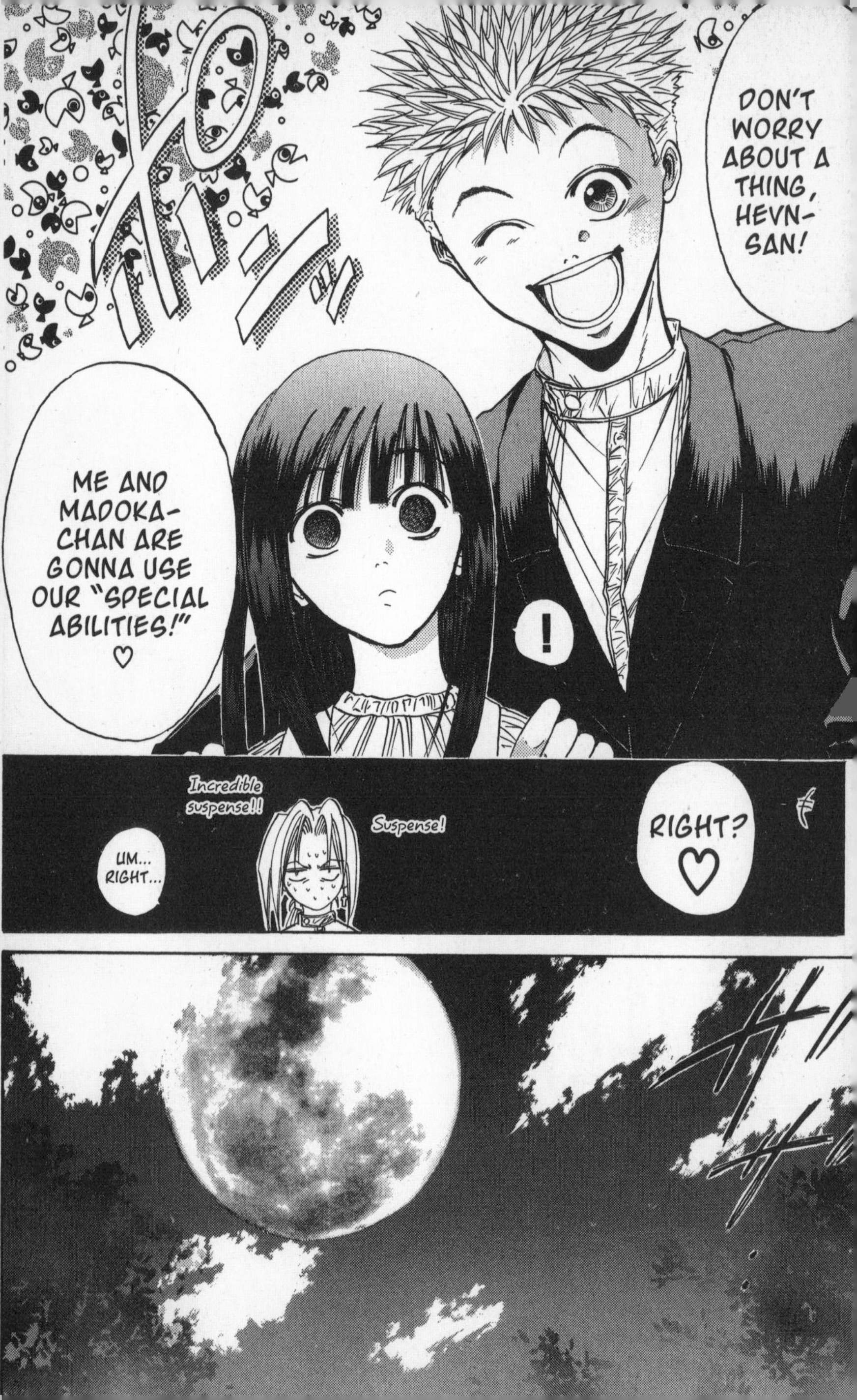
DON'T WORRY ABOUT A THING, HEVN-SAN!
ME AND MADOKA-CHAN ARE GONNA USE OUR "SPECIAL ABILITIES!" ♡
!
RIGHT? ♡
Suspense!
Incredible suspense!!
UM... RIGHT...

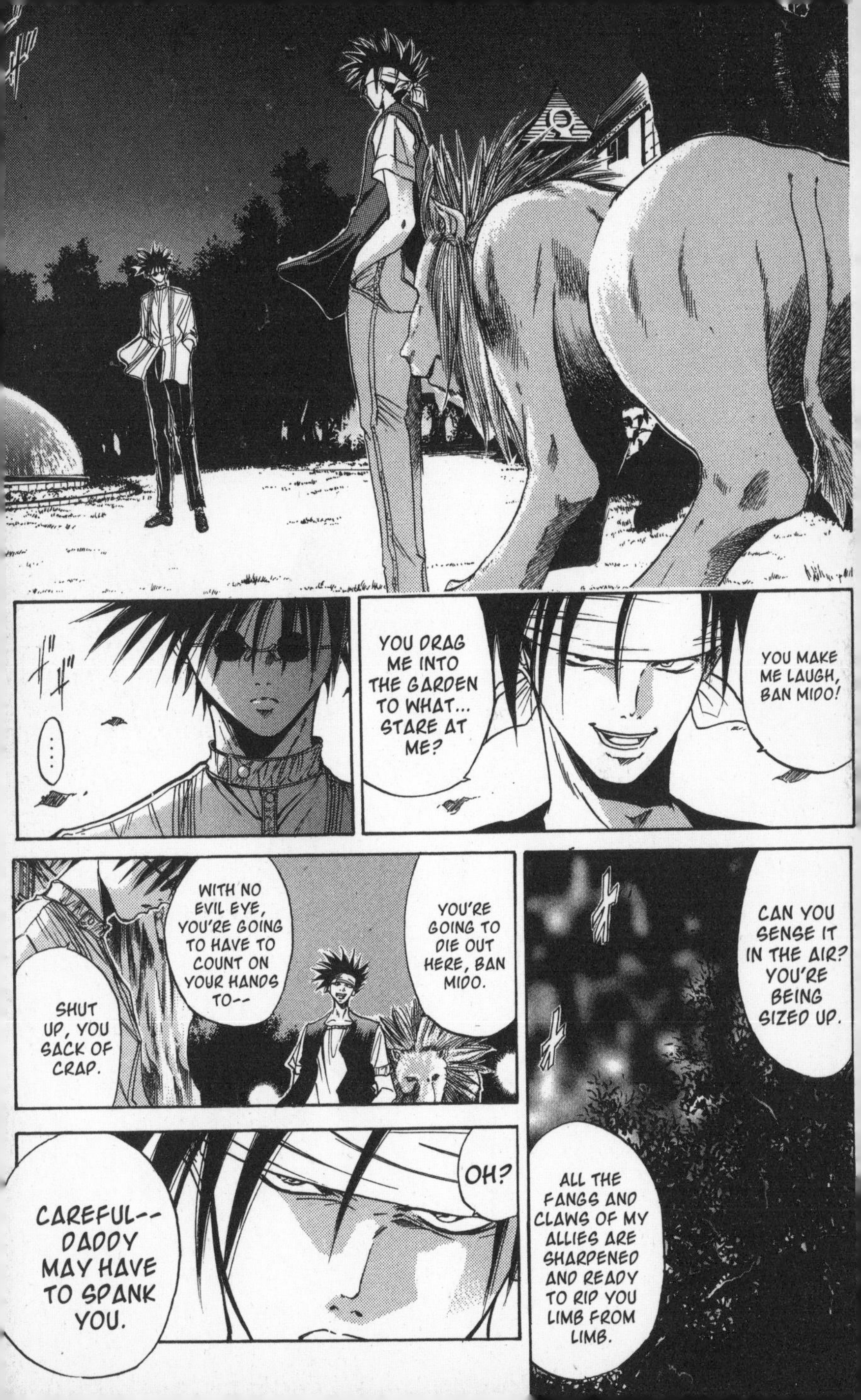
YOU MAKE ME LAUGH, BAN MIDO!
YOU DRAG ME INTO THE GARDEN TO WHAT... STARE AT ME?
....
CAN YOU SENSE IT IN THE AIR? YOU'RE BEING SIZED UP.
ALL THE FANGS AND CLAWS OF MY ALLIES ARE SHARPENED AND READY TO RIP YOU LIMB FROM LIMB.
YOU'RE GOING TO DIE OUT HERE, BAN MIDO.
WITH NO EVIL EYE, YOU'RE GOING TO HAVE TO COUNT ON YOUR HANDS TO--
SHUT UP, YOU SACK OF CRAP.
OH?
CAREFUL-- DADDY MAY HAVE TO SPANK YOU.

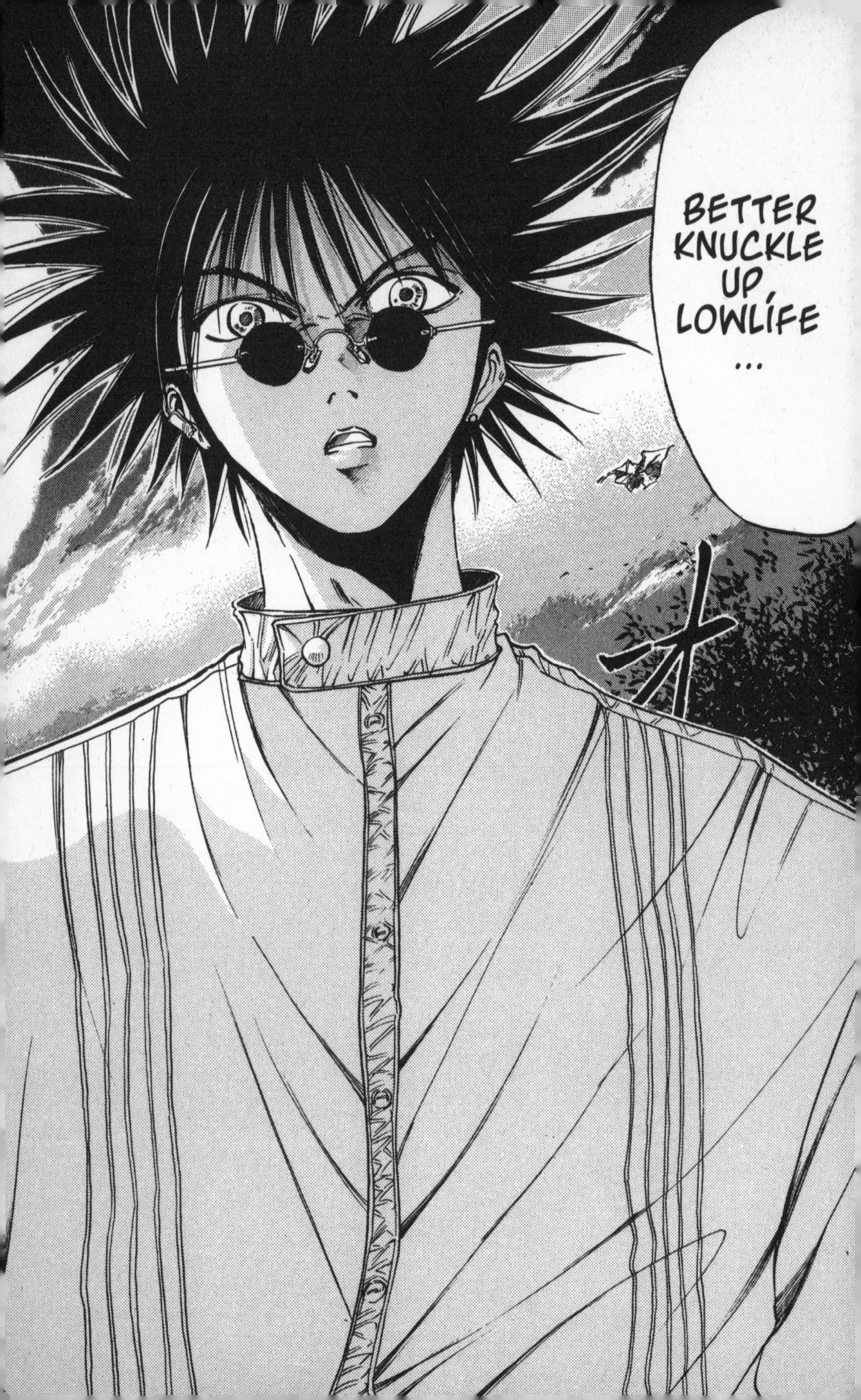
BETTER KNUCKLE UP LOWLIFE ...

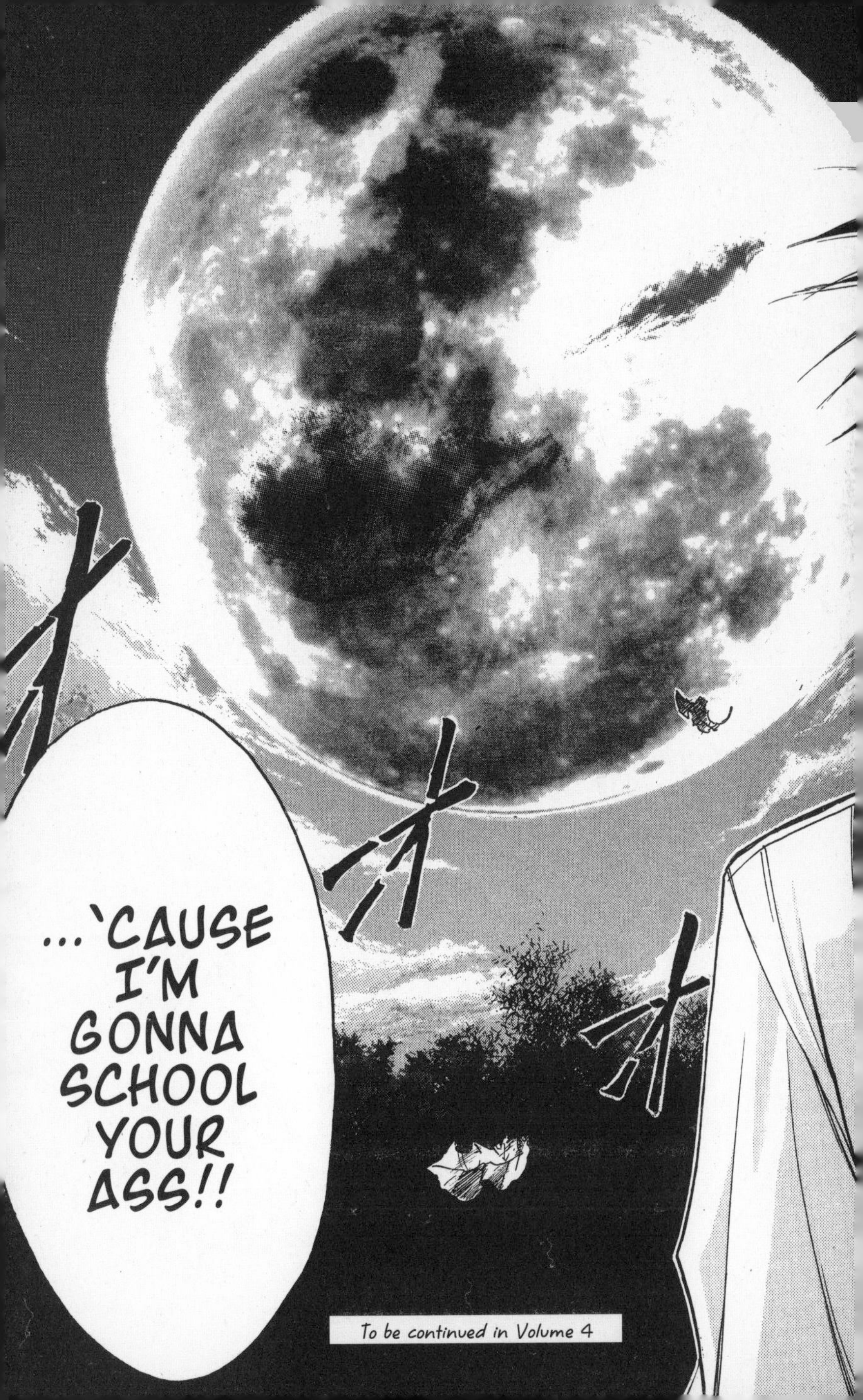
...`CAUSE I'M GONNA SCHOOL YOUR ASS!!
To be continued in Volume 4

スタッフ紹介(しょうかい) SUPPORT STAFF

伊川 良樹 YOSHIKI IKAWA

土屋 奈朋 NAHO TSUCHIYA

大久保 篤 ATSUSHI ŌKUBO

榎並 博昭 HIROAKI ENAMI

上村 聖史 KIYOSHI KAMIMURA

SPECIAL THANKS

横山 顕大 KENTA YOKOYAMA

戸嶋 久美 KUMI TOJIMA

EDITOR

SHIN KIBAYASHI

TOSHIMI HORIKAWA

KIICHIRŌ SUGAWARA

CHYONGHYON PAKU

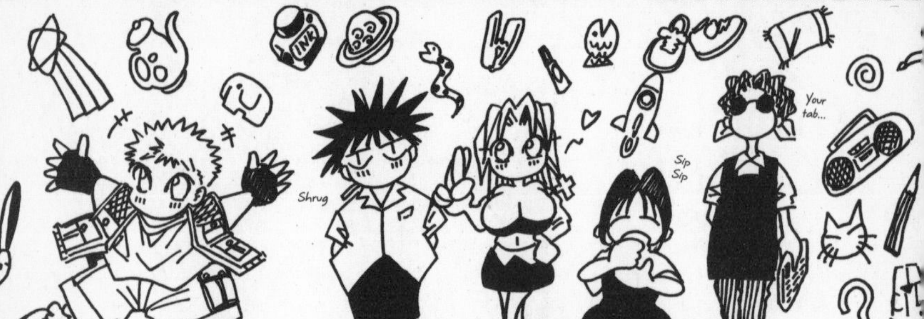
Your tab...
Sip Sip
Shrug

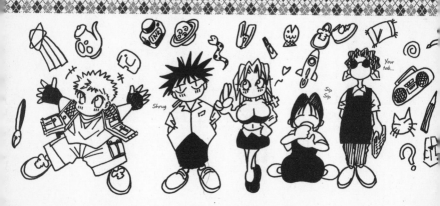

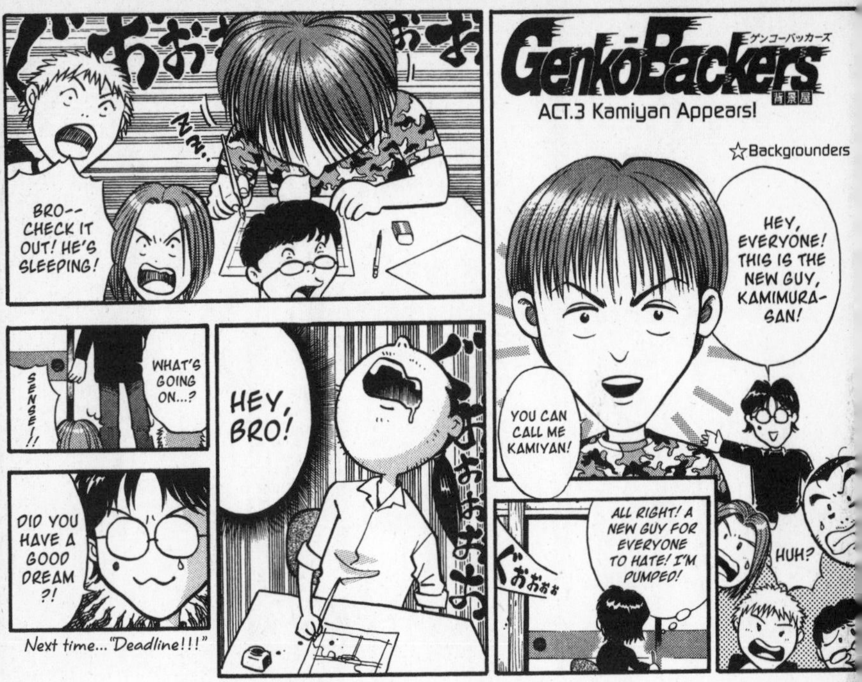
Genkō Backers
ゲンコーバッカーズ
背景屋
ACT.3 Kamiyan Appears!
☆Backgrounders
HEY, EVERYONE! THIS IS THE NEW GUY, KAMIMURA-SAN!
YOU CAN CALL ME KAMIYAN!
HUH?
ALL RIGHT! A NEW GUY FOR EVERYONE TO HATE! I'M PUMPED!
ぐおおぉ
ぐおおお
ZZZ...
BRO--CHECK IT OUT! HE'S SLEEPING!
ぐおおお
HEY, BRO!
WHAT'S GOING ON...?
SENSEI!!
DID YOU HAVE A GOOD DREAM?!
Next time..."Deadline!!!"

DRAGON ASH CALLED BREAD ♡

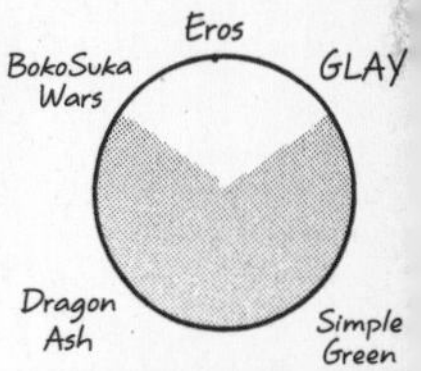
Eros
GLAY
Simple Green
Dragon Ash
BokoSuka Wars

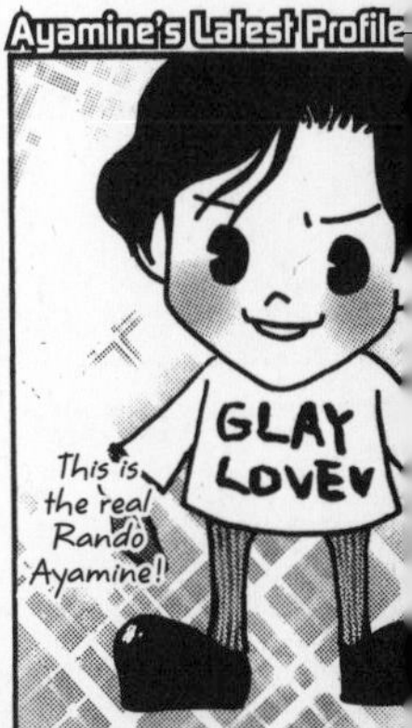
Ayamine's Latest Profile
GLAY LOVE♥
This is the real Rando Ayamine!

Fake Tsuchiya!

And he's so suave with the ladies! He's such a fashionable sensei, he can't even keep up with all the proposals he gets.

Girls, send your fan letters! And boys too, I guess...

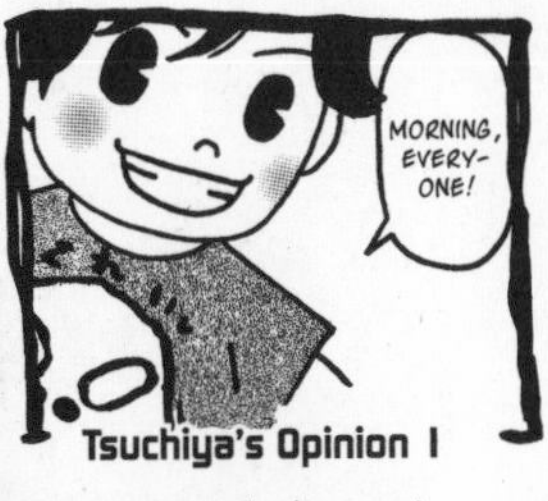
MORNING, EVERY-ONE!

Tsuchiya's Opinion 1

Attention all the boys and girls of the world--Ayamine-sensei is a really nice guy! His assistants all love him!

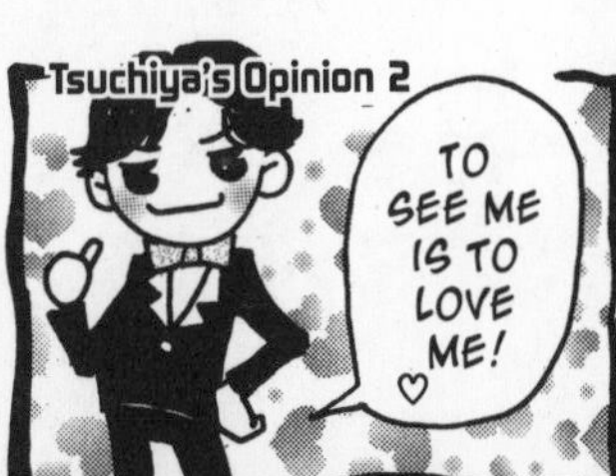
Tsuchiya's Opinion 2
TO SEE ME IS TO LOVE ME! ♡

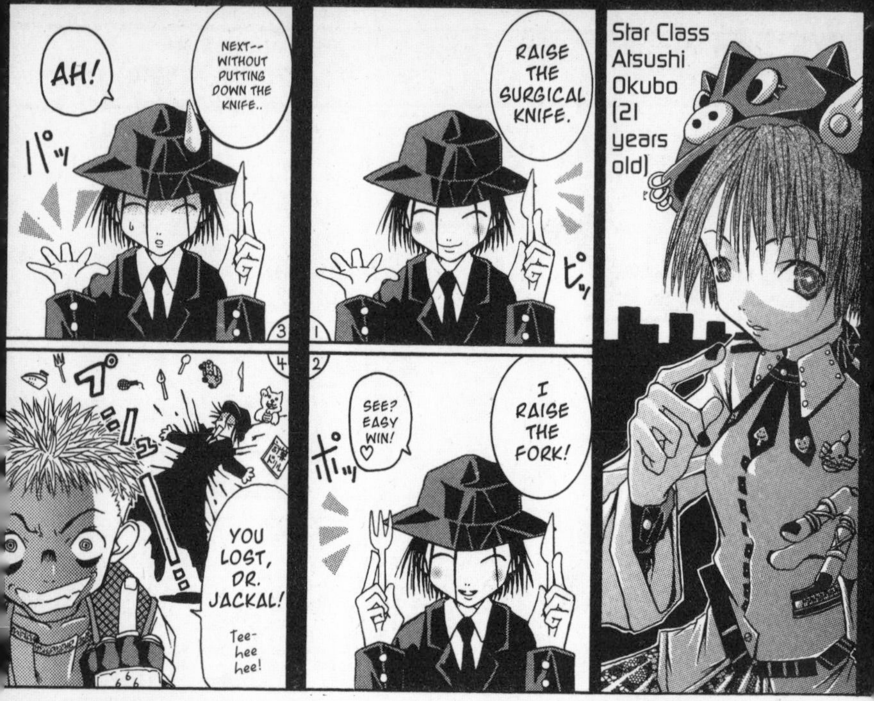
Star Class Atsushi Okubo (21 years old)
RAISE THE SURGICAL KNIFE.
ピッ
I RAISE THE FORK!
SEE? EASY WIN! ♡
ポッ
NEXT-- WITHOUT PUTTING DOWN THE KNIFE..
AH!
パッ
YOU LOST, DR. JACKAL!
Tee-hee hee!

The strongest carrier appears here! • Ashi Number Four • Hiroaki Enami

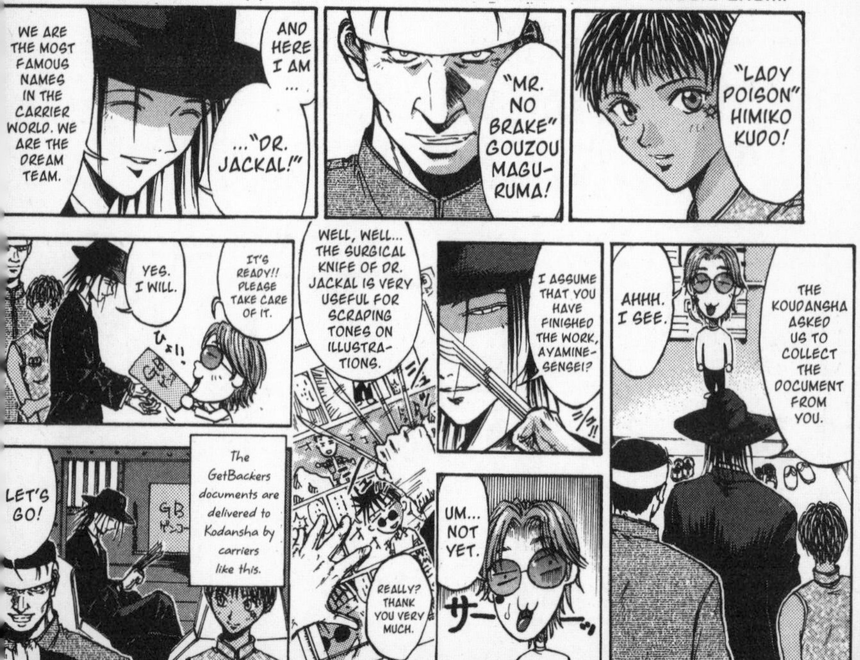
"LADY POISON" HIMIKO KUDO!
"MR. NO BRAKE" GOUZOU MAGURUMA!
AND HERE I AM ...
..."DR. JACKAL!"
WE ARE THE MOST FAMOUS NAMES IN THE CARRIER WORLD. WE ARE THE DREAM TEAM.
THE KOUDANSHA ASKED US TO COLLECT THE DOCUMENT FROM YOU.
AHHH. I SEE.
I ASSUME THAT YOU HAVE FINISHED THE WORK, AYAMINE-SENSEI?
UM... NOT YET.
サー
WELL, WELL... THE SURGICAL KNIFE OF DR. JACKAL IS VERY USEFUL FOR SCRAPING TONES ON ILLUSTRATIONS.
REALLY? THANK YOU VERY MUCH.
IT'S READY!! PLEASE TAKE CARE OF IT.
YES. I WILL.
The GetBackers documents are delivered to Kodansha by carriers like this.
LET'S GO!

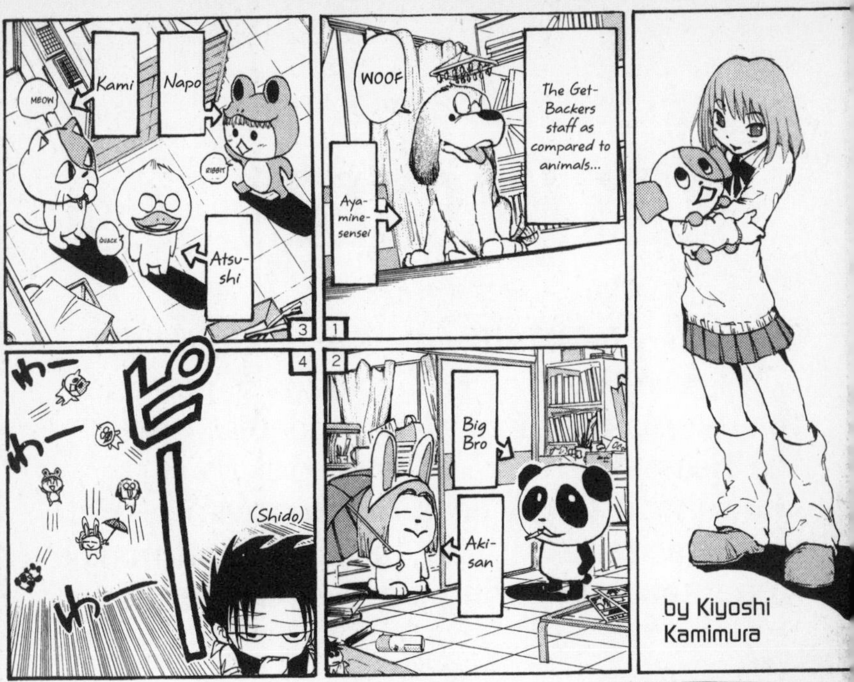
by Kiyoshi Kamimura
WOOF
The Get-Backers staff as compared to animals...
Aya-mine-sensei
Big Bro
Aki-san
Napo
Kami
MEOW
RIBBIT
QUACK
Atsushi
ピー
わー
わー
わー
(Shido)

THE ROOM OF AYAMINE

Hi, Minami-kun. How are you? I am doing my best Rumi-Chan Kaoru-Kun impersonation! Thanx for the doll! I'll put it in my room.

I am sorry I haven't replied to the fan letters like I said I woul in Volume Two o GetBackers.

To: Harue-chan
I use COPIC for choosing colors. I sometimes pick silver and (?) without thinking. I have no sense of differentiating the colors.

The message of Aniki C3-PO doesn't come out from Pepsi...

The cockroach came out at my work place and the scream of people echoed.

Lately, I am even working in my dreams. I can't take it when the paper is still blank when I wake up from such dreams.

Since I haven't drawn much lately, I've actually forgotten how to draw the GetBackers costumes.

What I thought when the Volume two of GetBackers came out... To everyone who bought the Volume Two of GetBackers, Thank you very much. I will improve my illustration skills more and for now...

Lately, I come out of my room only when I have a meeting with other people.

I get a lot of questions from fans about character profiles. So...I will create a character profile page soon.

Yoshiyo-chan, Kei-chan-- I am sorry I haven't replied to your letters yet. I will respond when I am on my break. I want my break!

I like my father and my mother as well.

I am sorry that my messages look rough, but I am serious about every message.

To the people who sent me fan letters-thank you so much! Your letters have really motivated me to work harder!

The reason I'm moving to a new place is because my resources got expanded, and I need extra space. Resources = Porn books.

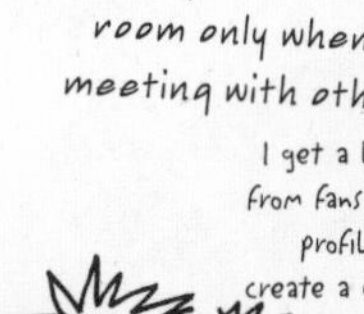

In the next electrifying volume of

GETBACKERS™

Ban Mido faces off with one of Ginji's old allies. Fresh out of Evil Eyes, is it possible for the master of illusions to defeat Shido, the Beast Master? And what exactly is Ginji's plan to get back the Stratusmix– uh... Stradivarius? All these questions (and maybe some new ones) will be answered next time.

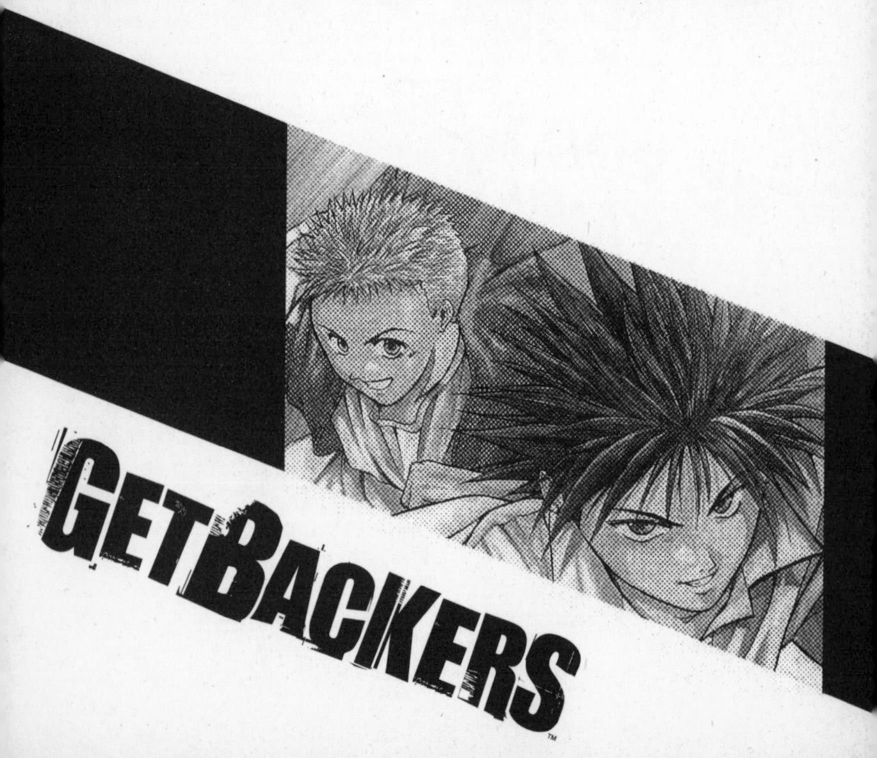
GETBACKERS™

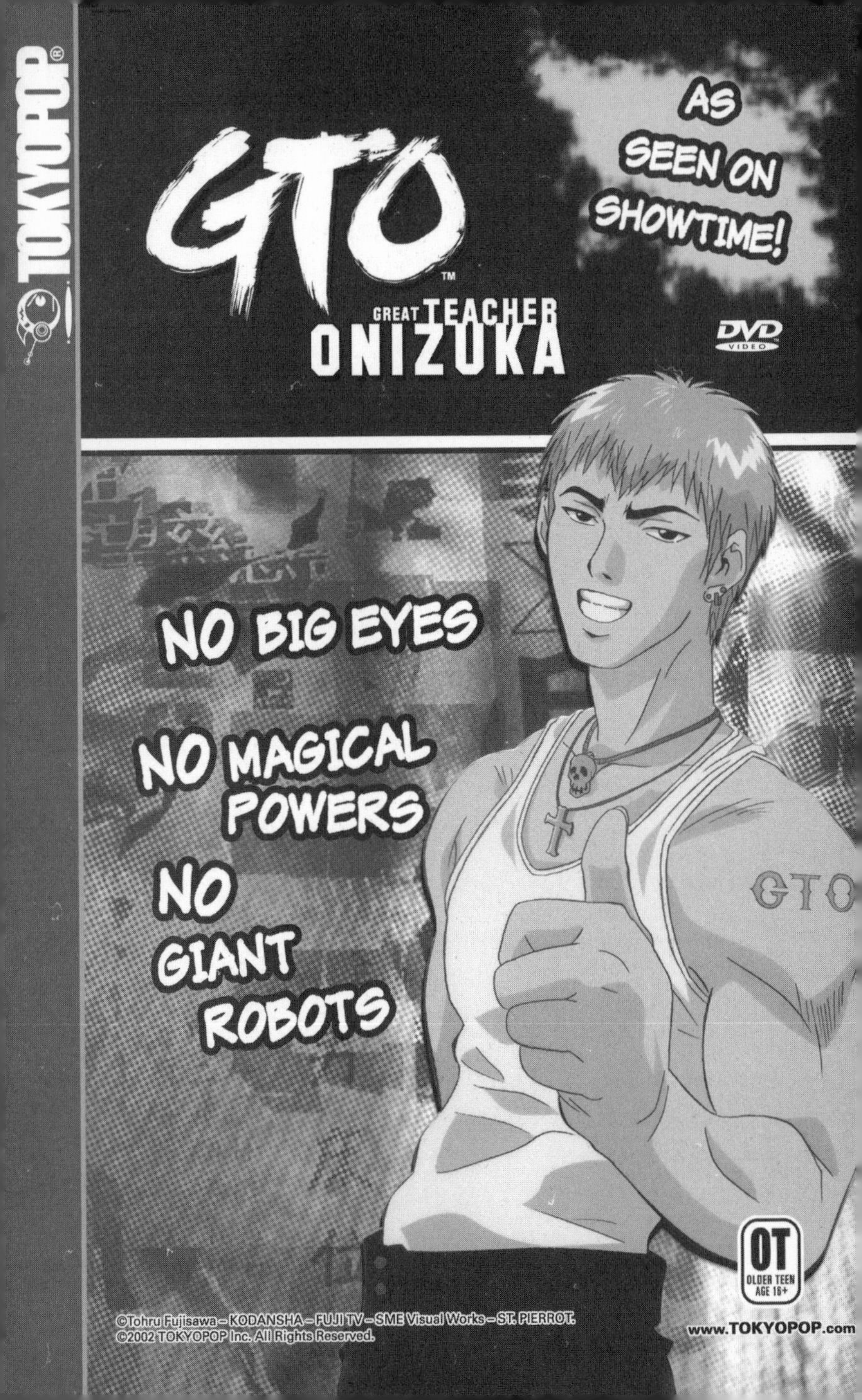
TOKYOPOP
GTO
GREAT TEACHER ONIZUKA
AS SEEN ON SHOWTIME!
DVD VIDEO
NO BIG EYES
NO MAGICAL POWERS
NO GIANT ROBOTS
GTO
OT OLDER TEEN AGE 16+
©Tohru Fujisawa - KODANSHA - FUJI TV - SME Visual Works - ST. PIERROT.
©2002 TOKYOPOP Inc. All Rights Reserved.
www.TOKYOPOP.com

ALSO AVAILABLE FROM 🌀TOKYOPOP®

**For more
information visit
www.TOKYOPOP.com**

03.30.04T

ALSO AVAILABLE FROM TOKYOPOP®

MANGA

.HACK//LEGEND OF THE TWILIGHT
@LARGE
ABENOBASHI: MAGICAL SHOPPING ARCADE
A.I. LOVE YOU
AI YORI AOSHI
ANGELIC LAYER
ARM OF KANNON
BABY BIRTH
BATTLE ROYALE
BATTLE VIXENS
BRAIN POWERED
BRIGADOON
B'TX
CANDIDATE FOR GODDESS, THE
CARDCAPTOR SAKURA
CARDCAPTOR SAKURA - MASTER OF THE CLOW
CHOBITS
CHRONICLES OF THE CURSED SWORD
CLAMP SCHOOL DETECTIVES
CLOVER
COMIC PARTY
CONFIDENTIAL CONFESSIONS
CORRECTOR YUI
COWBOY BEBOP
COWBOY BEBOP: SHOOTING STAR
CRAZY LOVE STORY
CRESCENT MOON
CROSS
CULDCEPT
CYBORG 009
D•N•ANGEL
DEMON DIARY
DEMON ORORON, THE
DEUS VITAE
DIABOLO
DIGIMON
DIGIMON TAMERS
DIGIMON ZERO TWO
DOLL
DRAGON HUNTER
DRAGON KNIGHTS
DRAGON VOICE
DREAM SAGA
DUKLYON: CLAMP SCHOOL DEFENDERS
EERIE QUEERIE!
ERICA SAKURAZAWA: COLLECTED WORKS
ET CETERA
ETERNITY
EVIL'S RETURN
FAERIES' LANDING
FAKE
FLCL
FLOWER OF THE DEEP SLEEP
FORBIDDEN DANCE
FRUITS BASKET
G GUNDAM

GATEKEEPERS
GETBACKERS
GIRL GOT GAME
GIRLS' EDUCATIONAL CHARTER
GRAVITATION
GTO
GUNDAM BLUE DESTINY
GUNDAM SEED ASTRAY
GUNDAM WING
GUNDAM WING: BATTLEFIELD OF PACIFISTS
GUNDAM WING: ENDLESS WALTZ
GUNDAM WING: THE LAST OUTPOST (G-UNIT)
GUYS' GUIDE TO GIRLS
HANDS OFF!
HAPPY MANIA
HARLEM BEAT
HONEY MUSTARD
I.N.V.U.
IMMORTAL RAIN
INITIAL D
INSTANT TEEN: JUST ADD NUTS
ISLAND
JING: KING OF BANDITS
JING: KING OF BANDITS - TWILIGHT TALES
JULINE
KARE KANO
KILL ME, KISS ME
KINDAICHI CASE FILES, THE
KING OF HELL
KODOCHA: SANA'S STAGE
LAMENT OF THE LAMB
LEGAL DRUG
LEGEND OF CHUN HYANG, THE
LES BIJOUX
LOVE HINA
LUPIN III
LUPIN III: WORLD'S MOST WANTED
MAGIC KNIGHT RAYEARTH I
MAGIC KNIGHT RAYEARTH II
MAHOROMATIC: AUTOMATIC MAIDEN
MAN OF MANY FACES
MARMALADE BOY
MARS
MARS: HORSE WITH NO NAME
MINK
MIRACLE GIRLS
MIYUKI-CHAN IN WONDERLAND
MODEL
MY LOVE
NECK AND NECK
ONE
ONE I LOVE, THE
PARADISE KISS
PARASYTE
PASSION FRUIT
PEACH GIRL
PEACH GIRL: CHANGE OF HEART
PET SHOP OF HORRORS

03.30.04T

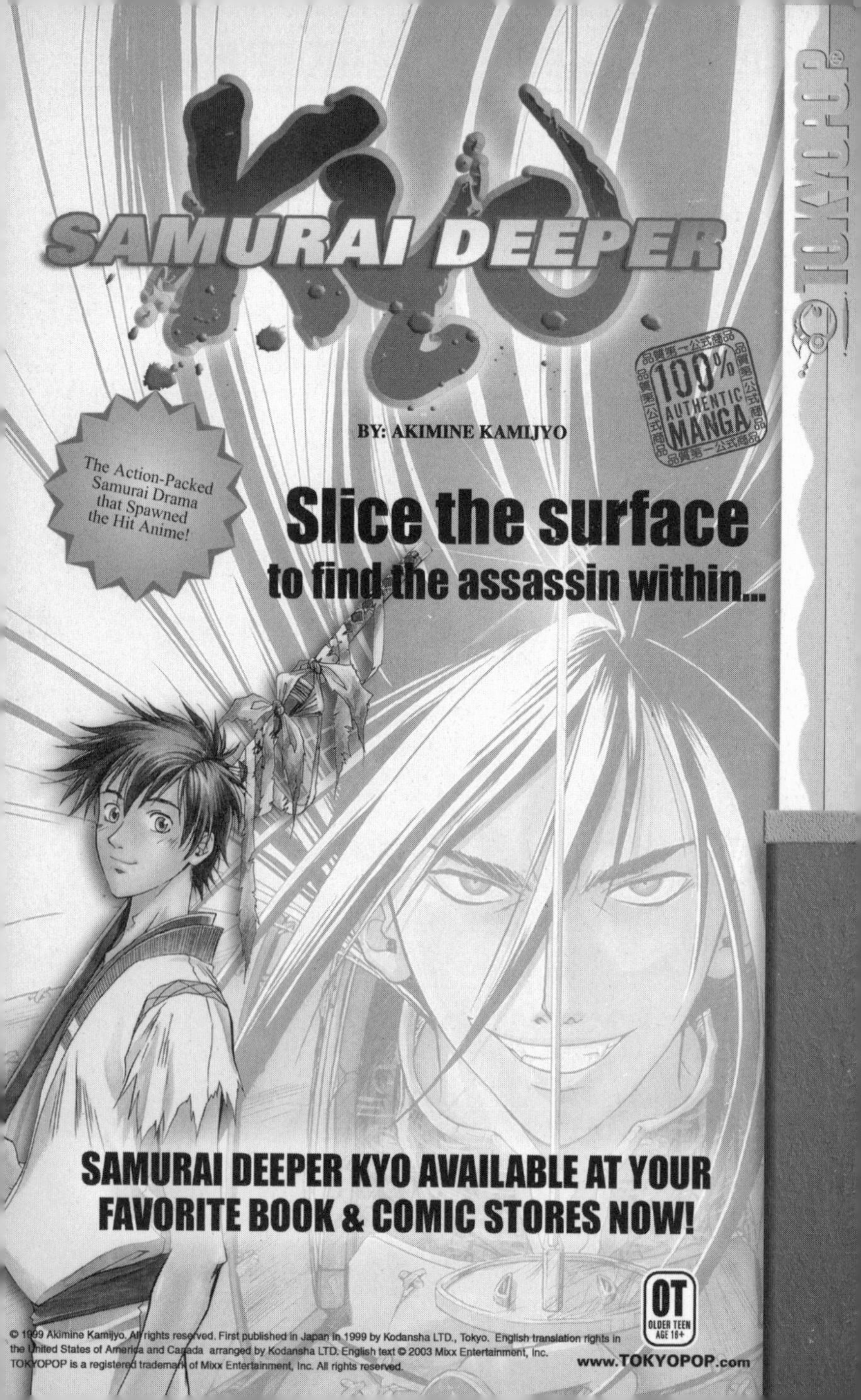
TOKYOPOP
KYO
SAMURAI DEEPER
100% AUTHENTIC MANGA
BY: AKIMINE KAMIJYO
The Action-Packed Samurai Drama that Spawned the Hit Anime!
Slice the surface
to find the assassin within...
SAMURAI DEEPER KYO AVAILABLE AT YOUR
FAVORITE BOOK & COMIC STORES NOW!
OT
OLDER TEEN AGE 16+
© 1999 Akimine Kamijyo. All rights reserved. First published in Japan in 1999 by Kodansha LTD., Tokyo. English translation rights in the United States of America and Canada arranged by Kodansha LTD. English text © 2003 Mixx Entertainment, Inc.
TOKYOPOP is a registered trademark of Mixx Entertainment, Inc. All rights reserved.
www.TOKYOPOP.com

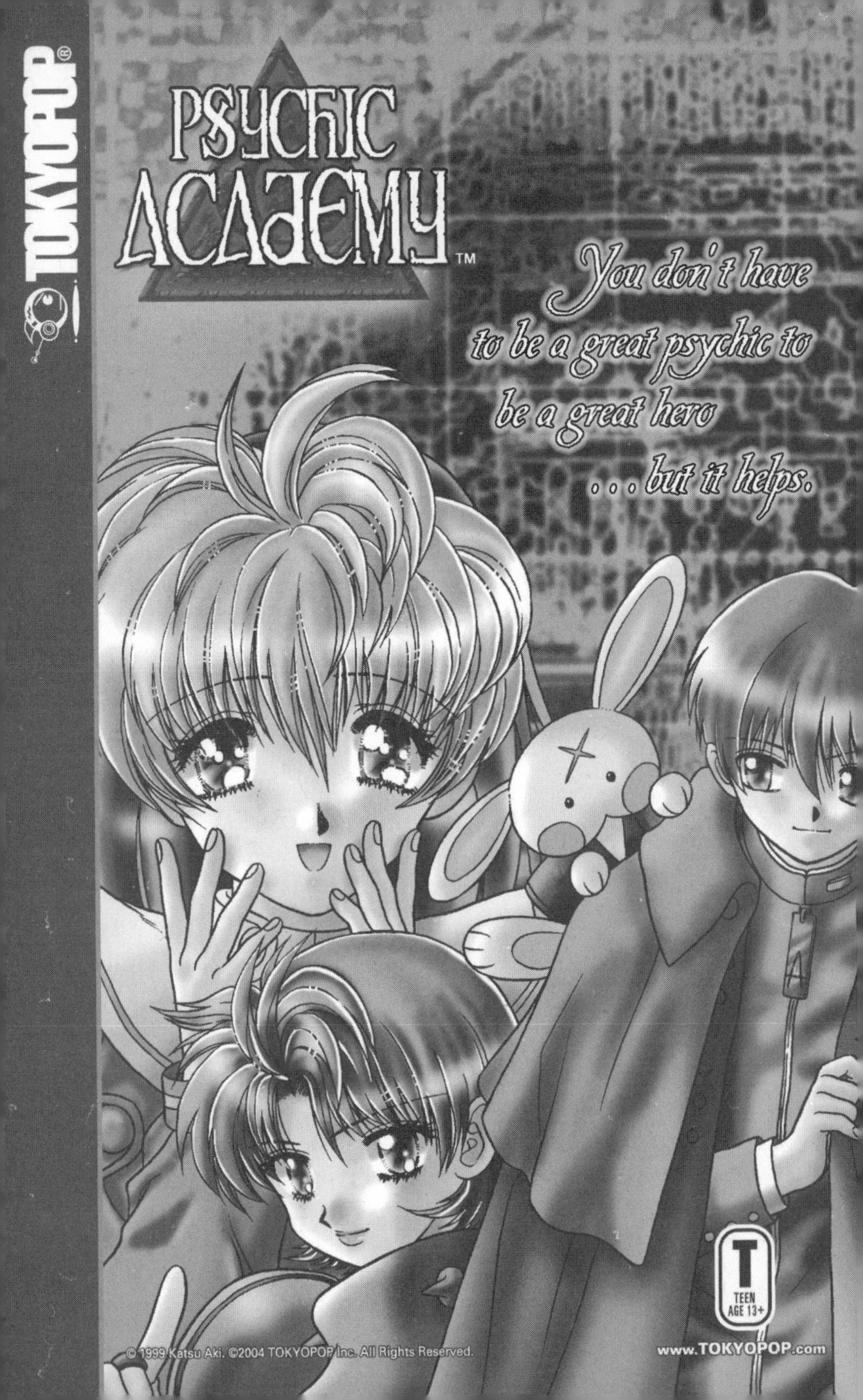
TOKYOPOP
PSYCHIC ACADEMY™
You don't have to be a great psychic to be a great hero . . . but it helps.
T TEEN AGE 13+
© 1999 Katsu Aki. ©2004 TOKYOPOP Inc. All Rights Reserved.
www.TOKYOPOP.com

STOP!

This is the back of the book.
You wouldn't want to spoil a great ending!

This book is printed "manga-style," in the authentic Japanese right-to-left format. Since none of the artwork has been flipped or altered, readers get to experience the story just as the creator intended. You've been asking for it, so TOKYOPOP® delivered: authentic, hot-off-the-press, and far more fun!

DIRECTIONS

If this is your first time reading manga-style, here's a quick guide to help you understand how it works.

It's easy... just start in the top right panel and follow the numbers. Have fun, and look for more 100% authentic manga from TOKYOPOP®!